internally and was challenged by powerful forces from within the Wall Street community and from Washington. Today, as four decades ago, "The Exchange," as it likes to style itself, is a troubled and harried giant attempting to preserve itself and some of its perquisites in an industry that is in the midst of the most profound changes of all.

This new book on the modern history of the Exchange, written with access to its records but not under its direction nor subject to its approval, traces the origins of the N.Y.S.E.'s problems and the dilemmas faced by its leaders during the last forty years. It provides a perspective that is essential to an understanding of what is happening on Wall Street and within the American business community today.

N.Y.S.E.

By the same author:

HERBERT HOOVER AT THE ONSET OF THE GREAT DEPRESSION, 1929–1930

THE ENTREPRENEURS

THE MONEY MANIAS

FOR WANT OF A NAIL. . . .

THE AGE OF GIANT CORPORATIONS

CONQUEST AND CONSCIENCE: THE 1840S

MACHINES AND MORALITY: THE 1850S

AMEX: A HISTORY OF THE AMERICAN STOCK EXCHANGE

THE CURBSTONE BROKERS

PANIC ON WALL STREET

THE GREAT BULL MARKET

THE BIG BOARD

THE ORIGINS OF INTERVENTIONISM

N.Y.S.E.

A History of the New York Stock Exchange 1935-1975

Robert Sobel

Weybright and Talley

NEW YORK

Weybright and Talley
750 Third Avenue
New York, New York 10017

Library of Congress Cataloging in Publication Data

Sobel, Robert, 1931 (Feb. 19)–
N.Y.S.E. : a history of the New York Stock Exchange,
1935–1975.

Bibliography: p.
Includes index.
1. New York. Stock Exchange—History. I. Title.
HG4572.S673   332.6'42'0973   75-8876
ISBN 0-679-40124-5

MANUFACTURED IN THE UNITED STATES OF AMERICA

To:

William O. Douglas for his heart, and
William McChesney Martin for his head

Preface

The New York Stock Exchange has long occupied a special niche in both the hagiology and demonology of capitalism. Among other things, it is the centerpiece for that great symbol Wall Street, a major tourist attraction which draws hundreds of thousands of visitors each year to lower Manhattan. At a time when power is distrusted, some come to see a fabled place from which their nation is supposed to be controlled. German and Japanese businessmen arrive in groups. They enter the N.Y.S.E. as they might the Louvre, whisper to one another rather than talk aloud, listen carefully to their guides and take notes and photos, scoop up brochures and ask about souvenirs, and watch the trading from the Visitors Gallery in awe. Those from the USSR and other socialist countries enter the N.Y.S.E. as an American might go to Lenin's Tomb—to see the source of power and inspiration close up, to wonder, to try to understand better the people who revolve about the institution.

The Exchange is indeed an impressive place, as well as a fine symbol. Constructed at the turn of the century at a cost of $2 million—a large amount of money in the days of the good five-cent cigar—it was meant to monumentalize the nation at a time of great confidence and patriotism. Its designer, George B. Post, had been the architect of Grace Church and St. Patrick's Cathedral, and there were touches of both to be seen on the N.Y.S.E. façade. Today the Exchange presents onlookers with a picture of strength and magnificence.

The picture deceives. Once it might have been argued that Wall Street was the power center of the land, but that period ended with the advent of the New Deal and the Great Depression. Pennsylvania Avenue in Washington, not Wall Street in New York, is the proper symbol for America in its imperial age.

If Wall Street was the major power hub of the nation at one time, this no longer is the case. As for the N.Y.S.E., it evoked images and provoked controversies, but more often than not it was misunderstood, being praised and condemned for the wrong reasons. The Exchange was and is a rallying point, a place where the major forces in the district transacted a part of their business, an institution that marketed wares, and a potent symbol. This is not to say the N.Y.S.E. was unimportant but rather that its significance in the scheme of things is often misunderstood and exaggerated.

This book is an attempt to understand and place in proper perspective the history of the Exchange during its most turbulent era. This period, spanning the years from 1935 to 1975, divides roughly into three phases, and so this work follows a similar organization. In the first phase, from 1935 to 1941, the Exchange survived and changed, with the latter necessary in order to obtain the benefits of the former. Under the leadership of Charles Gay and William McChesney Martin, the N.Y.S.E. came to terms with the New Deal and the depression. With the collapse of the speculative urge and the weakness of the investment banks, the Exchange became the preserve of the specialists, the men who dominate the floor, who remade the institution in their own image to serve their needs. Toward the end they took power for themselves and presided over a small and rather insignificant market, but one which they had led to safety.

The second phase, which covers the years from 1941 to 1966, might be considered the greatest age in the history of the Exchange, and perhaps of Wall Street as well. To be sure, both had great power during the Age of Morgan, but America was a second-rate nation at that time, and London, not New York, was the world's major financial center. If Wall Street did not lead the nation from 1941 to 1966, America led the world. It was a period that began in uncertainty which was transformed, in the early 1950s, to assurance and self-confidence. The changes were unexpected, for most at the N.Y.S.E. had been resigned to the belief that they would never again see a bull market like that of the 1920s.

Then it arrived, and not only was the new market mania more impressive in depth and breadth than the earlier one but it was longer lasting and helped reinvigorate and alter the economy as well.

In the process, the comfortable, well-functioning but somewhat exclusive market dominated by the specialists was called upon to fulfill demands for an entirely different kind of clientele than that for which it had been designed. Large institutions and tens of millions of small investors came to the market, straining its facilities—and the imagination of its leaders. These problems were not evident during the presidency of Emil Schram, a hard-working man who had been selected for the position for the wrong reasons, but performed satisfactorily nonetheless. Then, in 1951, the board selected G. Keith Funston as Schram's successor, and shortly thereafter he became a major national figure, the super-salesman of People's Capitalism, widely billed at the time as America's alternative to communism.

Meanwhile, weaknesses appeared in the Exchange's fabric, and no significant attempt was made to correct them. The system was showing signs of failure when Funston left his post in 1967. The period of stress and slow change that followed makes up the last section of this book. It is an era that has not ended, for the resolution of major problems has not been completed. Indeed, many otherwise astute observers of the financial scene appear to have misunderstood or have become confused by the ramifications of these highly significant changes and the issues in question.

They deserve attention and careful study, not only in order to comprehend the evolution of power in a small part of the tip of Manhattan but for a larger set of reasons. There rarely has been an important national event that has not affected the N.Y.S.E. Often the Exchange has served as a mirror for America, a reflection of its values—perhaps more a thermometer than a barometer. Major developments in the nation resulted in changes on the Street, which in turn had their impacts on a majority of Americans. The growth of large financial institutions, the appearance of rival markets, the sudden decline of the small investor, the uncertain role of Washington, the search for a new structure to serve both the old and new needs of the district—all of these concern Wall Street today and have analogues in other aspects of our society. It may be too much to hope that the resolution of the N.Y.S.E.'s concerns may in some way be reflective of the situation in the nation.

Two final observations should be made. The N.Y.S.E. administration and staff have been most cooperative and generous in assisting in the preparation of this book. But it does not reflect their views on many subjects. Whatever flaws, inconsistencies, and conclusions are found herein are my own. Finally, the Exchange did not subsidize this work in any way, shape, or form. This is not an "official history."

ROBERT SOBEL
Hofstra University
February 1, 1975

Contents

Part One

THE HARSH YEARS

1935-1942

Prelude

The Dow-Jones Industrial Index closed at 102.88 on Wednesday, January 23, 1935, up slightly more than a tenth of a point for the day. N.Y.S.E. volume was 620,000 shares. The *Wall Street Journal* called the trading "normal."

The Index was twice what it had been during the bleak early summer of 1932, when a decline of two points could chop almost 4 percent from the total value of all listed shares. There were several such days then, with the few remaining brokers and their clients almost too numb to notice. The feverish, panicky atmosphere that had prevailed in the early winter of 1929 had been replaced by a chill foreboding in June 1935, a striking contrast of climate and attitude. It was as though the district suspected it had contracted a fatal disease and simply was awaiting official confirmation of the fact.

Prices were in the doldrums in early 1935, and interest in them almost nonexistent. The January volume was 19.5 million shares. Six years before, in the same month of the last year of the great bull market, volume had been 110.8 million shares. When the bear market of 1930–1932 scraped bottom in July 1932, over 23 million shares were traded for the month, and on two occasions, over 2 million shares changed hands. There were no such days in January 1935. The last 2-million-share session had been in July 1934, and the next would occur in the following May.

Wall Street's professionals liked to see prices rise. Bull markets meant happy clients who would trade with brio, their accounts lubricated by profits. This created new business and commissions for investment bankers, brokers, and specialists. Price and volume statistics were watched carefully, and the former were the more significant in their view, because they influenced the latter. In 1929, when over 1.1 billion shares were traded, a Big Board seat changed hands at $625,000. Volume in 1934 was 324 million shares, and a seat could be had for as low as $70,000.

Owners of N.Y.S.E. seats had the right to participate in Exchange activities, serving clients and, in the process, their own interests. In the late 1920s, the financial district and the Exchange floor had become the symbols for reckless gambling as well as investment, and stress was on the former. They appeared as a great financial pump that helped prime the economic boom. Then, as stock prices declined sharply from late 1929 to mid-1932, the N.Y.S.E. became a scapegoat for every ill that beset the land. It was utilized in this way by Democratic Presidential candidate Franklin Roosevelt in 1932, and by New Dealers during the following year, when they framed and help pass legislation correcting abuses in the financial district. By 1935, however, the Exchange no longer was the symbol for prosperity or the focus of attacks on plutocracy. Rather, it was ignored, by-passed, almost the subject of ridicule. Along with Herbert Hoover, prohibition, and Queen Marie of Romania, it appeared a vestige of a previous age, no longer worthy of serious interest. In mid-1929, strangers would ask one another how high they thought the market would go. Three years later they might talk of a possible bottom to stock prices. By 1935, securities no longer were subjects of cocktail-party chatter or idle conversation elsewhere. Such New Deal agencies as the National Recovery Administration appeared central to American life by then; if N.Y.S.E. were the initials for 1929, N.R.A. were those for 1935.

Stock Exchange leaders realized this, and in early January launched an advertising effort aimed at interesting people in investments once more. N.Y.S.E. President Richard Whitney spoke of the new vigor of American capitalism and set out on a speaking tour of the nation to sell investors on the idea, and Exchange advertisements were placed in magazines and newspapers. These were either ignored or became the subject of satire. Comedian Eddie Cantor, who earlier had written humorously of his not-so-humorous losses in the Great Crash, thought that conditions indeed were getting better—all the brokers who planned to jump out of windows had already done so. Joe Penner added that he might buy stocks if the broker who sold him a bundle of losers in 1929 would buy his old certificates, which were presently serving as wallpaper in his bathroom.

In January 1935, radio commentary on the stock exchanges appeared on variety and comic shows, not in news and analysis programs. And none were more devastating than Fred Allen, whose Ipana–Sal Hepatica Hour was a Wednesday night favorite. Allen enjoyed poking fun at such targets, more often than not in the form of skits and mock newscasts. On January 23, he offered his commentary on the N.Y.S.E. advertising campaign:

ALLEN: New York City, New York. The New York Stock Exchange plans to present a radio program to further its educational and good-will campaign. Town Hall News presents the type of program brokers will probably favor. Be prepared for this—

ANNOUNCER: Hi Low Everybody! This is the Voice of Wall Street, folks, and the program tonight begins with a few words from our guest star, Mr. Lester Fidget.

MR. FIDGET: Thank ya, folks! I'm the guest star and I hope ya won't mind my comin' to the studio in my union suit. I lost my shirt in the market. All I gotta say is if I'd been playing golf as long as I been playin' the market I'd be Bobby Jones today.

ANNOUNCER: Thank you, Mr. Fidget. Thousands of satisfied customers say the same thing. Folks, in hundreds of homes around the country scenes like this are happening every minute—

MARY: John, John!

JOHN: Yes, Mary?

MARY: The landlord's coming up the stairs!

JOHN: I hope it's a social call. I ain't got the rent.

(knock at the door)

JOHN: Come in, Mr. MacGregor.

MACGREGOR: I'm in. I'm a man of few words, Mr. Smith. Aye want me rent!

JOHN: We can't pay, MacGregor.

MACGREGOR: Thin out ye go!

MARY: No! No! You can't turn us into the street.

MACGREGOR: Business is business, lass!

JOHN: Alright! As soon as the kid comes home from school, we'll go!

MARY: What will little Bobby say?

(knock at the door)

MACGREGOR: If that's the boy at the door, ye can ask him and SCRAM!

(door opens)

BOBBY: Mamma! Daddy! Look! I made a million dollars!!

MARY: You haven't been tossing pennies, Bobby?

JOHN: Where did you get this million dollars, son? Honor bright!

BOBBY: I knew you didn't have the rent, Daddy, so I took a dollar out of my bank to play the stock market. I made a million dollars in ten minutes!

MARY: My darling!

JOHN: My son!

MACGREGOR: My rent!

ANNOUNCER: And you too can make a million dollars playing the stock market. Ask your broker about margin, spelled M-A-R-G-I-N. Earn while you learn to play! This is the Voice of Wall Street signing off as the Singing Players give you their theme song—

SINGERS: The Old Oaken Bucket Shop,
The Old Oaken Bucket Shop,
The Old Oaken Bucket Shop
At Broad Street and Wall.

The advertising campaign was a miserable failure. (Although the Fred Allen broadcast had a large audience, it probably had no effect on the market. In any case, the Dow Industrials fell less than half a point the next day, on a volume of 437,000 shares. On five occasions in January, more than 1 million shares were traded. There were only two such sessions in February and three in March.)

In early March, several N.Y.S.E. leaders suggested that a "czar" be appointed to guarantee the Exchange's honesty to the public. The Securities and Exchange Commission did exist, of course, and under its first chairman, Joseph Kennedy, had in a sense "certified" part of the district's operations. Wall Street was still in the process of getting used to the regulatory body, and two years later the initially skeptical editors at *Fortune* would call the agency "the New Deal's most successful reform." But in March 1935 it was still viewed as an interloper. The N.Y.S.E. wanted "self-regulation," and hoped to do the job itself. Given public attitudes toward the financial district as well as the atmosphere in Washington, this was not feasible yet. Thus, the willingness to accept an outside, non–Wall Street but also nongovernment, dictator for the district. It was not an unusual idea or a radical solution. After all, when Hollywood was in the midst of scandal, the studios banded together to select Will Hays, who functioned as a czar of the movies, and baseball, in the aftermath of the Black Sox scandals, chose Kenesaw Mountain Landis for a similar position. This, said the N.Y.S.E. figures, was what Wall Street needed.

Like previous suggestions and programs, this one was received with jeers. The *New York Sun*, generally viewed as a probusiness and conservative newspaper, printed its reactions to the idea in the form of a poem:

We need a czar, a pleasant one,
Like Landis or like Hays,
To step into the Stock Exchange
And bring it better days;
A czar who knows the public mind,
And who can skilfully

Present us in the public eye
The way we like to be.

We need some glorifying done,
And need it badly now;
Oh, won't some volunteer step forth
And kindly show us how?
We want that chilly mask removed—
That manner cold as ice;
The public should be made to feel
We're really very nice.

Judge Landis bless'd the game of ball,
Will Hays made Hollywood;
Oh, why can't we be sanctified
And made correct and good?
The Stock Exchange is just a place
Where stocks are traded in.
Why should it be regarded as
Some dark abode of sin?

Come on, oh, czar, and do your stuff
To put us over right!
Our heart is in the proper place,
Our motives lily white.
Wash off our look of cold reserve—
Our highbrows high pull down!
Repaint us in the public eye—
We want to go to town!

Take charge! Do with us what you will—
Change body, speech or dress;
If there is anything we need
It is a friendly press.
A broker's just like any man,
And in these bitter days
No feller is in greater need
Of just a little praise.

Come, glorify the "put and call"
And sing the praises of
The "bid and asked" in accents sweet
Enough to 'waken love!
Give character to ticker tape,
And paint the ticker, an
Abused and slandered instrument,
That does the best it can.

Put laurel on the plus signs and
Praise well the minus too;
Do justice by "when, as and if"—
Give high and low their due.
Wax lyrical of margin calls
And let it be your song:
"No matter what the market does
It never does you wrong!"

Strew flowers on the market floor,
And teach that in a chart
One sees the very highest form
Of most instructive art;
Oh, educate the public well—
This moral tale unfold:
No matter what the ticker does,
It has a heart of gold!

For most of its existence, the New York Stock Exchange had been viewed as a symbol of capitalism in America. For good or evil, it was painted as the center of finance, the stage upon which the nation's major financiers played their parts. From the time the New York banking community had bested its Philadelphia rival during the Jacksonian period a century earlier, the corner of Wall and Broad and other stock exchange locations in lower New York had been seen as a significant part of the national power structure. Abraham Lincoln had railed against the investment bankers, brokers, and speculators during the Civil War, calling them ghouls who made fortunes from the blood of Union soldiers. William Jennings Bryan concluded that the N.Y.S.E. was the heart of the American plutocracy, where the cross of gold was fashioned, and upon which the laborers and farmers of the land were crucified. The institution was defended and attacked during the progressive period, and in the 1920s it was viewed as having international power.

In early 1935, the Exchange seemed irrelevant.

CHAPTER 1

A Time for Survival

Charles Richard Gay was sixty years old in 1935, and was weary. Those who knew him said he seemed to be "carrying the weight of the world on his shoulders" when he appeared in public, and especially among strangers. On such occasions he would stiffen, listen carefully, and wear a slight, clearly painted smile on his face. He could relax among friends, however, and was rumored to have a fey sense of humor.

Gay was given to dark-blue suits, often with herringbone patterns, and maroon ties, selected by his wife. He was well known in his Flatbush neighborhood. His father, Charles A. Gay, had been a partner in T. B. Coddington & Co., importers of English terneplate, and had settled in Brooklyn prior to his son's birth.

Charles R. Gay liked his neighbors and was satisfied with his modest home. It had a small garden, and he would plant a variety of flowers in it in the spring, and carefully cultivate them after working hours and during weekends. Gay was also a talented amateur photographer, and had a fully equipped darkroom in his cellar, where he developed both his still and motion-picture films. These were his only pastimes.

On warm summer evenings the Gays would take walks, and on summer weekends they would go to the Brooklyn Botanic Gardens to admire the world-famous flower beds, and Gay would take pictures of them to show his friends and add to his collection. Keenly interested in charities, and considering himself a good citizen, Gay was a trustee of the Methodist Episcopal Hospital and a director of the Brooklyn Association for Improving the Condition of the Poor, as well as a long-time advisor for the Flatbush Y.M.C.A. The Gays owned a summer home in Huntington, Long Island, and Gay belonged to several golf clubs. But the Huntington home was rarely used, and although Gay played golf on occasion, he did so more for business reasons than any other.

The Gays did not engage in a hectic social life. They had a few old friends and a handful of relatives and business associates, all of whom shared their interests, backgrounds, and values. They had one child, a son, William, who entered his father's business after graduating from college in 1927. William visited his parents several times a month, and on such occasions, Mrs. Gay would cook a special meal. Charles would stop by the neighborhood delicatessen to pick up a few items for his wife, waiting his turn with the rest, making small talk, and then carrying the packages home. The Gays had no servants for such tasks.

Charles Gay considered himself a good, hard-working man, and one who was an idealist. "Consciously or unconsciously the average man has a desire for something fine, something beautiful, something ideal, something noble," he later wrote. Gay had an unabashed love of country so common among middle-class people who came of age at the turn of the century. "Know America," he told a group at a Y.M.C.A. meeting. "Think of America as an entity to which you belong and which belongs to you; an entity which you can wound or heal, honor or disgrace, make absurd or magnificent by your own opinions and efforts. Do not postpone your love for America until it is taken away from you." Charles Gay liked to talk of the wonders of America, where a person with ambition and a willingness to work hard could get to the top.

On May 13, 1935, Charles Gay was elected president of the New York Stock Exchange.

On the surface at least, it would appear an American dream come true. Gay's predecessor, Richard Whitney, was an aristocrat. Whitney had attended Groton. Gay went to Public School 35 in Brooklyn. Whitney went on to Harvard, and upon graduation founded Richard Whitney & Co., a firm with close connections to the House of Morgan, where brother George was a partner. Gay graduated from Brooklyn Polytechnic Institute, then took a job as a three-dollar-a-week office boy. Later on, Gay joined a coal company, worked as assistant secretary for Long Island Loan & Trust, and in 1911, when Wall Street was in the doldrums, purchased a N.Y.S.E. seat for $65,000.

Gay was an outsider and could expect few favors. So he began work as a two-dollar broker—one who executed orders on the floor of the Exchange for others. In March 1915, he joined with another marginal figure to form Gay & Goepel. The company did well, as did other such firms during the war. Gay developed contacts with several major houses, did his work efficiently, bowed to their dictates, and in every way indicated that he knew his place and would remain content to accept crumbs from the tables of the mighty. In 1918, Gay bought out his partner's interest and changed the firm's name to Gay & Co. Soon after, one of his major cooperating houses, Whitehouse & Co., approached him with an offer of a partnership. Whitehouse was an old, prestigious company which, though a minor force on the Street, was close to some of the larger commission firms and at times engaged in underwritings with them. Gay accepted, and in 1919 he was named senior partner at Whitehouse. Four years later, the quiet and ambitious Gay was elected a governor of the New York Stock Exchange.

The title was more impressive than the position. Governorships were nonpaying posts, often given to minor figures who could be counted upon to go along with the dictates of their betters. The presidency was another matter, while the truly powerful men at the N.Y.S.E. found their ways to the Governing and Law committees. Gay served as governor from 1923 to 1935, and at no time was part of this power nexus. On the other hand, his position enabled him to make good contacts for his firm, and was not to be despised. Gay would vote with the mighty, and in return they would give him business. It was a good and satisfactory arrangement for all concerned.

Like most N.Y.S.E. members, Gay admired Richard Whitney, and accepted him not only as a major spokesman for the Street but a leader of the anti–New Deal forces in the nation. The aristocratic Whitney was pleasant to Gay, who clearly knew his place and had few pretentions.* An unselfconscious patrician, Whitney seemed almost bred for the position of Stock Exchange president; he was the kind of person who had occupied that post for as long as most members could recall. Whitney held a membership at the Knickerbocker Club, but more often than not could be found in his leisure time at the New York Yacht or Turf & Field. There he mingled with others of his circle and status—E.H.H. Simmons, Seymour Cromwell, William R. Remick, H. G. S. Noble—all of whom had occupied the presidency before him. Gay knew these men from Board meetings, and on such occasions he would sit quietly, smiling at the aristocrats, proud to be admitted into even that part of the circle. He said little and did what was expected of him. Gay was "safe." He knew it. So did the aristocrats.

Now Charles Gay was president himself, and he would hold that position until 1938, serving three terms. Had his election occurred at almost any other period, it might have indicated a democratization of the N.Y.S.E. The distance from Whitney's mansion on East 73rd Street in Manhattan to Gay's home on East 19th in Brooklyn was generations apart socially. But the mid-1930s were not normal times, and the membership had not turned to Gay in a positive fashion. Nor had it rejected Whitney, who ran for a governorship and won it with a larger vote than that given Gay. Whitney would serve on the Law Committee, and his friends dominated the Governing Committee. The

* The best study of Whitney is John Brooks, *Once in Golconda: A True Drama of Wall Street, 1920–1938* (New York, 1969).

Whitneyites suggested to Gay that he name Simmons as vice-president. This was done promptly. The floor of the Exchange belonged to Whitney, the most popular man there. Gay was a new façade for the S.E.C. and other interested agencies to report upon. Yet the change was significant, for it indicated the uneasiness, fears, and hopes on Wall Street at the beginning of the second year of the New Deal.

The front and financial pages of the nation's newspapers made clear that Wall Street was in trouble in 1935. What with the antibusiness attitude of many New Dealers, legislation enacted and enforced to regulate the exchanges, and the persistent depression—already affixed firmly in the national conscience to the 1929 crash—the district's reputation was shattered. It had lost the battle of the marketplace in 1929, the struggle for recovery during the next three years, and then the conflict with the reformers after the 1932 elections. Wall Street either would die or become nationalized. This, at least, was the popular impression early that year.

As with most such beliefs, this one was exaggerated, incomplete, and, in large part, false. The use of terms like "financial district" and "Wall Street" distorted reality, giving readers and even casual students the idea that there was such a thing as a monolithic entity called "American Finance." Such was not the case: the commercial banks, investment banks, insurance companies, brokerages, and trust companies that were located at the tip of Manhattan—many on Wall Street, but most elsewhere—often were at odds with one another over policy and practice, and even within each group there were rivals and enemies, either striving for the same goal, or seeking opposite prizes for themselves and the industry. There wasn't even a close-knit exchange community, for leaders of the N.Y.S.E., the Curb Exchange, the regional markets, and the over-the-counter market had their differences. The Curb, long the "little brother" of the Big Board, had its own handsome building on Trinity Place, and although it had always bowed to the dictates of the N.Y.S.E. Establishment in the past, it had already come to terms with the New Deal, having written a new constitution and having made internal reforms demanded by the Securities and Exchange Commission. The over-the-counter market, a more amorphous organization than any of the established exchanges, contained a range of opinions regarding reforms and the new Administration in Washington. Some over-the-counter brokers feared the N.Y.S.E. and considered it a logical enemy, while others relied upon Big Board commission houses for most of their business. As for the regional exchanges, they considered the N.Y.S.E. a rival, one that already was sending agents into their territories seeking new business.

When successful, they would put additional dents into the regional exchanges' already sagging operations. The N.Y.S.E. was supposed to despise the New Deal, and reserve particular hatred for the Securities and Exchange Commission. In contrast, while most regional exchange leaders had voted against Roosevelt in 1932, they now viewed the New Deal and the S.E.C. as protectors against the depredations of the New Yorkers.

If there was no unified financial district or even a real rather than symbolic Wall Street nexus of power, at least there was the New York Stock Exchange itself. The building certainly existed, with its magnificent Renaissance façade and main entrance—not on Wall Street, however, but on Broad. The institution could trace its origins to 1792 and, with some effort, even earlier, so that it could claim to be older than the nation itself. Most Americans knew of the Stock Exchange and used the term as a symbol for the district and even American capitalism itself. On occasion they identified an individual with the organization, thus employing a double symbolism. Accordingly, J. P. Morgan in his prime was supposed to speak for the N.Y.S.E. and, through it, for the Street, district, and capitalism in general. It was a neat and pat symbol, but as is so often the case with symbols, it was used to mask ignorance and misunderstanding. Morgan did not appear on the floor of the Exchange and had little to do with those who did, men he viewed as hired hands and lackeys. Rather, he operated from offices in his investment banking house, as did his peers, and pulled strings at corporation headquarters and in Washington and Albany. Morgan would use the Big Board to create markets for securities, but had little interest in day-to-day operations on the Exchange itself. Only when the N.Y.S.E.'s ability to absorb new issues was crippled, or when panics threatened the calm he so loved, would he interfere in its operations. In other words, the true power on Wall Street and in the district was not on the Exchange floor or in its upstairs offices but rather in the paneled boardrooms of investment banking houses, where powerful men guarded their privacy; they seldom appeared in the marketplace atmosphere of the floor and used the N.Y.S.E. through emissaries. J. P. Morgan organized United States Steel at the House of Morgan, with occasional state visits to the offices of other investment bankers. He sent his man, James Keene, to the N.Y.S.E. floor, to promote the securities, to "make a market" for "Big Steel," and assure its success among investors.

Richard Whitney was more akin to Keene than to the elder Morgan. Whitney first achieved important public attention during the October 1929 crash, when he appeared on the floor to rally support for the market. There were vivid memories of the tall, impressive Wall Streeter, strolling to the U.S. Steel post and asking its price. On learning it had last traded at 205, but was down a few points since then, Whitney smiled gravely and then put in an order for 10,000 shares at 205—thus indicating his confidence in the stock. Whitney continued to do the same for several other key issues, and the market rallied for a while. As far as the general public was concerned, Whitney had tried to save the day—he had acted in 1929 as Morgan had during the 1907 panic. In 1907, however, Morgan did not appear on the floor; he sent his representatives. And this was the situation in 1929 as well. Thomas Lamont of J. P. Morgan & Co., Albert Wiggin of the Chase National Bank, William Potter of the Guaranty Trust, George F. Baker, Jr., of the First National Bank, Seward Prosser of Bankers Trust, and a handful of other financial giants of the day—men who controlled over $6 billion in assets—gathered at Morgan headquarters and put together a pool of some $20 to $30 million, which was to be used to support the market. Then they sent their man—Richard Whitney—to the N.Y.S.E. floor to place the orders.

Within a year, Whitney was N.Y.S.E. president and spokesman, but from the first to the last he had no real power but rather was the errand boy of the mighty. Still, to the public at large, Whitney was the symbol of the Stock Exchange and Wall Street and was the most dramatic defender of American capitalism in the first years of the New Deal.

People confused the image with the reality, a confusion that began when the investment bankers needed a spokesman and, in effect, hired one, who happened to be a key N.Y.S.E. figure and later president of that institution. The identification was enhanced by newspapers, magazines, and radio, as reporters and editors went to Whitney whenever a statement in defense of finance capitalism was needed. Whitney himself came to believe it, although bankers knew that his brother, George, was far more powerful in the district than he. Even the New Dealers, and the President, acted as though Whitney spoke for a unified financial community.

So it was that Whitney was called to Washington to meet with F.D.R. in April 1933 to offer his ideas on legislation affecting finance. Whitney came out strongly in favor of "self-regulation." Allow the district to police itself, he said, and all would be well. Roosevelt disagreed, as did the district's critics in Congress. Throughout 1933 and early 1934, Whitney shuttled back and forth between the Exchange and Washington, speaking before congressional committees and with Administration leaders, hoping to convince them of his point of view. On other occasions he would travel to business conventions to bring the message of self-regulation, write articles for influential magazines, and speak before radio audiences.

In the end he was defeated; the Securities Exchange Act passed and was signed into law on June 6, 1934. The Securities and Exchange Commission was established, with Joseph P. Kennedy—a former stock speculator and, in the view of the Establishment, an *arriviste*—in command. Whitney could barely hide his displeasure as he showed Kennedy and other commissioners around the Exchange, and he continued to speak out against federal intervention. As before, the public assumed he was speaking for the institution, the Street, and the district. Such was not the case.

Stock Exchange members could agree that most people had lost confidence in the institution. They could measure this quantitatively in terms of trading volume, prices, and their own business losses. Or they could read the comments and listen to the commentaries of formerly friendly newspapermen and newscasters. The 1932 election results could be interpreted as a mandate for change on Wall Street, and even the signal for an antibusiness crusade not unlike the one their fathers suffered through before World War I. The nation was in a depression and needed a scapegoat, said some members, and business was to be it, with Wall Street and the N.Y.S.E. both the symbols of the disease and the cancer to be removed before a cure could be affected.

What was to be done in the face of this? Most members defended their institutions and actions, and they applauded Whitney's vigorous attack on the New Deal. Emotionally, at least, they were for the status quo and resented attempts on the part of Washington to interfere with what they considered a private business. But some—perhaps a majority—realized that the New Dealers would not be denied and that some reforms would be necessary. Whitney's self-regulation would not be enough; the N.Y.S.E. would have to accept the S.E.C. and work with the commissioners in much the same way perhaps that the railroads had come to terms with the Interstate Commerce Commission years before. There was no hard and fast boundary between the standpatters and the members who looked upon the New Deal as a needed cathartic for the district; rather, there was a continuum of opinion, in which members glided from a tendency in one direction to the other, depending upon mood, New Deal measures, trading volume, and other external developments.

There was another division of opinion at the N.Y.S.E., this one based on still more subtle distinctions. The Wall Street Establishment—including the major banks and particularly the key investment bankers—tended to oppose the New Deal and external regulation. Of course, not all felt that way; the oldest, Lehman Brothers, was a citadel of reformist sentiment, for example. But in the main, the struggle seemed to be between Wall Street and the White House. Each side had supporters. Wall Street's major investment banks had the look and sound of legitimacy in the mid-1930s, even though they had been scarred in the early years of the decade, and there were many small houses eager to ally themselves with the district's leaders and speak against "outside meddling." One could not hope to associate professionally, not to say socially, with the leaders of the House of Morgan, but at least one could take up that firm's banner, and so be known as a "Morgan-ally," and perhaps even win a nod from a junior partner on the N.Y.S.E. trading floor. Such was the real and psychic currency at Wall and Broad. Whitehouse & Co. received part of its bond business from J. P. Morgan & Co.; Charles Gay was considered one such Morgan satellite in 1935.

Maverick companies, in particular those whose origins were in other cities and which still maintained significant non–New York operations, often favored a degree of outside regulation, if only to curb the impulses and actions of a group to which they did not really belong. Kidder Peabody of Boston, an important underwriter of industrial securities at the turn of the century, had by 1935 become a supportive rather than initiating concern. Halsey, Stuart & Co. of Chicago, which in the 1920s dared challenge Morgan itself in utilities underwritings, had been forced to bow to New York power. Blyth, Witter & Co., a West Coast firm, had always viewed the Establishment in a guarded fashion. The Harriman interests, as much a Philadelphia-based operation as one of New York, had a record of independent actions. These and other such non–New York firms were bases for reformist sentiment, derived in part from a belief that change was needed, but also from a desire to humble the Establishment.

As important as ideological and geographic considerations—and in terms of distinction more precise—was that of function at the Exchange. To the general public, all Stock Exchange members were alike; although some were more distinguished and wealthier than others, they all performed similar tasks. In fact, there were three basic roles played on the floor, and some members attempted successfully to assay two of them.

The specialists were a key group, one with a set of interests the general public ordinarily identified as the "Stock Exchange mentality," although it was more complicated than that. Specialists were members whose function was to "make a market" in one or several stocks. They did this by maintaining an inventory of shares in an issue and standing ready to buy and sell from and to other members. Thus, a specialist might be asked, "How's XYZ?," and reply—translating the shorthand of the floor—that he would buy at $45 a share and was prepared to sell shares at $45.50. At that moment, the specialist in XYZ would not know the intentions of the questioner. The response might be an order to buy 100 shares, in which case the transaction would take place between $45 and $45.50 a share plus commission.

The specialist would also accept orders at fixed prices. Thus, a second member might place an order to sell 1,000 shares at $50, and this would be executed if and when XYZ reached that price, while a third could place an order to buy 1,000 shares at $42, which would become operational at that price. These orders would go into the specialist's "book," and this information about bids and offers would give specialists a knowledge of the market for their stocks that could prove useful to insiders. Indeed, the specialists could buy and sell for their own accounts, in this fashion making greater fortunes from the market than any other group. This part of the specialist activity had been criticized long before the 1929 crash, and the response was always the same: the specialist had to buy and sell for his account in order to maintain his inventory of the stock, and this was necessary so as to maintain an orderly market in the shares.

On other occasions, specialists worked closely with private traders—members who did not specialize or execute orders for the general public but rather used their memberships to deal for their own accounts. The great plungers of the 1920s—Jesse Livermore, Arthur Cutten, Ben Smith, and others—were private traders. The most successful of the group had a keen sense of the market and an ability to manipulate and bluff that would have served them well in Las Vegas today. But to shorten the odds, they would enter into relationships with specialists in the stocks in which they were interested, in order to learn about the demand for the issue on both the buy and sell sides, and then would use the information in their dealings.

The specialists were at the Exchange throughout the day and had no direct dealings with outsiders, operating instead among their peers. The private traders were out to make their own fortunes, counting upon public ignorance, stupidity, or foolishness to assist in their work. In terms of their functions alone, neither group had much interest in the individual investors, the people who had been so badly burned during the crash and afterward. Although the specialists earned part of their incomes from public transactions, they could survive without them. In 1935, it appeared that they would do so, and in collaboration with the private traders. In the second half of the year, according to an S.E.C. report, almost a quarter of all transactions were accounted for by members acting for themselves. This activity was concentrated in popular issues; over 30 percent of the volume in the twenty most active stocks came from members dealing for their own accounts. At the time there were 450 N.Y.S.E. firms, and of these only 172 received more than 85 percent of their income from brokerage commissions. The report indicated that only 66 of the houses did not trade for their own accounts. Of those that did, 80 had partners who traded at least 5,000 shares each in one month, while one had a partner who traded 910,000 shares for his own account in a single month. It was clear, too, that these private deals were profitable, and perhaps based on inside information obtained from specialists and other sources. During the 139 trading days in the second half of the year, the private traders were with the trend for 90 days, and against it for only 49. Finally, although specialists and private traders accounted for only half the N.Y.S.E. seats, two-thirds of the governors came from these two groups. News such as this substantiated widespread beliefs that the N.Y.S.E. was being run as a private club with little concern for the general welfare.*

The third group—the commission brokers—had a direct interest in the public, since most of their earnings were dependent upon orders from the so-called little guy. These were the men for whom the volume figures told the important story, and who hoped for bull markets in order to draw people to the Street. Small investors had little confidence in securities in 1935 and were uncertain regarding the integrity of the N.Y.S.E. Ever since the 1929 crash, newspapers and magazines had run stories of stock manipulations, and the small investors were surprised to learn that little of this had been against the law or even in violation of N.Y.S.E. rules.

The Exchange leaders attempted to regain confidence both through prosecutions of brokers and specialists for infractions of rules and through the promulgation of new regulations. On February 13, 1934, the Governing Committee prohibited members from participating in pools, syndicates, and joint accounts "organized or used intentionally for the purpose of unfairly influencing the market price of any security," and then forbade specialists from "disclosing to any person, other than certain committees of the Exchange, any information in regard to orders entrusted to him." Finally, "specialists [are] prohibited from acquiring or granting any option in the stocks in which they specialize." Other internal reforms followed, all in the spirit of self-regulation, but it is doubtful they had a significant impact on the public. Clearly, in a depression, few had money to invest or with which to speculate. But of those who did, many must have viewed the Exchange's reforms as a sign that it had been a dishonest institution in the past, when it also claimed to have been an equitable marketplace.

In effect, the organization's leaders were in a no-win situation. If they sponsored reform, it would be taken as an admission of prior guilt and perhaps present corruption, while a lack of action might be interpreted as a refusal to own up to abuses. In either case, the result would be a loss of public confidence, and this would harm the

* Richardson Wood, "New York Market," *Review of Reviews* (Vol. 94, No. 11, November 1936), pp. 40–44.

commission brokers more than the specialists, and the private traders least of all. Cooperation with the S.E.C., which might lead to an official endorsement of the Exchange and a New Deal imprimatur on securities dealings, was desirable. The others might hold out against reforms; the commission brokers would capitulate to Washington in the hope of regaining a portion of their old business, without which some might be forced into liquidation.

The reformist commission houses had articulate spokesmen. Paul V. Shields, one of the few Wall Streeters of prominence who had backed Roosevelt in 1932, was one of these, and a man with friends at the Securities and Exchange Commission. W. Averell Harriman, considered a flighty outsider but the possessor of a potent name, was another who was in the process of going over to the New Deal. E. A. Pierce, one of the district's leading figures, often spoke of the need for *rapprochement* with Washington. John W. Hanes of Charles D. Barney, who had been a candidate for the N.Y.S.E. presidency in 1935, was edging closer to the reformers, although still uneasy regarding a major challenge.

These, then, were the divisions at the N.Y.S.E. in 1935. Financial writers and several prominent Wall Street "insiders" considered them deep. There was some talk that the conflict between the reformist brokers and the Establishment might divide the district into warring camps, leaving whatever remained in chaos, a fit area for government intervention and even control. It was a dramatic time, when it was fashionable to speak and write as though most of the nation's key institutions would be cleansed and transformed by the New Dealers, who would work with allies in all parts of the country and in all areas of American life. The national struggle would be one between standpatters and reformers, and on Wall Street, between the Old Guard and the New Deal. Richard Whitney, who spoke of defying the specter of collectivism, reinforced the belief, as did fiery statements by such S.E.C. figures as William O. Douglas regarding a "break-up of the center of finance capitalism and its dispersion throughout the nation." But underneath the public images and discounting hyperbole, there remained a community of interest at the N.Y.S.E. in the mid-1930s, while the S.E.C. was, from the first, a moderate and rather conservative organization insofar as its leadership was concerned. It was so under Joseph P. Kennedy (1934–1935), and James Landis (1935–1937), and even under Douglas (1937–1939).

There simply was no place for radicalism or extreme liberalism in the Wall Street power centers of the time. There was much talk of the "Shields-Pierce-Hanes reform element," as though these men were interested in leading a movement to crush the Old Guard and, with the aid of the S.E.C., take its place. Yet Shields considered Felix Frankfurter and his associates—rumored to be the "real power" in Washington and in favor of a strong S.E.C.—harmful national influences. Pierce had backed Hoover in 1932, as had most of his friends. When he spoke out in favor of a Wall Street czar, Pierce added, "It should be someone along the lines of former President Coolidge." Pierce had loaned money to Whitney, and the two men belonged to many of the same clubs. As for Hanes, he was particularly close to the House of Morgan, and as a conservative southern Democrat, was shocked in 1933 by what he termed "the excessive zeal of some of Roosevelt's men." Before 1934, he had been on good terms with Whitney. Then, when Barney & Co. came close to failure that year, and Whitney refused to use his influence in its behalf, the two men grew apart. When Hanes agreed to run for the presidency in 1935, it was at the behest of conservative N.Y.S.E. leaders who wanted, of all things, to work with Joseph Kennedy and defy Whitney, who seemed to grow more intransigent every day.

At first, the district did not know what to make of Kennedy. Wall Street had been shocked by the nomination, and afterward fearful of what he might do. A well-known private trader in the 1920s and early 1930s, he seemed just the kind of person any reform movement would try to eliminate from the marketplace. It was observed that most of the manipulations and schemes that resulted in the Kennedy fortune were now illegal under laws he was supposed to enforce. Standpat conservatives, like Whitney, viewed Kennedy as a brash outsider who certainly was not of their kind, either socially or in a business sense. The more liberal Wall Streeters, such as Paul Mazur of Lehman Brothers, thought Kennedy was one of the most devious men in American finance. Both groups were angered by and admired the nomination; F.D.R. had not only rewarded his supporter but set a fox to catch the foxes. As much as anyone, Kennedy knew where the bodies were buried on the Street, and could dig them out. The Old Guard might fool an idealistic college professor, work with a reformist lawyer, or come to terms with a bureaucrat, but none of them would cooperate with Kennedy if he really wanted to transform the district.

But he didn't, as the N.Y.S.E. leaders quickly learned. Kennedy was concerned with the so-called strike of capital, by which investment banks seemed to be refusing to underwrite new debt and equity issues until they were more confident of the climate in Washington. In particular, the district was disturbed about some of the provisions of the Securities Act of 1933 and the Banking Act of that same year. Under their terms, underwriters had to submit to a long list of regulations, while commercial banks were obliged to divest themselves of their investment banking affiliates. Kennedy was charged with carrying out these provisions as well as recommending new legislation to regulate the district in general and the exchanges specifically. In 1934 it appeared that few men were better equipped than he to get around such regulations, and therefore it appeared reasonable to assume that Kennedy, perhaps more than anyone else, would be able to prevent abuses if he were of a mind to do so.

Kennedy delighted the district's leaders by taking a moderate position on reform. Some at the S.E.C. wanted to punish the exchanges, and there was even talk of nationalization if opposition to reform continued. Instead, Kennedy concentrated on assuring Wall Street he would undertake no punitive expeditions. After three months of tactful handholding and restraint, the chairman won over a sizable number of Stock Exchange moderates. The *Magazine of Wall Street* reported that "more intimate contact with the commissioners seemed to have produced confidence that the new S.E.C. rules will involve no unnecessary harshness." The strike of capital ended, and for the rest of his stay at the S.E.C., Kennedy continued to earn the moderates' trust, not so much for what he did as for what he might have done but didn't.

Kennedy called for self-regulation, but he meant something different from Whitney's use of the term. The N.Y.S.E. spokesman wanted the Exchange to make policy and carry it out, while the chairman would have the Commission formulate rules and leave enforcement to the exchanges. But Kennedy did not press his point, content merely with setting the stage for others and establishing a beachhead in the district. Most Exchange leaders recognized the difference between rhetoric and action.

Whitney was not among them. He remained adamant, insisting on responding to almost all of Kennedy's speeches and refusing to concede the government a role at the Exchange. Whitney rejected talk of reform; "The Stock Exchange is a perfect institution," he said. And initially, he had the membership with him.

In its first annual report, issued in January 1935, the S.E.C. found the nation's exchanges badly in need of change. The 1929 debacle had been caused by abuses, and these remained five years later. In particular, nothing had been done to curb the power of private traders and specialists. The report was less critical of the commission houses. By then, Kennedy recognized that whatever reform sentiment existed at the N.Y.S.E. was there, and, in effect, he gave men like Hanes and Shields ammunition to use in their attempts to reform the institution. Kennedy would do all in his power to help them. But if they failed, the S.E.C. would enter the picture and do the job for them. This appeared to be the threat in 1935. The reformist commission brokers understood this and continued their efforts. President Gay recognized the situation, but felt he could do little about it without the support of the Governing and Law committees. Both of these remained true to Whitney, and he not only rejected Kennedy's recommendations, but seemed to welcome the chance to enter the lists against him.

The two central issues in 1935 were a proposal to segregate broker and dealer functions and another to curb specialists and private traders. The former was an "inside" matter in that it was not recognized as a problem by most Americans, while the latter was discussed not only by financial columnists but on the front pages of the New York press.

The so-called segregation question was based on the operations of brokers and investment bankers during the 1920s. During the wild bull period of that decade, investment bankers would agree to sell an issue of stock and then proceed to help create a market for it by buying and selling the security. Thus, the same broker who had underwritten the stock, and through his customer's men had told the investors it was a fine investment, might be selling it at the Exchange to unload his shares. Or he could manipulate the issue, causing it to rise, and so lure other investors into purchases. These practices were obvious abuses of power, and the S.E.C. felt they had to stop. The brokers, on their part, argued that they could not simply underwrite an issue unless they also made a market in it, at least during the underwriting, so as to ensure liquidity. Unless buyers and sellers knew that there were others prepared to sell and buy, they wouldn't purchase new issues. And unless they did, private capitalism couldn't function. In effect, they insisted that if the segregation proposal went through, it would destroy liquidity and, with it, the securities markets. If they went, America would be well on the road to communism.

The curbs on private traders and specialists derived from Section 11 (a) of the Securities Exchange Act of 1934:

> The Commission shall prescribe such rules and regulations as it deems necessary or appropriate in the public interest or for the protection of investors, (1) to regulate or prevent floor trading by members of national securities exchanges, directly or indirectly for their own accounts or for discretionary accounts, and (2) to prevent such excessive trading on the exchange but off the floor by members, directly or indirectly for their own account, as the Commission may deem detrimental to the maintenance of a fair and orderly market. . . .

Some ardent S.E.C. lawyers recognized that given the small staff and budget, it would be impossible to enforce the provisions of the section. They offered a solution to the problem: end the specialist system and ban private trades. In effect, they would give the specialist a new set of standards, one that forbade him from dealing for his own account. In the future, they said, the specialist would act as a broker for the public—he would bring together buyer and seller on the floor and receive a commission for his work. He could not buy and sell stock for his own account, to add or subtract from his inventory. Let the law of supply and demand operate, went the argument, even though it would mean large jumps in the prices of securities. At a time when much of the public had left Wall Street, the S.E.C. felt little compunction to protect the arena for gamblers (as many S.E.C. figures believed those who "played the market" were).

This would sacrifice the "fair and orderly market" mentioned in the Securities Exchange Act, however, and the N.Y.S.E. had always claimed this was the major reason for the system. A second alternative —and a more realistic one considering the circumstances—was to convince the exchanges of the desirability of self-regulation. But to accomplish this, the government would have to accept the core of the Old Guard's position, including the specialist system. It was a complex problem, with no solution in sight in 1935.

At first the S.E.C. reformers tried to persuade the Big Board that there must be strict curbs on specialist activities and an end to private trading. All transactions would be for the public; a N.Y.S.E. seat would carry an obligation to serve investors and speculators. Members would be forbidden from using their positions to trade for their own accounts. If this were done, so the argument ran, the Exchange would be transformed from a private club into a truly public market. Once the alterations were completed and investors made aware of them, they would return to the markets, with the result being increased volume and benefits for all.

Increased volume was more important for the commission brokers than for the specialists, while it was of marginal interest to the private traders. The latter two groups rejected the S.E.C. argument. The actions being proposed would represent violations of their rights and major transgressions of their freedom to trade. Furthermore, the removal of private traders, and the possible curbing of purchases and sales by specialists for their own accounts, would result in a loss of liquidity, and this was to be avoided at all costs.

In this way, the segregation and specialist/private-trader issues were united. The N.Y.S.E. was charged with providing a market for stocks. In fact, this was spelled out in the constitution:

> Its objects shall be to furnish exchange rooms and other facilities for the convenient transaction of their business by its members; to maintain high standards of commercial honor and integrity among its members; and *to promote and inculcate just and equitable principles of trade and business* [emphasis added].

In the past, "equitable principles" had been interpreted as having two meanings. The first was that of an orderly market—liquidity—and the second of honor and integrity in dealings with the public. To violate either would be to say that the Exchange was no longer needed. Thus, the S.E.C.'s suggestions struck at the foundation of the institution, and the specialists and private traders were united behind Whitney in opposition to these fundamental changes.

There was yet another factor, one that interested the S.E.C. commissioners and led them to moderate their stance during the Kennedy years. The Commission had broad powers over the organized securities exchanges, and these might be regulated, since they were, after all, institutions in fixed geographic locations. The S.E.C. had less to do with the over-the-counter market, which functioned through telephone networks, without a trading floor, and would be close to impossible to regulate. Forbidden from trading at the N.Y.S.E., private traders would take their business to this market. Clandestine exchanges—almost like the speakeasies of the 1920s—might appear, and those, of course, would be uncontrollable, given the small S.E.C. staff and budget. Finally, segregation would be a dose of castor oil for the N.Y.S.E., but it well might doom the regional exchanges, since they were in worse financial shape than the Big Board. Thus, Kennedy, though willing and at times anxious to regulate this kind of floor trading, drew back from prescribing rules to enforce the change. His refusal to act drew criticism from other commissioners, and in particular angered the young New Deal lawyers who had entered the Commission hoping to use it as a weapon against the Wall Street Establishment.

Such individuals expected better from Kennedy's successor. James Landis had helped draft the securities legislation, and before that had been a law professor at Harvard, where he had been considered the protégé of Dean Roscoe Pound. But Landis was no radical, nor even a believer in thoroughgoing reform, while S.E.C. commissioner. He concentrated on gathering information, spoke of the Commission as a vehicle through which the district could cleanse itself, and refused to push for broker-dealer segregation. Max Lowenthal, a lawyer on Senator Duncan Fletcher's staff and a reformer who had hoped the S.E.C. would enforce strict rules on Wall Street, wrote of his disappointment to Frankfurter. "[His] tenure, however vernal may have been the hope with which it started, faded out in a dismal autumn fashion. . . . It has become increasingly clear that Landis likes the big boys and that the big boys like Landis." A. Wilfred May, a S.E.C. staff member, quit in disgust. Commission chief economist Kemper Simpson and his assistant, Wallis Ballinger, prepared a report recommending segregation, which Landis and the other commissioners rejected. Then Simpson and Ballinger leaked the report to the press, and were fired for insubordination. Landis supported the N.Y.S.E. on the segregation issue throughout his tenure. When the reformers tried to force the Exchange to stop trading unlisted issues, Landis intervened on its behalf.* Those who rejected this approach were silenced, quit, or were fired.

William O. Douglas survived the Landis era, in large part because he was able to adjust to the prevailing climate and could zero in accurately on the attitudes of those who had power over him and could offer rewards. Douglas had been a law professor at Yale when, in 1933, he was called to Washington to help frame the Securities Act. Later on he produced a study of protective committees and corporate reorganization under the Act. When Kennedy resigned, Douglas was named to the S.E.C., and in early 1936 was considered one of the "New Deal wild men" by the press.

Douglas was anything but wild during the Landis years. He came out against segregation and was on good terms with the N.Y.S.E. leaders. In mid-September, for example, he traveled to New York to meet with members of the Exchange's Special Committee on the Segregation Report, which was headed by Howland Davis. A week or so later—on September 21, 1936—Davis reported on a dinner he had had with Douglas at the Union League Club, one attended by several other S.E.C. and N.Y.S.E. figures. According to committee minutes:

> Mr. Davis said that he had the feeling that Mr. Douglas appeared to be quite fair and was searching for the truth as to the best interests of all. He also gathered from the discussion that the Commission was not inclined to hurry us at all but was really more anxious to get the facts, particularly as to the members' trading, even though it might take us a little time to do so. The [N.Y.S.E.] Chairman further states that the spirit of the dinner was very cooperative on all sides.
>
> Mr. Gayer Dominick stated that after the dinner he had driven Commissioner Douglas to the station and that about the last thing

* Michael E. Parrish, *Securities Regulation and the New Deal* (New Haven, 1970), pp. 209–15, is an excellent account of internal tensions at the S.E.C.

> the Commissioner said was, "It is quite clear to me that we will have to get additional information before we can come to any final decision and it will, no doubt, take some time to get that. However, you will probably hear from us within a week or ten days and we then may be able to let you know what we would like to have." *

Relations between Douglas and the Special Committee were cordial and occasionally friendly during the next three months, even though the Exchange provided the S.E.C. with little in the way of new information. Confidence was being restored on Wall Street. The N.Y.S.E. had come through the first reform wave, while at the same time business was recovering. Trading volume rose from 324 million shares in 1934 to 382 million in 1935, and then, in 1936, to 496 million. Specialists and private traders no longer feared for their survival; some commission houses instituted programs to train new brokers. Perhaps because of this the N.Y.S.E. leaders decided to hold the line against further reforms and, in fact, turn back the tide to the pre–New Deal situation as much as possible.

In Washington, Landis chafed at his job. Although concerned with setting up the regulatory apparatus and organizing his study groups, Landis was not really interested in administration. Nor had he shown any significant talents at politics or in dealing with Wall Street figures. Douglas and others at the S.E.C. knew that Landis ached to return to Harvard, and several New Dealers began jockeying to take his place.

Roosevelt had won an impressive mandate for reform in 1936. He swamped Alfred Landon, his Republican opponent, who had captured only two states. Economic recovery, which had been slow but steady since 1933, accelerated in the spring of 1936, due in part to the removal of some restrictions on production. From May 1936 to September 1937 the employment index rose from 96.4 to 112.2 and the payroll index from 84.4 to 109. Industrial production went from 101 to 117 in this same period. By almost any criteria, the Great Depression seemed to have been conquered.

It was at this point that Douglas began lashing out at the N.Y.S.E. Whether through conviction or a desire to take leadership of the S.E.C. "hard-liners," he was the one major figure at the Commission to demand a continuation of the reform effort. In January 1937 he asked for a new report on the segregation issue and indicated that he had gone over to the Simpson-Ballinger position. Two months later, in an address to the Bond Club in Chicago, Douglas criticized the lack of competition in investment banking and alluded to unfair practices at

* New York Stock Exchange, Special Committee on the Segregation Report, Minutes for September 21, 1936.

the N.Y.S.E. In April he told a group of trainees at a brokerage institute that "Our educational system has been too virile in the production of men immunized from a sense of feeling of social responsibility." Instead, it produced individuals "trained in the art of plunder in gentlemanly ways," who were "imbued with the false ideal that the American way means exploitation."

If F.D.R. intended to nominate an anti–Big Board figure to head the S.E.C. after Landis's departure, clearly Douglas would be his man. But this seemed unlikely in May, when the economic boom was still on, and Roosevelt had relented somewhat in his antibusiness crusade. Indeed, for a while it appeared a *rapprochement* between Roosevelt and moderate Wall Streeters was in the works. W. Averell Harriman, now a New Dealer himself, worked toward that end, and he urged Roosevelt to replace Landis with a prominent pro-Administration businessman if and when the chairman resigned.

As the S.E.C. prepared for a changing of the guard, and while the economic recovery continued, Charles Gay prepared his annual report to the membership, delivered on August 18. The Dow Industrials closed at 189.10 that day. Volume was low; only 702,000 shares were traded. This was quite a change from February, when there hadn't been a day when fewer than a million shares changed hands. Volume had declined markedly since then, and there was some talk that the economic boom might be peaking. Nevertheless, Gay felt he spoke from a position of strength, and devoted the first part of the report to the matter of N.Y.S.E.–S.E.C. relations. "That good has resulted from government supervision and regulation is granted," he said. "However, the time is here when we should assess losses against gains. If the result indicates that a broad and liquid national market is being impaired so that it does not function freely, it follows, of course, that it may cease to function in time of stress. Then, indeed, the public interest is being harmed."

Gay concluded that the public interest was best served by institutions like the Stock Exchange, while the S.E.C. had perhaps outlived its usefulness and, indeed, was a prime example of how regulation could be self-defeating and produce evil effects. At the crux of the matter was the segregation issue. "No dispassionate observer could fairly attribute these security market conditions entirely to any one cause or regulation," he said, after discussing the decline in trading volume over the past half year. "On the other hand, it seems clear that they are to a substantial degree due to various legislative and regulatory measures, which have had the effect of discouraging the buying and selling of securities." The New Deal, while perhaps necessary at one time, now stood in the way of recovery. Perhaps Roosevelt should consider disbanding some of the regulatory agencies established in

1933 and 1934 and encourage Congress to repeal or at least eliminate parts of laws passed during the famous first hundred days of his Administration. Gay did not say as much, but he surely meant the various laws regulating the securities industry, and the S.E.C. itself.

The Gay report was not unexpected; nor was its tone unusual. Richard Whitney had long said as much. But Gay was supposed to be somewhat different—a man who represented the N.Y.S.E. Establishment, but at the same time offered a new course and symbolized Wall Street's willingness to accept reforms. His August report signaled a triumph of conservatism at the Big Board, at least insofar as the public stance was concerned.

Landis announced his resignation on September 15, by which time the economic boom had ended, and it appeared a new downturn had begun. This had been caused by a tight-money policy at the Federal Reserve and a slowdown in government spending, which had not been compensated for by the private sector. On the day Landis resigned the Dow Industrials closed at 165.16, off more than 11 percent in the month since the Gay report.

Gay was asked to comment on Landis's resignation. The N.Y.S.E. president praised the man, but reiterated his earlier views: there must be a moderation of government activity in the economy if true recovery was to take place. The bulls were still to be found in the Street, and even though federal spending was down, the private sector could take up the slack—but only if confidence was certain.

On September 21—six days later—Douglas was appointed chairman of the S.E.C. The Dow closed the session at 159.26. Wall Street was uneasy. The time seemed ripe for a renewal of the New Deal's struggle with the business community, which once again had been singled out as the cause of economic hardship. Douglas would be well suited to head the Administration's attack.

And Charles Gay was Wall Street's most prominent spokesman, the defender of the Establishment against Douglas. Of course, it was the office he held, as much as the man, that was listened to, but, still, Gay had accumulated a following since becoming president. He knew, even then, that the economic decline had given heart to the reform elements and that the commission houses were lining up behind them. Hard-liners, also girding for battle, considered Richard Whitney their spokesman, with Gay merely a messenger boy, a cipher. Douglas appeared exhilarated, ready to put into effect ideas he had considered for the past four years, while to some it seemed Whitney was prepared to do battle with him.

Charles Gay wavered, wondering perhaps how he ever had managed to get into his position. In mid-September he told a reporter he hadn't planted his garden the previous spring. There would be no late fall blooms.

CHAPTER 2

The Advent of Reform

Few twentieth-century Americans have been as contentious as William O. Douglas. He took stands on most public issues, winning enthusiastic applause from some and bitter opposition from many—though the latter usually were individuals more concerned with appearance than reality, with rhetoric than performance. From the first, one heard words like "reformer," "liberal," "progressive," and even "radical" used to describe him. But if the adjectives were accurate—and there is disagreement on this—Douglas was all of these within a distinctly American context, one rather narrow as such things go. In reality Douglas was slightly to the left of Franklin D. Roosevelt, who described himself as being slightly to the left of center.

Douglas did not question the basic tenets of American capitalism in 1937, when, at the age of thirty-eight, he took command of the S.E.C., or afterward. He would regulate corporations, using the power of government to counter that of large aggregations of wealth, and enforce antitrust laws with vigor. But he would not nationalize industries; nor was he ever a socialist of any hue. Later on, Douglas spoke of a "creative tension" in American society, which prevented any one force from gaining dominance over the others, and he approved of this. He was in the tradition of Louis Brandeis (whom he would succeed on the Supreme Court) and Woodrow Wilson, laced with that of Herbert Croly and Theodore Roosevelt, with a sprinkling of Walter Lippmann and the surface glaze of Eugene V. Debs. He was nothing if not eclectic, as are most successful American politicians. In Britain he would have been a Liberal, and in Germany, a Social Democrat. In America, in the early 1930s and after, he was considered a radical.

The new chairman of the Securities and Exchange Commission wanted no revolution on Wall Street. Although a professed admirer of Louis Brandeis, he did not go as far as that reformer in asking for a breakup of corporate power and its scattering throughout the nation.

Douglas wanted the locus of national finance to remain where it was—on Wall Street—but he would insist that the district's leaders accept the letter and spirit of the Securities Act of 1933 and related legislation. Such an approach might win Douglas support from reformers at the commission houses, and even a few of the specialists and investment bankers. A moderate and conciliatory attitude could prod centerists like Gay to come to terms with the New Deal, especially if they could be made to believe that such an accommodation would lead to greater volume and even higher prices because of renewed confidence in the markets. Douglas wanted results, and the most important of these was a "clean" N.Y.S.E. that saw the virtues of regulation.

He was flexible as to means, however. On the one hand, he could mount a frontal assault against the Establishment. Kennedy had organized the mechanism for the attack, while Landis had gathered the ammunition. All Douglas had to do was give the word, and his eager young lawyers would swarm over the district, obliging N.Y.S.E. and other financial leaders to do their bidding. It would not be easy. As one of Douglas's friends and colleagues wrote, the S.E.C. would have difficulties "with its long drawn-out processes of constant vigilance, painstaking investigation, preliminary hearing, Commission hearing, Commission decision, possible appeal to the courts, and even to high courts." It would be much simpler and more direct for the N.Y.S.E. to handle such matters on its own, through self-regulation. Douglas wanted converts at the Big Board, not a host of vanquished and sullen foes.* In the beginning, then, he sought allies eagerly, employing charm, suasion, and good humor, while at the same time making certain the N.Y.S.E. knew that if these failed, a harsher, more thorough program would follow.

The Douglas views were clear, and made even clearer in September and October 1937 in a series of speeches and discussions. He called upon the Exchange to reform itself in almost all aspects of its organization, structure, and function. In the past, he claimed, the N.Y.S.E. served the needs and desires of its members, especially the specialists and private traders; it was, in effect, a "private club." Now it would have to serve the investors instead, and this would require changes. Private traders should be eliminated, said Douglas, with the N.Y.S.E. purchasing their seats and retiring them. The specialists should be obliged to meet new, stringent standards of behavior, with stiff penalties for breaches. The N.Y.S.E. administration itself should be scrapped, for it had always reflected the will of powerful specialists and investment bankers. In its place there should be a new administra-

* Fred Rodell, "Douglas Over the Stock Exchange," *Fortune* (Vol. 17, No. 2, February 1938), pp. 118–19, 120–26.

tion, with a paid president and staff, independent of the floor, with power over it. The president should be selected by a board, which would include public as well as private members—government officials, educators, and recognized men of character. The first order of business for the new administration would be to put bans on short selling and trading on margin, since both encouraged gambling, and so were not in what Douglas considered the public interest. Douglas felt that odd-lot dealers—houses that specialized in serving individuals who traded in less than 100 share units—were badly in need of regulation, and perhaps had always worked to cheat small investors. He would place curbs on the off-the-floor dealings of members, who had in the past used privileged information to make killings by buying and selling listed shares on the over-the-counter market. Finally, Douglas criticized the commission houses for being more interested in churning accounts so as to maximize commissions than in truly serving their customers.

It was a thorough program, one most N.Y.S.E. leaders thought extreme. The Whitneyites believed that, if enacted, it would not only destroy the Exchange but result in an end to liquidity in American finance, resulting in a Wall Street crash besides which that of 1929 would look like a minor tantrum. President Gay would not go so far—at least, in his public utterances. "My experience has convinced me that the Exchange is fully alive to its public function," he said. But he would cooperate with Douglas in "making the Exchange a more perfect institution." As for Whitney, he rejected S.E.C. controls and influence, stating that much of the nation's troubles were due to "interference" from Washington.

If the Whitneyites rejected the S.E.C. *in toto*, and Gay indicated—politely but firmly—that the Commission's attempts to change the N.Y.S.E. structure would be opposed, the reformers felt otherwise. Douglas had seemed reasonable enough in private conversations in the past, even though his public statements in September and early October were somewhat harsh. Taken together, they seemed to indicate a man who was willing to work with the Exchange for change, and even allow the members to decide tactical questions on their own, but would insist upon having the new regulations carried out. The commissioner's attitude and the impressions he made upon the N.Y.S.E. leaders also suggested that he was an able politician and one who would support reformers if they made their presence known.

Shortly after assuming office, Douglas received overtures from the reform element. Shields and Pierce in particular wanted to meet with him to discuss proposed modifications in the N.Y.S.E. structure and operations. Douglas granted them a hearing in late September, at which time the two commission brokers spoke of their willingness to join with him in a reform program. But there was an important condition. They would speak out in favor of changes within the Exchange in public and do all they could in that direction. Shields and Pierce would expect S.E.C. approval and support, but they—not Douglas—would decide how this was to be done. Reform was a touchy matter. If the N.Y.S.E. members felt it was being rammed down their throats, they would stiffen against it. They could be coaxed and wheedled into change, but only if they thought it came from their own kind, and not from a representative of "that man in the White House." In other words, Pierce and Shields had come to believe the Douglas program necessary and desirable for the Exchange itself—one that should have been adopted and even framed by the board had not the S.E.C. existed. They would dictate the form of new regulations, and would receive the credit (and abuse) for them. Douglas would get the substance of his desires.

The commissioner agreed. When he heard the proposal from the two somewhat uneasy men, he slapped his knee and chuckled. "Would you mind saying that again?" The commissioner extracted no promises or guarantees, and he didn't offer any of his own. For the time being, the S.E.C. and the Pierce-Shields group would play it by ear.

Had securities prices and volume stabilized in the late autumn of 1937, Douglas might have been content to let it go at that. Through attrition, ultimate victory was possible. John Hanes and others, who were sitting on the fence, indicated they would join with Pierce and Shields. The reform element was gaining power, though not nearly enough to mount an attack. Gay would be a candidate for re-election in 1938, for example, and he would run unopposed. There was some hope that he, too, might come to see the wisdom of moderate reform.

But the market collapsed. In mid-October, the nation underwent the worst panic thus far in the Roosevelt Administration. The Dow-Jones Industrials fell from 143.66 on October 11 to 136.30 at the close of Saturday trading on October 16. The reason was bad economic news, as well as fears regarding the President's conflict with the Supreme Court. Prices struck an interday low of 125.14 on Monday before closing slightly higher, and the following day they collapsed, declining almost ten points before a slight rally closed the gap somewhat. Volume was 7,290,000 shares, a figure not seen for more than four years. Although prices firmed and volume declined, it was clear that the bears had returned to the district in full force.

The market decline precipitated matters. It gave the Stock Exchange

Establishment ammunition in its fight against regulation. The collapse had been caused, it claimed, by undue interference from Washington. Even Shields and Pierce wondered whether their commitment to Douglas had been wise, and they sought out Joe Kennedy, who they hoped would act as a middleman between the two forces. Richard Whitney told the N.Y.S.E. board that the decline had "confirmed my worst fears" regarding regulation, and his power appeared to grow among its members. John Hanes voiced doubts, speaking out in favor of relaxation of some of the provisions of the 1933 and 1934 acts. The wavering on the part of Hanes and the stiffening of Gay's position against compromise were widely viewed as signs that Whitney was prepared to re-enter the lists and assume the presidency in 1938.

On October 18, the day of the Wall Street disaster, Shields went to see Kennedy, who assured him that Roosevelt was completely behind Douglas. Two days later Shields relayed this information to the N.Y.S.E. board members, who also knew that Douglas and F.D.R. were meeting at Hyde Park. The Exchange moderates—including Gay—wanted to extend an olive branch to Douglas, but Whitney opposed anything that smacked of "weakness." Instead, the board informed Douglas that it would take proposed changes in structure "under advisement"—nothing more. Then Douglas traveled to Wall Street and held a series of conferences with N.Y.S.E. leaders. No records were kept of the meeting, but reporters claimed that at them Douglas first attempted to convince the Wall Streeters that reform was not only necessary but was coming, whether they cooperated or not. Whitney rejected what he considered a bluff, while Gay, Simmons, and others wanted to take the matter "under advisement." "The job of regulation's got to be done," Douglas was supposed to have said. "It isn't being done now and, damn it, you're going to do it or we are." But even this brought no positive response from Gay and the others—but neither did it evoke a negative one, which would have been interpreted as a declaration of war. Instead, the board members, aided by N.Y.S.E. counsel William Harding Jackson, drew up a proposal which, in effect, called for further study and no action till the work was completed.

Douglas exploded. When Jackson asked if he would accept the proposal, the commissioner responded that "it is not satisfactory. The negotiations are off." Did this mean Douglas would go ahead with his own program? "You're damn right I will." To Jackson, this seemed to indicate government regulation of the N.Y.S.E., and even control of operations—though Douglas had never said he would ask for such power. "When you take over the Exchange, I hope you'll remember we've been in business a hundred and fifty years. There may be some things you will like to ask us." There was, said Douglas. "Where do you keep the paper and pencils?" *

Publicly, Douglas attacked the N.Y.S.E. on November 23, charging it with being little better than a gambling den. He threw down the gauntlet. Either the N.Y.S.E. would institute responsible self-regulation —with the S.E.C. being the judge of such responsibility—or face "an immediate and more persuasive administration by the Commission."

The Douglas statement galvanized the board into action. For reasons not understood at the time, Whitney was absent from several important meetings at which the Douglas statement was discussed at length. The board members were now convinced that the chairman not only meant what he had said but had complete White House backing. Some feared nationalization of securities trading—even though Douglas had never said as much while other members believed the time for self-regulation had come. Gay was present at all the meetings, and he spoke out more often than he had in the past. As much as any man, he said, he wanted to keep outsiders from interfering with the Exchange. He, Simmons, and others (he carefully did not mention Whitney) had done all they could to maintain N.Y.S.E. traditions and operations. But unless they gave in to some of the Douglas demands, they would lose all. Gay favored a tactical retreat, not capitulation, and would inform Douglas of his willingness to go along with "some elements [of his] recommendations."

The decision to compromise was made at a long meeting on November 26—just before Thanksgiving. Gay spent the holiday preparing a statement for release on the afternoon of November 29. It was discussed with Simmons, Jackson, and Hanes prior to release. In it, Gay indicated the N.Y.S.E.'s willingness to cooperate with the S.E.C.—in more detail and to a greater extent than ever before. He claimed the Exchange was "constantly improving its methods" but was prepared to work with "public authorities in every way for the better performance of those functions," and to do so "under the supervision of the Commission." In the long run, however, "the public interest can best be served by leaving to the exchanges . . . much of the regulation of their own business." Gay asserted that this stand did not represent a change in N.Y.S.E. policy; from the first, the Big Board had cooperated with the reformers.

> Mr. Douglas states that the rules now in force governing the trading activities of members of the Exchange are rules of the Exchange itself, enforceable primarily by it. This is true; but it is

* Ralph F. De Bedts, *The New Deal's SEC: The Formative Years* (New York, 1964), pp. 162–63; William O. Douglas, *Go East, Young Man* (New York, 1974), pp. 289–91.

also true that these rules prior to their adoption by the Exchange had been the subject of almost continuous interchange of views between the Commission and the Exchange. The Exchange stands ready to continue this interchange of views with the object of constantly improving trading methods. The Exchange is as anxious as the Commission to prevent any form of manipulation or abuse.

In this way, Gay co-opted a substantial part of the reformist position. For years, Pierce and Shields had been viewed as pariahs by a majority of the N.Y.S.E. leaders. Now many of their views—though not all, to be sure—would become part of the official line. Gay indicated that the Exchange would safeguard the public in many ways suggested by the Commission. But no compromise was possible on one key issue: the specialist system. "So far as we can see, they [specialists] are the fairest means which have yet been devised for handling the vast number of public orders to buy and sell securities." The president concluded that "if in the search for improvement, better methods can be found, the Exchange will adopt them. We do not feel justified, however, in undertaking more experimentation, because we *know* [emphasis added] that the general public would pay the price of mistakes and that price might be high." *

Some reporters read the Gay statement as an act of defiance, an indication that the Exchange's leaders were prepared to battle Douglas on the reorganization issue. In fact, it was a masked capitulation and a sign that the Establishment had thrown over the Whitneyites. Furthermore, it was acceptable to Douglas.

If the chairman would not insist upon the form of unconditional surrender and permit the specialists to maintain their power, the S.E.C. could have its other reforms. But these changes would have to come from the Establishment—including the specialists. Gay and his group would not accept an agenda from the commission brokers, although there was no sign then or later that Gay saw the problem as one in which either the commission brokers or specialists would defeat the other.

Douglas was faced with a clear choice. He could continue to cooperate with Pierce and Shields and, given Roosevelt's support, probably win. Then he would be able to formulate a new kind of exchange structure, one regulated by the government, perhaps without the specialist system, and certainly eliminating the private traders. Such a plan would bring opposition from the district's leaders, and might spark a new strike of capital at a time when a recession-ridden nation

* Statement by President Charles R. Gay, November 29, 1937.

could least afford one. Or Douglas could accept Gay's olive branch and permit the Establishment to remain in power, promising self-regulation, with the S.E.C. as judge of whether or not it was working satisfactorily.

The chairman opted for the Gay group. The man most Wall Streeters considered a dangerous radical rejected the form of complete victory for the substance of true reform. Notwithstanding his radical rhetoric, Douglas was a skilled politician and capable of major compromise. He had effectively undercut Whitney and his followers; Gay's statement in itself was a clear sign that the break had been made, and Douglas's acceptance an indication that he conceded district leadership to the Establishment moderates. The chairman did throw a sop to the commission brokers. On December 10, Roosevelt nominated John Hanes for membership on the S.E.C., filling a vacancy created by the resignation of James D. Ross. Then, apparently to balance this, F.D.R. selected Jerome Frank, a liberal New Dealer, to fill Landis's position.

Finally, as though to seal the arrangement between the N.Y.S.E. and the S.E.C., Douglas looked favorably upon a new rate schedule desired by both the commission brokers and the specialists, one that raised minimum commissions by almost 11 percent. The Committee on Quotations and Commissions recommended the increase on December 8, it was approved a week later and sent on to Douglas, who did not comment, his silence taken as consent. The revised schedule was voted upon and accepted on December 29 and went into effect on January 3.

Gay announced the formation of a committee to study "all aspects of a further development of organization and administration of the Exchange" on December 8. The committee would be headed by Carle Conway, chairman of the board of the Continental Can Co., one of the few important businessmen deemed acceptable to the New Deal, a close friend of Hanes, and a man who was known to favor Wall Street reform. Thomas H. McInnerney, president of National Dairy, and Kenneth C. Hogate, president of the *Wall Street Journal* (and of its parent company, Dow Jones & Co.) were "outsiders" considered favorable to the N.Y.S.E. Adolph A. Berle, Jr., one of the founders of F.D.R.'s brain trust, was named to please Douglas. The N.Y.S.E. members on the committee were John A. Coleman of Adler, Coleman & Co., a specialist firm; Maurice Farrell of F. S. Smithers & Co.; and William McChesney Martin, Jr., a partner in the St. Louis firm of A. G. Edwards & Sons. The other committee members did not own seats but belonged to firms that did. These were: Trowbridge Callaway of Callaway, Fish & Co., and also president of the Better

Business Bureau of New York; and John Prentiss, a partner at Hornblower & Weeks, a developing investment banking house and a former president of the Association of Stock Market Firms and the Investment Bankers Association of America.

The Conway Committee* consisted of men who reflected the views both of investment bankers and specialists who supported Gay, and those of the Pierce-Shields commission brokers, now united against the Whitneyites. Hanes was believed to be the prime liaison between the Commission and the moderate reformers, while Conway indicated his stance by traveling to Washington immediately after the formation of the committee to consult with Douglas on procedural and substantive issues. The chairman hoped the committee would begin its study immediately and have its final report ready in a matter of months. Conway told him that it had already begun to function. Callaway had been named vice-chairman, with Martin as secretary. An office had been obtained at 41 Broad Street and the staff was at work.

Due in large part to the committee's willingness to accept almost the entire Douglas program (with the major exception being that part dealing with specialist operations), there was no problem regarding ultimate objectives. Nor was there a factional clash on the committee; Berle and Farrell, considered at first the opposite extremes, worked well together. Conway was an able leader, but he left most of the operational details to Martin.

In mid-January, scarcely more than a month after having officially begun its work, Conway told the press that his final report was being prepared, and would be ready in a matter of weeks. At the same time, the Chicago Stock Exchange announced a major restructuring, with the introduction of a professional management and a paid president. Curb Exchange President Fred Moffatt indicated that he would ask his membership for similar changes, as it appeared practically the entire exchange community was rushing to accept reform.

Douglas remained in the background in January 1938. Conway informed him of the committee's work, and the chairman met with Martin and was impressed by him. Hanes reported on district sentiment. He noted that the Whitney group would not acquiesce to a radical revision of the constitution along the lines of the Chicago Stock Exchange document. If the Conway Committee called for sweeping changes in the power structure on Wall Street, and if the new N.Y.S.E. constitution reflected these recommendations, there might be another strike of capital. Already the Whitneyites were preparing for one which might cause a deepening of the recession. Hanes pleaded

* Its official name was "The Committee for the Study of the Organization and Administration of the New York Stock Exchange," but even in N.Y.S.E. documents, it was referred to as the Conway Committee.

with Douglas for moderation. The Dow Industrials had risen from 118.93 on December 28 to 134.31 on January 15. Volume was declining, but this time Wall Street was pleased with the lower figures, since it meant the end of panic selling. Hanes indicated such sentiment might return if the battle between the Whitneyites and Douglas were joined. He called for the tempering of S.E.C. rules, and perhaps an indication from Douglas that some of the more objectionable parts of the 1933 and 1934 legislation might be revised or at least softened.

Douglas rejected Hanes's advice and instead pressed the committee to complete its work as soon as possible. News of his attitude reached the N.Y.S.E., and it became evident that the S.E.C. would demand a major revamping of the constitution and the replacement of the old regime. This would mean not only the departure of the Whitneyites but of the administration moderates as well. On January 21, Gay told friends he would not be a candidate for office under the new constitution. "Having given fifteen hours daily to Stock Exchange work during one of its most arduous periods," he said, he hoped to step down. Mistrusted by both the reformers and the standpatters, Gay indicated he had a sense of relief at the idea of returning to the floor and office, and he later told reporters that he believed the presidency was a job "for a salaried career executive." Then, on January 24, the S.E.C. decided that short-selling rules would have to be changed even before the new constitution was ready. In the past the person entering into a short sale could not make it at a price *below* that of the last sale, so as to avoid the possibility of manipulation.* Under the revised rule, such sales could not be made *at or below* the last price. It was a minor issue, hardly worthy of special note, were it not for the timing and background. As the Conway Committee met and plans were being made to draft a new constitution, the S.E.C. signaled that it would remain a force on the Street even after reforms had been carried out. In addition, this was the first time the Commission had changed trading regulations without prior consultation with the N.Y.S.E. Had this occurred a year earlier, Gay or some other Exchange spokesman would have responded with charges of dictatorship. This time, Gay merely termed the new rule "a sincere effort of the Commission to deal with the problem of short selling." Then, on January 26, as though anticipating further S.E.C. actions, the Governing Committee formulated stricter regulations concerning who could and could not become a specialist.

* A short sale is the sale of a security the client does not own, and which is borrowed for him for that purpose by his broker. It is entered into in the belief the security's price will fall, after which the client will purchase the stock at the lower price, return it to the lender, and close the transaction with a profit. Prior to 1931, "bears" would use short selling to push a stock's price down, and so were guilty of manipulation.

The Conway Committee Report, addressed to Gay but in effect a manifesto to the Exchange, was released the following day. It was a short document, barely five pages long, a list of suggestions rather than a road map for change. The final version, drawn up by Martin, took pains to be conciliatory to both the N.Y.S.E. and the S.E.C.—the Conway Committee's two major audiences. "While the recommendations herein made would appear to involve a radical alteration of administrative machinery," it began, "the necessary changes really represent merely another step in the long evolutionary development of the Exchange as the Nation's primary securities market." This statement indicated that the report was consistent with Gay's often-discussed tradition of "progressive conservatism" and Douglas's frequently mentioned "self-regulation." In fact, its substance indicated an almost complete victory for the S.E.C., a matter the Whitneyites were quick to point out.

The report covered a variety of reforms, all of which fell into three basic areas: governance, problems for further study, and relations with the federal government. Insofar as the first was concerned, the committee urged the creation of a professional Exchange government, centered around a full-time president who, if a member of the N.Y.S.E. at the time of election, would step down before assuming his post. "We believe that the affairs of the New York Stock Exchange have now attained such significance and have so many ramifications, that the Exchange needs a President who, upon election, should divest himself of all other business interests of every kind. . . ." Power would be transferred from the old standing committees to a paid executive staff, created by the president. Furthermore, the Conway report recommended the reduction of the number of standing committees from seventeen to six, and among those to go would be the powerful Law Committee, which would be replaced by an Executive Committee with far less power. Similarly, the old Board of Governors, which had fifty members, would be replaced by a new one with just thirty-two. Only fifteen of them would be N.Y.S.E. members. There would be six nonmember partners of commission houses, six more commission brokers from out of town, three members in businesses other than securities (to represent the public interests), and the president and the chairman of the board.

In the past, the N.Y.S.E. presidents had served to carry out the will of the major committees, in what resembled, in some surface ways at least, a parliamentary form of government in which legislative and executive power were joined, with the latter dependent upon the former. In its place, the Conway Committee would erect a more presidential system, with the executive separate from and in most ways superior to the legislative. The expectation was that such a president, divorced from the powerful specialists, would be able to perform in the interests of all aspects of the district, as well as the public.

The Conway Committee recognized that any new government would have to deal with a variety of issues, and it recommended the creation of a committee of three to ease the transition. But it did isolate several major areas of concern. One of these was the "liquidity problem." The primary function of stock exchanges was to provide a place where buyers and sellers of securities could find one another, in this way making the selling of new securities all the more desirable, since the buyers would know that a market for them existed. The committee suggested the N.Y.S.E. study liquidity to make certain it was sufficient. It asked, "Was the Exchange performing as promised?" "We think . . . that the study must not be merely critical; it must also be constructive, so that whenever an existing part of the financial machinery is eliminated or slowed down, an adequate method of liquidity is substituted in its place."

The Conway Committee had several suggestions in this matter. Additional brokers might be admitted to membership by creating a class of associate members, such as then existed at the Curb—individuals with trading rights but without ownership privileges, who could trade but not participate in the governance of the N.Y.S.E. Full and associate members should be encouraged to deal with nonmember firms, even to the point of dividing commissions with them. "It has been suggested that issues of many more companies should have been admitted to trading on the Exchange."

Such changes would have benefited the N.Y.S.E. in that it would have obtained additional trades, at the expense of the O-T-C (over-the-counter) houses, which would find many of their issues now traded on the Big Board. On the other hand, N.Y.S.E. brokers would deal closely with nonmember brokers, and so give them business they had previously lacked. All of this would have pleased the S.E.C. One of the Commission's major problems was regulating the over-the-counter market. Now that market would be crippled, with many of its stocks and brokers at or affiliated with the Big Board. Had the Conway Committee's recommendations been elaborated upon and accepted, a unified national market could have emerged by 1940, and in the process most of the district's organizational headaches in the late 1960s and early 1970s would never have taken place.*

The report's final section involved the Exchange's relations with the federal government, and here the committee came down squarely in favor of self-regulation. "It is plain that standards of conduct must be largely self-executed, rather than imposed," said the report. "Particu-

* See Chapters 17 and 18.

larly in matters of policing business conduct, the Stock Exchange can act more swiftly and more surely than any government body." Closer relations between the S.E.C. and the Exchange would be desirable, and using language calculated to please N.Y.S.E. moderates, the committee argued that "Both bodies should work in harmony upon their common task of *gradually* raising the standards of finance and business *with a minimum of economic disturbance* [emphasis added]."

During the market's decline in late 1937, Gay had expressed his belief that the sharp fall-off had been caused by S.E.C. interference with the exchanges, while some S.E.C. defenders responded that there was evidence of insider manipulation of prices, and large-scale "bear raids" involving prominent N.Y.S.E. figures. In clear terms, the Conway Committee absolved both of responsibility.

> No cooperation is possible, however, unless there is general public recognition of one fact. Neither the Stock Exchange nor the S.E.C. can be held responsible for major fluctuations in the price of securities. These depend on fundamental business and economic conditions. The Exchange cannot be held responsible for corporate operations taken under existing corporation laws though it can, to a limited degree, indicate that extreme use of privileges granted by some corporation laws are looked upon unfavorably.

Douglas praised the report and urged the N.Y.S.E to enact its suggestions without delay. If this were done, and in a way to indicate acceptance not only of the letter of the report but its spirit as well, the S.E.C.'s regulation of the financial district's affairs would be minimized. In a speech the following week, the chairman reiterated his belief in self-regulation, but also stated he would not relax his vigilance.

> I do mean, first, self-discipline in conformity to law—voluntary law obedience so complete that there is nothing left for government representatives to do; second, I mean obedience to ethical standards beyond those any law can establish. . . . This type of self-regulation has unquestioned advantages. From the viewpoint of the business, they are obvious. Self-discipline is more welcome than discipline imposed from above.

The N.Y.S.E. Governing Board convened on January 31 to consider acceptance or rejection of the report. During the previous two days Gay had spoken out in favor of ratification, and together with other moderates had conducted an "education campaign." Gay did not pretend enthusiasm for the changes recommended by the committee, but he believed the N.Y.S.E. could "live with them." In any case, the alternative to acceptance was a greater S.E.C. presence in the district, and since only a few Wall Streeters seemed to want that, approval appeared a foregone conclusion.

The Whitneyites spurned this argument, and prepared to fight it out at the board meeting. During the last election this group garnered a major share of nominations and elections, and so it appeared rejection was a possibility. Whitney envisaged a coalition of specialists and floor traders that would defeat the moderates, then join with friendly investment bankers to frame a manifesto opposing the report, and finally declare "independence" from the S.E.C. It was a poorly thought out plan, one which had almost no chance of success, even if Whitney could have created his coalition—which he could not.*

The board meeting was portrayed as a showdown by the press, in which reformers and standpatters would clash, and a gathering the S.E.C. was watching intently. But such was not the case; from the day the Conway Committee had been named, ratification of a reform document was certain. The only question was the breakdown of the vote and the spirit with which reform would be accepted.

Whitney had advocated rejection prior to the meeting, but soon after it was called into session he seemed to realize that only a few members would support him in this. Instead of attempting to defeat the report, then, Whitney called for acceptance "in principle," and would leave it at that. It was clearly a maneuver calculated to anger the S.E.C., and perhaps precipitate a new struggle with the Commission. Gay recognized this and also saw that Whitney might win a sizable number of votes for his position. Never before had he opposed Whitney at a meeting, and in fact as presiding officer he wasn't expected to speak. But Gay left his chair, and going into the well of the chamber, he asked Whitney to reconsider his motion. In essence, Gay told him that the Conway Report would be adopted, that it was evident to the membership that the reforms were coming, and the only question was whether they would be imposed upon the Exchange or be in the form of internal change directed by the membership itself. Whitney conceded the point in a graceful response, but said he would vote against the report as a protest and recommended the same for others who felt as he did. Gay asked Whitney to abstain instead, for the sake of Exchange unity. He agreed to do so. Then the Governing Board approved the committee report unanimously—with one abstention.

The board scheduled a meeting with the members for later that week, in order to give them an opportunity to ask questions and make

* Notes on this plan are in the Leslie Gould papers at Hofstra University.

their views known. Only a handful of brokers attended, more out of curiosity than any other reason. Reform was a *fait accompli*.

Douglas was quick to respond to the news of the board action. "It does credit to the committee and to the New York Stock Exchange," he told reporters, and he termed the ratification a major step in the creation of "a truly effective system of self-regulation under government supervision."

The report recommended the creation of a committee of three members "which, in conjunction with counsel, should draft amendments to the Constitution which, when duly adopted would give effect to the recommendations herein made as promptly as practicable." In fact, what came to be known as the Special Committee of Three was to draw up the framework for a new constitution, and then submit it to the board for acceptance. E.H.H. Simmons, the former president and long-time friend of Richard Whitney, was named chairman of the body. Simmons had eased away from Whitney during the past few months for a variety of reasons, Stock Exchange reform being only one, and not an important one at that. Yet it was assumed at the time that Simmons had truly converted in order to salvage his own position in the district. The talk was that Simmons "went over the fence to the reformers so fast he left his pants hanging on the barbed wire." In any case, Simmons had little to do with the actual work, except to serve as a conduit for individuals who wanted their ideas considered. Charles B. Harding, the second member, was a young reformer who had joined Barney & Co. in 1922, had become a close friend of John Hanes, and received a partnership in the firm in 1925. Harding had purchased his seat in 1929, and since then had served on several committees including the Governing Board itself. He had remained quiet during the previous year's clashes, and so was acceptable to the Old Guard. On the other hand, his closeness to Hanes indicated a S.E.C. connection, symbolically if nothing else.

William Martin, who had gained in stature as a result of his work on the Conway Committee, was the third member.

The committee worked rapidly, in effect approving drafts Martin produced from his files which had been prepared during the Conway deliberations. The final report was delivered to the Governing Committee on February 21. It was printed and released two days later.

The report consisted of two parts. The first contained a "transitional article" which was to take effect immediately. "It directs that the Nominating Committee elected last January shall select nominees for a Chairman of the Board and for the twenty-seven elective members of the new Board of Governors." Thus, the Exchange prepared to create a new structure prior to approval by the membership. In the past, such a recommendation would have been debated for months, and would not have been finally passed without a membership ballot. In February 1938 it was accepted as a matter of course. As much as any other action or statement, this would convince Douglas and the public that the reforms were a foregone conclusion.

The rest of the report was an article by article dissection of the old constitution and suggestions for changes, all of which were to become effective after the annual election, scheduled for May. It was a fleshing out of the Conway Committee's recommendations with only one important addition—a new article providing for stiff expulsion and suspension rules.

There would be no change in the New York Stock Exchange Gratuity Fund, and none was expected. The Committee of Three thought that in the future the trustees might "hold coupon as well as registered securities," however.

The Gratuity Fund was hardly an important issue. It provided for the well-being of the families of deceased members, and as such was hardly a powerful or influential operation. Its six trustees were named by the Governing Committee, and always contained the president plus five of the N.Y.S.E.'s most respected and prestigious members. These men were responsible for the investment and disbursement of large sums of money, which they put into high-grade securities. The trustees were not compensated financially for this work; being selected was an honor, and considered a sign of status at the Exchange. E.H.H. Simmons was its chairman; former presidents often filled that post.

Richard Whitney was named a trustee of the Gratuity Fund in 1935, when he left the presidency. He was a trustee in 1938. His firm, Richard Whitney & Co., acted as its broker.

CHAPTER 3

A New Deal for Wall Street

In March 1937 the trustees of the Gratuity Fund decided to sell some $225,000 worth of bonds and purchase others. As was the practice, Richard Whitney was asked to handle the transaction. The order was not executed. Instead, Whitney kept the bonds and used them as collateral for a personal loan. Additional bonds were given to him for sale during the next few months, and Whitney repeated the performance. By late November, he had more than a million dollars' worth of Gratuity Fund money in his possession.

George Lutes, an Exchange employee who served as clerk for the fund, asked Whitney for the supposedly newly purchased bonds on several occasions, and each time Whitney put him off, saying he had forgotten to make the transfer and would get around to it shortly. Lutes did nothing and said nothing. "I was under him as an employee of the Exchange and I am only a clerk," he claimed later on. "Frankly, I was afraid of him."

The Gratuity Fund held its regular meeting on November 19, at a time when the Exchange's relations with Douglas were at their low point, when talk abounded as to the possible nationalization of the Exchange, and securities prices were plummeting. Whitney was unable to appear at the meeting. He had missed most of his committee sessions that month, sending substitutes and telling his colleagues that he was busy with other matters. They assumed these concerned the coming battles with the S.E.C., and nodded their understanding. Actually, Whitney was preoccupied with his own tangled affairs in mid-November.

The Gratuity Fund session began promptly and, as was usual, went smoothly enough, so that the trustees expected to complete their business in a matter of a few minutes. But Lutes, who was normally quiet at the meetings, added a new subject to the discussions. He informed the trustees of Whitney's failure to deliver the bonds and cash—$1,121,000 in all—to the account. Later on, Lutes said Simmons appeared "peeved," not so much with Whitney, but with him for implying that something was amiss. But the trustees voted unanimously to have Simmons contact Whitney that afternoon and ask him to deliver the bonds and cash.

Simmons tried to find Whitney, but failed. They did meet the following day, in Simmons's office. Whitney requested a one-day grace period in order to get the paper work completed. Simmons was unhappy with this, and urged his friend to complete the matter as soon as possible.

In fact, Whitney didn't have the money or the securities. They were gone, along with the more than $150,000 in bonds he had taken from the New York Yacht Club in his capacity as treasurer. The millions of dollars he had borrowed from friends over the past two years—with no collateral asked or given—were also gone.

Whitney had used the money to purchase shares in Distilled Liquors Corporation, a New Jersey firm he had helped organize in 1933 to cash in on the repeal of prohibition. Other liquor firms would have to age their stock before marketing it. Not Distilled Liquors, whose major product was Jersey Lightning, an applejack-based drink Whitney was convinced would sweep the nation. For a while, in 1933, the stock sold for as high as 45. Then, as Jersey Lightning failed to capture the public imagination, the price fell, reaching 9 by the time Lutes told the fund trustees of the missing bonds and cash. Later on, it was claimed that had it not been for the stock market decline of late 1937, Whitney might have emerged from his speculations a rich man. This was not so. Richard Whitney, reputedly a fine judge of securities and liquor, really knew little of either. In fact, Whitney had speculated on stocks throughout the 1920s and 1930s and had never done well. His major talent in finance proved to be an ability to extract loans from his friends and relatives.

Whitney went to his brother, George, at the Morgan Bank and told him of the Gratuity Fund situation. George was shocked—not only at the theft, but the fact that Richard had taken the money from the almost-sacred fund. He would help, of course, for if word of what had happened got out, all would be disgraced. The family's friends would cooperate, too, as would the Morgan Bank. Richard Whitney had no great ability for business but he was, after all, a gentleman, and such a person's associates could be counted upon to do the "right thing."

Only to a degree. Whitney & Co., still viewed as a major bond house and in the black, would have to be sold. George would try to sell the Distilled Liquor stock, though he had no idea who might want to buy it. The moneys thus obtained would pay Richard's debts, and perhaps there would be a little left over as well. That, together with his wife's money, would be enough to start Richard Whitney off in a new field.

The Whitneys met with Simmons and told him of the problem. Simmons was speechless, but indicated that he would keep the matter quiet until the brothers completed their transactions and returned the money. He realized too that George could not only be trusted but had the Morgan Bank behind him in his pledge. However, he drew back when George hinted that he—Simmons—might want to buy Whitney & Co. He knew nothing of bonds.

During the next three and a half months George tried to sell Whitney & Co. and the Distilled Liquors stock, and failed in both attempts. Showing a fine talent at juggling borrowings, Richard obtained millions from friends and commercial banks, turning his "accounts" over on an almost daily basis. He also borrowed against his wife's assets, and embezzled securities from Whitney & Co. accounts. The net borrowings came to more than $5 million. It wasn't enough.

Through all of this, Whitney found time to lead the Wall Street campaign against the Conway Committee Report. He would rush from friend to friend, borrowing and repaying, and doing so in a cool and dispassionate fashion, as though it was a matter of course, and of no true importance whether or not his friend gave him the money. The standard sum was $100,000, but some were asked for more—up to $250,000—and a few for as low as $50,000. Whitney also went to N.Y.S.E. members he didn't really know and casually solicited loans, implying they should be honored to be asked. They were, and most gave. If for some reason the would-be borrower hesitated, Whitney would smile and tell him to think nothing of it. A few individuals apologized for not having the money available, and went so far as to borrow from others in order to lend it to Richard Whitney who, after all, was still a major voice for and symbol of the Wall Street Establishment.

By mid-January, there were rumors of "troubles" at Whitney & Co., and some of these reached Howland S. Davis, chairman of the committee on business conduct. Davis, one of the Old Guard himself, took no action, but it happened that S.E.C. questionnaires on member firms' finances were being sent out. Whitney was not scheduled to receive the forms until May. Just to make certain all was well with the company, Davis directed they be sent to him on January 20.

Simmons delivered the report of the Committee of Three to Gay's office on February 21. The same day, Whitney returned the questionnaire to John Dassau, the Exchange's comptroller. It was a week late; Whitney had asked for and received an extension.

Dassau looked over the forms that evening and thought he spotted deficiencies and falsifications. Two days later—as the Committee of Three Report was being distributed to the members and the press—Exchange accountants were sent to Whitney's office to perform an audit. Whitney saw Davis the next day, admitted irregularities, and asked for time to correct them. Davis agreed, but the audit continued. On February 28 it seemed clear that Whitney had dipped into his customers' accounts. By March 3 the evidence was conclusive. Whitney went to see Davis to try to win help in keeping the matter quiet.

Davis might have agreed a year or so earlier, but by March 1938, reform was in command on Wall Street. Douglas's victory was assured, and the Old Guard which had so loyally followed Whitney in the past now acknowledged that Gay's approach would serve it best. Davis refused to help.

Nor would Gay, who saw Whitney in his office—once Whitney's office—on March 5. Gay was flustered, not knowing what to do or how to behave in the face of the collapse of a man who had appeared a giant. Gay had been president for almost three years, he had conferred with Roosevelt, and had met with Cabinet members. On one occasion he and Douglas drank and talked the night through, trying to come to an agreement regarding reform. He had handled himself well at such times. Not even F.D.R. could impress him. But Richard Whitney was something else. Roosevelt was President, but Whitney was a Wall Street aristocrat. Gay knew the difference. He too could be a president, but he would never be an aristocrat.

Whitney, in contrast, was calm. Conceding his crimes, he asked Gay's help in easing his exit from the Exchange. He would liquidate his holdings and sell his company and seat. But he wanted all charges against him dropped. "After all, I'm Richard Whitney. I mean the Stock Exchange to millions of people. The Exchange can't afford to let me go under." Gay refused. And he continued to do so each time Whitney raised the matter during the two-hour meeting. A specific set of charges would be brought against him on Monday morning, March 7.

More perhaps than the concessions to the S.E.C. and future changes, Gay's responses to Whitney marked the beginning of a major shift at the Exchange—the coming of the New Deal to Wall Street.

The charges were brought against Whitney that Monday. Howland Davis found additional inconsistencies in the firm's reports. Apparently it was bankrupt. Whitney did not deny it. Nor did Edwin D. Morgan, one of his partners. Two other partners, F. Kingsley Rodewald and Henry Mygatt, were called upon to confirm the fact. "Can your firm meet its engagements?" Together they replied, "No."

The Street buzzed with news of Whitney & Co.'s bankruptcy the following morning. At 9:00, Whitney's clerks called other brokerages to tell them that no security orders would be accepted. By the time Gay mounted the rostrum on the Exchange floor most present knew Whitney & Co. had locked its doors. This was unfortunate, but such closings had taken place before. Then, at 10:05, Exchange Secretary Robert Fisher rang the gong, calling for silence, and Gay read his statement, with visible emotion. Whitney & Co. was suspended. Then came the reason. "Conduct contrary to just and equitable principles of trade." *

Bankruptcy was not unusual in 1938 or earlier. But Whitney was not only bankrupt. He was disgraced as a crook. That had never happened before, not to a man of such stature, and it would never happen again.

Events moved swiftly after that. Whitney & Co. filed for bankruptcy the same day. Richard Whitney was indicted for grand larceny by one grand jury on March 10 and another on March 15. He pleaded guilty to both charges, and even volunteered additional unlawful pledges not covered by the indictments. He was expelled from the N.Y.S.E. on March 17, and on the same day Mygatt and Morgan were suspended for three years. Whitney was sentenced to from five to ten years in Sing Sing on April 12. The symbol of the old regime was gone.

There was a new regime, however, and a new symbol. The day before Whitney's sentencing, William Martin was nominated as chairman of the board.

Martin was a striking change from Whitney, even more so than had been Gay. The only thing about Martin that was ordinary was his appearance. He was of medium height, wore dark suits, usually with a vest, white shirt, and conservative tie. He rarely wore a hat until his nomination. Afterward, he always did. Martin could be counted upon to maintain correct appearances.

He would be quiet at business meetings, sitting back, listening carefully, taking notes, and should a speck of dust alight on one of the lenses of his rimless glasses, Martin would remove them and the speck with deliberation, as though pondering a weighty subject. He was only thirty years old when he took his post at the Conway Committee, but he behaved older than that. This was not because he was stuffy or aloof, although Martin gave that impression to many on the Street. Rather, he was without much of a sense of humor and had few of the social graces.

* Joseph Alsop and Robert Kintner, "The Battle of the Market Place," *Saturday Evening Post*, June 11, 1938, pp. 8–9, 77–80; June 25, 1938, pp. 10–11, 78–81.

He looked successful, as indeed he was. It was not the somewhat arrogant and spectacular success of a Richard Whitney, but rather that of a man who was completely confident of his abilities and background, and sublime about all that followed from them. He was not overly careful about the impressions he gave others, but at the same time he appeared to know that those around him were impressed by his bearing and knowledge. Martin seemed like the men who had surrounded J. P. Morgan the Elder at the turn of the century, while Whitney was of the kind Morgan used to front for him, but who was not of the inner circle. (As for Gay, he was more the "trusted employee" type who received a gold watch after being with the firm for twenty-five years.) Martin would have fitted in well as a second-level official in almost any Presidential Administration—in 1938 he seemed like the successful bureaucrat, but one who served in that post out of a desire for public service, not need. The New Deal was manned by young people who looked, sounded like, and even spoke with Martin's cadences. He was admired by old Wall Streeters for his abilities, and by Douglas for his progressive stances and willingness to act without hemming and hawing. Still, he did not fit into any particular mold.

Martin was a "loner," a man who seemed to have and need no close friends. He was a devoted son whose father, William McChesney Martin, Sr., was head of the Federal Reserve Bank of St. Louis, and the two shared an interest in economics and statistics. Martin went to Yale, where he majored in English—his father had suggested he get a broad education. After graduation in 1928, he worked as a clerk at his father's bank, and then took the post of chief statistician for the St. Louis brokerage firm of A. G. Edwards & Sons, which was owned by relatives. Martin became a partner in 1931 and was sent to New York, where within a month he handled the company's N.Y.S.E. operations. Despite misgivings, he found the work interesting, and he earned the respect if not the friendship of several Old Guard figures, even though he appeared more aligned with the commission house reformers. But he socialized with neither group. Instead, he registered for courses at the New School for Social Research, where he studied economics with Alvin Johnson and E. W. Kemmerer. Later on, he went to Columbia, where he took courses in contemporary politics with Raymond Moley, Leo Wolman, and others, as well as economics with H. Parker Willis. Almost all the work was with men who were deemed liberal, and several of his professors would soon after go to Washington to serve under Roosevelt.

Martin would take courses in the mornings, then rush to Wall Street in time for the opening, and then return to school after the close of trading. In the evenings he would go to the theater—at one point, he saw every show in the city—and he even wrote three plays, in addition to founding the *Economics Forum*, a magazine whose first issue contained articles by John Maynard Keynes ("A New Monetary Policy for England") and Josiah Stamp ("Our Price Level Problem"). At nights, after the show, Martin would go to Sardi's for a cup of hot chocolate, since he didn't smoke, drink, or gamble. Then, around midnight, he would go home—a room at the Yale Club—and call his father. Martin ate by himself, often at the Automat, seldom went to social functions, and seemed content to leave it at that.

Stock Exchange members considered Martin an intellectual, and the Big Board had had its share of them in the past. E. C. Stedman was a noted poet, Henry Clews had written several volumes of history and memoirs, and there were dozens of art collectors on Wall Street. Martin seemed different, however. There was nothing of the dilettante about him. This somewhat cold and thoroughly professional commission broker from the provinces, who attacked subjects in a calculated, almost bloodless fashion, awed even his associates on the Conway Committee. Whenever a fact was needed, Martin seemed to have it, or, if not, it would be in his possession at the next meeting. It was not that he was brilliant, but rather persistent and dependable, curious and intelligent. Martin wrote a clear, precise, but uninspired report. He was a "professional," but in a different sense of the term than Wall Street had been used to, since Gay and Whitney too were professionals, yet so unlike Martin. This young man relied upon knowledge—quantifiable knowledge, at that—and not friends, tradition, or shrewdness. Other major Wall Street figures had been known for their abilities to seize power and wealth, and indeed these had been the factors that made them great, and the reasons they came to the district. Martin did not appear interested in power or money, or even position and status. The Stock Exchange as an institution intrigued him, both as a practical and theoretical problem. He approached reform without the moral indignation of a Shields or the desire for integrity of a Hanes. Martin defended the N.Y.S.E., but not as a "perfect institution," as Whitney had called it, or with nostalgia and romanticism, as was the case with Gay. Instead, it was an institution that served a purpose, and one with several flaws that had appeared over time. It would be his task to update the N.Y.S.E.—not out of sentiment or revenge, but as a technician intrigued with a particularly complex malfunctioning.

Martin's selection as chairman of the board had been expected, and once it was announced, he was a prime candidate for the presidency under the new constitution. His work over the previous year had placed Martin in the reformer camp—close to Shields and Pierce, and a man who had Douglas's respect. By the time he had been named to the Committee of Three, the Old Guard had come to view him with a measure of distrust, but at the same time conceded that, unlike the reform leaders, Martin had been circumspect in his criticisms of the way the Exchange had been run in the past, indicating that it was the men, not the institution, that had caused most of the troubles. Martin favored the continuation of the auction market, complete with the specialist system. He believed the N.Y.S.E. should remain under the control of its members, while becoming less of a private club and more of a public utility. Douglas trusted Martin while knowing this, and Martin had the intelligence to counter S.E.C. attacks against the Big Board. At the same time, he was so obviously incorruptible and honest that he would inspire public confidence in Wall Street, winning support in any future encounter with the S.E.C. Six years earlier, Pierce had spoken of the need for a czar in the district, a man who could give the N.Y.S.E. a clean bill of health and attract investors once more. Martin would be no czar, but in terms of image and ability he was a vast improvement over Whitney, and more able to bring in a reform era than Gay.

As for Gay, he had become quite popular on Wall Street that March. With the Whitneyites routed and Whitney himself disgraced, the standpat element evaporated, leaving moderate conservatives like him the best hope—for the time being, at least—for a continuation of the old regime. The reformers credited Gay with handling the Conway and Committee of Three matters intelligently, while the others were pleased with the firmness and fairness he had shown during the Whitney crisis. Now that Whitney was gone, they no longer could call him "Charlie McCarthy" Gay, indicating their belief that he was only a puppet. The strings were cut, and Gay performed well on his own.

In March he told the members he would not be a candidate for the presidency under the new constitution, a foregone conclusion perhaps since at the time it was felt he hadn't a chance for S.E.C. approval. Dozens of individuals were rumored to have the inside track for the job, from the erratic and colorful Robert Hutchins, president of the University of Chicago, to O. Max Gardner, the former Governor of South Carolina and a man with close friends in Washington. The main question seemed to be: "Who has Douglas's approval?" Gay admonished the members to stop their speculation on the issue. It was meaningless, he said, since the new post hadn't even been created as yet. In any case, the Exchange members, not the S.E.C., would select the man when the time came.

*   *   *

On March 17, the same day Richard Whitney was expelled from the N.Y.S.E., the Governing Board approved the draft of a new constitution, one that accepted the Conway Committee's recommendations and those of the Committee of Three. The document, longer and more elaborate than its predecessor, was to go into effect on May 16, so Gay had to prepare the way for his successor during the next two months. He persuaded Howland Davis to leave brokerage and resign from the committee on business conduct in order to become a full-time executive at the Exchange, thus not only winning an important member of the Old Guard for the new dispensation but also showing the Whitneyites that no punitive expedition would be mounted against them. New special committees were formed, at the rate of almost one a week, to study such matters as short selling, the creation of associate memberships, the elimination of private traders' seats, and the like, as well as to draw up new rules by which the constitution would be made operational.

Gay worked well with Martin in this period, and the two men came to respect one another. Six years earlier, Martin had written an article under a pseudonym, "Martin Maxwell, Jr.," in which he called the N.Y.S.E. "one of the most marvelous mechanisms of the machine age." News of the article, and reprints of it, appeared on the Street that spring, and the talk was that Gay was responsible for its dissemination, knowing as he did that Martin would almost certainly succeed him. In April, Gay announced that the salaries of Stock Exchange employees would have to be cut due to the decline in business, and he did so in order to spare his successor an unpopular act.

On May 9, when elections were held for the new Board of Governors, there was talk that Douglas wanted Gay to allow his name to be placed in nomination and, in effect, continue his work under the new president. The S.E.C. issued a denial, but there was substance to the rumor, since by then Gay had come to lead those conservatives who had accepted reform. But Gay rejected the nomination, and all the nominees for the new board were from the reform element and, as had been the practice under the old constitution, ran unopposed. The members could signify their feelings by crossing off the names of those they disliked. Of the 1,375 members, 924 cast ballots, and Shields—considered little more than Douglas's stooge and a turncoat by the Old Guard—was crossed off the list by 161, the best indication of how many die-hards remained at the N.Y.S.E. by that time.

Three days later John Hanes, another reform leader, was named Assistant Secretary of the Treasury, to take office in early summer. One columnist wrote—jokingly perhaps—that Gay would soon have plenty of time on his hands and might take Hanes's place at the S.E.C. It was written in a humorous vein, but for a week was a topic of conversation at the N.Y.S.E.—which had seen Kennedy go from Wall Street to Washington, and knew of Gay's strengthened position in both the S.E.C. and the N.Y.S.E.

The constitution became effective at 3:00 P.M., on May 16, when the newly elected board met for the first time and selected Martin as president *pro tem,* an office he would hold, along with that of chairman, until formal elections were held on June 30. The board then approved a resolution praising Gay's "calm judgment and steadfastness of purpose" in a "period of profound difficulty." It was the kind of statement usually passed at such moments as a matter of course. This time, at least, it was more than mere rote.*

As though to indicate that what one columnist called "A New Deal on Wall Street" had really begun, Martin made several significant gestures. He dismissed the Exchange's long-time law firm, Carter, Ledyard & Milburn, one of whose partners, Roland Redmond, was Whitney's closest friend, and another, William Harding Jackson, who had clashed repeatedly with Douglas. It was replaced by Milbank, Tweed & Hope, an equally conservative house, one acceptable to the Old Guard, and founded by Jeremiah Milbank, the very symbol of Wall Street orthodoxy. In this way, Martin pleased both reformers and moderates.

Martin brought an air of informality to the office too. His door was always open—literally—so that anyone who wanted to see him could breeze right in. At times Martin would answer his own telephone, and he continued to lunch at plebeian places when not attending business-related meals. All of this was well publicized; the new president was on good terms with the press, and appeared at ease with reporters. This was the way to gain public confidence, and he was intent on obtaining it. Later on, Martin would show visitors around the trading floor, followed by reporters and photographers. Only four years earlier some members had protested when Whitney had permitted Kennedy and other S.E.C. people to come to the floor, which was reserved for members and employees only. Now Martin was opening it to all—or, at least, so it seemed. As with other such gestures, this was meant to indicate a new candor at the N.Y.S.E.

On June 3, and then again on June 8, the Exchange sponsored "round-table conferences" with the S.E.C. Martin, Shields (now chairman of the committee on public relations, another of Martin's gestures), and various N.Y.S.E. figures met with Douglas, Hanes, Ganson Purcell, then head of the trading division, and key S.E.C. executives to discuss future plans for the Exchange. Douglas wanted to talk about five major issues: a central depository for securities, problems

* Gay remained head of his brokerage, now Winthrop, Whitehouse & Co., and was there until his death in 1946, at the age of seventy.

of floor administration, bond trading, odd-lot trading, and commissions. However Douglas and Martin had already agreed that a central depository would be desirable, and a study group had been named to report on the possibilities, while the Brookings Institution had begun a study of odd-lot trading sponsored by three Stock Exchange houses. Little was accomplished at the round-table conferences, but the S.E.C. and N.Y.S.E. leaders had another opportunity to display their new friendship, and they posed for pictures showing them smiling at one another, shaking hands, and engaged in thoughtful conversations. "The day of the crackdown on Wall Street is over," said Douglas. When Martin was confirmed as president on June 30, Douglas sent his congratulations, pledging "our fullest cooperation, and our unqualified support." "The honeymoon is over," Martin told reporters. "Now I'll have to produce." Both men agreed that further changes would be necessary, and the new president said he would present an agenda for reform within the next few months, one that would convince even the most skeptical observers of the sincerity of the Exchange's moves in this direction.

A good part of their friendship was sincere. For over a year Douglas had worked to bring significant structural changes to the N.Y.S.E., and now that he had succeeded he could afford to be magnanimous. In fact, it was good politics: he would reinforce the reformers and at the same time mend fences with his former opponents. But there was the broader picture to consider as well. The 1937 recession had caused a crisis of confidence in the New Deal. Some New Dealers—among them Harry Hopkins and Leon Henderson—argued that Roosevelt would have to resort to even greater pump-priming, that business would not take up the slack left by the government's withdrawal from the private sector, and that Wall Street remained the New Deal's major antagonist and would have to be curbed, perhaps nationalized as well. Others, including Secretary of the Treasury Henry Morgenthau and Hanes, spoke for a balanced budget and a campaign to convince business it had nothing to fear from the New Deal in the future. Given this new confidence, business spending and investment would accelerate, and so bring the nation out of the recession. Hanes continued to advocate modifications in the securities legislation, and given his new post at the Treasury, he was expected to carry even more weight with Roosevelt than he had in the past.

As he so often did in such circumstances, Roosevelt put both approaches into operation at the same time. On the one hand, he increased spending programs through the W.P.A. and P.W.A., while a new A.A.A. was instituted under which farm subsidies were increased. In April he asked Congress for funds for an investigation of large-scale concentrations of economic power, and with it set up the

Temporary National Economic Committee, which many businessmen feared was the beginning of a new campaign against them, one that would end either in a massive antitrust crusade or socialism. But at the same time, through Douglas, he placated the Stock Exchange. Reform was still important, but so was confidence in securities. If and when investors felt the markets were "safe," they might come back, investing their funds in new issues of stocks and bonds, and with this cash influx businesses could expand operations, creating goods and jobs and taking the burden for both off the federal government's shoulders. Furthermore, a strengthened N.Y.S.E. might be able to end trading in listed stocks at unregulated over-the-counter markets, and so consolidate all operations under a single roof.

Both Douglas and Martin understood what was happening. The S.E.C. chairman, his eye already on a Supreme Court position, withdrew from public view during the next few months, as though waiting to see which of the New Deal factions would win. He could afford to do so, since Martin could be counted upon to support most of his old positions.

Martin was not a front man for the S.E.C., however, and although a reformer, he did not agree with all of Douglas's stands. He too wanted to restore trust in the N.Y.S.E., and sincerely believed that the old ways, as typified by Whitney, had to go. The private club atmosphere would be ended, and public confidence in the Exchange restored. But he still considered the system, in its essentials, to be far better than any alternative. Replace the crooked and inept with honest, intelligent specialists and brokers, and all would be well once again. This was quite different from what the S.E.C. had wanted, even though at the time the two men seemed to be working in tandem and thinking alike. Some Wall Streeters and New Dealers went so far as to call Martin the chairman's protégé, and Douglas's repeated praise of his performance gave the label believability. In fact, Douglas would shift from one point of view to another during the next year, especially on the issue of his successor, but for the most part he remained with the Hopkins-Henderson group, while Martin was close to the Morgenthau-Hanes leadership in the Treasury Department.

Martin's agenda for reform was released in a fifteen-point program on October 31. It was designed to provide additional protection for the public, enlarge the N.Y.S.E.'s operations, and make the nation aware of the institution's efforts to attract new business. It was not an agenda for action, however, for all the recommendations had been adopted unanimously by the Board of Governors on October 26. Rather, it was a report to the S.E.C. on what had been done, and to potential investors on the new climate at the Exchange. The new rules consisted of:

1. Reduction of the debt ratios of member firms from 20 to 1 to 15 to 1, effective January 1, 1939. This meant that brokerages would have to maintain a higher assets-to-liabilities balance, in this way assuring the public they were solvent.

2. Prohibition of loans, unless fully secured, by member to, or from, any governor, committee member, officer or employee of the Exchange. This might be called the "Whitney rule," and it made even clearer the separation between the administration and the trading floor.

3. Disqualification of any governor or member in the investigation or consideration of any matter relating to a creditor member or firm.

4. Answers by all member firms to "long-form" questionnaires at least once a year, and to "short-form" questionnaires quarterly.

5. Annual independent audits of the books of all firms doing a public business.

6. Reports to the Exchange from members, firms, and partners of all unsecured loans of more than $2,500 obtained from or made to any other member firm or partner.

7. Prohibition of member firms from carrying margin accounts, effective April 1, 1939, for general partners or any member firm dealing directly with the public.

8. Prohibition of member firms from carrying an account for a general partner of another member firm without prior written consent of a second partner.

9. No member doing business as an individual would be permitted to carry securities accounts for customers.

10. More intensive supervision by the committee on member firms of member-firm employees.

11. Stricter and more rigid supervision of member firms' business practices.

12. Weekly reports to the Exchange from member firms on their underwritings and net resulting positions.*

The final three points were more ambiguous, written as much to indicate a willingness to comply with S.E.C. desires as anything else. One dealt with tentative plans for a central securities depository. Douglas had long favored one, which would remove customers' securities from brokerages—where they might be used illegally, as they were by Whitney and others—and place them in a central vault. This plan was opposed almost universally by the commission houses, which claimed it demonstrated Douglas's lack of appreciation of their plight. Without such securities on deposit in their offices, they would be

* These points were enacted in Rules 518, 519, 531, 532, 535, 536, and 540.

unable to make short sales. In fact, Douglas did understand this; he also wanted to ban short selling.

The second point proposed the separation of capital employed by member firms as underwriters from that they maintained as dealers. This was to assure that investment bankers would not utilize funds in customers' accounts to support new underwritings without first having obtained permission to do so. If enacted, it would make for more responsible underwritings but at the same time limit the scope of the underwriters' activities.

Finally, Martin called for the increased use of supervisory audits of member firms by the Exchange itself. The implication here was that if this were done, the S.E.C. could withdraw from Wall Street more rapidly than might otherwise be the case. The member firms supported the objective but were generally unwilling to accept such supervision unless it was tied to decreased controls, and this Martin could not promise.

The Martin agenda was well received in the press, and Douglas called it "a good beginning." As far as the S.E.C. was concerned it was just that—a beginning—while Martin appeared to believe it the end as well. Nowhere in the agenda was there mention of the specialist system and the segregation of broker and dealer functions, problems Douglas still felt needed change. Now it was clear that Martin thought otherwise. The foundation for a new confrontation—this one between the S.E.C. and the Exchange's reformers—seemed to be developing.

The specialist system was hardly the kind of issue around which to launch a crusade against Wall Street, since so few Americans understood what it was and, by 1938, many of those who did cared little about investments. The first New Deal reform effort on the Street had been initiated by the Stock Market Crash, marked by the struggles against Whitney, and culminated in Whitney's disgrace. Now a fresh symbol was needed, and the Hopkins-Henderson group in Washington thought it arrived in the person of Robert Hutchins.

On September 28, Martin had announced the names of the three public governors who would complete the new board. They were: Carle Conway, Robert Wood (of Sears Roebuck), and Robert Hutchins. The Conway and Wood nominations had been expected. The Hutchins selection was a trifle surprising in that he had caustically criticized the fleshpots of high finance. But in another way it was not, for in this period the "boy president" of the University of Chicago was being asked to serve on a variety of boards and commissions. He was in great demand and high favor, especially in academic circles and among intellectuals. To many of them, Roosevelt had proved a disappointment. F.D.R. had compromised too much, had backtracked, had come to terms with conservatives, and in fact—on occasion—had appeared quite conservative himself. But he would leave office after his second term, it was thought, and in late 1938 Hutchins was one of those who appeared to have contracted the White House bug.

The 1930s, a period of great ferment, threw up more than its share of celebrities, most of whom would have remained relatively unknown were it not for the depression and its reformist aftermath. A handful of them—Douglas and Martin were two—survived the decade and were important public figures for years after. Most of them—and Hutchins was a prime case—proved to be men for that season alone, although they would linger on for a while, usually on the periphery of major happenings, a reminder of what might have been rather than what was or is. Yet in 1938, Hutchins's star seemed on the ascendant, while Douglas and Martin appeared to have "flattened out" in terms of their careers.

Hutchins had become president of the University of Chicago in 1929, at the age of thirty. He quickly scrapped the old curriculum, did away with most intercollegiate athletics, and created a new course of study, one geared to the needs of intelligent and ambitious students. He had come to office at the right time, for just after the Great Crash everything that smacked of the old system was being challenged, and Hutchins seemed vital, yeasty, and progressive. The society had lost its way and he and others like him would help find it again. Hutchins combined a reverence for tradition in terms of subject matter with a desire to find novel forms in the matter of organization. He would teach the classics, but in new ways (in fact, many of his reforms were actually re-introductions of medieval concepts, but they seemed fresh in the early 1930s). He was the most dynamic university president since Woodrow Wilson had headed Princeton. Like Wilson, he seemed a national leader in the making.

Martin considered Hutchins a fine catch for the board. He was just the kind of man to give it a cachet of progressivism. But he didn't last long. From the first he clashed with other board members, even the most progressive of them. Hutchins was irate that the N.Y.S.E. planned no further action against those involved in the Whitney affair. Hutchins, who had something of a Calvinist view of life and was intrigued with the idea of sin and salvation, thought the Exchange would have to scourge itself of its sins, and do so completely. It was a period of purge and scapegoats, of symbolic deaths and subsequent rebirths, and Hutchins wanted one for the Exchange. George Whitney and Richard Whitney's other partners would have to pay the price of collaboration with the criminal, as would all others implicated in Whitney's disgrace. The S.E.C.'s report on the Whitney failure had been released on October 27, and Hutchins was convinced there had been a coverup at the Exchange. He demanded an investigation of the matter, but found no support on the board. Hutchins introduced a resolution to that effect, which was defeated by a vote of 29 to 1. And with this, Hutchins resigned from the board.

Hutchins and Douglas were close friends even before they had come together on Wall Street. Their friendship may have been another reason for Hutchins's selection for the board. At one time, Hutchins had tried to woo Douglas from the S.E.C. with an offer of the deanship of the University of Chicago Law School, and the chairman, perhaps in a joking way, suggested in turn that the two of them might want to swap jobs. But the Hutchins resignation had little visible effect on Douglas's relations with Martin. On December 28, the Exchange completed a detailed investigation of charges against J. A. Sisto, head of the Sisto Financial Corporation, and found him guilty of manipulations. Sisto was expelled from the Exchange, and Douglas praised the action, calling it an illustration of the adequacy of Exchange rules covering investigations and punishment of wrongdoers.

The Douglas-Martin détente continued into early 1939, a period when economic recovery took place, but at a slower pace than was deemed desirable, and Thurman Arnold, head of the Antitrust Division of the Justice Department, embarked on a major trust-busting operation. Business confidence was shaken, but for the moment, at least, stock prices held firm. At the same time, foreign affairs became more important, with talk of a new war in Europe, one that might involve the United States. In Washington, Secretary Morgenthau warned that unless business recovery came soon, such a war would find America unprepared, and he urged Roosevelt to take steps to restore business confidence. This might require the scrapping of some New Deal measures, a step Morgenthau desired. "Does it contribute to recovery?" This should be asked of every old program and proposed new one. If the answer was in the negative, the program should be ended.

As the New Dealers contested with one another, Martin called a conference of stock exchanges, to meet in New York on March 18 and discuss common problems. Sixteen exchanges were represented, and after a two-day session they released a unanimous report. Most of the recommendations for change were innocuous, as for example a suggestion that corporate proxy statements be simplified. Others, on the surface at least, seemed to give the S.E.C. greater power. The Commission should define "bad manipulation," for example, and set down more concrete rules under which the exchanges would operate. This was not a call for an end to self-regulation, however, but rather a masked demand for increased freedom. The original Securities Exchange Act had been vague in certain areas, deliberately so, in order to give the S.E.C. a wide range of power for whatever problems it might face. Now, in March 1939, the exchanges asked for more clarity. A case in point was the ban on wash sales and manipulations, a practice in which speculators would conspire to buy and sell a security so as to give onlookers the impression of great activity and interest when none actually existed. This had been forbidden under the Act, and the N.Y.S.E. thought the ban reasonable. In the conference report, however, it requested an amendment which would require the S.E.C. to state, unequivocally, what actions would constitute violations. In other words, wash sales and related practices would be outlawed "in contravention of such rules and regulations as may be prescribed by the commission as necessary or appropriate in the public interest or for the protection of investors."

If the S.E.C. accepted this amendment, it would mean that manipulations would be unlawful if they violated a specific rule, but acceptable otherwise. All would be allowed except that which the Commission banned, where in the past the exchanges had to be concerned with those actions that might be interpreted as manipulations, in fear of S.E.C. retaliation. On the one hand, it seemed the exchanges themselves were asking for an end to self-regulation, a practice they had supported only a few months earlier, while on the other they were requesting clearer guidelines from the Commission. Underneath all was a subtle attempt to free the exchanges from even more of the S.E.C.'s control than existed under self-regulation.

Douglas saw through this and announced that the Commission unanimously opposed the recommendations. But on March 20, as though in defiance, the N.Y.S.E.'s Board of Governors ratified them. Another struggle between the Commission and the Exchange seemed in the making. S.E.C. moderate George Matthews saw Martin and suggested a new round-table conference between the Commission and the Exchange to smooth ruffled feelings. But the conference could not be called, for late that afternoon, Roosevelt announced his nomination of Douglas for the post of Associate Justice of the Supreme Court, to fill the vacancy created when Louis Brandeis retired.

There had been rumors of the nomination for several days before it was made, and it may have been that Martin took a strong position knowing he had Douglas in a corner. The S.E.C. chairman could hardly open a crusade against Wall Street at a time when he hoped to be leaving the Commission. In addition, the nomination would have to be confirmed by the Senate, and conservative Republicans there might cause trouble if they believed Douglas had taken a turn toward radicalism. For the time being, at least, Wall Street could expect little trouble from the chairman or the Commission, the former because of his ambitions, the latter because its members did not know who would succeed Douglas, and which direction the S.E.C. would take after he left.

Douglas delivered several speeches in early 1939, preparing the way for acceptance of his nomination, if and when it came. Almost all were conciliatory; the old calls for crusades, the note of stridency that often crept into his statements, were absent. Indeed, some sounded as though they had been written a decade before for Herbert Hoover. "We are a capitalistic economy and only so long as we remain a capitalistic economy will we remain a democracy," he said. "Capitalism and democracy are Siamese twins; they cannot live if separated." Government, he implied, was getting too big, and should be curbed. "Every . . . chore should not be left to government. Let us not look to government for leadership, except where self-help breaks down." In early 1939 he described himself as "really a pretty conservative sort of fellow from the old school, perhaps a school too old to be remembered." According to Douglas, he was not "advanced" at all, but rather "old-fashioned." Liberals hailed his nomination as another victory for their cause, while conservatives called Douglas a wise and prudent man who had matured considerably over the past two years. The nomination sailed through the Senate with no difficulty.

For the time being, Commissioner Robert Healy became acting chairman of the S.E.C., pending the selection of a permanent one. There were several candidates for the position, and, at first, Hutchins led the field. The International News Service said it was "in the bag" for him. And once he took office Hutchins would conduct a reform campaign on Wall Street that would make Douglas's seem tame in comparison. If there were no war in Europe, the 1940 Presidential election might be conducted on domestic issues, and economic recovery continued to be the key national problem. New York District Attorney Thomas E. Dewey, the man who had put Whitney in jail, was a prime contender for the Republican nomination, and he had little support in the financial district in 1939. If Hutchins became S.E.C. chairman, and then spent the next year as the scourge of Wall Street, in the process assuming leadership of the New Deal's left wing, he might well capture the Democratic nomination. And if this happened, the N.Y.S.E. could well become a prominent issue in the election. Of course, all of this was based on supposition and the possibility of a chain of events taking place, with the absence of a single link resulting in a new situation for 1940. But these were the kinds of thoughts running through the minds of Wall Streeters in April.

As was his practice on such occasions, Roosevelt said nothing in the face of dozens of rumors about Douglas's successor, while Wall Streeters and financial writers, as well as nationally syndicated columnists, offered their ideas on the subject. Clearly Hutchins was a favored candidate, but there were others. Healy was among them, as was Ganson Purcell. If Roosevelt meant to place a professional in the position, it could be one of them. Neither man had a significant political inclination, and such a nomination would have no ideological connotation. The *Wall Street Journal* of March 25 claimed that Douglas had recommended Jerome Frank, an orthodox New Dealer who was already on the Commission. This would allow F.D.R. to name still another commissioner, and so pay off two debts at once. But Frank was not a wealthy man, and he had already indicated a desire to leave government service for private law practice. In addition, Frank was Jewish, and there was some concern as to whether or not he could function effectively with the Wall Street Old Guard. Kennedy's Catholicism had been something of a bar; Frank's Judaism might be more than Wall Street could bear.

Leon Henderson, the New Deal economist, became a favorite as Hutchins's star waned in early April. He had little detailed knowledge of the financial district, however, and his abrasive manner would certainly bring the Douglas-Martin era of good feeling to a close. Adolph Berle was spoken of as a compromise candidate, along with Dean Acheson of the Treasury Department. Shields, Hanes, and others were thrown in as though to complicate matters. Meanwhile, S.E.C.–N.Y.S.E. relations were at a standstill, awaiting Roosevelt's decision.

On April 24, F.D.R. nominated Henderson to fill the vacancy created by Douglas's departure for the Supreme Court. Since the commissioners, and not the President, selected the chairman, this did not necessarily mean Henderson would assume that position. Walter Winchell, Drew Pearson, and other columnists predicted that Henderson would take leadership after his confirmation by the Senate, and then initiate a major reform effort. By this time, Hutchins had been forgotten, and there was some talk of Henderson moving from the S.E.C. to the Cabinet, or even obtaining the Vice-Presidential nomination in 1940. Thus, Wall Street and the S.E.C. became pawns in the larger chess game F.D.R. was playing with the press and nation.

But Henderson was not to be the Commission's leader. The S.E.C. met to select its new chairman on May 19, and at Roosevelt's bidding chose Frank for the position. In this way the President threw a sop—Henderson—to the more ardent reformers in his inner circle while at the same time indicating to Martin and others at the N.Y.S.E.—by the election of Frank—that cooperation would remain the keynote in the future, thus pleasing Morgenthau and Hanes at the Treasury.

Douglas's departure and the election of Jerome Frank were important benchmarks in the history of government–stock exchange relations. The Douglas chairmanship was the height of federal regulatory power on Wall Street. Frank proved an able chairman, but he didn't have Douglas's drive and ambition. Furthermore, conditions in 1939 were quite different from those of 1937. The N.Y.S.E. had survived the Douglas administration pretty much intact, with a new constitution but most of the old power alignments unchanged. Douglas had been unable to resolve the segregation and specialist issues to his liking, and at the time of his departure both appeared dead. In fact they were not; they would arise again in more serious and dangerous forms thirty years later. Along with the question of N.Y.S.E.–O-T-C relations, these were among the major pieces of unfinished business of the New Deal on Wall Street.

William Martin served the Exchange and the wider financial community well. The N.Y.S.E. had its czar, one who would not interfere unduly with essential floor operations but instead defend them—with an intelligence that Whitney lacked and a sense of style and politics foreign to Gay—against the S.E.C. and all comers. Perhaps now he could also increase business. If he did, Martin would be deemed a complete success. Failure in this area, however, could lead to his downfall and, ironically, give additional power to elements on the floor, the major specialists in particular. In 1939, as before, the Old Guard watched the volume figures, worried about a loss of business to other exchanges, and considered its powers sacrosanct. All else, so it believed, was peripheral.

CHAPTER 4

The Dead and the Dying

The conference of stock exchanges, called to consider recommendations for amendments to the Securities Exchange Act, convened a few days after the German invasion of Czechoslovakia. As the delegates met in New York, world leaders seemed all but convinced a major war would erupt that autumn. In the United States, President Roosevelt asked Congress for $552 million for defense, and was placing the nation on a war footing. The arguments regarding domestic reform were heard less and less that March, while America's political leaders turned their attention to world affairs. Much of the New Deal was dead; the 1940 Presidential election would not be conducted on the issues of domestic policies after all, and now it seemed possible Roosevelt would attempt to win a third term, citing the war as a reason "not to change horses in midstream." The reform wave, which in any case had crested long before, was clearly on the wane.

The Douglas-Martin clash regarding alterations in the law did not appear on the front pages of many newspapers. Nor was it analyzed with the care it might have received had the confrontation occurred a year before. Most of those who wrote about it believed the S.E.C. and the N.Y.S.E. were refighting the wars of the mid-1930s. The conventional wisdom had it that Martin was engaged in a struggle with the Old Guard, and that the latter had obliged him to assume Whitney's goals—albeit with a different stance—before the Commission. The direct assault hadn't worked; Martin was to try a flanking attack. And unless he succeeded in freeing the district from the Commission, he might be fired before the year was out. Arthur Krock, Drew Pearson, Walter Winchell—the gamut of analysts—took this view.

To be sure, many Wall Streeters had bridled at the S.E.C.'s regulatory actions, and even though they hadn't really changed the district as much as had been claimed, the idea of governmental controls still rankled. But the Douglas-Martin confrontation, cloaked as it might be in terms of legalities, was not really about government–private sector relations. Rather, it dealt with the all-important concerns of volume.

Douglas understood this, even while he vented his spleen during conversations with reporters on the conference report. "Looking at the end result, if you try to measure in terms of a program for business recovery, the report is a phony," he said. "Opening things up so that the boys in the Street can have another party isn't going to help recovery." Such statements aided Douglas later on, when his nomination for the Supreme Court vacancy was criticized by senatorial liberals who complained he had accepted "the Wall Street point of view." They demonstrated that Bill Douglas was as tough, as forceful, and as progressive as he had been in 1935. But he also recognized the motivation for the conference, and its recommendations. Martin and his colleagues wanted additional business for their exchanges. If greater regulation would bring in the customers, they would accept that. And if a lessening of standards would attract them, so be it. In his official response, Douglas showed an understanding of this:

> This proposal is presented on the ground that it will aid the capital markets. The S.E.C. is deeply concerned with the problems of maintaining a free flow of capital, from the savings of the investor through the productive channels of industry. To this end the commission is vitally interested in stimulating the confidence of investors in the securities of American industry. But this commission cannot stand idly by, while any attempt is made to bring investors back into the market on a 1929 basis. Such a proposal would redound only to the benefit of those whose primary interest is served by an increased volume of trading—the broker to whom more trading means quicker profits, the insider, and the market rigger—not American industry nor American investors. Sound recovery cannot be had through the use of injurious stimulants.

Yet by his espousal of self-regulation, Douglas had encouraged just such interests to be helped, such stimulants to be attempted. Whether or not a radical revamping of the N.Y.S.E. was needed or desirable was a matter that could be and was debated for years, but in fact such structural and attitudinal changes had not taken place during the New Deal. The kinds of men—and in some cases, the very individuals—who had power in 1929 retained it a decade later. They were annoyed by the New Deal, which had caused inconveniences and had obliged them to release information which in the past had been private, but other than disclosure, they operated pretty much as they did before the birth of the S.E.C. The reforms, considered radical at the time of their inception, proved moderate and bland in their adolescence, and even the S.E.C. appeared to be approaching a comfortable accommodation with the individuals and institutions it was supposed to regulate. Investment bankers had to offer a prospectus, with "full disclosure," to would-be purchasers of new bonds and stocks, but few clients bothered to read them. Specialists had to prepare and submit reports, both to the S.E.C. and the N.Y.S.E., but these revealed little and were poorly written and perhaps rarely read. The private traders were still there, and if the pool organizers and raiders were absent, one might note they seldom could be found when volume was low. Such individuals lived by shearing the sheep, and the sheep were elsewhere in the 1930s.

It should not have been surprising, then, for the Stock Exchange to do all in its power to increase business in 1939. The Douglas-Martin clash was, to that degree, a charade, with Douglas insisting that volume would rise when investors and speculators had confidence in the honesty of the market and the president saying, in effect, that other methods had to be tried to lure them back. Accommodation and self-regulation were still in the saddle. The imbroglio of March 1939 would have been quite different, in meaning and results, had a Hutchins encountered a Whitney. But Douglas and Martin were brothers under the skin. They knew it, and so did the Old Guard, which both disliked and needed the young president for these reasons.

Commission brokers and specialists didn't have to be told by newspapermen that their business was bad and getting worse. If anyone had doubts, he could consult the Exchange's own statistics for the dreary story. The number of listed issues remained fairly constant in the 1929–1939 period—2,710 in 1929 and 2,630 ten years later—as a result of a relaxation of standards both in the retention and acceptance of new issues and several raids upon the Curb Exchange, the over-the-counter market, and regional exchanges for listings. More often than not the new stocks carried lower prices than the old; in order to fulfill the minimum listing requirements, a few firms split their stocks before application. Some very inactive securities were retained on the list in the hope that in time they would attract investor or speculator interest. Thus, the 942 million listed shares of 1929 grew by almost 50 percent—to 1.5 billion shares—by 1939. The average price of a N.Y.S.E. stock in January 1929 had been $89.85. In June 1939 it was $26.51. In 1929 trading volume was over 1.1 billion shares, for a turnover rate of 119 percent. Slightly more than 262 million shares were traded in 1939, and the turnover rate of 18 percent was the lowest since 1922. Average daily trading was 4,276,808 in 1929.

In 1939, for the first time in sixteen years, the figure was below 1 million—954,570 shares.

Some shoddy merchandise could be found at the N.Y.S.E., but this was only part of the reason for the lack of investor interest. The depression and the scapegoat role Wall Street filled in the 1930s were more important. Still, the marginal issues didn't help, especially when the financial columns of leading newspapers ran stories on low quality and poor markets, as did the *New York Sun* on May 5, 1939:

> LIFE AMONG THE LOWLY
>
> Standard Commercial Tobacco lost half a point, or 40 per cent of its open market value, in the first few minutes of trading. Its low of around 75 cents a share was the poorest price ever paid for the stock. The company is in receivership. . . . Although the Stock Exchange has been looking into the advisability of removing Pirelli from the list, because of insufficient stock outstanding, nothing seems to have been done with Rhine-Westphalia Electric Power. Less than 10,000 of American shares are listed. The last sale was November of last year at $6 a share. Most of the time nobody has been able to get a bid on the stock. On April 21 the market was an eighth bid and none offered. Six days later the quotation was 3 bid and 5 asked, and that also was quoted two days later. On May 2 the market was 3½ bid and 5 offered. No bid, offer, or sale has been made since. A dividend worth less than an eighth of a point has just been paid. . . . In yesterday's dull market sixteen stock issues sold at or less than a dollar a share. Some of these stocks were in bankrupt companies, including a few railroads. A good purge of the penny stocks now might save the Stock Exchange a headache or two later.

But the N.Y.S.E. was in no mood to delist securities, not at a time when it was desperate for new business.

As might have been expected, the volume decline and the general air of pessimism on Wall Street were reflected in the price of a Stock Exchange seat, which sold for as little as $51,000 in 1939. Ten years before, just prior to a distribution of "fractional seats" to members in the Exchange's version of a stock split, the price had reached a high of $625,000.

Under Martin's direction, a special committee considered the matter of retiring some seats as they came to market. The reason given was conformity with the S.E.C.'s recommendations, but in fact the members were more concerned with supporting the prices of seats so they wouldn't fall so low as to spark new rumors about the district's decline. Many of these were not rumors, however; in 1942, N.Y.S.E. seats would sell for below the net assets behind each of them. In other words, the Exchange was worth more dead than alive.

Meanwhile, a second committee inquired into the possibility of selling associate memberships. Holders of these would not be owners of the N.Y.S.E., or of the real estate upon which the Exchange building rested, but would have the right to trade on the floor, although not to vote for the administration. Associates could not serve as specialists, and limitations on their rights to represent commission brokers were also to be established. They could, however, perform the functions of two-dollar brokers (making trades for others, for a fee), or service their own accounts. At a time when the S.E.C. was attempting to ban private traders, the Exchange considered a plan that would increase their numbers. The thought was that an associate membership might sell for a fraction of the current market price for a full seat, or that an annual fee might be charged the associates. Most important, however, was the new business such members might bring to the N.Y.S.E., especially from the over-the-counter market. The idea never progressed beyond the talking stage, but its consideration indicates how desperate the N.Y.S.E. had become for volume in 1939–1940.

In April the Exchange embarked on a publicity campaign. In the past, member firms had been forbidden to advertise in newspapers, with the exception of "tombstone" advertisements of underwritings and notices on financial pages of approved newspapers. Advertising, it was believed, was tantamount to solicitation, and such a practice was denied members of the higher professions—medicine, law, and brokerage. Now this too was overthrown in order to obtain new business. The committee on public relations announced on April 13 that it would encourage member firms to advertise "tastefully." It was a "liberal, realistic policy," and "broad latitude" would be granted those commission houses who wished to avail themselves of this new right.

Not many firms took advantage of it. Some were dubious as to the value of advertising, others weren't at all certain as to what to say—even though they were besieged by business-hungry advertising agencies who were sure that with the proper approach business would boom—and a few feared advertising would indicate they were in some way less than respectable. Fenner & Beane, a leading commission house, led the way. On May 4 it ran an advertisement in the *Wall Street Journal*, the *New York Times*, the *New York Herald Tribune*, and other leading newspapers throughout the nation. The quarter-page ad was entitled: "Why a Stock Exchange?" It proceeded to discuss the reasons for having a securities market. "When an investor purchases securities through a firm that holds membership in the New York Stock Exchange or the New York Curb Exchange, he is dealing with organizations that are financially responsible, for those Exchanges regularly review the financial status of all members and their financial requirements are high and rigid." Fenner & Beane also observed that the S.E.C. was on the job, to protect the investors. *"These safeguards for the investing public explain why most of the country's leading corporations list their securities on a recognized exchange, and why so many institutional and individual investors prefer to purchase listed stocks and bonds through member firms."*

This and future ads were concerned with the exchanges, and attempted to educate investors as to the functions of brokers and the safety of the marketplace. They were not offers of services, and certainly not solicitations. In this first ad, for example, there was no mention of Fenner & Beane in the body of the text, but rather a simple, distinguished signature at the bottom, containing the firm's name and its membership at the N.Y.S.E. and the Curb Exchange, with offices in other cities. The Big Board houses accepted advertising gingerly, and not for another decade would it be used in an aggressive fashion.

On April 14—the day after advertisements were permitted—the N.Y.S.E. announced the opening of a gallery and exhibition room, to be completed on May 1 as part of the celebrations surrounding the inauguration of the New York World's Fair. Martin called the new policy an indication of the openness of trading. For the first time, anyone interested in the Exchange could stand above the floor, in the gallery, and watch the specialists and commission brokers' representatives at work.* Many of the members were unhappy with the innovation, calling it an intrusion upon their privacy. As was usually the case, the opposition came primarily from the specialists, whose firms were quite small, had little overhead, and could survive if not prosper on low volume. The commission brokers, with higher costs and large payrolls, felt otherwise. By early April quite a few of them were placing employees on "Scotch weeks"—the euphemism for layoffs subject to immediate recall—while others cut their staffs through outright firings. More common was the practice of putting most employees on half time, and so preserving at least the semblance of their jobs.

The Exchange itself was in deep financial trouble. Throughout the middle and late 1930s, it showed net losses on operations, but always a rather small amount, due primarily to the cutting down of Exchange

* Educational groups had been permitted to view trading prior to 1939, however, but under the careful supervision of Exchange employees.

employees and other economies. In 1938, when expenses were below those of the mid-1920s, Gay reported a net loss of $140,377. The following year, the first under the new constitution and president, the loss was $1,149,373, a record. And what was worse, there appeared no other ways to eliminate expensive items, while the new methods of attracting additional business were unsuccessful.

In early May the S.E.C. disclosed that members trading for their own accounts were responsible for over 21 percent of all transactions in April, indicating that the N.Y.S.E. was still a private club. If this were so, it was not because the members didn't want public participation but rather due to indifference on the part of potential investors. In April 1939, 20 million shares were traded, against 111 million nine years earlier. Private trading declined in the interim, but public transactions almost vanished. The problem was to get the individual customers back.

On May 3 several commission houses presented a new plan designed to do this. They would offer "baby portfolios," consisting of a package of blue-chip dividend-paying stocks, which could be purchased as gifts or form the basis for a personal portfolio. These "packages" would range in price from a few hundred dollars to several thousand and would be available at reduced rates. In fact, the commissions would barely cover the costs of brokerage and handling. The brokerages were interested in the plan because they hoped it would attract new business, while the Exchange called it "a novel way" to invest. But as a writer for the *New York Herald Tribune* noted: "It seems that the scheme is more a frantic effort to aid brokers in keeping body and soul together than an invention that is likely to revolutionize investment practice." In any case, the S.E.C. frowned on baby portfolios, and the idea died.

Then there was the installment investment plan. Under this, small investors could purchase stocks—usually in investment trusts—with a down payment, the rest being loaned by the commission house and paid off in installments. The idea had first been suggested by John J. Raskob in 1929, when that General Motors executive originated the idea of "every man a millionaire." The program outlasted the bull market, and from 1929 to 1937, when it dwindled to little more than a few accounts, some $52.5 million had been invested this way. Given the general trend of stock prices in this period, about $17.2 million of this was lost.

The Exchange mounted a program for installment investments in mid-1939, but then the S.E.C. indicated its opposition. "In view of the various defects and problems pointed out as prevalent in this type of investment medium and in view of the actual experience of investors, it is questionable whether the installment investment plan as presently constituted, operated and maintained, involving the purchase of fluctuating common stock through the means of a 'trust on a trust' with high selling costs, maintenance fees, other loads and the duplication of expenses, fills an 'economic need' for these classes of individuals." The Commission went on to call the plans "fraudulent and misrepresentative," and with the issuance of the report, the Exchange dropped the idea.*

The N.Y.S.E. and the rest of the financial complex and community in lower Manhattan was in the doldrums in early 1939. This was a time when the nation was still emerging from the Great Depression, with fears of another dip, such as that which occurred in 1937, ever present. America's gross national product would be $91.1 billion in 1939, the highest since 1931, and it would top the $100 billion mark the following year. Almost 9.5 million Americans were jobless in 1939—17.2 percent of the work force—but this was below the 1938 figure, and the unemployment rate would be cut in half during the next two years. The depression was indeed ending, although this could be seen only in retrospect.

When Congress met in January, Roosevelt sent it his traditional message. "We have now passed the period of internal conflict in the launching of our program of social reform" he said. "Our full energies may now be released to invigorate the processes of recovery in order to preserve our reforms." But for the first time since his inauguration six years before, the President did not ask Congress for a legislative package, or even a single major piece of new legislation. The message seemed clear enough: the New Deal had run dry of ideas, not only for reform but recovery as well.

Foreign problems dominated Administration thinking, and as war approached, Roosevelt asked for additional defense appropriations. Military spending rose from $1.2 billion in 1938 to $1.4 billion in 1939, and then to $1.8 billion in 1940. This massive effort and others related to defense and war took the nation out of the depression and provided increased employment and a measure of prosperity not known since the late 1920s. During the period from 1933 to 1939—one of the great reform eras of American history—federal spending had risen from $4.6 billion to $8.8 billion, and the gross national debt had gone from $22.5 billion to $40.4 billion. Spending reached the $13.3 billion mark in 1941, and then went to $34.1 billion in 1942. As for the national debt, it was $72.4 billion in the latter year.

Federal spending, associated first with preparedness, then with the war itself, brought prosperity to most parts of the nation, but not to

* A variety of the installment investment plan would resurface after World War II as the Monthly Investment Plan.

Wall Street. There the hangover from the 1930s remained, and would linger long after the depression had been relegated to memories elsewhere in the land. Americans had been bitten by the bug of speculation late in the 1920s—the massive volume and large-scale public participation came toward the end of the decade. Then, even after the 1929 crash, many investors and speculators remained on the street, hoping to pick up bargains and make killings when prices rose once more. But they didn't, not until 1932, and the effect of this experience was to teach that generation of Wall Street amateurs a lesson: stay away from the stock markets. Wall Street professionals realized that most of the time individuals such as these arrived too late in bull moves to make much money and remained too long in bear sessions and so lost everything. Given the bull market of the 1920s and the bear market of the early 1930s, that group of amateurs received the bitterest lessons of any in the national experience.

The Great Depression, then, produced a generation of Americans who no longer believed in purchasing stocks and were interested in security, not windfall riches. Workers in defense-related and other industries made good salaries during the war, and they put their money into savings accounts (which rose from $2.2 billion in 1940 to $16 billion in 1945) and purchases of United States savings bonds (the holdings of which rose from $860 million to over $10 billion in the same period).

Little of this money would go to stocks. As early as 1939, America was becoming the "Arsenal of Democracy," and business was the foundation of that arsenal. The large companies whose securities were listed on the N.Y.S.E. made excellent profits during the war. Total corporation profits after taxes amounted to $3.3 billion in 1938, and rose to over $6 billion in 1939, and doubled once more by 1943. This situation was not reflected at the N.Y.S.E., despite massive efforts to make this story known. While the rest of the country put the depression behind them to fight the war against the Axis powers, Wall Street was still trying to live down the excesses of the 1920s.

Talk of the possibility of new European hostilities increased as the year went on, and it played a significant role in Wall Street thinking too. As might have been expected, many brokers recalled what had happened in 1914, when World War I erupted. It had come unexpectedly, and in fear of panic selling, Europe's stock exchanges closed, with the N.Y.S.E. following suit, and remained closed from July 31 to December 12, 1914.* In the interim, an outlaw market

* For an analysis of the situation on Wall Street in 1914, see Robert Sobel, *Panic on Wall Street* (New York, 1968), pp. 322–49.

appeared on New Street, where some stocks were selling lower than their closings on July 30, and others at premiums. It was an unprecedented situation; no one was certain then whether the war would present industry with huge profits or destroy capitalism. By early 1915 the latter possibility seemed unlikely. The Dow-Jones Industrials closed at 71.42 on July 30, 1914, and opened at 74.56 on December 12. Within the next twenty months, the average doubled.* The World War I bull market was in full swing, and it benefited not only investors and speculators but the brokers and specialists as well. Average daily volume was 270,262 shares in 1914. It more than doubled to 623,859 shares in 1915, and went to 842,873 shares in 1916. The war began in one of the slowest years in N.Y.S.E. history—in fact, average daily volume in 1914 was the lowest in the twentieth century—and in 1919, the first full year of peace, the average was 1,178,789 shares, a record that would stand for six years.

As war talk intensified in 1939, discussions of 1914 and subsequent years, along with the statistics, were bandied about Wall Street. There was one major difference between the situations in 1914 and 1939: in the latter year, the district was prepared for war, rumors of which caused prices to rise and volume to expand.

The bullish analysis of the war was simple enough: Europeans had liquidated their American and domestic stock holdings in 1914–1915 and had gone to gold, as was customary at such times. Then, seeing the growing strength of the American economy, they sent their gold to this country, both for safekeeping and profits in the American equity markets. European and American bulls provided the power for the massive upswing in 1915–1916, a period in which the United States went from being the world's leading debtor country to its major creditor. Now history was repeating itself. If a war erupted in Europe, there would be some liquidation of securities, and then the Continent's gold would come to America for investment in stocks and bonds in a rapidly expanding economy.

In late August of 1939, after the signing of the Nazi-Soviet Pact, war talk dominated the news. There seemed little doubt it would come, and most commentators appeared to agree that hostilities would begin with a German attack against Poland. The only significant question thereafter was the British and French response. Some believed Prime Minister Chamberlain would attempt further pacification of Hitler, while others were convinced that German aggression would signal an Anglo-French declaration of war against Hitler. What of the Russian role? And would the conflict last for long? There was a peace

* The Dow Industrials were recalculated, using a new base, in 1916. This statement refers to the old base, which stood at 152.10 on September 23, 1916, at which time the new average was 101.03.

party in Britain, another in France, and rumors of counterparts in Berlin and Moscow.

There seemed little doubt that a long war would be far more destructive than the 1914–1918 struggle had been, and perhaps more revolutionary. As for the United States, the nation still recalled the bitter disillusionment that followed the 1918 Armistice. Isolationist sentiment was strong in America, even while dislike of Hitler was more intense than it had been for the Kaiser a generation earlier. If America remained neutral in the war, Europe might be destroyed, leaving the United States rich, powerful, and secure. In such a situation gold would be a good investment, but American stocks and bonds even better.

War scares were endemic during the late summer of 1939, and they caused stock prices to decline erratically. In this period, bulls and bears presented their cases to investors, the former arguing that war would mean higher prices, the latter convinced a conflict would result in the greatest declines since 1937. Prices were jumpy in August, but closed on the downside, a sign the bears were winning the argument. On the other hand, volume was low; during the August 29–31 period, three days when talk of a German attack on Poland was discussed throughout the nation, trading volume didn't rise above a half-million shares a day, even while the Dow Industrials fell from 137.39 to 134.41. "A fair case can be made for the thesis that stock exchanges in general are permanently shrunken in economic importance in the last decade," wrote the *Christian Science Monitor* on September 2. "Wall Street argues that the 'thinness' of today's market is largely due to federal red tape, but thinness has been observed in foreign markets where the backward governments of Europe have failed to see the good in meticulous government regulation." Still, the hope persisted that war would result in higher prices and volume.

The Board of Governors prepared for the event. Recalling the 1914 experience, some members recommended the suspension of trading, while others thought limits should be set to declines, in the fashion of commodity markets. After discussion, it was agreed that prominent board members should go to the floor the moment news of war was heard and try to calm the traders. Martin and his staff would station themselves at trading posts and make certain harmony reigned. If there were heavy orders for certain stocks, trading would be suspended in them alone. It was a simple plan, one based in part on the experience of 1929. Martin was not sure it would work, but it was the best that could be done under the circumstances. The board did not want to close trading and so lose investor confidence and at the same time perhaps miss out on a bonanza trading opportunity.

Word of the German attack reached the floor an hour after trading had begun on September 1. Governors rushed to various trading posts, not certain what to do. The market was flooded with orders, both to buy and sell, an indication that investors and traders were confused about the impact the war would have upon prices. If Britain and France declared war, so the argument went, Hitler would be stopped and serious peace discussions would begin soon after. Thus, prices would rise. But the further appeasement of Hitler and a subsequent carving up of eastern Europe by Germany and the Soviet Union would be viewed as bearish news. Volume was almost 2 million shares that day—the highest in a half year—but prices rose by only slightly more than a point on the Dow.

The next day was Saturday, when the market was open for half-day trading. Rumors of an imminent announcement from London spread through the district. Volume was almost as high as it had been the previous day, despite the short hours, and the Dow rose by more than two points, closing at 138.09.

Britain and France declared war on Germany on Sunday, when the markets were closed, and they remained closed on Monday, Labor Day. Commission brokers were primed with purchase orders before the bell on Tuesday morning, while the governors, Martin, his staff, and S.E.C. representatives stood at the specialists' posts, prepared to offer assistance or close down if necessary.

Stocks opened higher—at 142.38—on very heavy trading. Prices rose sharply throughout the session, the average hitting 150.07 before closing at 148.12. Volume was 5,934,000 shares, the highest since the bottom fell out of the market on October 19, 1937, at which time prices declined almost ten points. Now the averages were headed in the opposite direction. The Dow Industrials reached an intraday high of 157.77 on September 12, and closed the month at 152.54. September volume was 57,089,000 shares, the best since January 1937. In late 1939 prices appeared low, prospects were good, and talk of a new bull move was heard throughout the district. Three N.Y.S.E. seats were sold on September 5, with the first going for $61,000, the second for $63,000, and the third for $65,000. One of the three buyers, reflecting on the situation and Martin's strong stand vis-à-vis the S.E.C., told reporters, "There might be some future in this business after all."

Stock prices and volume leveled off and then declined in October, as the "phony war" began along the Franco-German border, with little action anywhere on the Continent after the fall of Poland. Military analysts for major newspapers and radio networks predicted that the Germans would be unable to defeat the French forces at the Maginot Line, while the Anglo-French armies were incapable of strong offensive action. Trench warfare of a new kind would evolve, they said, of the kind that had destroyed all combatants in 1914–1917. Britain's World War I Prime Minister, Lloyd George, recalled this, and said peace negotiations were "not at all unlikely," and such talk was heard openly in the French legislature. In America, Roosevelt invoked the Neutrality Act, designed to keep the nation out of the war, but in a radio address told his countrymen that he could not expect them to remain "neutral in thought." Uncertainty put a damper on investor enthusiasm, but Bethlehem Steel doubled in two months, Anaconda rose from 21 to 39, Bendix Aviation from 16 to 31, Vanadium from 16 to 40, and du Pont from 126 to 188, all in the same period. Just before Christmas, a seat changed hands at $70,000, the high for the year.

In late November, brokerages began calling in those employees on Scotch weeks. They were on full time, so the saying went, not for the duration of the war but that of reasonably profitable markets. In a rare burst of optimism, several commission houses announced that they would pay year-end bonuses—for some, the first since 1933. Martin complimented the members on the orderly way they handled the influx of business in November, and S.E.C. Chairman Frank joined him in this. At the same time, both men denied that the Street welcomed the war—the market rise had inspired magazine stories about the "merchants of death" on Wall Street and in munitions plants, who profited greatly from armed conflict. "From an economic viewpoint there can be no real profit in war," wrote Martin in the first issue of *The Exchange*, which was released that December, the last of the major projects planned a few months earlier to publicize the N.Y.S.E. and help bring in new customers.

The war did not develop as anticipated, however. Instead of an Allied-German confrontation at the Maginot Line, there was little fighting anywhere in October and early November, while rumors of peace negotiations persisted. Stocks moved within a narrow range on low volume; the Dow Industrials rose 18 points in September, fell 7 in October and November, and rose 4½ in December. The only significant war news at this time was the Soviet attack on Finland on November 30. After suffering a series of initial setbacks, the Red Army defeated the Finns by March.

Wall Street was in the doldrums during the first three months of 1940, a period in which the Dow declined by 1.11 points and there were only four days in which over a million shares were traded. Investors and speculators awaited some dramatic event before moving, while military analysts wrote and talked of new forms of trench warfare to come along the Somme. In early April *The Exchange* ran an article by a long-time broker who had been on Wall Street since the

1907 panic, and in which he analyzed the reasons for the low volume and narrow price range. Business remained uncertain, he wrote, there was a lack of prospects for substantial profits, although taxes were sure to go up, and the war news remained unclear. The New Deal regulations and rules prevented chicanery and manipulation, and this was to the good, but at the same time they necessarily decreased interest in stocks and bonds. In other words, speculation had been checked, while investment was not yet seen as worthwhile. The writer did not offer a program for change. "There is a lot of hard work to be done," he concluded. "Let's get started—today!" * But how? The answer awaited war developments.

Shortly after the declaration of war, the Allied governments required their nationals to turn in their American securities to a previously established agency, which would sell them and use the money to purchase food, supplies, and arms. Financial analysts believed these sales would result in increased volume and lower prices at the N.Y.S.E.; such had been the case in 1915. This did not occur. Hoping to receive the highest prices possible, and feeling that the disposal of large blocks of stock in illiquid markets would depress prices, the Allies sold their American holdings slowly, and in most cases to institutional buyers, off the Exchange floor. The result was a stable price level—and a loss of windfall profits for N.Y.S.E. brokers and specialists.

The Dow Industrials closed at 148.17 on May 9, on a volume of 848,000 shares. In terms of prices, stocks had remained steady since early September. Germany invaded the Low Countries the following day, sweeping through with little opposition, clearly attempting to outflank the Maginot Line. This was a signal that serious fighting was about to commence along the French front. That same day the pound sterling fell sharply, and Winston Churchill replaced Neville Chamberlain as Britain's Prime Minister. The Dow responded to this news by falling more than 3½ points, with over 2 million shares traded for the first time since late September. Hitler launched his blitzkreig against France on May 12, a Sunday, and the Dow fell by 7 points on heavy volume on Monday, closing at 137.63. By June 3, when the British evacuation at Dunkirk was completed and it seemed that Germany might have won the war, the average was at 114.73. The Dow had lost 32 points in May; it was the worst month in these terms since 1931. Prices recovered to the 135 level by October, but then declined once more, and on low volume. After a year of war, Germany was in command of the Continent and deep gloom pervaded Wall Street.

* * *

* "Is It as Black as It Looks?" *The Exchange* (Vol. I, No. 5, April 1940), pp. 10–12.

There were compelling psychological reasons for the decline in securities prices in 1940. News of German victories on the Continent, the Luftwaffe's smashing assaults against Britain that autumn, and the Axis' consolidation of power in eastern Europe made it appear a German victory was in the making, while the Japanese occupied French Indochina, in what seemed a preparation for a western drive toward India. Many military analysts believed that only through a negotiated peace could Britain survive, for the air war over London was a preparation for an invasion, with one expected by the spring of 1941 at the latest. When asked to assess the war situation, Martin responded that he thought the war would end either in six months or two years—that there would be a negotiated peace, or that the British would turn the tide somehow. Could this be accomplished without American help? Martin thought the United States would have to supply England with arms, but added his belief that America would remain militarily neutral. In fact, Martin was an interventionist, and such statements were obligatory for individuals in his position at that time.

Uncertainties abroad were complicated by the Presidential election of 1940, pitting Roosevelt against Wendell Willkie. As was expected, Wall Street gave Willkie strong support. Willkie was a businessman who, as president of Commonwealth & Southern, a large public-utilities holding company, had battled Roosevelt over the Tennessee Valley Administration, and in addition he was generally viewed as a "Wall Street lawyer." But Willkie was not a bitter foe of the New Deal, or for that matter an opponent of F.D.R.'s program of helping the Allies. Rather, he would consolidate the New Deal programs and try to develop better relations between government and business. In other words, he was close to the Martin approach, though suspected of having a taint of radicalism by some Old Guard N.Y.S.E. members. At the same time, however, the district's more liberal elements were not as strongly opposed to Roosevelt as they had been two years before. By 1940 the New Deal had ended, and agencies like the S.E.C. were being defanged, while businessmen flocked to Washington to help in the defense effort as "dollar-a-year men." Thus, Roosevelt moved somewhat to the right politically, as under Willkie's leadership the Republicans ventured to the left. The result was a clash more of personalities than programs in the 1940 election, and this should have eased political pressures on stock prices. The markets disliked uncertainty, however, and the matter of who would occupy the White House in 1941 only added to the bearish sentiment.

As psychological factors depressed prices, economic forces should have countered them. By late summer of 1940, banks reported that demand deposits were $9 billion more than they had been at a comparable time in 1938, for a 66 percent increase, while the money supply was 43 percent higher. The excess reserves of member banks in the Federal Reserve System that June were $3 billion—134 percent higher than in 1938. Demand for consumer loans was rising, indicating confidence in the economy and a strong pull on the demand side. At the same time, industrial production, fueled by war-related orders as well as increased consumer demands, boomed. The Federal Reserve's index of industrial production stood at 148 that June, compared with 84 two years before. The future appeared bright. There was talk of a tax increase for 1941—after the election—but the gross national product would expand at an even faster rate. That June, the Exchange released a survey of first-quarter earnings, indicating that the net income for all listed companies was 24.2 percent over that of the previous year. Railroad earnings had climbed by 659 percent, steel by 90 percent, retail merchandise operations by 82 percent, and construction firms by 78 percent. These figures were released on June 24, 1940, at which time the Dow Industrials stood at 123.76, with trading volume at 472,000 for the Monday session, and 15,570,000 shares for the month as a whole. Two years earlier, on June 24, 1938, volume had been 2,291,000 shares, and the Dow was at 129.06, with volume for the month at 24,368,000 shares. All the economic preconditions for a bull market were present in 1940—there were higher earnings, good dividends, fine prospects for the future, and surplus capital available for securities purchases. Fears of inflation were replacing the chill of depression, and this too was expected to provide an impetus for a major bull move.

But it didn't, and the lackluster performance buttressed the claims of long-time critics who said that the exchange system was obsolete and indeed dead, and awaited formal burial, which would come soon. The coffin had been fashioned during the 1929 crash and subsequent declines, sealed by New Deal reforms, and interred by the Whitney disclosures. Martin was admired, but he couldn't raise the dead; nor could good economic news stir activity for more than a few sessions.

The argument was both simple and convincing. For years critics had charged that only gamblers and speculators would deal in common stocks, with the unwary investors sucked in during bull moves, more through fantasy and hard sell than for sensible reasons. The Great Crash had shown the vast majority of Americans that investments in common stocks didn't pay, and the lesson was reinforced in the depression by bear moves. At the same time, New Deal reforms rid the district of many speculators—those not ruined by the crash—and put a bridle on the others. Martin's reform era had come too late; the

N.Y.S.E. no longer had credibility with the former investors, while it was too honest by 1940 to attract speculators. Full disclosure, higher earnings, advertising, a vision of a prosperous America—none of these had been able to create an enlarged public interest in securities. The business of Wall Street remained—corporations would seek financing there, and the large bankers had nothing to fear. Perhaps in the hope that he could develop a climate for investment in equities, Martin came out in favor of increased participation by the private sector in the defense effort, and delivered several speeches on the subject in late 1940. Indeed, Roosevelt did encourage private business to expand, but it did so through borrowings from banks and government agencies, not the flotation of new stock, since the prices were so low. The one-time investor would buy government bonds and put his money into a savings bank, and the government and the banks would finance the war effort. The N.Y.S.E. was no longer needed. Or so it seemed in late 1940.

CHAPTER 5

A Farewell to Reform

The New Deal was the most far-reaching American social reform movement in the twentieth century, one that altered society, and was directed by and helped create a distinctive kind of public servant: the New Dealer. No less than participants in other major upheavals, these men seemed to be cut from a limited number of patterns. Just like the Abolitionists of the 1840s and 1850s and members of several protest movements of the 1960s, they appeared to conform to circumscribed standards of dress and behavior, spoke a common language that sounded a trifle alien to outsiders, and had similar backgrounds. The quintessential New Dealer was a graduate of an Ivy League law school who then went on to corporation practice or taught in his own or an equally prestigious institution. His income placed him in the upper middle class, his artistic tastes in the aristocracy, his sympathies with the proletariat. The New Dealers tended to come from old-line Protestant or *arriviste* east European Jewish families, with a sprinkling of Irish on the periphery. They were liberal to radical in conviction and confident of their own intelligence and abilities. They yearned for power and recognition; the New Deal presented them with the opportunity to obtain both.

Not all New Dealers fit this pattern, and each had his own distinctive traits. But somehow they could be spotted in a crowd—or at least, that was the claim of veteran Washingtonians, some of whom swore this could be done after a thirty-second conversation on any topic. Later on, the New Dealers would be caricatured, and people with highly idiosyncratic attitudes would be squeezed into the same category. Exaggeration and distortion were liberally employed, but as is the case with all such caricatures, underneath it all was a core of truth.

Certainly Jerome Frank, general counsel for the Agricultural Adjustment Administration at age forty-four, was of the type. He was a successful lawyer whose talents had been recognized early. Frank's book *Law and the Modern Mind*, had won high praise from Felix Frankfurter, who was in the process of dispatching young lawyers to Washington to help create the New Deal. Frank was a pragmatist with a strong conviction that intelligence could move the world, and that he and others like him possessed that intelligence, and the world was ready to be moved. Of course, he knew next to nothing about farming, but this was not a necessary talent for the job. "What we need are brilliant young men with keen legal minds and imagination," he told a fellow New Dealer. Knowledge was not as important as freshness, and lack of experience could be overcome by innovation and intelligence. Frank found compatriots who felt as he did. Adlai Stevenson, Abe Fortas, Alger Hiss, Lee Pressman, Thurman Arnold—all of whom had similar backgrounds, were of the same generation, and worked together for reform—entered the A.A.A. at that time.

America seemed to teeter on the brink of momentous change, and Washington was crammed with bright, dazzling lawyers, the cream of the country, who would dictate the tactics of the transformation, men more interested in results than philosophy. These New Dealers—the descendents of the Progressives, the ancestors of the New Frontiersmen—were cocky and confident, certain of their own talents and convinced that those who opposed them either were foolish or evil.

Brilliance and hard work were not enough, however. The A.A.A. also needed people who were experienced in farm problems, and these were in short supply at A.A.A. headquarters. The program failed, for this reason among others. The young lawyers were assigned to other positions, with Frank moving to the S.E.C.

By 1937, and after four years of practical experience in government, Frank was a more cautious and less certain individual. The following year he published a new book, *Save America First*, which was a call both for domestic reform of a modest nature and an argument against foreign entanglements—and crusades. Frank would limit the power of large corporations—but he would not destroy them. The man who a few years before had spoken confidently of the virtues of socialism now asked for higher wages for workers and lower prices for consumers, both of which could best be accomplished through the free-enterprise system. Frank was still brilliant, often caustic, and never dull. But the fires of reform had been banked by 1938. The new chairman of the S.E.C. would castigate the public-utility holding companies, toy with the idea of eliminating new corporate bond issues and replacing them with common stock expansion (he was not serious in this), and try to convince the N.Y.S.E. of the need for a central depository for certificates and "brokerage banks." The major struggle of the Douglas era—for control of N.Y.S.E.—had been resolved, with both Wall Street and Washington accepting the principle of self-regulation. The segregation of specialists' functions as broker and dealer had been of major concern before the 1937 collapse. Afterward, in the becalmed markets of late 1937 and early 1938, the matter appeared of less importance. Segregation might be possible in a vigorous market, with high volume, so that the implementation of the change would not cause anyone to suffer unduly. The markets were quite different in 1938, and the dangers of manipulation to the detriment of investors small—since there were clearly so few of that species to be found at the commission houses.

Thus, Frank's arguments with the N.Y.S.E. were minor compared with those of Douglas. Yet because the Wall Street community was by then accustomed to viewing any conflict between the Commission and the Exchange as being significant, they were publicized and hotly debated, as philosophical matters if nothing else. Given Frank's temperament, he relished the struggle.

This was the situation in regard to the brokerage banks. Traditionally, commission firms had used customers' certificates in short sales, for example. In addition, clients' cash balances were commingled with holdings of the brokerages. In the cases of reputable firms, these practices represented no real problem, and, in fact, most investors were unaware that they were the rule. If any had doubts as to the honesty or solvency of their broker, they could obtain their certificates and cash simply by asking for them. Many steady traders did not, as a matter of their own convenience and the result of the trust they had in their brokerages.*

Douglas had spoken of the possibility of forming brokerage banks, and Frank revived the idea soon after assuming the chairmanship. For a while it appeared he would make the drive for segregation of specialist functions and the organization of independent depositories a major goal for 1939. In a speech delivered on June 23, he called for the establishment of brokerage banks, controlled by private interests, which would hold customers' cash balances as well as their certificates. If the Frank plan were accepted, the commission houses would not be able to utilize clients' certificates in making short sales, and would be obliged to turn over to the depository funds that were not theirs but which they had used for corporate purposes. Frank went further. He

* This confidence was merited. Stock Exchange houses had a superior solvency record than banks and trust companies. Despite the mythology that had grown up about the Great Crash, few had declared bankruptcy in 1929–1930, and in 1931, when one out of every ten banks was insolvent, the N.Y.S.E. reported that over 95 percent of its members had come through the year intact, and there were no insolvencies from 1935 to 1937. The commission houses pointed proudly to this record, but the very fact that Douglas, and later Frank, had raised the issue contributed to the generally poor reputation the N.Y.S.E. had in the nation.

wanted the brokerage banks to have the power to pay interest on deposits and make loans to clients, enabling them to buy securities on margin. If this were put into effect, the commission houses would lose a good deal of their business in lending money at interest to margin customers. "An end to broker's free credit balances and broker's loans would wipe out half the commission houses in the Street," thought the *New York Sun*, while the *Wall Street Journal*, concerned but less troubled, believed the Frank attack against the commission firms was "as significant, in its own way, as Douglas's crusade against the New York Stock Exchange." *

Frank's speech afforded Martin an opportunity to defend the interests of the commission houses, as he had in the past fought for the specialists and private traders. In a letter to Frank, written on July 14, he said, "We have examined carefully your recent suggestions as to the possible advisability of establishing 'brokerage banks.' These suggestions, which are receiving our open-minded consideration, present a problem of the utmost importance to the brokerage business which, as you know, is already struggling under reduced volume and increased costs." In the past, Martin had met with Douglas at round-table meetings to hammer out differences of opinion and come to conclusions. This time, however, Martin took another path. "In the interest of this common objective, I have invited Messrs. W. Randolph Burgess, Carle C. Conway, Walter J. Cummings, and Roswell Magill to serve as a PUBLIC EXAMINING BOARD in connection with this entire matter and related aspects of our business." Martin said that the Exchange would use its final report as a basis for reforms, if indeed any proved necessary.

This initial encounter between the new S.E.C. chairman and Martin indicated that the Exchange wanted to declare its independence of Washington and practice true self-regulation. Round-table conferences were out; Martin wanted no compromise, no conceding points to what he was increasingly coming to view as an outside agency. He had worked with Douglas because it had been necessary to preserve the Exchange, and he had succeeded in his objective: moderate reform and N.Y.S.E. autonomy. The reforms were over, and the Wall Street Establishment felt it was time to roll back some of them, certainly not an occasion to concede further powers to the S.E.C. The main issue, then, was not brokerage banks, a minor matter at best, but the degree of control the Commission would have over the district during the Frank era and beyond.

* * *

* Broker's free credit balances refers to customers' cash remaining idle in brokerage accounts, while broker's loans was money brokers borrowed to help finance underwritings.

When Martin announced the establishment of the Public Examining Board, Frank responded that he was pleased and would assist the board in its studies. Government lawyers did meet with the board, but it soon became evident that the examining group had little concern with brokerage banks as a means of safeguarding the public interest. Tensions developed between Washington and Wall Street over this issue, with the press generally siding with Martin. Douglas had come to Wall Street at a time when change was in the air, and he had a knack of getting along well with reporters, massaging their egos, and being "good copy." Frank was not as fortunate. The reform wave had crested long before he arrived in the district, Frank had no use for reporters, and in fact engaged in abstract and often pointless correspondence with some of the Street's most influential commentators, and was rather dull compared to his predecessor.* By the time the board made its report—September 1, 1939—it was clear that Martin meant to ignore the S.E.C. In any case, there was little public interest in such matters on the eve of World War II.

The report opened by observing that "The Stock Exchange has been remarkably free from failures," and that in no way were its recommendations to be interpreted as an indication that major problems existed. It went on to reject the idea of brokerage banks. "Our consideration . . . has led us to the conclusion that the best results will be obtained through strengthening the regulations of the Exchange in a series of particulars . . . rather than through the institution of a brokerage bank." The body of the report contained fourteen specific points. In one was a proposal that customers' cash balances left in brokers' hands should be segregated and deposited by the brokers in commercial banks, but there was no hint that these moneys should not be used for brokers' loans. Also, it was suggested that commission houses separate their brokerage and underwriting businesses, and incorporate each individually. This would seem a restatement of Douglas's old call for segregation, but in fact the Public Examining Board did not go on to recommend complete divestiture. Instead, it implied that the same individuals could serve on the governing boards of each new corporation, and that the two units could work in harmony with one another. Segregation here was not asked for in order to reform operations at the N.Y.S.E. but to protect customers' cash balances in brokerage accounts from losses in underwriting operations.

The P.E.B. recommended that the Exchange and the S.E.C. join to work for an amendment to the federal bankruptcy law "to make it clear that balances so segregated and securities held in safekeeping and

* A lengthy correspondence between Frank and Leslie Gould, financial editor of the *New York Journal American*, can be found in the Gould papers.

in segregation are not subject to the claims of the broker's general creditors in case of his insolvency." The commission houses should be audited regularly, on a surprise basis, and each firm should distribute annual financial reports to clients. The audits and supervision should be conducted by the Exchange, not the S.E.C.

The report took cognizance of the N.Y.S.E.'s financial problems and called for a new tax on transactions, which would go to the Exchange and be used to increase the staff. "Since the Stock Exchange's examining force and periodic inspections are its principal mechanism for self-supervision, we recommend further strengthening of the examining staff."

Martin hailed the report as a progressive document, and said it would be used as a basis for further discussion and eventual action. Copies were forwarded to the S.E.C., but without an indication that comments on its form and substance were needed. Nor did Martin attempt to set up a meeting with Frank to discuss future actions.

The report, then, was significant in three major respects. In the first place, it demonstrated a desire to reform the commission houses; no future changes appeared to be contemplated in specialist activities, and the specialists, then as before, remained the power group on the trading floor. Next, acceptance of the report, which did not include a recommendation for a brokerage bank, demonstrated that the Exchange would not consider such institutions. Finally, throughout this period Martin had remained cool toward Frank, and his independent course of action indicated that he felt the time had come to consolidate his power and diminish that of the S.E.C. in the district.

Martin had come to office as the candidate of the moderates, an outsider who was relatively unknown to the major specialists and not of the reform element in the commission houses. During the Douglas era he had defended the specialists, and in the process had won the support and trust of many powerful men on the floor. Now he was speaking out for the commission houses, and indicating that he, and not the S.E.C., was the major force for reform in the district. Douglas had willingly relinquished a portion of his constituency and mandate to Martin prior to his having gone to the Supreme Court, in part for political reasons but also because he seemed to trust the new president. Now Martin was acting to wrest a good deal of the remaining S.E.C. power from Frank.

The S.E.C. acknowledged receipt of the report, but declined comment upon it, except to say it was gratified to note that the board had concerned itself with customer protection. Speaking for himself, Frank told reporters he was willing to compromise on the issue of brokerage banks, and was prepared to consider "reasonable alternatives." The matter should be discussed, he said, at future round-table meetings, such as those that had proven fruitful during Douglas's tenure.

Apparently Martin did not agree, for no additional conferences took place, even though Frank indicated on several occasions they would be desirable. Instead, the Exchange moved ahead on its own, creating committees to consider the recommendations. By mid-October, Martin had seized the initiative from Frank. Now he was hailed by both the Old Guard and the reformers as the most "constructive" force in the securities field.

As though in response to this challenge, and perhaps in an attempt to oblige Martin to accede to a new meeting, Frank initiated an ill-conceived campaign of his own. Throughout 1938 and into 1939, N.Y.S.E.–based commission houses had increased their activities on the regional stock exchanges. In their search for new business, they would buy and sell securities whose primary listings were in New York. The Big Board had fought such practices throughout its history, at times expelling members for refusing to deal only in New York. In the early part of the century, reformers charged the Exchange with attempting to form a monopoly, and, in fact, this was the case. In 1939, however, monopoly was not at issue. The N.Y.S.E. specialists, already suffering from the decline in trading volume, demanded that the commission houses cease the practice. And the board complied, on September 1, with a new rule to that effect. Almost two months later—on October 25—and only after vainly attempting to organize a new meeting, the S.E.C. requested the Exchange to rescind the rule.

The ban on trading in N.Y.S.E.–listed stocks at other exchanges did not violate the Securities Exchange Act, although a case against it might have been made under the terms of the antitrust statutes. Thus, Frank had selected weak ground for his attack. Martin realized this and asked for a full statement on the matter. In the meantime, the Exchange would suspend the rule.

While the report was being prepared, Frank announced, on November 16, that brokers and dealers could not commingle the securities of different customers as collateral for a loan without the consent of each customer. In addition, a broker or dealer could not commingle his customers' securities with his own under the same loan pledge. This announcement apparently was meant as a countermove against the P.E.B. report, and an indication that the S.E.C. was moving forcefully in the field.

It had an opposite impact. Martin calmly stated his agreement with the new regulations and noted that they had already been prohibited by the Exchange's rules, adopted more than a year earlier. The implication was clear: not only was the S.E.C. behind the times insofar as reforms were concerned but its members weren't even certain of their own areas. It was at this point that several newspapermen suggested that S.E.C. staff personnel had been selected on a political basis, and that many of them had little knowledge of the industry they were supposed to regulate. Frank defended his agency in a series of lengthy letters to financial columnists which, however, he refused to allow them to quote. The attacks continued in the press, while the chairman defended his work in private, hoping without success to convince his critics that the Commission was in excellent shape.

On December 11, the Board of Governors informed the S.E.C. that it would not rescind its rules regarding members trading in its stocks on other exchanges. Nine days later, Frank formally requested a reversal of this policy, citing sections of the Securities Exchange Act as justification and asking for a response by December 28. Once again, the Exchange and the Commission headed toward a confrontation, but by then it seemed that no matter what the outcome Frank had lost his bid to take Douglas's place insofar as power and prestige were concerned. The S.E.C.'s momentum had been stopped, and the key to the defeat was not trading regulations but Martin's unwillingness to negotiate, an implied belief that the S.E.C. could not dominate the district as it had in the past. Also, Martin was preparing to turn to new matters, most of them concerned with the impact of the war on Wall Street and the continued problem of low volume, while Frank, as though speaking with accents of 1935, still wanted reforms. Frank hoped to iron out matters at a new conference, and Martin rejected the idea. "The SEC has never abandoned *its* use of the 'round-table method,' " the chairman wrote to Norman Stabler, financial editor of the *New York Herald Tribune*, on November 25.

> There are certain areas of Exchange activity with respect to which we have no power to issue regulations, but which affect the public interest. In those areas, the round-table method has meant prior discussion with us before the Exchange issues its own regulations. The Exchange is not required thus to consult us, but, until recently, has deemed it wise . . . twice this month it has made rules without prior consultation.*

Frank had been outmaneuvered; his tenure as S.E.C. chairman was almost devoid of accomplishment. In part this was due to his own inabilities to learn the terrain before acting, or to develop the political skills necessary to cope with the Wall Streeters. He still seemed to

* Letter from Frank to Stabler, November 25, 1940, in *Leslie Gould Papers.*

believe that a fine intelligence was all that was needed for the task, and that experience and personal relationships were secondary. Frank was arrogant with newspapermen and clumsy in his dealings with the financial district's leaders, and as a result columnists who had criticized Martin toward the end of the Douglas era defended him against Frank in late 1940. Such an attitude had wrecked the A.A.A. It had a similar, though less devastating, effect at the S.E.C.

The reason for this was the Douglas legacy and the times. As for the first, Douglas had been so successful that there really wasn't much more required in the way of reform. As *Fortune* put it in June 1940, Frank's main task seemed to be to "refrain from doing anything that might upset the S.E.C.'s big cart of liberal apples. They took too long a time to ripen." Yet Frank was an activist by nature, and insisted on remaining so even when this quality was not needed. The times called for a caretaker, not a reformer, and Frank was unsuited for the role.

The times, too, worked against him. Douglas had arrived on Wall Street at the flood tide of reform, while Frank was named to his post when the tide was ebbing. The war, not domestic reconstruction, occupied the nation's thoughts in 1939. Even Frank recognized this in his non-securities writings, such as *Save America First.* Careers and reputations would be made in defense-related agencies, not the old New Deal ones. Frank arrived in the right place, but at the wrong time. He came to realize this in February 1941, as the hearings bogged down in trivialities; the S.E.C. would win a victory, but it would be close to meaningless. Working through his friends in Washington, Frank began seeking a new position. In April he was named to the Federal Circuit Court of Appeals for the Second District. On April 9, the S.E.C. announced the election of Edward C. Eicher as its new chairman. Eicher was a former congressman from Iowa, a member of the House Committee on Interstate and Foreign Commerce, and a staunch New Dealer, who was known for his knowledge of finance and abilities at administration, and had been a member of the Commission since 1938.

Joseph Kennedy was a political associate of Roosevelt's as well as a famous man of Wall Street. Landis, Douglas, and Frank were important New Dealers, men who had come to Washington with F.D.R. and clearly were "the President's men." Eicher was a strong supporter of New Deal measures, who had a successful career in Iowa before being elected to Congress in 1932, at which time he was fifty-four years old. He was a lawyer and a politician, not a Wall Streeter, and certainly not one of Roosevelt's bright young men. Nor was he a prominent, or even interesting, person. His was a political appointment, and a sign that the S.E.C.'s vitality had all but gone.

On May 29, Roosevelt announced the nomination of Ganson Purcell to take Frank's place on the Commission. Purcell was a true professional, an able bureaucrat who had risen through the ranks and was deemed the most knowledgeable man at the S.E.C. Both Landis and Douglas had relied upon him for the framing of new codes and regulations, and he did the same for Frank. On December 30, after serving as chairman for only nine months, Eicher was named Chief Justice of the District Court of the United States for the District of Columbia, and in late January, Purcell was elected to take his place as S.E.C. chairman.

The Commission passed beyond politics to administration with the coming of Eicher, and with the selection of Purcell it entered an age of bureaucracy. Not for another generation would the Commission be a moving force in lower Manhattan.

On November 19, 1940, while still parrying with Frank, Martin said he would leave for a ten-day trip to the West Coast on December 1. While there he would deliver major addresses in Portland, Seattle, San Francisco, and Los Angeles. Purportedly, the trip was being made to organize the Exchange into a more effective national unit. Paul Shields, then chairman of the committee on public relations, would accompany Martin, along with several other key personnel. The announcement underlined the belief that the S.E.C. challenge was not serious, and did not require Martin's presence in New York. Thus, in yet another way, Wall Street indicated that the era when Washington mastered the financial district was coming to an end.

The question of trading volume was a more important consideration, however. The trip had been planned in late October, when volume was low. With the coming of the European war, trading expanded. During the eleven full-time trading days after October 30, volume was over the million-share mark. Then it fell off drastically, so that on the day Martin made his announcement, volume was only 703,000 shares.

Martin was not traveling to the Coast to signify his independence of Washington; nor was this a good-will trip. Rather, he would use his platforms there to speak to Washington, to demand additional considerations, while at the same time attempting to draw more business from the West to the East.

The trip was well-prepared from a public relations point of view. It was covered extensively in the West Coast newspapers, and Martin was greeted as though some latter-day, Americanized, incarnation of the Prince of Wales. Here was this young, dynamic, attractive bachelor from New York, arriving with his full retinue to take the West Coast by storm. Or, at least, so it seemed from a reading of front-page stories in California, Washington state, and Oregon. Actually, the shy, diffident Martin was somewhat embarrassed by the fuss, which made him seem more like a motion-picture star than the serious man of business he had come to consider himself.

The trip opened inauspiciously in Portland on December 1, where Martin spoke on "The New York Stock Exchange: Crossroads of the World." On the surface it appeared a pedestrian effort, and was delivered in a dull monotone; afterward, little was heard of the "glamorous New Yorker." But, in fact, it marked a new declaration of independence on the part of Wall Street.

Martin said he hoped the government would allow private enterprise to take a major share in the mobilization effort. Arms would have to be paid for through higher taxes, "but to tax too heavily in the early stages of intensive factory operations would be to discourage capital now at work, and, perhaps, disturb long-term production." Although he did not say as much, Martin apparently felt Roosevelt was about to embark on another phase of the New Deal, with the Reconstruction Finance Corporation and other federal agencies financing the defense program. If this were done, the private sector would seek support from Washington, not Wall Street, and this would deal the financial community yet another blow. It was the 1932–1934 struggle all over again. Speaking for private enterprise, Martin was saying that the investment bankers could provide adequate capital for the rapidly expanding war industries, in this way anticipating an attack from the federal agencies, which was already being mounted. Thus, the N.Y.S.E.'s leader asked for a maintenance of the present rate of taxation, hoping that if this were done, Roosevelt would not have sufficient funds to finance a federal program in the defense area.

Of course, this presented problems. Many Americans still talked of the "merchants of death," and were convinced businessmen—and Wall Street in particular—had lured the nation into World War I. Only a few years before there had been a movement to "take the profit sign out of war," and Martin seemed to want to put it back in. Anticipating this argument, Martin noted that without profits, business could not function, and without business, America could not arm. If the government tried to finance the defense effort on its own, the result would be destructive inflation or prohibitive taxation. The only sensible alternative was reliance upon the private sector, and in his role as spokesman for one of its major institutions, Martin was prepared to cooperate.

He would do so in the spirit of reform. Martin had no desire to wipe out the changes brought by the early New Deal. "Government regulation is here to stay," he said, although he hoped some of the provisions of the securities laws would be altered and others eliminated entirely. In the main, however, regulation helped the financial district clean its own house. But the task was done, and now the Washingtonians should withdraw, albeit in triumph, and leave the job of running the nation's financial establishment to the private sector. Regulation, he said, "should be salutary and not of a hindering nature."

> In addition to a policing business, government should do its best to build business. If it doesn't, you may see the picture of a national income perhaps rising from $70 billions to the goal of $100 billions but with an attendant lower standard of living for the individual.

In this way, Martin set forth a challenge to the government which, it would appear, was as much to the Reconstruction Finance Corporation as to the Securities and Exchange Commission. He felt he had won the battle against Frank and was now moving on to present a view of a different kind of America, one in which business was curbed in its excesses but given freedom and full rein at other times. Martin did not return to this theme in his future speeches on the West Coast, and indeed would not do so until after the war. Events of the next nine months made this difficult, if not impossible. But the challenge was made and was noted at meetings in Washington.

Martin was in Seattle the next day to speak on "The Stock Exchange in a Changing World." This was a short, informal history of the institution, with special emphasis on how the Exchange met the crisis of trading that followed the German attack on Poland. Stress was placed on the safeguards afforded investors at organized securities markets, and the lack of them elsewhere. Martin alluded to the difficulties in policing the over-the-counter markets. And it was with this that he indicated the major reason for his trip, and for his desire to speak to a national audience from the West Coast. The N.Y.S.E. was asking for a major revamping of the securities market system in America, and a change in securities law.

An increasing number of shares of N.Y.S.E.–listed stocks were being traded at the over-the-counter markets in 1940. There was no way of knowing how many, but some estimates ranged as high as 30 to 40 percent in active issues. It was already known that British investors were selling their shares off the exchanges, and that N.Y.S.E. firms were suffering a loss of business as a result. Pressures could be brought to bear against New York–based commission houses, obliging them to use N.Y.S.E. facilities, but little could be done about the Midwestern and West Coast houses, which had a long record of independence from, and even antagonism toward, Wall Street. By traveling to the Coast, Martin was indicating a desire to create a better spirit of cooperation with the regional exchanges. He was calling for no less than an alliance of stock exchanges against the over-the-counter market, to bring pressure upon the government to pass legislation that would put a halt to its trading in listed securities, and this in the name of increased investor protection.

Martin would take yet another step in the struggle. All companies whose stocks were listed on the Big Board or the regional exchanges had to complete questionnaires, and in addition fulfill S.E.C. requirements as to full disclosure. Unlisted companies were exempted under existing legislation. Martin, speaking from Seattle, called for "equalization."

> Under law, registration by corporations with securities in the hands of the public with the Securities and Exchange Commission is required only of such corporations as list their shares on a national securities exchange or those which made a public offering of securities since 1933. The great majority of corporations whose securities are dealt with in the unlisted market are, therefore, not required to make broad disclosures of their progress—of their earnings and assets. Corporations which do not elect to register, a process which entails the making public of prescribed facts about themselves and the filing of ample reports with the Securities and Exchange Commission, include many prominent companies.
>
> The Stock Exchange desires an equalization of these opposed situations. The registration of all publicly owned corporations would result in better service to investors, among who the exercise of judgment depends vitally upon adequate facts.

If these recommendations were acted upon, fewer companies might have been able to float securities, since many that did were small firms selling minor issues privately, or in other ways did not come up to minimum S.E.C. requirements. But virtually all stocks that did meet the requirements and so were floated would qualify for listing, and presumably would wind up on an organized market. In 1940, many over-the-counter stocks refused to submit information to the S.E.C., and so were effectively banned from the Exchange. If the law were changed, and the reports required, presumably listing would follow soon after. This would cripple, and perhaps even destroy, the over-the-counter market, not only as the repository for unlisted stocks but as a rival to the N.Y.S.E. for listed trading.*

* Thirty-two years later these ideas would surface in the famous *Martin Report.* Consistency was always the president's strongest suit.

The over-the-counter dealers responded to the speech, charging that, in effect, Martin was asking for the destruction of the small businessman in America. Many new firms, they said, obtained financing through the issuance of stock, and did so in a fashion that was within the law. If the law was changed, and these firms obliged to submit information, the costs might prove prohibitive, and in addition, the marketability of their shares would be effected. Martin was not interested in protecting investors, they claimed—with justification—but only in increasing the power and business of the N.Y.S.E. This was understandable, said the O-T-C houses, but should not be confused with reform.

Martin continued the attack in San Francisco, on December 4, where his topic was: "The Significance of the New York Stock Exchange." He stressed the high standards of the N.Y.S.E., as though to contrast them with those of the over-the-counter houses. "The subsequent listing of well-managed, eligible corporations, we are positive on the basis of long experience, would further marketability of their securities, promote wider ownership, and ensure a desirable price publicity when securities change hands," he said. "The thing that has caused the most trouble for American business is trying to hide things nobody cares anything about anyway. The more business can disclose without misleading people, the better off it will be."

Martin had hoped to form an alliance with leaders of the San Francisco Stock Exchange on the equalization issue. But that organization's leaders were not interested in discussing equalization, at least not until the question of multiple trading had been settled. Martin was asking the San Francisco brokers to join with him in a struggle against the over-the-counter houses at a time when N.Y.S.E. members were forbidden from dealing in Big Board stocks at the San Francisco Exchange. George N. Keyston, president of the San Francisco Stock Exchange, had been a leading force in the attempt to remove the ban, and in protest against it, did not attend the Martin speech. But other brokers did, and during the question period wanted to talk about the ban. "I won't say anything about it," was Martin's response, and he noted that the Exchange would make its position clear "within a few days." (This came on December 11, of course, when the N.Y.S.E. reiterated the ban, a move that further angered the San Francisco brokers, but by then Martin had left California.)

The N.Y.S.E. contingent then moved on to Los Angeles, the last stop on the tour. In an address entitled "The Real Significance of the Stock Exchange," Martin restated most of the points made earlier and also called for a diversification of business to the West Coast. In the end, he returned to the theme of equalization. "So long as the present unequal situation exists between registered and non-registered securities, the public will remain hampered in its need of many facts that are essential to reasoned investment."

Martin was back in New York on December 14, where he faced a mixed reception. Most of the major specialists—leaders of the Old Guard—cheered him on. Ironically, the men who had castigated the S.E.C., calling it an invasion of their privacy and rights, now saw the Commission as a powerful weapon to be used against those O-T-C market-makers who were taking their business from them. Martin's call for full disclosure and his attempts to draw additional issues to the Big Board struck a responsive chord with them. After seven years of conflict, the specialists had become supporters of the S.E.C., though many felt rather strange about their new position.

The commission brokers—men who had earlier called for a greater reform effort in the district so as to draw customers to the markets—felt otherwise. Many of them were deeply involved in over-the-counter dealings in unlisted issues and in bonds, and they made larger commissions than would have been possible under N.Y.S.E. rules. These were the men who had helped put Martin into his post and had applauded his reform efforts on the floor. But now he was treading dangerously on their preserve, and they would have none of it. Speaking through their organizations—the Investment Bankers Association and the National Association of Securities Dealers—the commission houses raised the cry of "double-cross." "We're going to kick Martin out," one of the leading commission brokers was supposed to have told *New York Times* columnist Burton Crane. The political waters, then, were quite muddied in late 1940. Both commission houses and specialists supported Martin in his contest against S.E.C. Chairman Frank, while the former group spoke of ousting the president because of his stand on the issue of equalization. Some of the regional exchanges, along with the Curb Exchange, were sympathetic to Martin's desires to draw business from the over-the-counter market, but the regionals would not cooperate on this issue until and unless Martin removed the ban against N.Y.S.E. members dealing in listed shares on other markets.

All contenders in the struggle invoked the public interest to buttress their positions, as though principle, not profit, would decide the matter. But in late 1940, survival and volume, not ethics and theory, dominated the securities markets.

The situation worsened in early 1941, indicating the failure of Martin's efforts and the debilitated condition of the market. On

December 27, 1940, the Board of Governors had announced it would not rescind the ban against members trading in listed issues on other exchanges or markets, although it would continue to remain inoperative so long as the S.E.C. opposed it. Frank responded by scheduling hearings on the matter, to begin in Washington on January 21. These continued for nine months, at the end of which the S.E.C. ordered the N.Y.S.E. to amend its constitution in such a way as to permit members to trade at other markets. The board accepted the decision; although it might have appealed, it declined to do so.

In this period the British sold hundreds of large blocks of stock in America, almost all of which were handled by New York brokers and investment houses, but few appeared on the N.Y.S.E. floor. These foreign sales represented a bonus for the brokers, while volume at the Exchange drifted lower. There was nothing Martin could do about this. On March 4, for example, the British sold 203,000 shares of United States Steel off the floor, and the transactions, worth some $11.5 million, were handled by sixty brokerages, all of which were N.Y.S.E. members. That same day, volume at the Big Board was 288,000 shares, and the most active stock—U.S. Steel—traded only 9,000 shares. Scarcely a day went by without another block reported, while N.Y.S.E. volume remained low. It was little wonder that Martin was frustrated. "We have Hitler to one side of us and the government to the other, and we are fighting to preserve our way of life," he said on March 5, in an uncharacteristic burst of anger. Unless the low volume could be corrected, the Exchange would wither, and if this occurred, free enterprise was doomed. The low volume, he said, was due to three factors: the war, taxation, and the S.E.C. The Commission responded promptly, calling the charge "ignorant," and this set off an exchange of abuse that continued for three weeks. Although relations between the Big Board and the S.E.C. had been poorer in the past, it had never reached the level of vituperation of early 1941.

Tax problems also became pressing. The city and state tried to increase taxes on transactions, but Martin was able to block the attempts, largely by threatening to move the N.Y.S.E. elsewhere. The federal government was another matter. The new excess profits tax went into effect on January 1, and this did not trouble the Exchange, which in any event had no profits at all. But Martin had been counting upon excellent first-quarter corporation reports to boost investor interest in securities, and now, due to taxes, these would not come. The Committee on Stock List suggested that corporations list excess profits taxes separately from the rest of their income taxes, as though to indicate that profits would have been higher without them. In the meantime, Martin continued to press for abolition of the tax, with the government permitting private enterprise a larger share in the defense effort. And this too failed.

The challenge here came from the Reconstruction Finance Corporation and its powerful leader, Jesse Jones. Unlike the S.E.C. leadership, the R.F.C. was directed by businessmen who had come over to the New Deal in 1932–1933. Jones himself was a Texas tycoon, who had been a lumberman in Dallas in the 1890s and then entered banking, real estate, newspapers, and oil. He was a liberal Democrat of the old school, which meant he had opposed William Jennings Bryan in 1896, had supported Woodrow Wilson in 1912, and had contributed mightily to the party ever since. At one point he had Presidential ambitions of his own, but by 1932 these had faded, and when President Hoover asked him to join the board of the Reconstruction Finance Corporation, Jones accepted. Thus, he arrived in Washington before the New Dealers, and as a prominent Democrat, he was made its chairman.

Under Jones, the R.F.C. grew and soon became a major New Deal agency, outgrowing the more modest ambitions held for it during the Hoover years. Jones proved skillful at political infighting, defending his realm against the young, brash New Dealers, while at the same time expanding his power into their areas whenever possible.

The war presented Jones with an excellent opportunity to do so. In early 1940, the R.F.C. requested the right to make loans to defense companies to enable them to expand their facilities. Congress responded in June by extending the life of the agency and increasing its lending capacity by $1.5 billion. Roosevelt funneled much of the new defense spending through the R.F.C., so that by late 1940 Jones was being talked of as "the Bernard Baruch of World War II." By February 1941, almost 800 defense plants budgeted for more than $2 billion were under construction, financed by the Reconstruction Finance Corporation—and not by equity and bonds floated by the New York financial complex.

Martin and other N.Y.S.E. leaders had been able to mount offensives against the S.E.C. and deal adeptly if not always successfully with its leaders. Jones and the R.F.C. were another matter. In the first place, Jones understood business through practical experience, even though Houston practices differed from those of New York. Then, too, Jones presented Martin with a *fait accompli*, and one outside of his special area of power as a leader. It was well and good for the Big Board's president to battle with Frank over market policy, but to enter the lists against Jones on the matter of corporation financing was something else altogether. In early 1941, Martin was a spokesman for a major segment of the financial community, but he could hardly claim the same position in regard to the larger business complex of the nation.

Jones's abilities to deal with big corporations had been honed by a half century of experience in private enterprise and seven years at the R.F.C. Faced with the choice of floating new bonds or stocks in an uncertain market, or getting a lump sum from the government in the form of a long-term, low-interest loan, business seemed to prefer the latter. Conservative columnists would complain—but to no avail—that these businessmen—who included not only defense-plant executives but those in steel, aluminum, railroads, oil, and chemicals as well—were selling their souls for a mess of pottage, and that the growth of R.F.C. power signaled the coming of a dangerous federal power.

Martin did not criticize the R.F.C. or Jones directly; he knew he hadn't support for such an attack. Furthermore, it was becoming evident in early 1941 that the New York financial community was in no shape to handle the massive financings that would be needed by American industry in the months to come. Already there were signs that not all the foreign sales could be handled expeditiously. A British offering of a block of Consolidated Edison, for example, could not be disposed of for almost a week due to the unwillingness of investment banks to take it on. There were reports that some brokerages and investment banks were withdrawing from the markets, since they lacked sufficient capital to deal with the large blocks, or were fully committed and would not venture further. A handful of brokerages, including Merrill Lynch, E. A. Pierce & Cassatt and Ladenburg Thalmann, began to concentrate on marketing British-owned securities, but in order to do so, they had to refrain from accepting business in other areas of the market.

Given this situation, could the New York investment community finance the defense effort? The answer seemed to be that it couldn't, having been weakened in the early 1930s and never having fully recovered. The decline in business in the mid-1930s had led most investment houses to cut back on operations. Now that new business was coming their way, they could not take advantage of it.

The specialists at the N.Y.S.E. were in a similar situation. The decline on the floor had hit them hard, and they too cut back, not only financially but psychologically as well. The U.S. Steel specialist was used to thinking of a 9,000-share day as being heavy, and of feeling his heart skip when a 300-share order came his way. How could such individuals handle big blocks? Could they commit funds—assuming they had them—to support markets where thousands of shares would have to be digested? The answers to such questions were known to Martin, the community, and to Jones as well. In late February, Jones suggested that the R.F.C. lend money to public utilities, some of which were having difficulties in marketing new equity and debt issues. This offer, if accepted, would have marked a major federal challenge to Wall Street, and more importantly, a sign that Washington's control over the economy was expanding at a rapid rate. This was a more radical suggestion than anything Douglas had proposed at the flood tide of the New Deal. Yet it drew no protest from the N.Y.S.E., although some journalists called it a native form of fascism designed to help businessmen friends of the Democrats. By then, however, the New York investment community could offer no viable alternative, and Jones knew it.

The Exchange's 1940 financial statement reinforced this gloomy sentiment. Released in mid-February, it showed that volume was at its lowest level in nineteen years. A drastic cost-cutting program had shaved $461,000 from expenses, and the sale of a property at 39 Broad Street added $400,000 to the Exchange's account. At the end of 1937, the N.Y.S.E. had 2,336 employees; in late 1940, the number was 1,665 and further cuts were impossible if operations were to continue. Also, by then the Exchange had sold all its non-securities–related businesses and properties. Still, it reported a deficit of $246,000 for the year. Martin announced that a building at 41 Broad Street, which housed brokers' offices, would soon be sold, not only to obtain funds but because it was no longer needed. Brokers as well as the Exchange had cut back to that point. "Business is at low ebb on the Stock Exchange for reasons which are thoroughly well-known—war and fear of its expansion, the inevitability of increased taxation and the present capital gains tax, political uncertainties in many countries, and domestic regulation which discourages risk capital," he said. "When events justify changes for the better, the New York Stock Exchange which, alone among the world exchanges is still functioning freely, should speedily benefit."

When would that time arrive? Brokers and specialists had been assured that when economic recovery was certain, business would improve. Then they were taught that the war would bring profits, just as World War I had benefited Wall Street. Neither of these predictions had come true. Now they were told that better times were coming "when events justify changes for the better." What did this mean? In February 1942, a N.Y.S.E. seat sold at $20,000, the lowest price since 1898, and it dipped to $19,000 by May, at which time there were only eight bids for seats, at prices ranging from $14,000 to $18,000. The low price for a sale that year was $17,000. In 1940, trading volume had been 207 million shares, the worst showing since

1921, when fewer issues had been listed. The turnover rate for 1940 was 12 percent, the lowest in the century. In early 1941, it seemed that record would be broken.

Specialists would stroll from post to post during the trading day, gossiping and sharing rumors. There were sessions when many specialists had no trades at all. They would read newspapers and wonder about stories devoted to the economic boom. The want ads indicated that unskilled laborers at defense plants could earn as much as N.Y.S.E. specialists.

The customers' men were in equally bad shape. They would search out "prospects" as though they were selling insurance. It was not unusual for a customers' man to make dozens of blind telephone calls each day, hoping that one of them would result in a hot lead. Then he would make an appointment to see the man at his office or home, cultivate him for a few days, all in the hope of handling an odd lot of American Telephone, worth a few dollars in commissions. It was no time to enter Wall Street. The Stock Exchange Institute, a school run by the Exchange, discontinued operations in May. The reason was not given, but it was known that the Institute had too few students to make its work worthwhile and that economy moves were necessary.

Martin had blamed the war, taxes, and the S.E.C. for the decline in business, and most Wall Streeters could agree that all had hurt them. To this list, some would add another factor: William Martin himself. The president had taken office in a bad time, and had been hailed as a miracle worker, a young genius who would defend the financial district against the New Deal and, most importantly, provide the N.Y.S.E. with a shining symbol of integrity that would attract investors. He had done and been all of that, but it was not enough.

Martin had performed better than his resources at the Exchange might have indicated he would. He had put the new constitution into operation, organized an effective and efficient staff, and had proved adept at winning the confidence of both the reformers and Old Guard in New York and the S.E.C. in Washington. In 1938 it appeared federal control of the exchanges was possible; this kind of talk was no longer heard in early 1941. Instead, the Exchange had become master in its own house, while the S.E.C. was in decline. Martin had failed in his attempt to end multiple trading, and did not succeed in uniting the nation's exchanges against the over-the-counter markets, but he did open the issue and, given the situation at the time, did as well as might have been expected. The same was true for the excess profits tax and the increased role of the R.F.C.

Martin took the presidency when the Exchange was in political difficulties and trading volume was low. He had helped resolve several thorny political problems by early 1941, but volume was still poor;

indeed, the average daily trading had declined more than 25 percent since Gay had left office. In the most vital area of Exchange business—the only important one insofar as profits were concerned, but also the one Martin had least control over—the president had failed. Had he proved a blunderer, while at the same time, due to events over which he had no control, business improved, Martin would have been hailed as a savior. Instead, the opposite had occurred, so that by February 1941 Martin's reputation was on the decline. He could no longer influence events, and his constituency was melting.

Martin was never one to overstay a welcome. On February 27, he announced that he had been reclassified 1-A by his local selective service board and would soon be drafted. The Exchange set about seeking a new leader, spokesman, and symbol. Martin had served well the requirements of 1938–1939. The N.Y.S.E. needed his counterpart for the war years.

CHAPTER 6

The Schram Era Begins

Richard Whitney thought of newspapermen as either prostitutes or crude hacks, not worth conversing with seriously. When he wanted or needed press coverage for a N.Y.S.E. event, or hoped for columns favorable to his point of view, he would try to get the message across through underlings. On occasion he would speak directly to newsmen, but these were rare indeed, for although Whitney affected an air of easy informality, it was usually more akin to a noble asking one of his serfs the way through the woods than a discussion among equals. The financial reporters recognized this and resented the attitude. As for Whitney, he couldn't care less. Even during his worst period, after the disclosure of wrongdoing, he refused to go out of his way to curry favor with reporters and columnists. The journalists may have disliked and even hated the man, but many admired his sang-froid.

Charles Gay was an altogether different kind of person, one who almost feared the press, treated reporters with deference, and stood in awe of certain columnists. He would answer their questions politely, go out of his way to get them information, and tried, usually unsuccessfully, to become "one of the boys." It didn't work, and although some reporters were amused by the efforts and joked about them, most considered Gay a decent enough person, certainly a relief after the Whitney era. In general, they respected Gay's sincerity and basic integrity, even while they believed him an intellectual lightweight. This attitude did not change until Gay's last days in office, and by then it made little difference what reporters thought of him.

In many ways, the transition from Gay to Martin was as great or even greater than that from Whitney to Gay, or at least so the newspapermen seemed to believe. Martin knew more about Exchange operations, and was more thoughtful in his analysis of events and men, than Whitney, and was as much a symbol of integrity as Gay. He enjoyed the world of ideas, appeared at ease with reporters and columnists, and often would seek them out at gatherings in preference to the company of Wall Streeters. In part, this was the result of a conscious effort at wooing reporters. In addition, Martin was a reformer and activist, and the Wall Street news corps, by and large, was agreeable to that point of view. Because of these factors, Martin always enjoyed a "good press." Such influential columnists as Leslie Gould of the *Journal American*, Burton Crane of the *Times*, Charles Donnelly of the *World Telegram*, Ed Collins of the *Herald Tribune*, George McDonald of the *Sun*, and Sylvia Porter of the *Post*—all of whom had favored the S.E.C. in its conflicts with the Exchange during the Whitney and Gay administrations—backed Martin in his struggles with Frank. And later on, when Martin worked for a freer hand on Wall Street, which seemed to some a call for an end to the S.E.C.'s regulatory functions, the columnists were sympathetic. As far as they could see, Martin was the enemy of the Old Guard, of reaction, and for that reason alone they would support him. At the same time, the president was accepted by all factions in the district insofar as his reforms were concerned. Their only quarrel with Martin was over his failure to increase their business. In part, politics consists of the art of appearing to be different things to different people. Martin was a good politician, Gay a mediocre one, and Whitney simply didn't care.

On March 4, 1940, Leslie Gould wrote an impassioned, friendly letter to Martin, who only a week before had announced his forthcoming departure for the Army. "Maybe I am seeing things under the bed," he said, "but I think I see signs of a move to restore to the seats of power of some of the old faction that mismanaged the Exchange under Richard Whitney. To my mind, it would be fatal for the Exchange to go back to that kind of leadership. If that were to happen, the government might well step in and take over. That would be a tragedy for all concerned." Martin would soon leave, but before he did, he could indicate the direction the Exchange should follow in the future and help select a suitable successor.

Martin replied the following day. "On the whole I think there is considerable merit in what you say, and although you will not agree with some of the points I make, I am confident we are both working for the best interests of Wall Street." *

Gould's suggestion showed naïveté unusual in a man of his experience and knowledge. Martin was in no position to dictate to the board which, after seven years of the New Deal, was still dominated by the Old Guard. Nor could he oblige the members to select his candidate for the succession; the Old Guard would do that. Charles B. Harding, chairman of the board, announced he would not stand for re-election, since he expected to be called into the service. His place

* *Leslie Gould Papers.*

too would be filled by the powers on the board. The great reform era was coming to a close, on Wall Street as in Washington, and the outgoing president knew it.

Yet Martin would make one last effort to preserve the spirit of moderate reform. If some of the powers held by the members and the board were relinquished to the professional administrators, he said, the N.Y.S.E. might be able to deal more effectively with Washington. Everyone at the Exchange understood that if this were done, the Old Guard would lose power to the new Martin bureaucrats.

On March 5, the president offered his program. He suggested that the board be reduced from thirty-two members to sixteen and that the seven standing committees be combined to form three. In the process, the executive committee would cease to exist and many of its functions would be assumed by the president's office. The new board was to work more closely with the administration than previously had been the case, and in the future all members of the board as well as the administration were to receive salaries. Considering the poor livings many were making on the floor and in the offices, board membership might easily become a full-time occupation, and the positions, which so often went to wealthy older brokers, might be prized by younger, more aggressive and reform-minded men.

The board approved the selection of a special committee to prepare amendments to the constitution. Robert Stott was selected as a member, as were John A. Coleman, Paul Shields, and others sympathetic to Martin's approach at the time, and who were also acceptable to those on the floor. The special committee was named on March 12, went to work soon after, and on July 23, delivered its report, one that indicated Martin had been defeated and a power shift from the administration to the board was taking place. The committees would not be restructured and the board members would not receive stipends. Rule-making authority would be transferred from the committees to the board, an alteration Martin hadn't requested. According to the ballots sent to members in late July, the constitutional amendments needed to put the changes into effect would make the Exchange more representative, centralize administrative authority in the presidency, and establish the board "as the Exchange's sole policy-making body." The new board, reduced in size to twenty-five, would dominate the N.Y.S.E., given a strong chairman and a pliant president.

Martin had hoped to bequeath to his successor a strengthened administration, one that could act more independently from the membership than previously had been the case. During his first months in office, he had great de facto powers. The membership had acceded to Martin's wishes in the hope that by so doing they could "save" the institution from Douglas and the S.E.C. radicals. In effect, they would sacrifice the front office to preserve the floor. Martin had succeeded, but as the New Deal's interest in reform waned, the membership began demanding a return of its powers. Increasingly, Martin faced opposition, first from one faction, then another. The uprising of commission brokers in late 1940 was one such revolt. Unless the president was free to ignore special interests, Martin believed, he could not develop a program for the common good. Restructuring was one method for reform, and now this had failed. Martin would leave for the Army on April 16, three months prior to submission of the special committee report and the revision of the constitution. Asked his comment on the revisions, Private Martin declined to speak.

When interviewed in early March about the best man to succeed him, Martin had said he should not be a politician. Such an individual, he added, would "not be able to resolve the Exchange's problems." Martin worked for the nomination of a Wall Streeter who understood the district. There is no indication, however, that he had ever singled out a candidate, or that if he had, his opinion would have carried much weight.

A nominating committee was selected, and despite efforts to "crack" it, confidentiality was maintained. But from the first it seemed evident that the N.Y.S.E. would look to Washington, not Wall Street, for its new president.

Had Martin resigned a year before he did, the Exchange might well have canvassed the S.E.C. for his successor. By early 1940, however, that agency was in decline, while the Reconstruction Finance Corporation had become a major force in the district, in large part the result of its willingness to undertake corporation financings. Jesse Jones remained the key figure at the R.F.C., a man who had weathered the New Deal storms to emerge as a powerful leader in the early days of World War II, when F.D.R. sought men with business experience to replace the intellectuals and lawyers of the reform period. Jones was named head of the newly created Federal Loan Agency in 1939 and also retained his seat at the R.F.C. He had positions at the Export-Import Bank, the Home Owners Loan Corporation, and the Federal Housing Administration. There was talk in Washington of a Jones Presidential bid if Roosevelt decided to step down in 1940. Of course, he was one of many mentioned in the press, and Jones always insisted he was not interested in the White House. But the impression remained that he had great power and was a man to be placated by all institutions having dealings with Washington.

Jones had several protégés, most of whom were moderate-to-conservative in ideology. They had made the R.F.C. and other Jones-influenced agencies strongholds of the "Old Democracy" and so were suspected of lacking proper reformist zeal in 1933–1939. John Snyder, the future Secretary of the Treasury in the Truman Cabinet was one of them, and Clifford Durr, who later became head of the Federal Communications Commission, was another. Sam Husbands, Frank Ronan, and John F. Coleman—these were not people known to the public, but in their own spheres they exercised a great deal of control over financial decisions in Washington. Tommy Corcoran, who at the time was close to Roosevelt and considered a reformer, was the liaison between the White House and the Jones forces, and, in particular, worked closely with Emil Schram, who early in the game was singled out for the Stock Exchange presidency.

Schram was forty-seven years old in 1940, had been in government service throughout the New Deal, and was one of its more important bureaucrats. Schram received regular promotions from his grateful chief, and yet he was an anonymous man, who labored in Jones's shadow and was content to remain there. He was a powerfully built man of medium height with a receding hairline and an open if bland face, one that rarely showed emotion. Schram had no gift with words, either in the written or spoken form, and was uncomfortable when called upon to chat with strangers. He was known as a meticulous person, one who didn't take chances, a man of modest ambition who, perhaps, had already risen higher in his career than he had ever anticipated. If Charles Gay had gone to Washington, he might have been Emil Schram. In short, he was a decent, honest, apparently mediocre and unimaginative individual who could be depended upon to perform as promised, but no more than that.

Schram was a native of Peru, Indiana, a small town from which he had never expected to venture. He went to the local schools and, upon graduation from high school, went to work as a bookkeeper for a nearby coal and lumber dealer. A few years later he obtained the job of draining some swampland in Illinois, and from this work became chairman of the National Drainage Association. While serving in this essentially honorary position, Schram managed grain elevators in Hillview, Illinois, and served as director of the Hartwell Drainage and Levee District, where he was when the depression struck.

Schram was not a political man, but when Jesse Jones called him to Washington in 1933 to take charge of the R.F.C.'s drainage, levee, and irrigation division, he came. While Jones was busy politicking, Schram and others at the R.F.C. took care of the agency's work, and shortly after he arrived, Schram was ensconced as Jones's righthand man. The ebullient Texan and the plodding Indianan worked well together, and in 1936 Schram was named to the board of the R.F.C. While there he took charge of the Electric Home and Farm Authority, which made loans to several hundred thousand tenants and farm owners, averaging around $150 each. It was complicated and difficult work, which demanded long hours from a prudent person, and the former bookkeeper from Peru, Indiana, was the right man for the post. In addition, Schram understood the political ramifications of the job. The E.H.F.A. was funded by the Treasury at $850,000, was under the nominal control of the Tennessee Valley Authority, and was to report to the R.F.C. Schram had to serve three masters—the conservatives at the R.F.C., the reformers at the T.V.A., and the middle-of-the-roaders at the Treasury. In the end, he pleased all groups, an indication that he had learned more than a little about politics.

In effect, Schram was the keeper of a financial pump. The E.H.F.A. would borrow money from Wall Street bankers—often as much as $15 million at a time—and then use it to make loans to clients. Schram was accepted by the New Yorkers, who were then in the process of learning that conservative small businessmen from the Midwest were their natural allies against the more radical New Dealers. While traveling from Wall Street to Washington, Schram told a reporter that he hadn't done badly for the grandson of a German immigrant, only two decades away from the offices of Cole's lumber and coal yard. It was one of the very few times he allowed himself such a boast. For the most part, Schram remained self-effacing. Only when the E.H.F.A. was liquidated and not only returned its original capital to the Treasury but showed a profit did Schram hold a press conference.

When Jones became administrator of the Federal Loan Agency he insisted that Roosevelt permit him to choose his successor. This was granted, and Jones selected Schram, who moved to the chairmanship of the R.F.C. Within a few weeks, he was also named to the Export-Import Bank, the Federal National Mortgage Association, the Federal Prison Industries, Inc., the Rubber Reserve Company, and a half dozen other federal agencies. For the first time, Schram became a fairly well known person in Washington, although clearly not yet of the first rank. He was not recognized at fine restaurants, in part because of his blandness but more obviously because the Schrams ate at home. Emil Schram was not a wealthy man, and in February 1940, while head of the R.F.C., his salary was $10,000 a year—more than comfortable by the standards of the day but hardly grandiose.

At the time, William Martin's salary at the N.Y.S.E. was $48,000 a year.

Schram was concerned about his future. He held an important position, but it was a political one. If F.D.R. left the White House, either by refusing to run for a third term or being defeated at the polls in November, Schram might be out on the street looking for employment. What could he do then? He was an able man, to be sure, but without an education, the kind of background that suited him for corporation board rooms, or money. With the exception of Corcoran, he had no close friends at the White House, and so no one there could be counted upon to find him an outside job. And even Corcoran, who by then had decided to leave government service, was finding it difficult to get a position. There was Jesse Jones, of course, and Schram told Jones that he was interested in a nongovernment position, preferably one that paid a suitable salary. If Schram had had a law degree, Jones might have been able to place him on the federal bench, but clearly that was out of the question. For a while it seemed Schram might be named to head the Federal Reserve Bank of Chicago, but Marriner Eccles, then chairman of the Federal Reserve Board, hadn't forgotten that at one time F.D.R. had tried to ease him out and name Jones as his successor. Eccles would not accept a Jones protégé for the Chicago position, and so the search continued. Jones let it be known that anyone who found Schram a suitable position would have a call upon his gratitude.

Paul Shields understood the situation. Ever since 1934 he had shuttled between Washington and Wall Street and was known as one of the district's leading reformers, accepted but not completely trusted by either community. Without contacting Jones, Shields spoke to the N.Y.S.E. nominating group about Schram. Here was a man of executive ability who, however, knew next to nothing about the Exchange. Some Wall Streeters had met Schram, and had found him to be likable enough. But could they in conscience name a man who was ignorant of the methods and men of the Exchange? The committee was not even certain Schram had ever been inside the building, and he had no background in the securities business. Indeed, his sole recommendation seemed to be that Jesse Jones would be pleased by the selection.

That sufficed. The Exchange announced Schram's nomination and acceptance on May 6. The appointment was ratified two weeks later. Schram took office on July 1.

At no point had Jones been consulted regarding the nomination; the Exchange had contacted Schram directly. But Shields and his colleagues knew Jones would be delighted. "The governors of the New York Stock Exchange are to be congratulated upon securing the services of Emil Schram as president of that important institution," he told reporters. "Mr. Schram has had a wide experience in dealing with business and finance in his eight years with the Reconstruction Finance Administration. Every imaginable problem has come before him for consideration. He is unusually capable and well qualified for this position of great trust. All of us in government will miss Emil."

In this way, the N.Y.S.E. took as a leader the protégé of the man whose policies at the R.F.C. threatened it. Jones was no longer at the commission in 1940, but its board was dominated by his friends, as well as those of Schram. No promises were asked for or given in 1940, but clearly the Exchange accepted Schram in the hope that he would be able to bring an end to government attempts to finance companies directly, and in general smooth matters for Wall Street in Washington.

Schram's selection completed a revolution in N.Y.S.E. leadership that had begun only five years before. Anthony Stockholm had been the Exchange's first president, being selected for that post in 1817. From that time to 1935, every president had been a member of the Exchange and, more important perhaps, a representative of its leading specialists and most prestigious investment banks. It had been a job for men who were the reflection of Wall Street power. Charles Gay represented an important break from tradition. He was a parvenu, who had not attended the same schools as the aristocrats; nor did he belong to their clubs. His son did not mingle with their sons, and would not marry one of their daughters. Gay knew his place, however, and the Old Guard noted that he was a N.Y.S.E. member, after all, even though the first nonaristocrat to occupy the presidency. As for William Martin, he was the first non–New Yorker to become president of the Exchange, as well as the first to be paid for his work. Martin had varied interests, some of them quite exotic as far as Wall Streeters of the late 1930s were concerned. Still, he had been a member and was considered an expert in the field of exchange finance and development.

Now Emil Schram was to be president. He was not an aristocrat nor a New Yorker. Schram had never been a member of the Exchange and knew nothing of its functioning. All of this would be learned in time, and Schram was a quick study, a person of some intelligence and ability. One might easily have named a dozen other men far more suited for the job than Schram—and, indeed, Martin had done so. But in the end, Schram had no rival. He was selected to please Washington, not the Exchange members. If Martin had come from the N.Y.S.E. as an ambassador to Washington, Schram was accepted on Wall Street as its hostage against adversity. Richard Whitney had been the last aristocrat to serve as president, Gay the last New York broker in the post, and Martin the last Wall Street professional. From the time of Emil Schram to the present, the position has been filled by men who have never served on the floor.

* * *

Schram proved an able if unimaginative politician—he had, after all, survived the New Deal, and in 1940 that spoke volumes. He readily admitted his ignorance of Exchange procedures, but somehow made it appear that such admissions were a Will Rogerish sort of poking fun at the "city folk." Schram made much of his Indiana background, of his need for advice and guidance from Wall Streeters, and his expectation of putting in long hours on the job. To one reporter he joked that although he knew the Stock Exchange was at Wall and Broad, he wasn't certain of the location of the main entrance to the building, never having been inside. This kind of façade served him well; the financial press portrayed the president-elect as a shrewd, intelligent, and able administrator, who was much more sophisticated than was believed.

On June 25, the Exchange hosted a dinner in Schram's honor at the Hotel Commodore, to which 1,650 members and guests were invited. The presidents of most of the regional stock exchanges attended, as did leaders of the S.E.C. Schram sat at the center of the dias, flanked by Donald Hardenbrook, a N.Y.S.E. member who served as toastmaster, and William Martin, on leave from basic training. Robert Stott, the new Stock Exchange chairman, was on Hardenbrook's left, while Jesse Jones was on Martin's right, a symbol of Washington's power. As Jones beamed at Schram, and the two men exchanged pleasantries, the guests knew that without the Commerce Secretary, Schram would not have been there.

Schram delivered an intelligent, carefully written speech to the audience, one that contained concepts few could argue with, along with hints of programs and developments to come that would work well for the financial community. He spoke of continued cooperation with the S.E.C. "I earnestly believe that the S.E.C.'s regulations, together with your own, have afforded that strong measure of protection which is essential to the public interest." Schram praised the Exchange. "I do not expect that my administrative task will be easy. But neither do I expect that it will be too difficult, because I recognize that both of the essentials to a successful administrative program are conspicuously present in your organization: I refer to the integrity of the Exchange and to that deep desire, which I know pervades your entire membership, to operate it in a manner to serve best the public interest." He alluded to his work at the R.F.C., comparing the N.Y.S.E. to the government agency. Both performed worthy public services, and he was fortunate to be moving from such a central government commission to one at the heart of the free-enterprise sector; he called the N.Y.S.E. "the public square in the business community of America." Schram told two humorous stories, said some complimentary things about Martin, exhorted the members to new efforts ("I expect to bend the oars, but if you should cease to row, our craft will only move in a circle"), and closed with a modest aside—"I am no Aladdin with a magic lamp, no Moses promising to lead you out of the wilderness."

The speech was greeted with a standing ovation, and there were good notices for Schram in the financial press the following day—even though some critics noted that the new president hadn't offered any substantive proposals. It was, after all, a maiden speech, and the dinner was not the proper occasion for such matters to be presented. The Schram program would come later on, and when it did, relations with Washington would improve, investors would have a new confidence in securities, and volume and profits would increase. These were Schram's major objectives—at least they were the reasons for his having been selected for his new job.

There was little cause for celebration on the floor the next day. Prices declined, and volume stood at 635,000 shares, in what the *Wall Street Journal* called "a typical session." What could Schram do to turn this kind of market around? Indeed, could any administrator have an effect on quotations and volume? Many N.Y.S.E. members seemed to think one could—that Schram would prove to be an Aladdin or Moses. This was the residue of faith, however, and not of experience.

Robert Stott, who had succeeded Harding as chairman of the board, understood the hopes of the membership, but had little confidence in Schram's abilities at attracting new business. Along with the rest, he had supported the nomination of the R.F.C. head, but more to placate Washington and for the sake of appearances than to draw investors and speculators to the Street. Other methods would have to be found to increase trading volume and underwritings. Such a task would require the efforts of a professional, and by no stretch of the imagination could Schram be considered one.

As a member of the special committee charged with selecting Martin's successor, Stott had recommended Schram for the position. Only forty-one years old in 1941, Stott was considered one of the district's most promising young men and a rising leader of the Establishment. This in itself was rather unusual, for Stott was no patrician. Instead he was a man of middle-class origins who had attended public schools in Brooklyn, did not go to college afterward, and began his Wall Street career as a clerk at the age of eighteen. Then he worked his way up the ladder, a model of the Horatio Alger hero Wall Streeters of the time so admired. He purchased his Exchange seat in 1929, just after the crash, and six years later was named to the board. In 1941, Stott was head of the specialist house of

Wagner, Stott & Co., and defended the interests of his group against the reformers both on Wall Street and in Washington. By no means was he deemed a spokesman for the specialists' cause, however, but instead an able, intelligent individual who could get along with all groups and had a clear command of the facts. In this period, Stott seemed to combine Gay's practicality and Martin's knowledge with the support of Whitney's constituency. He was able to attain position and power because that constituency, like almost everything else in the financial district, had undergone changes since the mid-1930s.

The Old Guard of the early 1930s consisted of gentlemen who graduated Ivy League colleges and then entered the brokerages and investment banks controlled by relatives and friends. They were clubmen, and many were only part-time businessmen, not particularly famous for their acumen. In 1930, they dominated the N.Y.S.E. administration, serving on committees after hours for the prestige involved. Meetings often were poorly attended, especially when some major social function was at hand. That year, fully 72 percent of the N.Y.S.E. governors were listed in the social register. Richard Whitney was not only first among equals at the time; he was a typical governor and member of the Old Guard.

In 1941, only 33 percent of the governors could point to listing in the social register, which in any case no longer carried the cachet it did in the pre–New Deal years, and Robert Stott, not a carbon copy of Richard Whitney, stood for Old Guard interests. Indeed, it would be wrong to consider that group as having any power at all in the higher reaches of the Exchange's government. Of all the governors serving at the time of the 1929 crash, only Raymond Sprague survived. Howland Davis, who had left Whitney at the last moment, was a paid executive vice-president in 1941. Of the other influential Old Guardsmen of the pre–New Deal period, none remained in office. They could be found on the floor, however, and in the executive offices of investment banks, but even there they did not hold sway. One could afford an amiable dabbler in good times, but when business was poor, expert and professional leadership was needed. So the Old Guard accepted new blood—and Robert Stott came to the fore, while Emil Schram would be an agreeable front man for the group.

In introducing Schram at the dinner, Stott spoke highly of the new leader, but there were hints of a change in attitude in his remarks. "We have made Mr. Schram our spokesman—before the public, with the press and in Washington," he said. Schram was to be a spokesman then—nothing more. The board—dominated by new Old Guardsmen like Stott—would take care of internal matters. It, and not the administration, represented and defended the interests of the members.

"It is entirely proper for you to give the management of the Exchange the benefit of your views and suggestions at any time, or to criticize and find fault if you wish," Stott told the members. "All we expect is that these suggestions and criticisms shall be expressed through the proper channels." These channels, needless to say, led to the chairman's office.

The Stott introduction was as clear and blunt as could be. Now the specialists would take direct command of the Exchange and organize it to suit their interests before all others. These men liked Schram, but had little confidence in his abilities to operate effectively within the building. Indeed, in this respect he was exactly the kind of person they wanted. Schram recognized his limitations, and understood why he had been chosen for the position. He would do what he could with his old comrades in Washington, utilizing his knowledge of the Rooseveltian labyrinth to the Exchange's benefit. If he was also able to increase public confidence in the markets and so attract new business, it would be a bonus. Schram would have little to do with internal affairs, and when he spoke out on such matters, it would be as the voice of the board, and only after long consultations with leaders of the new Old Guard.

Stott was one of them, and it would be his task to lead in the restoration of members' powers and privileges. His vehicle would be the chairmanship, a relatively minor office during the Martin era, and his arena would be the floor. Any attempt on the part of the professional administration to act independently of the floor would be met with anger and rebukes—and dismissals. This is not to say that Schram and Stott anticipated problems with one another, or that a clash was inevitable. Rather, by 1941 the pendulum of reform and centralization of power in the hands of advocates of change had begun swinging the other way, on Wall Street as in the rest of the nation. The much-vaunted New Deal revolution had come to an end, and Schram, no less than Stott, was a sign of this.

There would be no return to the old regime as it had existed during the early 1930s. The reforms forced upon the district by the New Dealers had been digested, and in such a way as not to disturb the established power groups unduly. Their influence had been circumscribed somewhat, but for the most part they were intact. The more radical suggestions of the early New Deal, which included a drive to "break up Wall Street," either were never considered or had been transformed into little more than placebos. The S.E.C. was enfeebled; the R.F.C. would be dissuaded from significant action by Schram; Franklin Roosevelt was raiding Wall Street for talents to mobilize the war effort in 1941, just as eight years earlier he had gone to the Ivy

League for help in creating the New Deal. The next important series of changes for the district would come from the leaders at the N.Y.S.E. and other institutions in lower Manhattan.

The New York Curb Exchange was one of these latter organizations. Even more than the Big Board, the Curb suffered from declining business. Trading volume had peaked at 476 million shares in 1929, was halved in 1930, halved again in 1931, and once more in 1932, when volume reached 57 million shares. There was a recovery to 135 million in 1936, and then a new decline. In 1940, trading volume had been 43 million shares, and from all indications, 1941 would be even worse. In the spring of 1941, when N.Y.S.E. members ate in public restaurants, no longer able to afford the private clubs, Curb brokers were going without lunch, or carrying sandwiches in paper bags.

The Curb's internal structure was separate from the N.Y.S.E.'s but in such a way as to make it a satellite of the larger institution. Both exchanges had their own stock lists and specialists to handle them—with the Curb's stocks and specialists deemed inferior to those at the N.Y.S.E. But they differed insofar as the commission houses were concerned. The major brokerages considered themselves part of the N.Y.S.E., even though they traded in listed shares at other markets, such as the regionals and the over-the-counter. This, after all, was what Martin's crusade against multiple trading had been about—it was an attempt to bind the commission houses still closer to the N.Y.S.E. at the expense of the regional exchanges and the over-the-counter markets. The Curb stood between the brokerages and the Big Board on this matter and could not afford to take a stand. On the one hand, some 80 percent of all Curb transactions originated at the Big Board brokerages, while on the other, the Curb had always existed at the sufferance of the senior market. In 1941, prudent Curb officials and members made few important moves without first consulting leaders in both camps.

Two years before, the Curb wrote and ratified a new constitution, one that created a professional administration. George Rea, a former bank president from Hawaii who earlier had been founder and president of the Buffalo Stock Exchange, became the first paid president of the Curb. Fred C. Moffatt, one of the Curb's elder statesmen, took the chairmanship, and together they worked to increase volume.

Rea was intrigued with an idea put forth by Amyas Ames in late 1940. Ames, an executive at the commission house of Kidder, Peabody, was also a member of the N.Y.S.E. Board of Governors. He was a leader against Martin in the struggle over multiple trading and had always been aloof from the Old Guard, considering himself more a representative of the non–New Yorkers, the Boston aristocracy in particular. He had received graduate training at the Harvard School of Business Administration, and in 1941 was deemed one of the district's most original thinkers.

Ames believed that the N.Y.S.E. specialists were doing an inferior job and that better executions of orders could be had in the over-the-counter market. In serving his clients, Ames often took his business there rather than to the N.Y.S.E. floor, a fact that angered the Big Board specialists and made him a renegade in their eyes. Ames gave little evidence of concern with this, but he did develop an idea to combine the N.Y.S.E. with the over-the-counter market. As he saw it, the floor provided a perfect meeting place for buyers and sellers, far more convenient than the O-T-C telephone network. The markets on the floor, however, were poor. Thus, he asked, why not permit the O-T-C traders access to the floor? The Stock Exchange could charge them a fee for entry, and perhaps one on each transaction. This would combine the benefits of the Big Board with those of the over-the-counter markets and in the process increase business for specialists.

Ames's suggestions—and they were no more than that—were misread by the Curb's leaders, who believed that he had spoken with the support of the board. In fact, Stott and others were angered by the idea. They still hoped to end all member trading with O-T-C houses, and under no conditions would admit them to the floor. To do so would be to end the rationale for the specialist system, at least in part. After a while, given the Ames proposal, N.Y.S.E. specialists might become wholesalers of securities to the over-the-counter market, which would handle the retail business by dealing directly with the commission brokers. If this happened, the Exchange would surely dwindle in importance and perhaps in time even go out of business.

Rea and Moffatt did not seem to understand this. Sensitive to the ideas emanating from the commission houses, they seized on the Ames suggestion and made it the core of a far more elaborate plan. On May 12, 1941, they called a press conference to release details of their proposal, which they said was the result of a four-month study and had recently been submitted to the S.E.C.

The Rea-Moffatt plan called for a stimulation of the commission brokers through the incentives implied in the Ames suggestion. It is apparent, they began, "that interest in securities can be aroused when a sales organization is given the opportunity of reasonable compensation for its efforts and that the public's interest in securities, and the resultant transfer of idle funds into a share in the ownership of industry, can be stimulated." Then Rea presented his plan which, he said, was intended to serve merely "as a basis for discussion and further study."

In May 1941, the specialists were doing a meager business, while the O-T-C dealers were getting quite a bit of the transactions in N.Y.S.E.–listed stocks. Some claimed they were doing a greater volume of business than their Exchange counterparts. Whether or not this was true, it bothered the specialists, and Rea offered a way out of their difficulties. The Curb president suggested that if the specialist saw there were no buyers or sellers, he could offer shares to O-T-C dealers at a discount and in quantities and under terms of his own making, and that this information could be carried on the N.Y.S.E. tape. Since almost all the O-T-C dealers "traded off the tape" anyway, this would be a major convenience for them, and in addition legitimize actions they had long engaged in albeit in a "masked" fashion. Thus, the specialist in ABC might offer to sell 1,000 shares of ABC at 29, less one point to dealers who took the entire amount, which would make the net price 28 or, in this case $28,000. He might do this to obtain business or simply to lighten his inventory situation.

O-T-C dealers throughout the nation, who would have access to the tape through rentals of the equipment, would see this offer. One or more might decide to make the purchase, which would go to the first whose representative contacted the specialist on the floor. Such a dealer might have several customers who were interested in ABC, who would gladly take shares at 28½, in this way saving themselves a half point from the floor quotation at the time. The O-T-C dealer could sell them as much of the 1,000 as they wanted, making a profit of $.50 for each share he disposed of.

As Rea saw it, this would make the 2,500 or so O-T-C dealers agents of the exchanges, and spur them to recommend listed stocks to their clients. No longer would these dealers compete with N.Y.S.E. and Curb specialists. Instead, their fortunes would be wedded, with one dependent upon the other for volume. The Exchange specialists would obtain additional business while also disposing of potential or real rivals, and the O-T-C dealers would acquire a new legitimacy and a source of shares more dependable than what existed at the time. In the process liquidity would be increased, and so "better markets" would be made in stocks. When markets were thin and specialists edgy and unwilling to take chances, large jumps in prices were common. Seeing these unsettled potential investors kept them from the exchanges—or at least, so it was believed. The more prosperous specialists would be able to absorb stock in falling markets and supply it in rising ones, and this would redound to the benefit of all, said Rea.

The National Association of Securities Dealers, which represented the O-T-C firms, would meet regularly with representatives of the exchanges. All N.A.S.D. members in good standing would become associate members of any exchange they did business with—including the N.Y.S.E.—for the payment of a fee. Rea also believed the commission schedule should be raised, so as to compensate specialists for their loss of business to the O-T-C market.

The plan met with a good reception. Ames thought it worthwhile, as did members of other large commission houses. Although the S.E.C. asked for time to study the proposal, individual Commission members indicated interest and favor.

At first the N.Y.S.E. said nothing of the Ames-Rea-Moffatt ideas. The Exchange was in a state of flux. Schram had just been selected to replace Martin, but would not take command for several months. Eicher had been in office for little more than a month, and there was no clear indication of the S.E.C.'s direction under his leadership. But the proposal demanded a response from the Big Board, and Stott, who had only recently been elected chairman, spoke for the Exchange and did so obliquely.

Stott observed that the Exchange had been successful in handling many large secondary distributions during the past few months, referring perhaps to the sale of formerly British-held securities, but not adding that even more of these had been handled by the O-T-C dealers. He noted that he had only taken office on May 12 and could not speak authoritatively yet, and would not do so until May 28, when the new Board of Governors met. But he would be interested in seeing a second market in operation on the trading floor, one that functioned alongside the familiar auction market. Stocks there would be sold at the established price at the auction quote less a discount. But he would go no further than this.

There was no mention of the O-T-C dealers in the Stott message. Instead, he indicated that this second market would involve only N.Y.S.E. members. In other words, the commission brokers would be able to purchase large blocks at discounts and then sell them to customers. The specialists would be in firm control of both trading areas and have the right to shift offers back and forth between them according to their own needs and judgments. He hoped that commission brokers who frequented the second market would use the money saved by so dealing to increase expenditures on merchandising and advertising. By placing both floors under the supervision of the specialists, he expected to assure their continued domination of the Exchange and the nation's trading. Under the Ames-Rea-Moffatt proposal, the N.Y.S.E. specialists would tend toward the wholesale business; under the Stott suggestion, the specialists would dominate both wholesale and retail, functioning in whichever market offered the greatest profits and opportunities, and doing so when they felt it wise. The Curb plan might have resulted in an increase in business for the O-T-C dealers at the expense of the N.Y.S.E. specialists; the Stott proposal would have opened business formerly handled by the over-the-counter houses to the N.Y.S.E.'s commission brokers and specialists.

Stott's response was well considered and intelligent from the point of view of the N.Y.S.E. It was the kind of plan and the result of a variety of analyses that Schram did not yet understand, and perhaps never would. On the one hand, Stott indicated an interest in the new ideas and even in helping to work out a new means of bringing customers back to Wall Street, while on the other he made certain the N.Y.S.E. would dominate the talks and benefit from whatever alterations were made.

On May 20, leaders of the N.A.S.D., the Curb, and Stott attended a "Town Hall Meeting" at the Downtown Athletic Club to discuss the matter further. The meeting was sponsored by several commission brokerages, including J. S. Bache & Co.; Eastman, Dillon; Fahnestock & Co.; and A. M. Kidder. Ganson Purcell was also present, representing the S.E.C. The participants considered the various plans, the kinds of discounts to be offered, and methods of operation. Rea was enthusiastic about the conference and predicted that implementation of a new trading plan was less than a year away. Purcell was silent, but indicated that the S.E.C. remained "interested" in the ideas discussed. The N.A.S.D. representatives wanted to hear more about the plans before commenting. Stott said little, except to approve the idea of higher commissions.

Within a few months the idea was dead. Chairman Eicher left the S.E.C. for the federal bench and Purcell took his place. He had gone to the meeting to hear an idea which purportedly came from the Wall Streeters. If they would not press the matter, neither would he. As far as Purcell was concerned, the plan was in abeyance. Rea and Moffatt said no more about it, at least not publicly, perhaps because they had learned that the N.Y.S.E. wasn't that interested in their ideas. The N.A.S.D. let the matter drop. By the time Schram was in office, Stott had organized an Exchange committee to study the question of a second market. This committee met a few times and disbanded without returning a series of recommendations.

Stott had helped kill an interesting idea, a variety of which would reappear in the 1960s, but which in 1941 seemed detrimental to the interests of the N.Y.S.E.'s specialists—the men who were the backbone of the organization. It had been done with finesse and quietly, in such a way as to escape the attention of the Wall Street press corp, busy covering Schram's election, wondering what he would do once in office. Financial writers had little doubt he had much to learn about the workings of the Exchange, but appeared certain he would become a power on Wall Street. This was not to be. Rather, Robert Stott, who had proven himself shortly after assuming the chairmanship, would become the leader for the floor brokers even while the public and Washington looked to Schram as the symbol of the Exchange.

CHAPTER 7

The Nadir

Stott had no intention of cooperating with the over-the-counter dealers and certainly would not advocate a pact with them. Even meeting with their representatives in a public forum, as he had in May of 1941, was viewed as a bold and perhaps unwise move by several of the Exchange's more conservative and tradition-bound members; it was as though Churchill had agreed to debate the issues with Hitler at that juncture.

The over-the-counter markets had long histories, and, indeed, some of them might have justifiably claimed earlier origins than the N.Y.S.E. itself. They were vague, often amorphous affairs, not really one market, as was commonly believed, but several, containing different communities that overlapped each other. The highest grade federal, state, and municipal bonds were traded over-the-counter. So were extremely speculative stocks, unapproved by the S.E.C., which couldn't meet listing requirements at even the most marginal exchange. Some O-T-C brokerages were highly rated and quite respectable, while others were little better than bucket shops of the kind that lined lower Broadway at the turn of the century. Were it not for the fact that several O-T-C houses were making fine markets in N.Y.S.E.–listed issues, the Exchange might have ignored the traders, as it so often had in the past. This O-T-C network, larger than the Exchange in the aggregate, was considered a racy place, not only by Wall Streeters but most investors. Somehow the specialist, offering the same prices to all who asked him, was deemed more respectable than the trader who telephoned several of his fellows attempting to obtain the best deal available. The trading floor was the status symbol of the Establishment; the bank of telephones remained the plebeian mark of outsiders and interlopers. Allow the latter access to the floor, and the distinction would be on the way to obliteration. Not even the S.E.C., in its wildest period, had seriously suggested this possibility. For the N.Y.S.E. to accept the Ames-Rea-Moffatt proposals in 1941 would be to open the door to a far more radical structural change than any adopted in the

1930s. Gay had rejected milder notions while on the defensive; Stott would not countenance such changes at a time when the Exchange was intent on recapturing a sizable portion of the powers lost to Washington during the New Deal. Had he proved more pliable, Stott would have lost much of his constituency. In any case, he did not intend to cooperate with the O-T-C traders. Rather, he would indicate a willingness to listen to all sides and consider other points of view. No action would be taken, however, unless it preserved the Exchange's integrity while at the same time brought additional business to the floor. If Stott could accomplish these goals, he would not only become the most popular figure at the N.Y.S.E. but one of its major powers.

Alternative plans already existed. In late 1939 and early 1940, when foreign purchasers attempted to buy large blocks, while at the same time the British were liquidating much of their holdings of American securities, the board developed techniques to handle the additional business. Under one suggestion, members would be permitted to gather small lots from several buyers to create a block of stocks that would then be offered to potential purchasers. Or the purchaser would make his desires known to a member, who then would gather the block together. In each case, the purchaser would be charged a smaller commission than was customary. The method was never used, however, due to the inability of N.Y.S.E. members to put together sufficient capital and signs of opposition from the S.E.C.

When the British sold their large blocks, the N.Y.S.E. put forth a plan to take the business from the O-T-C market. Temporary consortia of brokers would be formed to pool their assets and take the stock—at reduced commissions. Then they would try to sell the issue gradually, in such a way as not to depress its price on the open auction market. This method might have won S.E.C. approval and even a change in laws against such group activities, but the floor brokers objected to the technicalities of the plan and it was rejected.

Both ideas were revived in May of 1941, and after drastic reworking, were set forth as the N.Y.S.E.'s answer to the Ames-Rea-Moffatt proposal. The plan was given several names at the time, but was best known as "special offerings" or simply "specials."

The special offering was designed to be the most drastic institutional change in trading methods at the N.Y.S.E. since the specialist system had been accepted shortly after the end of the Civil War. Under the rules and traditions of the late 1930s, the specialist and the commission broker were there to serve the public. In theory, at least, prices were to be determined by a formal exchange of orders. Neither commission broker or specialist was supposed to be a salesman or act to "push" a stock. To be sure, specialists would attempt to lighten loads or accumulate stocks, while commission brokers would call their customers and try to induce them to buy or sell stocks. But these practices were not entered into for the benefit or detriment of one issue or another. The commission broker did not receive a larger commission for selling a particular stock, and the same principle held true for specialists.

The special offering broke with this tradition. It occurred when a potential seller of a large block appeared at a brokerage to ask its services in disposing of his shares. Given the thin markets of the time, such a sale might create havoc on the floor. For example, the stock of ABC might have last traded at 32, and have a volume of only 200 or 300 shares a day during normal sessions. The seller might wish to offer 5,000 shares. He would understand that the demand for them was low and that conventional N.Y.S.E. selling would depress prices. Thus, he would be willing to accept a lower net price for his block in order for it to be sold. In 1941, such a person would be driven to the O-T-C market, where the dealer would purchase the entire block but at a reduced price. While negotiating, the dealer would try to scout up customers for parts of the block, a practice denied N.Y.S.E. specialists, who because of it were losing business to the O-T-C dealers.

The Exchange retaliated, and did so by adopting some of the methods of the O-T-C traders but not the men themselves. Under the plan, the commission broker would approach the board and ask for permission to make the special offering. If granted, the news would be flashed to the membership via the tape. The brokers and specialists would learn that ABC was being offered at, say, 30 net by way of the special offering. This meant that while the offering was on, the price would not vary; normal specialist dealings were suspended. Commission brokers would receive a special fee for their sales of ABC to their clients, which could run as high as 2 percent, almost four times the ordinary commission at the time. Finally, the customer who purchased ABC by means of a special offering would pay no commission.*

The Exchange hoped that special offerings would entice new customers to the securities market and at the same time convince some of the old to leave the O-T-C brokers and return to the N.Y.S.E. A potential customer might receive a telephone call from his Big Board broker and be told that instead of having to buy ABC at 32 plus commission he could have it for a limited time at 30 and no fee. The broker might urge him to buy, knowing that his commission on the deal would be substantial. The seller of the block would be content,

* The special offering should not be confused with the secondary distribution, which was a well-established convention during the great bull market of the 1920s and before. Secondaries were offered off-the-floor, often by the issuing company, while specials were on-the-floor and offered by other holders. In addition, secondaries were made after the floor was closed for the day, while special offerings were handled during regular trading hours.

understanding that even though he would receive only 28 or so net for his 5,000 shares, it was a better price than could have been obtained at the O-T-C market, or if sold the regular way at the N.Y.S.E.

The O-T-C brokers protested the plan vigorously, arguing that it was clearly designed to destroy them, and in any case was a violation of S.E.C. requirements. The Commission disagreed—this was viewed at the Exchange as the first fruits of having selected Schram as president—and the special offerings method was ratified in February 1942. The plan went into effect on February 16. Three days later the board approved a special offering of 2,958 shares of Bon Ami at 37⅜, for which the brokers would receive a special commission of $1.00 a share. The offering was taken in a matter of hours, on a day when total N.Y.S.E. volume was only 345,000 shares. Of the next eleven specials that month, only two could not be made satisfactorily, and had to be withdrawn, although the experience during the rest of the year was better.

Special trading was the first program put into effect by the resurgent Old Guard. Stott and Schram hailed it as an effort to reinvigorate business at the N.Y.S.E. and serve the public. It came too late to accomplish either objective. Had the Exchange developed and presented the technique in 1939, it could have captured the bulk of the foreign business that year and in 1940, and so diverted a bonanza from the O-T-C houses. By 1942, however, the British selling had been completed, and there was little business left. There would be seventy-three successful offerings in 1942, sixty-nine the following year, and seventy-three again in 1944. Then the number dropped sharply, reaching twenty in 1946 and not recovering for more than a decade. In early 1943, Stott was obliged to concede that the impact of special trading had been "picayune."

All indications at the time were that those individuals who had purchased stocks by participating in special offerings were not traders, to be lured back into the market as though the offerings were "loss leaders" at a department store. Rather, they were cautious individuals who might purchase sound issues at bargain prices but would rarely if ever again call their brokers. The sellers tended to be large institutions hoping to dispose of their blocks quickly and at a decent net price. The Stock Exchange's leadership, intent more on preservation than expansion and wary regarding innovation, was content to let it go at that. Given their natural inclinations, special trading was a bold step, but it still did not answer the needs of the N.Y.S.E. for increased volume.

Slightly less than 800,000 shares were handled through special offerings in 1942, and these were worth $22 million. No wonder, then, that Stott called the trading picayune, even though in 1943 the volume topped the 1 million mark—a record that would last for a generation.

But to some of the members, 800,000 shares was not picayune at all. In 1942, only 125,700,000 were traded, the lowest since 1914—a year when the Exchange had been closed for five months. The turnover rate in 1942 was 9 percent, the worst in N.Y.S.E. history. Average daily trading for the year was 455,000 shares, the lowest in more than a quarter of a century. For specialists and brokers operating in this kind of market, the 800,000 shares transferred through special offerings was not to be despised. It could be the difference between solvency and failure.

At the height of the 1929 bull market, some 125,000 people were employed in the securities industry. In late 1941, the number was 33,000, and their salaries were far lower than they had been a dozen years earlier. An experienced commission broker earned $35 a week in 1941, assuming business was average, and if it were not, he might be fired before he could quit. During the last stage of the bull market, that kind of money might be given a broker by a grateful client as a tip, and then considered too small by men taking in thousands of dollars a week. There were 665 member firms operating at the N.Y.S.E. in 1929, with 541 of them in New York itself. In early 1942 there were 417 in the city and 557 nationwide. This was the result of an amalgamation movement that began in the late 1930s and continued throughout the war. It was not unusual for two weak brokerages to merge in the hope of forming one strong one, but instead develop into a bigger and weaker entity, which would in turn be taken over by a strong, major firm. Or a small specialty brokerage would acquire a larger company at bargain prices, with the pledge to retain top management at current salaries. Then, shortly after, the leaders of the new firm would fire almost all the customers' men and clerks who had worked at the larger operation, sell off assets, and emerge a bigger company than it had been originally at little cost, since the returns from the sale of assets more than covered the purchase price. On other occasions two undercapitalized specialists would come together, pooling their funds and personnel, in an effort to retain all of their stocks. In general, of course, it was a case of the strong engulfing the weak. During the first six months of 1941, 219 N.Y.S.E. firms showed an aggregate loss of $5,292,000, 14 broke even, and 264 showed profits of $6,682,000. Some newspapers reported that the community had a profit of $1,390,000 for the period, which though true enough was certainly deceiving, to say the least. Among the profitable firms, 136 had earnings of $4,055,000, and these received more than half their business from secondaries and specials and underwritings of new securities. Had they reported their brokerage revenues alone, most would have shown deficits.

Just before the 1929 crash, there were 1,658 branch offices of member houses throughout the nation. Twelve years later, the number was 875, while the tickers in use declined from 9,707 to 2,219. In 1928, 17 percent of Harvard Business School's graduates entered the investment field. Only 4.4 percent went to Wall Street in 1940, and a survey of the 1941 class indicated the figure was below 2 percent.

Business in all its phases was moribund. After so many years of depression, the investment community had become wary of change, frightened of innovation, uncertain of its own powers and abilities, and awkward in its actions. Large underwriters who in the 1920s would bid on multimillion-dollar offerings with a sense of abandon, and then sell the issue to customers in a matter of hours, to return to competing for still larger issues the following day, had retrenched by the mid-1930s. Even then, however, they would join with others to bid for the few underwritings that came their way, and the stronger firms could afford to spend days and even weeks in the distribution. It was different in 1941. Underwriting groups were hard to form for the best issues, and several industrial firms were obliged to look for funds elsewhere, either from the government or private sources. Late in the year, insurance companies seeking investments began bidding against underwriters for new issues, indicating perhaps a desire to enter the brokerage field. This was not so, however. The insurance firms, which had always been content to pay commissions to Wall Street houses for portions of large underwritings, were by then obliged to buy the entire issue, primarily because they had no alternative in seeking large block investments. If they did not take them, no one would; the underwriting houses would let them pass, unwilling to assume the burdens of distributing a million dollars or so worth of securities to an almost nonexistent community of investors.

The floor was a quiet place, with only a fraction of the specialists and representatives there at any given moment. Most would remain in their offices, reading newspapers, making telephone calls, or simply passing the time of day with their partners. Others would lounge outside the building, in the smoking room, or pay a visit to a local saloon, while their clerks remained at their posts to take messages. If a buy or sell for 100 shares came down, the clerk would rush out the door to find his employer, who would scurry back to fill the order and then return outside to celebrate. It was a period during which the active issues would trade fewer than 8,000 shares on most days, when a specialist could spend an entire session on the Street and fill only a dozen or so orders.

Speculation used to thrive in thin markets, when it was relatively easy to corner a stock. The markets were thin in 1941, but due to disinterest more than anything else; in any case, the S.E.C. forbade cornering techniques. But even if all regulation had ended, it would have been senseless to corner a stock, since there were so few speculators and manipulators in the district competing against each other, trying to fleece the lambs or being fleeced themselves. The giant speculators and private traders of the 1920s had either retired or were dead, while a few remained in business, but as brokers and underwriters, not floor managers. Their replacements were of a more modest breed. Financial writer Washington Dodge wrote of one in a survey of the Street in late 1941:

> The last of the diehards is the "Boy Trader," a rather corpulent young man who on occasion will swoop down on the Floor and indulge in a veritable orgy of buying. There are two schools of thought about him. One is that he only appears when his trust-fund income arrives and disappears as soon as it is lost. The other theory is that nobody could actually be so careless as he appears to be and that when he is buying in quires he is probably selling, through others, in reams. Last summer in that stronghold of speculation, Southampton, Long Island, the following conversation was heard between him and his less spectacular brother:
>
> "Was that you running up Steel at the close because I'm short?"
>
> "No, I swear I didn't touch Steel all day long."
>
> But these reactionaries are in the very, very small minority, and what Floor trading remains is on a small, sharpshooting scale.*

Dodge noted that conditions were so bad that brokers, specialists, and private traders could not afford to dine at the Exchange's Luncheon Club. As a result, the restaurant showed deficits and met the emergency by opening its door to "all classes of practitioners of the financial arts." To some of the older members, this action, more than anything else, was a sign that their time had indeed passed.

* Ever since the mid-nineteenth century, the short sale had been a classic tool of the speculator. During the 1920s market manipulators like Arthur Cutten and Jesse Livermore would sell a stock short—selling shares they didn't own at current market prices with the promise to return them afterward. Then they would force the price down through massive selling, after which they would purchase the borrowed stock at the lower price and return it. This is what the "boy speculator" and his brother were discussing. There were days in the late 1920s when the short interest was estimated to be well over 10 million shares. On December 31, 1941, however, the short interest was 349,000 shares, a record low, and yet another indication of the lack of speculative interest in stocks. Washington Dodge II, "Letter from a Blighted Area: Wall Street," *Fortune* (Vol. 54, No. 11, November 1941), p. 46.

At that, the N.Y.S.E. was in better shape than the regionals, some of which closed down or combined operations with other ailing exchanges. The Curb was the subject of many rumors in 1941–1942. Several members actually suggested abandoning its building at Trinity Place, allowing the creditors to take over, and then recommencing trading in the open air, where it had been conducted prior to the move indoors in 1921. Curb seats sold for $650 in 1942, when average daily volume was less than 90,000 shares, and the most active day of the year saw only 387,000 shares change hands. The situation was mixed at the O-T-C houses. Those specializing in industrial and railroad securities did poorly, but others interested in government bonds reported good business. In any case, overhead at the O-T-C markets was far lower than that at the N.Y.S.E. and Curb, and this was pondered by several of the more radical reformers in the district. Let the Curb go outdoors, they said, and the N.Y.S.E. could relocate to modest quarters in another state, where rent would be cheap and taxes low. There was no indication that such moves were contemplated, but the rumors caused a brief period of anxiety at City Hall.

Throughout his career, Mayor Fiorello La Guardia inveighed against "the interests," one of which was the investment community in lower Manhattan. He was on good terms with many of the district's leaders, however, even when he understood they were helping to finance the campaigns of his political opponents. Like most of his predecessors, La Guardia knew that Wall Street was a central part of the city, and one of the main reasons New York occupied its preeminent position. If the securities market moved to another location, a major shift of financial focus would be initiated and lower Manhattan could become a business desert. This was recognized in Albany as well. From time to time—usually in election years—political leaders would discuss new taxes they hoped would be imposed upon stock transactions. The presidents and chairmen of the N.Y.S.E. and Curb would issue opposing statements, and the battle lines would be drawn. Then there would be a rumor of a possible move elsewhere, complete with stories about sites in Newark or some other city. On occasion the N.Y.S.E. would even put deposits on land. Then both sides would back down and a compromise would be reached.

Real estate prices in the financial district declined steadily throughout the depression, a period when it was not unusual for a quarter to a third of an office building to be unoccupied. Hundreds of brokerages went out of business in the 1930s, and many more were compelled by the shrinkage of operations to move to smaller quarters. The decline in office space used by N.Y.S.E. firms alone was impressive, with the accepted estimate being a 60 percent fall-off from 1933 to 1941.

The business slump presented La Guardia with a problem. On the one hand, he hoped to keep the financial district in the city and on a thriving basis so as to be able to collect taxes to help run New York, while on the other, the slack rental situation meant that the net tax revenues fell steadily over the years. The mayor could either lower taxes in the hope of attracting new business, or raise them in order to keep the total tax income steady. Given La Guardia's beliefs and the nature of his constituency, he opted for the latter course of action. By 1941, real estate valuations for tax purposes on most Manhattan properties were at approximately the same levels as in 1926, while office buildings in the financial district were being taxed at a rate some 17 percent higher.

Exchange spokesmen protested this situation, and in mid-1941 took their case to City Hall. At the time it was claimed that the break-even point for rental property in the financial district was approximately $2.00 a square foot, and that space could be had for below that level in several buildings that had rented for $8.00 in 1929 and over $3.00 as late as 1936. But the city's leaders were unmoved, for even then, a minor realty boom was starting in lower Manhattan. Government agencies, most of them connected in one way or other with the war effort, were leasing entire floors, many of which had been abandoned by companies in the financial industry. Already advertisements for office space were down, and there were many signs that prices were firming and would soon rise. Threats of removal to other states did not have the same impact on City Hall in 1941 as they did a few years earlier. La Guardia appeared to believe that if the stock exchange complex left the city, the slack could be taken up by federal spending, and, indeed, New York might become a more important administrative center than any other city except Washington, and in time might even eclipse the Capital. To do this, office space would be needed, and lower Manhattan was a prime location. The federal government had begun its life there a century and a half before; part of it might well return in the early 1940s. This, at least, was the message City Hall was sending the N.Y.S.E. in late 1941 and early 1942.

Whether or not it was a bluff is hard to say; certainly La Guardia and his circle were skilled at the game. Still, the threat had credibility in late 1941, and even more after the Japanese attack on Pearl Harbor on December 7 and America's entry into the war as a belligerent. The taxes remained at the same levels, the N.Y.S.E. stopped talking about a move, and federal employees outnumbered financial workers in lower Manhattan from 1942 to 1945. Now the N.Y.S.E. was an orphan in its own backyard.

Not only was the Exchange no longer considered a central institution in New York but its function as a barometer of change and sentiment for the nation had been eroded during the depression, when through economic circumstance and other reasons the number of shareholders and accounts declined drastically. Although there was no census of stockholders in 1929, American corporations reported that there were some 20 million individuals on their books as certificate owners. Allowing for duplication, one scholar estimated that the total number of shareholders was in the neighborhood of 9 million, while another thought the figure closer to 15 million. That same year, N.Y.S.E. commission houses claimed that approximately 1.5 million active accounts were being serviced, while some 600,000 of them were involved in margin buying. While these statistics do not portray an entire nation hell-bent on speculation, they were far higher than those at the beginning of the decade. The depression ended all this. An S.E.C. study of shareholders, completed in mid-1941, indicated that there were slightly more than 4 million owners of securities listed on the N.Y.S.E., and less than a half million owners of shares on other exchanges or traded over-the-counter. At the same time, N.Y.S.E. commission houses reported that they were servicing only 394,000 accounts, and most of these were inactive.* Furthermore, declines in the number of accounts had been posted for every year since 1936, and there seemed no reason to believe the trend would not continue.

This was why stock prices were not viewed as an indicator of sentiment regarding the European war in 1939–1941. After the British selling was completed, prices moved in a sluggish fashion, generally downward but without a sign of panic. (Indeed, there could be no panic without volume, and trading fell steadily in this period.) Disinterest, not efficiency, enabled the N.Y.S.E. to maintain a steady course during the many military crises of 1939–1941.

Some Wall Streeters feared the Japanese surprise attack would precipitate a financial panic. Stock prices had risen earlier in the month in the hope that Japanese-American relations would improve. The Dow Industrials had closed at 116.60 the previous Friday, with volume at 519,000 shares. That Sunday evening there was talk of suspending trading should an anticipated selling wave eventuate. But a telephone survey of the commission houses that evening indicated they were in good shape to handle an influx of orders, while some specialists could do the same given help from the Exchange. Business was brisk at the brokerages prior to the opening on Monday, but not as much selling as

* John Sears, *The New Place of the Stockholder* (New York, 1929), pp. 35–37, 60; "Appraising the 1941 Investor," *The Exchange* (Vol. II, No. 6, June 1941), pp. 11–12.

expected was reported. Trading began at the usual time, and stocks traded in a narrow range that session: 111.53–115.46. At the close the Dow stood at 112.52, down only 4 points, small under the circumstances. Volume was high at 2,028,000 shares, but this had been anticipated.

The war news was generally bad in December, and yet the Dow Industrials closed the month at 110.75, for a loss of only 3 points. Volume was 36,390,000 shares, in a year when only 170,603,000 were traded. It had been the Exchange's busiest month since May of 1940, when it appeared the Axis powers might win a complete victory in Europe.

Seeking an indication as to what might be expected in the way of Wall Street developments, economic and financial analysts explored the World War I experience to find parallels to the situation in early 1942. Several appeared interesting. The United States had been in a depression in 1913. Then, with the coming of war in Europe, there was a brief panic on Wall Street, which was followed by confidence and prosperity as war orders spurred consumption and investment, and in the end, enlarged profits. To this was added America's own preparations for war, which placed additional demands upon the economy, created new opportunities, and resulted in still higher sales and income. All of this was reflected in stock prices, which rose sharply and steadily during the 1914–1917 neutrality period, a time when high volume and good profits were the rule at the N.Y.S.E.

The situation changed during the war itself. Shortly after President Wilson had received his war declaration from Congress, the economy was mobilized and profits curtailed through new taxes. Although trading volume continued strong at the Exchange, neither 1917 nor 1918 could match the 1916 highs. In addition, the bull market came to a slow end. The Dow Industrials (new base) traded in a range of 65.95–110.15 during the American participation in World War I, but was at 88.06 just prior to the Armistice in 1918, for a loss of more than 6 points for the war period.

Recitations of this experience were made by several journalists and economists in early 1942, most of whom used it to justify predictions of a generally narrow market during the new war. As had been the case in 1914, the American economy was in a depression when war erupted in 1939. Then, with the arrival of military orders, the situation began to change. Corporation profits after taxes rose from $3.3. billion in 1938 to $6 billion in 1939, a year when the impact of European war orders was beginning to be felt. Then, in 1941, profits reached the $9.5 billion level. Most other statistics were equally impressive. But the good economic news was not reflected in stock prices. The Dow was at 135.25 just prior to the German invasion of Poland, and stood at 116.60 when the Japanese attacked Pearl Harbor.

If the surging economy of 1939–1941 could not spur a bull market, argued the analysts, certainly the war itself would result in a decline. The December 1941 experience seemed to indicate this would be the case. The combination of poor war news, rumors of a "conscription of capital" during the conflict, and the generally sober mood of the nation in 1942, as contrasted to the exuberance of 1917, also supported this view. In fact, 1942 was a bad year, at least insofar as volume was concerned, while the Dow fell from 113.00 on January 1 to 92.92 on April 28.

That spring, it appeared the more pessimistic analysts had been justified in their views of the wartime market. Business at the Curb had almost ended, while the N.Y.S.E. floor often seemed deserted, as for the month of April, average daily volume was only slightly above 300,000 shares. Commission brokers and specialists traded information on how best to obtain a commission in the armed forces instead of shouting quotations to one another. Patriotism impelled many to volunteer that season, but at the same time those who left Wall Street probably felt they would not be missing much by being away from the district for the duration of the war. Perhaps those who remained envied their friends who were off for what appeared a more exciting and important experience. There had been an exodus of Wall Streeters for the Civil War, and another for World War I. On each of those occasions, however, those who left were confident they would assume their old positions after the war. Quite a few of the Wall Streeters who served in World War II were not at all certain they wanted to take their old posts after the fighting, or indeed whether there would be a financial district worth returning to.

In the face of predictions of stagnant prices and a general aura of gloom and doom, a bull market began in late April. Volume and prices both rose in 1943 and 1944. On August 31, 1945, the last trading day prior to the end of the war, the Dow closed at 174.29, having almost doubled its April 1942 lows. Volume was high that day, at least by 1942 standards, at 1,110,000 shares, but it was below the year's average daily trades of 1,422,085 shares, which was the best in seven years. If Wall Street was not euphoric during the war, at least it did not stagnate or die, as had been feared in early 1942.*

* * *

* If one considers World Wars I and II as complete entities, and does not separate each into the periods during which the United States was neutral and the belligerency phase, the performances were similar. During World War I, the Dow rose from 71.42 to 88.06, and in World War II, the average went from 135.25 to 174.29, practically identical percentage rises.

The Exchange's brokers and specialists earned decent livings during most of the war period, and the N.Y.S.E. too showed a good advance. In 1941 it had a net loss on operations of $629,560, and an additional loss of $1.6 million on the sale of property. This was followed by a deficit of $815,972 in 1942. Then, in 1943, the N.Y.S.E. reported a profit—the first since 1936—of $676,508. Business was such that Exchange personnel received a general wage increase, this too the first since 1936, and one that helped stave off a strike of financial workers. As though to indicate their appreciation of Schram's efforts—and implying that in some way he had been responsible for their prosperity—the members voted to increase the president's salary from $48,000 to $55,000, but this was rejected by the Treasury Department, which at the time had control over such matters (in November of 1945, Schram's salary was raised to $100,000 a year, however). Institutionally, at least, there no longer seemed any question that the Exchange would survive, and might even flourish.

There was yet another issue that could not be resolved so happily. Did the N.Y.S.E. fill an economic function? To put it another way, would American finance be much different without the Exchange than it was with it? During the 1920s, the last great era for Wall Street, such a question would not have been asked. In that decade, over 80 percent of all new capital needed by domestic corporations had been raised through the issuance of bonds and stock, and without the marketability provided by the N.Y.S.E. and other financial markets, such paper could hardly have been sold easily. The situation changed drastically in the 1930s, when not only did the need for new capital decline but private placements became more common, while the refinancing of debts became less and less important. Thus, in 1930–1934, 75 percent of new capital was provided by stocks and bonds, and in 1935–1939, only 30 percent.

The Exchange had developed, grown, and prospered because there had been a demand for such an institution, and its members had justified their existence and earnings by taking note of this. By the late 1930s, however, the N.Y.S.E. was on its way to becoming a self-serving organization, one where investors and speculators sought financial gain, with brokers and specialists there to cater to gaming instincts. To some, the difference was not evident, but it was to others who pondered such matters during the depression. If the Big Board was indeed a financial pump for American capitalism, then the work of Wall Street bestowed prestige, power, and self-satisfaction on the men of the N.Y.S.E. If it were not, then the Exchange was little better than a gambling den. Indeed, this charge was often made during the early New Deal days, and was denied vigorously by Wall Street spokesmen.

Yet this was what the Exchange was turning into in the 1930s, and the transformation continued during the war. From 1940 to 1944, less than one-third of all new capital required by American corporations was provided through the issuance of stocks and bonds, and only a quarter of that was in the form of common stocks—which were, in effect, the "merchandise" of the N.Y.S.E. In 1941 some $301 million worth of new equity was floated by Wall Street investment bankers, this in the form of seventy-six separate underwritings. During 1942, only $80.7 million of equity was floated by twenty-three companies, with half the amount accounted for by four issues of public-utility preferred stock. The situation in bonds was no different. In 1941, $2.091 billion were sold on the Street; in 1942, the amount of bonds was $1.250 billion.*

This was still another sign that power was ebbing from the financial district, and becoming more centralized in Washington. This shift, which had begun in 1933, appeared to have been halted in 1938. With the coming of war, it started again, this time in a more dangerous fashion insofar as the district was concerned. One might argue against the New Deal in the name of freedom and democracy in peacetime. This could hardly be done during the greatest war of the century, when Wall Street, no less than every other part of the nation, pledged support of the national government.

In 1940, Martin had suggested that Wall Street be permitted a major role in the defense effort. As he saw it, the alternative was federal financing, which would entail a massive increase in taxation and large deficits, both of which would unsettle the economy in such a way as to wipe out all gains made since the early 1930s. That year, federal expenditures rose to $9 billion, the deficit to $3.9 billion, and the national debt to $43 billion. There seemed every indication that the spending and deficits would be still larger in 1941.

Roosevelt rejected Martin's idea, but even had he accepted it, the Wall Street investment banks were in no shape, either financially or psychologically, to undertake ventures of the scope needed. As a result, preparation for war was financed by higher taxes and greater deficits. Expenditures rose to $13.3 billion in 1941 and the deficit to $6.1 billion.

Upon America's entry into the war, it became evident that the tax structure would have to be revised in order to raise funds and at the same time stem inflation. Secretary of the Treasury Morgenthau agreed and suggested a revival of the excess profits tax used in World War I, whereby corporations would be taxed heavily on their profits after a certain point. Morgenthau was erroneously quoted as saying

* Charles C. Abbott, *Financing Business During the Transition* (New York, 1946), p. 101; *New York Times*, January 3, 1943.

that no firm should earn over 6 percent on investment for the duration, and this caused a dip in stock prices at the N.Y.S.E. Thus, businessmen were prepared for a radical measure when Roosevelt offered his tax proposals in April 1942. The President asked for a 100 percent tax on corporate profits beyond an "excessive" amount, but he would go no further than that. In addition, he wanted a limitation on individual incomes to $35,000 after taxes, authority to fix wages and prices, to ration scarce goods, and a host of related measures. Clearly this was a "maximum" program, and Roosevelt realized compromises would be needed if the bill were to get through Congress in any meaningful form.

Congress modified the President's requests, and in October passed the Revenue Act of 1942, which F.D.R. promptly called "the greatest tax bill in American history." Under its terms, the excess profits rate was set at 90 percent and the maximum corporate rate was raised from 31 to 40 percent. In addition, Congress passed the authorization for a "victory tax," a 5 percent surcharge, as well as several other measures designed to raise revenues. The victory tax would be refundable after the war, as would part of the excess profits tax. Additional revenue measures were passed in 1943 and 1944, but the 1942 Act set the tone for business during the war and provided corporate accountants with both a guide and philosophy for the duration.

The excess profits tax encouraged corporations to minimize their profits and change their bookkeeping procedures so as to shift profits into various capital accounts. The same held true for "cost plus" contracts signed with defense corporations, under which the supplier was guaranteed a profit in excess of costs. In such cases, the corporation was encouraged to undertake expenditures that would enrich its net assets, for use after the war, although these items were generally hidden in the balance sheets. Needless to say, the excess profits arrangements also encouraged waste; it enabled some firms to embark on risky ventures, knowing that the costs were being paid by the government, since if the company did not spend the money, it might be taken in the form of taxes.*

In all, the government's wartime tax program should have indicated to sophisticated readers of financial statements that net profits were no longer meaningful guides as to the true performance of American corporations. For that matter, other aggregate figures for the war period also had to be viewed with caution. Just as many firms changed their accounting procedures during the 1930s in order to report higher earnings, in this way boosting their prices of stocks and bonds, so they squirreled away profits in wartime to avoid taxes and set their houses in

* For an informed summary of the law by one who participated in its framing, see Randolph E. Paul, *Taxation in the United States* (Boston, 1954), especially pp. 294–348.

order for what many analysts believed would be a major postwar depression. Net corporate profits, as reported to the government, rose from $6.9 billion in 1940 to $11.1 billion in 1942, reached a peak of $12.1 billion in 1943, and then declined. By most measures, 1944 was the high point for wartime production, and in that year, profits were $11.7 billion.* But the statistics for retained earnings show a different side of the picture; they rose from $710 million in 1940 to $3.6 billion in 1944.**

The giant American corporations expanded rapidly during the war, becoming the backbone of what was termed "the arsenal of democracy." Standard Oil of New Jersey, for example, had $822 million in sales in 1941, and $1.618 billion in 1944; General Electric's sales went from $412 million to $1.5 billion in the same period; and General Motors' from $2.4 billion to $3.1 billion, while relatively small I.B.M.'s sales went from $19.6 million to $72.3 million. But the reported earnings of these and other representative companies did not rise at anywhere near the same rates. Nor did their dividends climb, in part because they were controlled by the government for the duration but also because the corporations wanted to retain earnings for the postwar period. Standard Oil of New Jersey earned $5.15 a share in 1941, paid a dividend of $2.50, and traded in a range of 33–46⅞. The company earned $5.64 a share in 1945, traded at 56–68⅞, and paid the same $2.50. General Electric's 1941 statistics were earnings of $1.99 a share and a dividend of $1.40, while trading at 24¾–35⅛. In 1945, the earnings had fallen to $1.96, the dividend was up to $1.55, and the trading range was 37⅞–49⅝. As for General Motors, earnings fell from $4.44 in 1941 to $4.07 in 1945, and the dividend also declined, from $3.75 to $3.00. But the stock rose, from 28⅝–48½ in 1941 to 62–77⅞ in 1945. The same kinds of figures could be given for most major firms, with similar results. Reported profits stagnated, as did dividends, while prices rose at the N.Y.S.E. Either investors understood the financial byplay in regard to taxes and so accepted the earnings as understated, or they had developed a greater confidence in stocks and bonds than they had in the last years of the depression. Given the low volume at the Exchange, and the fact that most former investors were drawn to defense and war bonds, both for patriotic and financial reasons, the former explanation appears more likely.

During the war, many large corporations paid off portions of their debts, or at the very least, entered into few refinancing operations.

* United States Department of Commerce, *Historical Statistics of the United States from Colonial Times to 1957* (Washington, 1960), p. 580.

** Abbott, *Financing Business*, p. 43.

Some purchased their own common stock so as to lower their capitalizations. When they needed additional capital, they tended to borrow from the government, where they could obtain lower interest rates, faster action, and were not troubled by unsold and undigested securities, as might have been the case on Wall Street. Government construction of defense plants and their leasebacks to private concerns were commonplace, as were loans at low rates earmarked for specific projects. Federal expenditures were $34 billion in 1942, and in 1943, $79.4 billion. The figure grew to $95 billion in 1944, and then rose slightly to $98.4 billion in 1945. The bulk of this money went to finance the war effort, and so was used to purchase arms and other equipment from American corporations.

A new economic and business pattern appeared to be developing during the war, one that made the New Deal seem a minor foray by comparison. In the earlier period, most of the nation's corporation executives were allied with Wall Street in opposition to the more radical reformers in Washington, who occasionally seemed about to take command of the New Deal. Although it was attacked in the press and abandoned by many investors, the N.Y.S.E. could at least be certain of its status in the business community. If corporations had not utilized Wall Street's services as much in the 1930s as they had earlier, this could be blamed on the depression and the strict enforcement of S.E.C. regulations. When economic recovery came, so it was believed, the corporations would finance their operations—and in particular, their expansions—by the issuance of equity and debt through investment bankers, and these in turn would be traded at the N.Y.S.E. Perhaps at that time, thought the more conservative Wall Streeters, a united business community could mount a counterattack against the New Deal "radicals." After all, the great period of progressive reform, begun in the cities and states in the late nineteenth century and symbolized on the federal level by Theodore Roosevelt and Woodrow Wilson, had come to an end with World War I, and after the war, America turned to Warren Harding and Calvin Coolidge. Perhaps the same scenario would be followed after World War II. At least, this was on the minds of some in the district during the war.

By 1944, however, conditions had changed drastically. As a result of their financial policies during the war, many large corporations were extremely solvent. In 1939, for example, nonfinancial corporations had $10.9 billion in cash items, and this stood at $23 billion at the end of 1944, while in the same period their holdings of government securities rose from $2.2 billion to $20.8 billion. Total current assets of these corporations went from $54.6 billion to $98.8 billion from 1939 to 1944, while current liabilities rose to only $53.3 billion from $30 billion.* The firms behind these figures would not require the services of investment bankers as much as had been believed in 1939, or even 1941. This would mean fewer stock and bond flotations, which would cut down on the number of shares listed at the N.Y.S.E., and indicate that major corporations would no longer be so concerned about the prices of their securities or, for that matter, whether they were traded at the N.Y.S.E. Already there were signs that this was occurring. Even during the depression, the total number of listed shares rose, going from 757 million in 1929 to 1.424 billion in 1939. In 1945, however, the number was still close to the latter figure—1.492 billion shares—having stagnated throughout the war period.

Finally, concerned brokers noted that the Roosevelt Administration had ceased being an anathema to manufacturers and other businessmen. Instead, the policy of harmony begun in 1939 continued to develop and was being sealed by the experiences of national emergency. There seemed no reason to doubt that government agencies would continue to finance business if called upon to do so after the war.

Herbert Hoover had warned against this close government-business nexus during the 1932 Presidential election. At the time, he indicated that such cooperation would stifle freedom and be a prelude to a domestic form of fascism. During the early New Deal, some reformers hoped to construct just such an alliance, but they failed. One of the reasons the N.Y.S.E. selected Emil Schram for the presidency was its hope that he could influence his former Washington associates to permit the Street a greater degree of freedom, and also to allow the district's banks a larger share of the business than they had in 1940. To do so was beyond his powers, or those of any other person who might have occupied his position at the time. It would appear that the Wall Street financial community—including the N.Y.S.E.—might well become a major institutional casualty of the war. The Big Board, which many had believed would not outlast the depression, did so, though it hardly came through unscathed. Unemployment, economic stagnation, and the greatest reform effort of the century, one which made the N.Y.S.E. the symbol of failure and chicanery, had left the district dispirited and shabby. Recovery to its earlier period of glory seemed out of the question in the early 1940s. Survival, not prosperity, was the fondest hope entertained at the N.Y.S.E. in the gloomy first days of World War II.

Given the situation at the time, such an attitude was understandable. Like so many other organizations and institutions in America, the N.Y.S.E. had become accustomed to preparing for the worst during the depression. What kind of a situation would it be in, however, if

* Abbott, *Financing Business*, p. 31.

prosperity did return, a boom greater in every respect than that of the 1920s? Although the N.Y.S.E. had been restructured during the 1930s, and the S.E.C. had helped create a new Wall Street, many major issues of the decade had not been resolved. The list was long—segregation of specialists' functions, creation of brokerage banks, financing by banks and government agencies, multiple trading of N.Y.S.E.–listed stocks, relations with the over-the-counter market, the level of commission rates, the apparent inability of the N.Y.S.E. to trade in large blocks without creating a disruptive market, and even the relationship between the specialists and the commission houses and the powers of the administration. All of these issues and problems had been raised during the 1930s, and none of them successfully resolved. They did not seem important to the men of the early 1940s, not when survival was at issue. Because they could not or would not come to terms with them, all would reappear, many in the same form, a quarter of a century later.

Part Two

THE GOLDEN GENERATION 1942-1961

CHAPTER 8

With the Tide

Little is known of David Clarkson, a broker of no great business distinction whose death sometime in the middle of the nineteenth century went unrecorded in the major newspapers of the time. City records indicate that he had an office on Broad Street and was a member of the New York Stock and Exchange Board, the earlier title of the N.Y.S.E. Along with some two hundred others like him, Clarkson tried to make a living from the buying and selling of shares for others. He probably traded for himself as well, though prudently. David Clarkson must have been a conservative and trusted broker, for he never went bankrupt or failed to deliver on pledges during the many panics and depressions of the time. Nor did he close shop during slack trading periods, when reported volume often fell below 2,000 shares a day. Like most brokers, he probably had other interests to tide him over—insurance and real estate perhaps—and on occasion he might have taken flyers in underwritings, commodities, and arbitrage in foreign currencies. However he managed it, Clarkson survived in the young, frail, brokerage business of more than a century ago.

In all probability, Clarkson lived a middle-class existence, for he is not mentioned in the press or the few histories of the period as one of the leading men of the district. Jacob Little, Samuel Ward, and a dozen or so "Young Napoleons of Finance" captured the public imagination from time to time, but Clarkson was not one of them. We do not know where he lived, whether or not he was married, and if so, whether his sons followed him into the business—although other Clarksons do appear on the membership roles in the second half of the century.

Yet David Clarkson must have been well known in his own small circle, and even respected. From 1837 to 1851, he served as president of the Stock and Exchange Board. None of his predecessors had occupied the office for more than six years, while two-year terms were the rule afterward, with exceptions made only for unusual men or circumstances. Richard Whitney, president from 1930 to 1935, held the twentieth-century record, but not for long. Emil Schram occupied the presidency for more than ten years, and then put in a brief stint as consultant before retiring to his midwestern home. Were it not for illness, Schram might have remained at the job, for he had won the respect and trust of his constituency at the N.Y.S.E. At a series of farewell dinners, parties, and meetings, he was praised for his intelligence, abilities, and warmth in glowing phrases, even allowing for the hyperbole of such moments. Some Wall Streeters noted his tenure, but at least insofar as reported tributes are concerned, none made mention of the fact that save for David Clarkson, he held the record. The reason was obvious. Except for the length of his service, Clarkson had done little to distinguish himself on Wall Street.

Without being unduly harsh, and always remembering the difficulties of the job and the problems of the period, future historians of Wall Street may make the same assessment of Emil Schram. Indeed, even those of his contemporaries who worked closely with Schram, who always supported the man and have never had a critical word to say about him, are at a loss when asked to discuss—or even name—some of his accomplishments. The responses to such questions are blank stares, anger and accusations of insensitivity on the part of the questioner, and statements about Schram's personal qualities, not his programs and activities. Some will suggest that Schram's most important contributions came in his relations with Washington, although few will say how these helped the N.Y.S.E. or Wall Street in general. Those who do, make observations about Schram's lobbying activities during the war. In particular, they cite his work in the capital gains area. But his efforts in the postwar era pass without comment.

Schram was a visible president in that he often went on the road to deliver speeches before chambers of commerce, fraternal organizations, and the like, and appeared to offer testimony before various congressional committees. As a spokesman for Wall Street in Washington, Schram was informed and intelligent if not wholly effective. Time and again he demonstrated a grasp of the issues and a knowledge of complex financial and political matters beyond those of the congressmen and senators who questioned him, and indeed of staff experts and other witnesses. Schram may not have been flashy and articulate, but he was hard working and particularly impressive in technical areas.

In his public speeches, Schram tended to concentrate on national questions, such as the problems of business in general, the nature of the postwar world, government-business relations, and the role of the Stock Exchange in America. Not once during his presidency did Schram call for a major reform—with the exception of demands for revision of tax laws. He was no innovator, and if he had flashes of imagination and intriguing insights, he kept them to himself. Schram seemed content to come and go with the tide, to gain small victories in the hope that, taken together, they might conserve that which was worth keeping and rectify minor flaws that needed correcting. William Martin had sponsored changes, obtained some of them—along with a powerful group of enemies—and then left Wall Street, a contentious figure, after less than four years. Schram remained in office more than twice as long, and accomplished less than a quarter as much as Martin. But he survived, even though a generation after his leaving young men and women of the district hardly know his name. The same was true of David Clarkson. Going with the tide may not earn one a special niche on the Street, but it does seem to help assure longevity in office.

This is not to say that Schram should have acted otherwise. After all, he had been "hired" to perform exactly as he did. Schram was a figurehead, a defense against New Dealers, a symbol of rectitude alloyed with reformism, and a spokesman for "enlightened business." As previously indicated, the actual governance of the N.Y.S.E. was left to Stott and others, who together constituted a new Old Guard. All seemed pleased with the arrangement, and all performed their tasks as expected.

Schram's first significant undertaking was to influence Washington during the formulation of the Revenue Act of 1942. During his initial year as president, Schram spent almost as much time in Washington as in New York, and there he collared senators and representatives, discussed common problems with lobbyists, offered testimony before several congressional committees, and did all in his power to obtain a tax measure in keeping with Wall Street's view of the public good.

Along with some three hundred and fifty others, Schram testified before the House Ways and Means Committee during the hearings on the 1942 bill. Some witnesses—the National Association of Manufacturers and the United States Chamber of Commerce among them—argued in favor of a sales tax as the best means available for raising the huge sums of money needed by the government to fight the war. They accepted the notion that if America was indeed to become the arsenal of democracy, its leadership would have to emanate from Washington. Schram was one of the handful who spoke against the idea, advocating instead proposals Martin had first enunciated three years before. To maintain freedom and at the same time encourage efficiency, business should have a major role in the arms effort. Investment would have to be stimulated, and the capital markets prodded into action. One method to accomplish this would be through a lowering of the capital gains tax and the passage of supplemental legislation to permit individuals and corporations to use specified short-term losses to offset long-term gains. Schram offered the then-unusual notion that the lower tax rates would bring in a greater amount of revenue than would the far higher ones advocated by the Treasury Department.* He conceded that a lower capital gains rate would be beneficial to the N.Y.S.E., and that he as its president might be expected to support it because of this. But Schram went on to note that unless investors were given a reason to buy stocks and bonds, corporations would lack the incentive to float new issues, and without the funds obtained through such flotations, private enterprise could not be expected to shoulder much of the burden of the arms effort.

Schram was an able advocate. While at the R.F.C. he had learned to parry and thrust with legislators, and he showed his skills at the public sessions, where with a blend of empirical evidence and vague generalities he made a strong case for his point of view. His old friends on Capitol Hill welcomed him, and he may well have convinced some of them to support portions of his program. Of course, he never had a chance of obtaining agreement for his plan to lower taxes; the entire drift of public opinion and Presidential thinking was against him here. But he did salvage the capital gains revisions. Under the terms of the new Revenue Act, capital gains would be taxed at a maximum of 25 percent, while in some instances, short-term capital losses could be used to offset long-term gains.

The New York financial press greeted these changes as signs of Schram's influence in Washington and his abilities at persuasion. It was a minor victory, considering the problems of Wall Street in 1942. In addition, there was some question as to where the credit for the capital gains provisions should go, since several Treasury figures had favored this revision in the law too.** Finally, trading volume and underwritings did not rise with the passage of the new rates. Later on, when business did improve, Schram claimed that the six months' waiting period needed to establish long-term capital gains status helped deter speculation, but there was no evidence to support this, especially since the N.Y.S.E. did not develop a speculative fever during the war, and where raids were conducted, the O-T-C, and not the N.Y.S.E., was the arena.† For the rest of his tenure, however, Schram would carry the reputation of having helped write the pro-investment features of the 1942 Revenue Act, and even now, this is singled out by his friends as one of his most significant accomplishments.

* Some economists, of all ideological hues, noted that revisions in the tax laws in the early 1920s did result in higher net revenues. At the time, however, this was considered an incidental factor in the use of taxes to increase revenues.

** Paul, *Taxation in the United States*, p. 300.

† "The tax law since 1942 has said that money realized from the appreciation in securities held for more than six months is taxable not as income . . . but as a capital gain. . . . Astonishingly, many people of wealth and acumen seem unaware of this." "The Wall Street Situation," *Fortune*, March 1945, p. 121.

That same year Schram worked to assure harmonious relations between the Exchange and the S.E.C. Martin had avoided a round-table conference with Frank; Schram sought one with Purcell in order to guard against S.E.C. "attacks" on the N.Y.S.E. The two men had respect for one another that dated back to the time when they were young New Dealers in 1934. Both Schram and Purcell were technicians rather than ideologists. Each man had reached the height of his ambition; neither wanted to press ahead, for personal or political reasons. Too, the war bound them together. When they met in New York in July, they issued a joint statement regarding the need for cooperation "in the face of the current emergency." The two men and their aides and allies discussed such matters as war financing, the uniform reporting of financial information to federal and state agencies, accounting procedures, wartime coordination between the exchanges, and the allocation of securities under the provisions of the legislation banning holding companies in utilities. A second meeting in August concluded with a statement of agreement on all outstanding issues, and both Schram and Purcell told reporters that new meetings would be scheduled when needed. But there were no others, for from that time on, until the end of the war, Schram was able to act without important reference to the S.E.C. If the period of reform had ended in the late 1930s, Schram and Purcell signed the peace treaty between Wall Street and Washington in 1942.

Finally, Schram worked to assure harmonious relations with Albany. In February he appeared before the Assembly to ask for relief from the state's stock transfer tax in the face of declining business. Without this, he said, operations at the Exchange would be crippled, with brokers and specialists unable to earn sufficient profits to stay afloat. As would be the case in Washington later in 1942, Schram presented a well-reasoned brief, but he could not obtain the hoped-for revisions in taxes. He had failed, but so for that matter had his predecessors who had gone to Albany before him.

Schram alluded to the state taxes in his annual report, issued on February 27. The N.Y.S.E. showed a net loss of $2,229,560 for 1941, compared with less than $1 million for 1940. Expenses had already been cut as far as they could, and relief from outside sources could not be expected. Thus, Schram called for a revision in the rate structure.

The idea of rate revision was not new; nor did it originate with Schram, but rather from the floor, being transmitted to the administration through Stott. The new rates increased commissions by from 10 to 25 percent.

Having thus afforded the brokers a measure of relief, the board acted to assist the specialists, some of whom were on the edge of failure. Under the terms of a series of constitutional amendments "to provide a fair allocation of charges in relation to the services and benefits received," the fee for a post-space on the floor was lowered from $1,000 a year to $500, and in addition several minor charges were either eliminated or reduced. In all, these changes saved the average specialist around $20 a week—a pittance in the 1920s, but a considerable amount of money for some specialists in 1942. A cut in the annual dues from $1,000 to $750 provided a bonus for these marginal brokers and specialists.

The Exchange itself needed financial help and so was obliged to ask for special assessments from its members, as though taking a portion of the reduced fees in order to share in the largesse. All specialists and odd-lot brokers and dealers were to pay an annual fee of $150, while associate and relief personnel operating in the capacity of specialists would be assessed $10 a man. Finally—and most importantly—a charge of not more than 1 percent was authorized to be assessed on net commissions received and retained by each member and member firm. The rate would be reduced by half once $500,000 was collected in any given year, and removed when the sum reached $750,000.

These were small sums for the once-powerful N.Y.S.E. to seek, but there was no room for embarrassment regarding such matters on Wall Street in 1942. A decade earlier, Richard Whitney had been able to borrow as much money as would be raised by the special assessment, while his friends had thought little of signing over $100,000 or so on his word. In the first year of America's participation in World War II, the gathering of several hundreds of thousands of dollars required maneuverings and efforts, complete with long talks with members, some of whom felt the added assessments were unfair and didn't mind saying so.

The hard times of the war years accelerated the process of *embourgeousement* that had begun in the mid-1930s and was signaled then by Gay's election. By 1942 the clubby atmosphere of the old N.Y.S.E., though discernible, was rapidly fading. Many of the old-timers who had dominated the institution prior to the 1929 crash were still active, but they had lost power, and they lacked the will, stamina, and perhaps intelligence to attempt a revival. No longer was brokerage a profession for gentlemen alone, a dignified if somewhat rowdy one at times, for among other things, the pre-1929 concept of what constituted a gentleman appeared antique during World War II. Certainly few members could afford to treat the business as a part-time pursuit, a prelude to a late afternoon at the club, and one that could be left safely to clerks while senior partners vacationed at Newport or traveled to the south of France. The upstairs eating club, a symbol of the old days, still accepted outsiders, much to the chagrin of some veterans, but the Luncheon Club had no alternative but to continue the practice in order to obtain needed revenues, while on the floor, the new men were coming to dominate affairs, lead committees, and receive the respect of the men they had replaced.

There is such a species as a "new old-timer," men who had always emulated and admired the Establishment, and who after a period of rapid change came to direct it. At times advocates of change arrive to preserve, not alter, institutions. This was the type of man who gained control at the N.Y.S.E. during the war. Just as the reformers had their period of domination in the 1930s, the new old-timers had their day in the 1940s.

Many were self-made men who had begun their careers as clerks in the 1920s, and at that time had no greater ambitions than to serve the Establishment. Then, when the 1929 crash, depression, and New Deal—as well as the trauma of the Whitney disgrace—destroyed the old regime, they filled the places vacated by their former masters. The newspapers talked of the reformers of the Martin era as though they were "the wave of the future," and given a longer period of peace as well as economic recovery on the Street, they well might have been. But the new old-timers were gaining power too, if not in a flamboyant fashion, at least behind the scenes, on the lesser committees at first, and then the board. For the time being they cooperated with the reformers, but when the opportunity presented itself, they took command.

Schram and Stott were their prototypes. Capable, shrewd, hard working, and ambitious, they accepted the pre-1929 doctrines of free enterprise capitalism while bowing to the inevitable in the form of regulation. Given a chance they might have forced the reformers from the district, if not from Washington, but they knew this was out of the question. On the other hand, they had contempt for the playboy specialists and brokers of the 1920s, the sons of wealthy men who hadn't bothered to learn the business before coming to power. These new men worked with the reformers, usually in such a way as to preserve as much of the form and content of the old district as was possible. In 1935, it seemed they might be able to invigorate the old forms. In 1942–1943, evidence of a rebirth could be seen on the board and in the presidency.

More important, however, the new Old Guard dominated the floor, making certain that favored specialists received the best of the few new issues approved for trading, and doing what they could to aid their allies at the commission houses. These activities were known to members and most financial reporters and columnists, but the public had little knowledge of the changes. This was not the result of a conspiracy, but rather a lack of interest in such matters. Schram would make the headlines from time to time, and as far as most readers of newspapers were concerned, he was in command at the N.Y.S.E. But true power was in the hands of these new men.

John A. Coleman was undoubtedly the most able and powerful of the group. For a longer period than any other figure in N.Y.S.E. history, he dominated the floor, even while he avoided headlines and his influence was known to few outside of the district. Coleman was also a significant behind-the-scenes force in local and state politics, as well as one of the city's most prominent Catholic laymen.

Coleman was born in New York in 1901 to religious, middle-class parents. His father, a policeman, was stationed in the financial district. Coleman attended local parochial schools and, in 1916, took a job as clerk at the offices of E. H. Stern & Co. for sixteen dollars a month.

This was a period when boys with his background flocked to the area, most hoping for senior clerkships after twenty or so years in back offices. The New York Curb was the only exchange where east European Jews and Irish Catholics held positions of power, and that outdoor market was considered a financial ghetto by the Big Board. The senior market would deal with the curbstone brokers, but at a distance, and seldom as equals. A few Curb members managed to make the jump to the N.Y.S.E., usually as representatives for commission houses. Promotion to the specialist ranks was a rare occurrence.

By 1922 the Curb was indoors, and Stern & Co. was willing to purchase a seat for Coleman, who would serve the company's interests there. He did well, and in 1924 he was made a partner in the company and moved to the N.Y.S.E. Stern retired in 1928, and the firm was reorganized by Coleman and Paul Adler—who had been second-in-command in the old company—as Adler, Coleman & Co.

The tall, powerfully built Coleman was an exceptionally talented, stubborn, and tough man. He was also open and direct, with little of the deviousness and servility the Old Guard had been accustomed to finding in newcomers whom they considered their social and economic inferiors. For his part, Coleman was not interested in joining their clubs or attending their parties. He would mingle with the Old Guard during business hours and then devote his evenings to his family, church, and charitable functions. Whitney and his circle respected Coleman and the few others like him at the N.Y.S.E., but clearly would not admit these men to the inner circle of power. Had it not been for the crash of 1929, Coleman might never have advanced beyond the status of one of the lesser specialists.

Adler, Coleman & Co. survived the crash and managed well during the early depression years. In this period, men of Coleman's integrity and conservatism were prized, and so he rose rapidly in status and power. In 1937, Pope Pius XI appointed him a knight of St. Gregory. That same year, at the age of thirty-six, Gay selected Coleman for a place on the Conway Committee.

Coleman worked well with the other members. Reform was in the air and he realized that it made no sense to fight it. In addition, the somewhat puritanical Coleman must have relished the idea of driving the lax, inefficient, and morally corrupt Old Guardsmen from the Exchange. The system was good, he thought, but controlled in the past by the wrong kind of people. While Conway and the S.E.C. seemed to believe that decent men were not to be found in the district, and so large-scale institutional changes might be needed as well as outside regulation, Coleman was convinced that all that was necessary was a cadre of men of integrity. Ironically, the son of a New York policeman was becoming the ideological heir of J. P. Morgan the Elder.

Richard Whitney's illegal activities were uncovered in 1938, and the man who more than anyone else symbolized the Old Guard went to jail. That year, Coleman was elected for the first time to the Board of Governors. Three years later, he was elected vice-chairman and, in 1943, he became chairman. Given Schram's personality, as well as his limited knowledge of the Exchange's internal operations, Coleman became the most powerful executive there. The other board members —William Haffner, Ernest Jones, Sylvester Larkin, Robert Boylan, and Irving Fish among them—followed his lead. Like him, most would not have achieved prominence were it not for the decline of the Old Guard in the late 1930s.

By itself, the N.Y.S.E. could not have hoped to inspire interest in investing, even though Schram and others tried to convince the public that prices were low and investing safe. By 1943, however, even these attempts waned. Coleman and his circle, specialists for the most part, recognized that the Big Board might never again witness a major protracted bull market such as those of the past. Even if one did develop after the war, so it was believed, the market would not resemble the prototype of the 1920s, when it seemed everyone was making money. The commission brokers—the men who had accepted reforms in the mid-1930s and were allied then with the S.E.C.— operated at markets that competed with the N.Y.S.E. for business. These were chancy allies in any future contest with Washington. Furthermore, a new generation of Americans had grown to maturity since the 1929 crash, people to whom the N.Y.S.E. was a symbol of broken promises and depression. Finally, whatever interest in securities that might have developed in the late 1940s had been quashed by the war, when even the Exchange's leaders appeared on radio to urge Americans to purchase war bonds, not corporate stocks.

Faced with this situation, Coleman and his associates retrenched. Men who could not have hoped to lead the Exchange in its glory years now held sway over a much less powerful institution, and they seemed content to let it go at that. John Coleman had become the man to see if a specialist hoped to be assigned one of the few new issues that came to the floor.* He dominated the arena; with the exception of a handful of independent men who usually minded their own businesses and tried to steer clear of him, Coleman set the tone for the N.Y.S.E. He would leave his Park Avenue apartment at 7:00 each workday, attend church services, and arrive at his office at 9:00, and the Exchange floor fifteen minutes later. After the 3:30 closing he would return to his office for a few hours of work, and then leave for home, where he would spend the evening when not occupied with various charitable and political activities. From time to time, Coleman would play a round of golf, but other than that, he seemed to have no hobbies. Work and service—not play—were his interests.

Coleman was loyal and could be trusted to deliver on pledges. While he dominated the floor, specialists who had earned his favor received benefits in the form of new listings; those who transgressed obtained little, and at the height of his power Coleman was capable of driving such men from the Exchange. He frowned on members who violated breaches of faith, but could be lenient to one who ignored minor S.E.C. regulations. Coleman was a man of Wall Street, proud of his accomplishments and suspicious of outsiders.

In this way, and under the guidance of such a man, a new age of puritanism dawned at the N.Y.S.E., one that was narrower than any of the past. Perhaps this was so because Coleman had been trained on the floor, and was most comfortable there. Unlike previous Exchange giants—Jay Cooke, Morgan, Schiff, Baruch, Livermore, and even Martin—he was not an investment banker, speculator, or commission broker. These men, by virtue of their occupations if nothing else, had to be concerned with the larger outer world. Coleman lacked this broader outlook; imagination and innovation were not his strong suits. But given the nature of the times, perhaps these qualities were not badly needed. In this era, the N.Y.S.E. seemed an antique backwash and not a major bauble of American capitalism.

* * *

* In the process, Coleman became one of the N.Y.S.E.'s leading specialists. By 1947, when he left the chairmanship, Adler, Coleman & Co. was specialist for forty-seven stocks, including American Tobacco, Armour, Wilson, Liggett & Myers, International Minerals, Curtiss Wright, and General Public Service.

Just as the wartime period helped produce such men as Stott, Coleman, and Schram—intelligent and able people if not individuals of great vision and daring—so it provided an arena for the first of the "new breed" of speculator, although he was not recognized as such then. Almost all of the district's major speculators and manipulators have been "outsiders"—men from the provinces or overseas—who have angered and irritated the established powers or, in the case of Coleman, the new Establishment. They often arrive in groups, and their coming signals the beginning of a major bull move, almost as surely as the swallows of Capistrano indicate the advent of spring. But Serge Rubinstein, who arrived in New York shortly before the outbreak of World War II, held the stage alone.

Later on, Rubinstein told reporters that his father had been Rasputin's financial advisor, and his family one of the wealthiest and most powerful in Czarist Russia. Whether or not this was true is difficult to say, for Rubinstein was a master confidence man, wholly convincing when he applied his charm, but often discovered in lies.

He was born in 1908, in a country recovering from war and revolution and about to undergo more of the same. "The first thirty years of my life have been chaos," he said. Rubinstein claimed his family was the object of a massive hunt by the Soviets, and escaped to Finland with the Bolsheviks at its heels. From there the Rubinsteins went to Sweden, then to Geneva, and on to Vienna. While in Austria, at the age of sixteen, Serge participated in a jewelry swindle—his first major business operation. Then he left for Britain, enrolled at Cambridge, and graduated in 1920 with a degree in economics. Rubinstein wrote his thesis on dormant Swiss bank accounts. In the process, he earned several thousand pounds by contacting rightful heirs and owners, obtaining their money for them, and sharing in the proceeds. "Mr. Rubinstein never seemed to be short of cash—he had more than the other students," recalled one of his Cambridge friends.

Shortly thereafter, Rubinstein took control of a Korean gold mine, the Chosen Corporation, doing so through manipulations at a French bank. The mine was sold to the Japanese in 1933 for some $3.4 million in yen. With the aid of Japanese associates, Rubinstein smuggled most of the money into the United States, and then traveled to Shanghai and afterward to Macao. There he bribed officials into granting him a Portuguese passport. Then on to Canada. In April 1938 he entered the United States at Buffalo as Sergio Manuel Rubinstein de Rovello. He left after a short stay, returning in September. Apparently Rubinstein was occupied at this time in transferring his holdings to American banks. This was accomplished by late 1938, when he opened accounts at several major Wall Street commission houses.

Rubinstein speculated in a minor way at first, learning the intricacies of the American financial complex. At the same time he participated in refugee relief programs, dabbled in Presidential politics (contributing $10,000 to Roosevelt's 1940 campaign and becoming friendly with several senators and representatives), and sought women. Money, power, women—these fascinated Rubinstein, and he was intent on possessing all of them he could.

In 1942 Rubinstein was the "boy wonder" of Wall Street, its most famous and mysterious speculator. However, this reputation was not as great as might seem, since there were few like him in the district. Also, his manipulations were conducted off the trading floor, even when they involved N.Y.S.E.-listed stocks, for Rubinstein preferred secrecy and did all in his power to avoid contact with the S.E.C. By dealing with principals, he obtained control of Panhandle Producing and Refining Company, a listed firm that was a minor force in the oil industry. Panhandle was to act as a catch-all for several Rubinstein properties and speculations. At the same time, he dabbled in other securities—including the BMT subway in New York, about to be taken over by the city—and the arbitrage of foreign currencies. Afterward he would go to the nightclubs, prowling for women and contacts, and several times a year, Rubinstein sponsored costume parties at which he always appeared as Napoleon. He eluded the S.E.C., but had troubles with the Selective Service Commission, which seemed intent on drafting him into the Army. To avoid this, Rubinstein purchased a large part of the equity of Taylorcraft Aircraft Co., a small defense contractor, and claimed he was vital to the war effort as its guiding force. Still, the draft board persisted, even after Rubinstein's attempts to bribe some of its officials into granting him an exemption.

In 1944, Rubinstein obtained control of James Stewart & Co., a large construction firm. Then the Stewart family issued objections, and for the first time Rubinstein found himself in a proxy fight. Too, Rubinstein discovered that Stewart was in unsound financial shape and would show major deficits for the next few years. In fact, the company could drain off all of his assets and still fail, leaving Rubinstein bankrupt. This situation, added to growing desperation regarding the military draft, forced Rubinstein to the N.Y.S.E. floor. He merged Stewart into Panhandle, announced the formation of a construction operation that would undertake gigantic programs after the war, and tried to boost the price of Panhandle, then around $2.00 a share, at the Exchange, after which he intended to get out.

The campaign began in April 1945. Rubinstein cultivated the friendship of securities analysts at the commission houses and fed them optimistic reports regarding Panhandle. The market was rising anyway, and in the buoyant atmosphere of the day, they recommended the stock, which rose above 6 by mid-summer. Laird & Co. released a major advisory on the company, calling it a firm with "promising potentialities." In the fall, Panhandle announced the purchase of new properties in Throckmorton County, Texas, and the *New York World-Telegram* wrote glowingly of its potential, while the *Sun* reported that several new wells were about to gush. The *Wall Street Journal* thought the number would be seven. "It's pretty safe to figure Throckmorton'll return 15 million barrels," Rubinstein told reporters, as he handed out geologic surveys and maps to men who couldn't understand them but were impressed nonetheless. By October, Panhandle common was over 10. Then Rubinstein influenced friends at Naess & Cummings, a major advisory concern, who boosted the stock in reports. The stock rose again, and Rubinstein, overjoyed, began to sell.

And with his first sale, Panhandle dropped sharply. Given the small volume of the time, Rubinstein's "dump"—some 37,000 shares—forced the price down by more than a point.

This was Rubinstein's initial contact with the N.Y.S.E., at least as a plunger, manipulator, and speculator. All of his other deals had been conducted away from the floor. Now he had to master it if his fortune was to be preserved, and he didn't have the time to learn its lessons. So he hired an expert to do the job for him. Frank Bliss, known as "The Silver Fox of Wall Street," had been one of the most skillful floor managers for the syndicates of the 1920s. It was said that Bliss could dispose of a million shares of an issue in a week without disturbing its price. Bliss would buy and sell, buy and sell, always with an eye toward dumping the whole block in the end, but orchestrating the campaign with finesse. Naturally, Bliss had been in semiretirement throughout the 1930s—the markets of that decade could not absorb large blocks, even if there were syndicates to float them. From time to time, Bliss would travel to other exchanges in the hope of finding a situation from which he could profit. While in London speculating in gold, Bliss met Rubinstein. The two men only shared a few meals, but each took note of the other's interests and abilities. Now the boy wonder contacted the old man and asked his help in disposing of Panhandle shares. Bliss was eager for a last manipulation and agreed. On October 18, 1945, he conferred with Rubinstein to plan strategy, and on the following day Rubinstein met with associates to assure them he would hold on to his shares. On October 20, a Saturday, Bliss began selling.

The market was rising at the time, and on heavy volume. Bliss sold a total of 80,000 shares at an average price of around 10, without anyone the wiser. Encouraged, Rubinstein planted additional stories about the company. Bliss was able to sell another 28,000 shares at an average of over 11 in November. He disposed of 60,000 shares in December, accounting for half the Panhandle sales, even while the stock's price rose to 13⅝ as a result of Rubinstein's rumors. Standard & Poor's publication, *The Outlook*, publishing a favorable item on the company that month, spread news of a special dividend. In January, Bliss sold most of the rest of Rubinstein's holdings. By the end of the month he reported a total of 246,000 shares disposed of in two and a half months. Rubinstein had 50,000 shares remaining, and he held them until April 1946, when he resigned from the company. Even then, there was no inkling of what he had done.

The Rubinstein-Bliss distribution was the first major coup of its kind since the establishment of the S.E.C. Neither the agency nor the N.Y.S.E.'s floor observers took note of the activity in the stock. Nor was any taken of further activity later in 1946, when Rubinstein sold Panhandle short in anticipation of the stock's collapse. In all, the financial manipulator made more than $3.5 million on the stock during the four years he was associated with it and the company. And almost nothing of this was known in the district or in Washington.*

The Panhandle episode indicated that neither the Exchange nor the S.E.C. was capable of policing the district, and that given a major bull market, gross speculation and manipulation might well develop. It showed, too, that both the government and the Exchange had permitted their guards to drop. Considering the situation during the previous three years, this was understandable.

By 1943, the N.Y.S.E. appeared in a somnolent state. Like most wartime homefront organizations, it was staffed by old and middle-aged men, with some women being admitted to the floor due to the exigencies of war. (On April 28, 1943, Helen Hanzelin, a Merrill Lynch telephone clerk, became the first female employee of a member firm to work on the Exchange floor. Some specialists observed that such an innovation *would* come from a commission house.) The new generation of specialists and commission brokers were off to war, and of those who returned safely, many were expected to enter fields other than those related to the Exchange. Washington no longer viewed Wall Street as a serious power; even the S.E.C. began to slumber.

Trading was sluggish in the summer of 1943, and yet few specialists went on vacations. Some remained at their posts because they could not afford to leave, others had trouble finding sufficient fuel for their cars, or replacements on the floor. The tide of war appeared to have turned in Europe. That summer the *Exchange* magazine ran articles on the safety afforded investors by railroad bonds, the promise of

* The Rubinstein story has never been fully told, and since so much of the material is unknown to this day, it may never be. The best study is Gene Smith, *The Life and Death of Serge Rubinstein* (New York, 1962), pp. 126–57.

electronics (stressing such emerging firms as Crosley and Sparks-Withington), and the success of the third war-loan camapign. In August, analyst Frederick W. Thoben noted that the end of a major war often brought a bull market in its wake, and in September, the magazine ran an article entitled: "What Investors May Expect in Early Peace Days . . . Analysts' Viewpoints." Edward Barnes thought "the transition from war to peace will not halt the declining trend in the ratio of profits to sales and services." Barnes was not hopeful; a major bull market did not appear to be in the making. Lucien Hooper, though somewhat more optimistic, feared several basic weaknesses in the economy which, he wrote, "indicates somewhat lower stock prices over the near term—prices which will afford an opportunity to make some highly profitable investments for the postwar period." The market was sluggish. The Dow Industrials seemed rooted in the 140 area, with small price changes on low volume the rule.

This situation changed in 1944. As it became evident that an invasion of France was being prepared, possibly for early spring, and that the European war might come to an end the following year, Wall Street buzzed with talk of conversion to a peacetime economy. Fearful perhaps of what the changes would mean, while at the same time eager to capitalize upon them, large and small businesses hastened plans for the peace. Huge amounts of money would be needed, even if the government continued its financing efforts, which seemed unlikely. These firms turned to the Wall Street investment banks for aid, and beginning in July—after the D-Day invasion of Normandy—the volume of new financings began to grow. In September, some $418 million worth of new securities were floated, the highest amount for any month since 1940. In early October, *Business Week* reported that an additional $800 million might be offered before the sixth war-bond drive got under way in late November. Especially significant from the N.Y.S.E.'s point of view, many of the underwritings were for "war baby" companies, who for the first time were selling equity.

Almost all of the new issues were traded at the O-T-C markets. If previous experience held, some of the firms would seek listing at the Curb Exchange and then, after "seasoning," would transfer to the Big Board. Eager to hasten the process, the Exchange ran a series of advertisements publicizing listing requirements. Schram sent a notice to all members outlining the qualifications and procedures, and had the letter reprinted in *The Exchange* in order to give it wider circulation. In its small way in 1944, the N.Y.S.E. prepared for an influx of business after the war. At the time, it was believed that as the war ended new firms would list shares, while the public, though holding their war bonds, might be persuaded to buy stocks once more.

There was no appreciable increase in listings in early 1945, but trading volume rose sharply. Almost 39 million shares traded in January, a figure not seen since before the war, and in June, after victory in Europe, the volume was well over 41 million. For the year as a whole, average daily volume was 1,422,085 shares, the highest since 1937. Stock prices rose too, with bullishness intensifying as the war drew to a close. On August 14, the day Japan surrendered, the Dow-Jones Industrials closed at 164.79; a year earlier, it had been 146.77. The swift and unexpected collapse of Japan gave added drive to the bull market. In early January 1946, the Dow crossed the 200 mark headed upward, amid widespread cheering at the Exchange and headlines in the financial press. The last time the average had been at that level was October 1930, and then it was plunging lower.

The Stott-Schram-Coleman group had assumed leadership when business was poor, with little hope in sight for a change. With great skill they managed to keep the N.Y.S.E. afloat, adjusting well to the poor volume and lack of new listings. Having done this, they were confronted with what appeared at first to be a rampaging bull market. The additional business was welcomed, to be sure, but would the N.Y.S.E. be able to handle it, and adjust once again to a bullish mentality? Furthermore, would the market continue upward? The situation was uncertain in early 1946. By then, public support of President Truman had begun to wane, the reconversion effort had cost jobs, and some economists were predicting a depression to match that which followed World War I. Indeed, the nation's gross national product was shrinking, both in terms of constant dollars and those unadjusted for inflation.

Inflation was a major problem, as wage and price controls were abandoned on a piecemeal basis, contrary to Truman's desires. Wholesale prices rose almost 70 percent from the end of the war to 1948, the worst in American history to that time. This was followed by a period of recession, during which Congress passed a tax bill lowering corporate rates, doing so over Truman's veto. In all, the domestic political scene was in shambles, with the Republicans capturing control of Congress in 1946. By then, some members of his own party were calling for Truman's resignation or, if that were not forthcoming, his impeachment. At the same time, the great debate in the area of foreign policy was won by the "cold warriors," and the nation, having just concluded a major war, was obliged to turn once again to foreign affairs.

There was bullish economic news too. Although industrial production dropped by almost a third in 1945, burgeoning civilian demand for autos, housing, clothing, and other products took up much of the slack.

The Federal Reserve acted to increase the money supply, and at the same time, private corporations went to the capital markets to raise additional funds, which were added to retained wartime earnings and used for plant expansion. Private investment advanced by more than 500 percent from 1945 to 1950, as the nation's businesses went on a spending spree that rivaled the one of the late 1920s and early 1940s. Fears that government agencies would continue their wartime financings proved unfounded. Not even the greatest wave of labor upheaval in the nation's history—in 1946 there were some 5,000 strikes involving approximately 15 percent of the labor force—could dampen the boom.

This mixed picture befuddled many in 1945 and 1946. On the one hand, there was a measure of political instability and uncertainty, while on the other, the economy was clearly moving ahead, despite dislocations and fears of further inflation.

Faced with this situation, prices at the N.Y.S.E. jumped irregularly, confusing investors and market professionals but adding to public interest. Quotations rose sharply in March, April, and May of 1946, and then fell in June and July, collapsing on heavy volume in August and September. That summer a majority of stock analysts argued that a new bull market was in the making; they reversed their field in early autumn, after which prices declined once again, this time on low volume, reaching the 163 level in mid-May 1947. In all, it was a difficult market to predict and interpret, both in terms of prices and volume.

The active, vigorous markets of 1945–1946 did spark interest in Wall Street, and for the first time since 1937, young college graduates indicated desires for financial careers, with large numbers of them coming to the district seeking employment. In 1946, many brokerage houses resurrected their training programs and developed new ones. The increased volume seemed an indication the public was coming back to the markets, and they prepared for the move. By then, the veterans had returned too; the wartime fear that the young, talented specialists and commission brokers who were serving in the military might not come back to Wall Street proved unfounded. Their presence seemed to insure the continuity of experienced personnel necessary for smooth operations during the bull phase of 1945–1946.

At the time it appeared that the financial district might yet see a new era of glamor and high profits, something to match that of the 1920s, if without the wild speculation of that decade. There had been false starts toward bull markets in 1937 and 1942, but the first ended with bad political and economic news, the second with wartime setbacks. Wall Street had not seen a large-scale advance since the relatively laissez-faire days before the coming of the S.E.C., and some on the Street believed that Washington would act to quash any speculative move that might develop.

All the preconditions for a long-term bull market were there to be seen: an optimistic economic view, potential investors and speculators with plenty of money, Treasury and Federal Reserve policies supportive of prosperity, and an end to wartime controls and taxes. America was clearly the only major economic power in the world, even more so than it had been after World War I. The war had ended the depression, and now the war itself was over, with no new depression in its wake. Many waited for history to repeat itself—a post–World War II bull market to rival that of the post–World War I period.

The market rose, to be sure, and brokers appeared cheerful. Still, the district's confidence was thin, liable to rupture at the first sign of unpleasant economic or political weather. Old-timers still carried scars from the 1930s and were wary of talk of prosperity. Some anticipated a crash, even when corporate earnings proved good in 1946 and set records in early 1947. When stock prices began to slide rapidly in August 1946, and then accelerated in early September, they nodded to one another and spoke of their fears that this was the signal for a new collapse. On September 3, the Dow Industrials fell 10½ points on a volume of less than 3 million shares. Congressman Al Sabath of Illinois requested an investigation, charging that the market was being manipulated to effect the coming congressional elections, and for the next half year would repeat this belief in Congress and on the stump. In August 1947 the S.E.C. reported that "nowhere does it appear that the overall market action resulted from planned or concerted action by any group; nor do the activities of any group seem to have amounted to more than the free play of different opinions as to when to buy and when to sell." Further, it "found no evidence that market prices depended at any moment on manipulative activities." Thus, the N.Y.S.E. was exonerated of Sabath's charges that it harbored manipulators, but the episode indicated that the Exchange and the district were under careful surveillance. Sharp moves in any direction could result in an investigation, or a series of them. A generation of legislators had grown up knowing that Wall Street had become a favorite whipping boy for the nation's assorted ills. The anti–Wall Street mentality had been held in abeyance for the duration of the war. The Sabath attack indicated that even if a depression did not return, antibusiness attitudes still carried political clout. As a result, stock prices and trading volume failed to respond to good news and tended to decline on bad. By mid–1947, the price/earnings ratios for leading stocks were at their lowest levels in recent history.

Some Wall Streeters noted the disparity between the economy and the markets. Patrick McGinnis, leader of a medium-sized commission house, Pflugfelder, Bampton & Rust, had long urged investors to buy railroad stocks, and through public lectures and market letters managed to stir some interest in them. Charles Allen, the head of his own investment house, specialized in taking over sick firms, renovating their managements and balance sheets, and then, after a publicity campaign, selling a portion of their stocks to the public. Allen dabbled with such speculative issues as International Telephone & Telegraph, United Cigar-Whelan, and Wickwire Steel. Toward the end of the war he bought large blocks of Benguet, a Philippine gold mining operation, whose price rose when General MacArthur recaptured the islands. Allen concentrated on underwritings in 1945 and 1946, especially those for small "war baby" stocks. He spoke forcefully of his belief that the market rise of 1945–1946 was genuine. "Pretty soon we will go beyond the 1929 quotes," he told reporters in 1946. "There is nothing phony about this market. An investor who selects carefully can make some good buys at current levels."

Allen, a man given to hyperbole, hedged by indicating that selectivity was the key to successful investment in the postwar market. McGinnis said as much by recommending railroads, not industrials. Even the few speculators who made their appearance in the postwar period, capturing the attention of newspapermen and, for a while, congressmen like Sabath, did not operate as though believing a broad-based advance was possible.

Morris Blumberg—known by friends and reporters as "Little Blumberg from Brooklyn"—was one of the more colorful of the speculative crowd. He dabbled in stocks in the early 1930s, seeking bargains but rarely finding them. During the 1937–1942 slump, Blumberg worked as a label promoter for the International Ladies Garment Workers' Union, returning to the Street during the short 1942 bull market. He remained there throughout the war, and after Japan's surrender, Blumberg began speculating in low-priced "special situations," such as Fansteel, Raytheon, Childs, and Leonard Oil. The markets for these issues were thin, and so Blumberg had little difficulty in obtaining a commanding position in some of them. He would cause their prices to rise by buying shares steadily, then wait for good corporate news to push prices upward (or plant the news himself in the columns of friendly journalists), and then sell, just as carefully. Blumberg concentrated on over-the-counter issues, for some of his operations went beyond the purview of the law in relation to organized exchanges. Thus, his operations had minor impact on the N.Y.S.E. But Little Blumberg and others like him did serve to advertise securities, perhaps better than all the N.Y.S.E.'s campaigns. Through wheeling and dealing, Blumberg managed to parlay a $1,500 stake in 1942 to several millions of dollars in 1946. "You haven't seen anything yet," he would scream at reporters, as he prepared for his next coup.

Little Blumberg was small fry compared with the great plungers of the 1920s—Jesse Livermore, Arthur Cutten, Percy Rockefeller, and George Breen, for example. He provided comic relief and good copy, but Blumberg was not a man to inspire awe. He did not possess that air of mystery and aura of power that master manipulators exuded. And there had never been a major bull market without such individuals.

Even Serge Rubinstein had left the scene temporarily. Shortly after concluding the Panhandle operation he was tried for draft evasion, found guilty, and sent to jail. He was released in 1948, re-entered the market and scored several new victories. Once again he was in trouble with the law, this time for manipulations. After a series of legal suits—as well as one in which the government tried to force him to leave the country—Rubinstein emerged wealthier than ever. He did not survive to participate in the next major bull market, however. Rubinstein was murdered on January 27, 1955, and the case was never solved. Some newspapermen compared the dead man with the giants of the past. His coming, they thought, was a sign that the bull market was dawning; the writers implied that other speculators, like Rubinstein, would soon make their appearances.

They were wrong—or, at least, those speculators and manipulators who did operate in the market in the late 1950s and throughout the 1960s were of minor importance. A bull market was in the making, but it would be different from any of the past. Serge Rubinstein and Little Blumberg were not the heralds of speculators yet to come, but rather throwbacks to those of the past. The next bull market would have its plungers and moving forces, but they would not be lone individuals with millions to back their bets. Rather, they would be faceless individuals, trustees of institutional wealth measurable in the billions of dollars. A new kind of economy was being created in America, and a new kind of prime investor. It would be several years, however, before this was recognized.

CHAPTER 9

The Outlines of Change

Economic and political news during the last half of the 1940s was not monotonous. Instead, conditions were either better than had been anticipated or far worse. Unexpected events also fell into these categories. If the nation did not undergo the much-forecast depression, it did suffer through one of its most severe periods of inflation, which by 1947 appeared incapable of solution. Although Harry Truman did not prove the blunderer many feared he would be, political uncertainty and economic crossfire marked his first years in office. These were further complicated by the dawning of the Cold War and the great debate over internal security.

The pent-up demands for goods and services continued to bolster the economy, as money in the form of savings and higher wages was plentiful and appeared to arrive in a never-ending stream. President Truman seemed unable to cut back on spending, while the Federal Reserve cooperated with the Treasury in maintaining low interest rates. Federal Reserve Chairman Thomas McCabe defended this stance. In May of 1949 he said: "I am convinced that we could not have abandoned our support position during this period without damaging repercussions on our entire financial mechanism as well as seriously adverse effects on the economy generally." Former Chairman Marriner Eccles, who had resigned over this issue, responded: "In making a cheap money policy for the Treasury, we cannot avoid making it for everybody. All monetary and credit restrictions are gone under such conditions; the Federal Reserve became simply an engine of inflation."

Americans seemed unsure as to how long the apparent prosperity would last, unclear as to the meaning of the international situation, and lacking in confidence in the nation's leadership. On the one hand, the gross national product rose from $210.7 billion in 1946 to $259.4 billion in 1948. But when adjusted for inflation, the figures for the two years were almost the same, as was real income per capita, which rose by only ten dollars in the span.

The Republicans could hardly have hoped for a better political situation. After sixteen years of the New Deal and Fair Deal, they seemed certain of retaining control of Congress and capturing the White House in 1948. The party selected Thomas E. Dewey and Earl Warren at its convention and then settled back to await the November victory celebrations. The Democrats—divided, dispirited, and resigned to defeat—nominated Truman with little enthusiasm.

On the whole, Wall Street welcomed the anticipated change. There was talk of a "baby bull market" early in the year. Automobile sales were strong, and despite uncertainties regarding price supports, most farmers appeared optimistic. The excess profits tax, first enacted in 1940, was repealed on the last day of 1947, while at the same time Cold War defense orders were rising. The profit situation was excellent. All that was lacking was political confidence, and that would come after the November elections.

The Dow Industrials were at the 180 level in early January. The market declined to 165 by mid-February and then began to climb on higher volume. In late May, the average was over 190, and there was talk of a 230 Dow by election day. Prices retreated in the summer, however, as though expecting a rally in the fall. It arrived in October, gathering steam as election day approached. The Dow closed at 189.76 at the pre-election session.

The market collapsed when Truman was elected; the next day the Dow fell more than 7 points on a volume of 3,237,000 shares, the busiest in a half year. Prices declined for the rest of the month, leveled off, and fell again. By June 1949 the Dow was in the 160s and apparently headed to still lower levels. Once more, Wall Street had seen a false start toward a boom era.

The news was bad that summer. It was a recession year, and although inflation was no longer a major threat, unemployment took its place and was even more ominous. The jobless rate was 5.5 percent, the highest since 1940, and during the summer it reached beyond 6 percent, with over 4 million workers seeking jobs. The gross national product declined, both in terms of current prices and those adjusted for inflation. Now stories of labor unrest appeared. The newspapers spoke of the possibility of a new wave of strikes. Congress had approved the Marshall Plan, the North Atlantic Treaty Organization had been formed, and there were other signs that the Cold War was intensifying. The communists seemed on the brink of success in China; late that year, Chiang Kai-shek would be forced to flee the mainland. In Washington, Truman was barely more popular than he had been the year before. Despite his victory, he lacked a strong mandate. Never a charismatic leader, he went about his work scarcely seeming to care about public reactions.

Money was tight in the early summer of 1949, even though the discount rate was 1½ percent—where it had been since August of the previous year. The Treasury reported difficulties in selling long-term bonds, and there was talk that interest rates would soon rise, causing further complications. This seemed to indicate that stock prices would decline, and short selling began in earnest, a sign that whatever confidence in securities that still remained was being eroded.

On June 14, 1949, the Dow Industrials had an intraday low of 160.62. Volume was 1,345,000 shares—very high for the period, and in a down market, since the Dow fell 3 points. There was nothing extraordinary in the news—the United States was continuing its troop pull-out from Korea, the Berlin blockade seemed on the verge of ending, and the trial of American communist leaders continued; baseball activities appeared as interesting as those in other parts of the national spectrum. At the Exchange, Emil Schram was delivering a speech urging reductions in the capital gains levy and a 10 percent credit on dividends to taxpayers as a step toward the elimination of double taxation. The board approved the creation of a new public relations committee, on which John Coleman, now the past-chairman, would serve. Upstairs at the N.Y.S.E. the accountants were completing a report on activities during the first half of the year. Even then, it was certain operations were at a loss, although conditions seemed to be improving.

Bull markets usually end with a bang—a panic, a collapse, the failure of a leading bank or industrial enterprise, the coming of a war—and even though prices may recover thereafter, the spirit seems gone and the decline or stagnation begins. Thus, October of 1929 stands out as the symbol, if nothing else, of the end of the bull market of the 1920s. This was followed by a generation of false starts, minor bull moves, and then sharp falls, after which the cycle would repeat itself.

Brokers and specialists can recognize the conclusion of a bull market and know what stagnation and false starts are, at least in retrospect. But they cannot determine the time a major upward sweep begins. Years later, when such individuals were asked to select an event, or a date, that marked the initiation of the bull market of the postwar era—greater by most measures than that of the 1920s—they expressed puzzlement, and even wonder, that a person could be interested in such matters. Some would opt for one event or another, few could agree on a single one, and in more cases than not, their recollections were incorrect. This is not surprising, for bull markets—even the most important of them—had usually had inauspicious beginnings.

No single happening or date can be isolated and set down as the first day of the great rise. It was called later on "The Eisenhower Bull Market," but in fact it did begin during Harry Truman's second administration and was in full flower when the Republicans recaptured the White House in 1952. Yet so disliked was Truman at the time—by the press no less than by the public—that it was not given his name. For want of a better date, June 14, 1949, might be selected as a starting point, for the averages would never again touch that low point. For reasons no analyst could have predicted, prices began to rise in mid-June and they continued upward for every month of the next twelve, completing the first leg of the recovery on June 12, 1950, at which time the Dow Industrials stood at 228.38. In the space of one year—minus two days—the average had risen 67.76 points, and the Street was optimistic once more.

Viewing the period retrospectively, it would appear that the great bull market of the 1950s and 1960s was preordained by the economics of the situation. Given excellent and growing corporate profits, America's pre-eminent position in the world, federal acceptance of deficit spending as a legitimate device, as well as close to universal agreement that a major depression must not be allowed to reoccur whatever the cost, and the appearance of new technologies and merchandising techniques to stimulate consumption and production, the prices of common stocks were "bound to rise" and the general public "drawn to the market."

This is an attractive and plausible argument, but one that is not wholly convincing after a study of public attitudes of the time. Furthermore, there have been periods of prosperity during which stock quotations fell or stood still, and many when prices did not reflect the movement of the economy insofar as magnitude of advance or decline. If investors were logical and students of finance, the market would not have risen on heavy volume in the late 1920s, stagnated in 1939–1942, or behaved so erratically in 1972–1974. Indeed, had investors been swayed by economic conditions and had prices reflected "realities," the great upward move would have begun during the war, paused perhaps to test the wind in 1945–1946, and resumed the following year. Instead, it began in 1949. Why? And still more interesting a question, why did the lack of a major bull market not surprise Wall Streeters? Finally, why did the financial district in general and leaders at the Big

Board take so long to recognize the configurations of the new era in investing?

Some of the reasons and parts of the answers have been discussed already. An entire generation of investors had been frightened from the market by the decline of 1930–1933, which followed the crash of 1929. The long depression of the 1930s served to cement attitudes, and by the early 1940s the 1929 crash had taken on an almost mythological quality. Historians and journalists described it as one of the major turning points in American history, something akin to the battle of Lexington in 1775 or the firing upon Fort Sumter in 1861, while Franklin Roosevelt took on the aura of a Washington or Lincoln, with Herbert Hoover cast in the role of George III at worst, James Buchanan at best. In other words, 1929 had become more a symbol than an event, and the crash and depression that followed were magnified and enhanced in the recitation to the potential investors of the 1940s, young people to whom the crash was a dimly remembered occurrence. Thus, one generation was repelled by the market, and that generation taught its children to avoid Wall Street. During the war and even in the immediate postwar period, these people awaited a market decline. For them, good news was to be discounted and the bad magnified. In time, such individuals would be drawn to the market, but they would come with no small amount of trepidation, prepared to leap away at the first sign of "another 1929."

Political uncertainty also played a role. The situation might have been different had Roosevelt lived to serve out his term, for those who disliked the man and his policies, and even distrusted him, conceded that he was a strong, able, charismatic leader, one who could rally a nation and had proven it on several key occasions. Harry Truman inspired no such sentiments. He seemed erratic and, after three terms of F.D.R., "a little man." His clashes with Congress, his inability to hold together the Roosevelt coalition, and his outbursts of temper disturbed those who felt that a strong White House was necessary for national confidence, while the Cold War and the specter of the atomic bomb added to the uncertainties. Harry Truman may not have resembled the caricature of Hoover that had evolved by the mid–1940s, but he was no Roosevelt either.

There was a recession in 1949, a mild one to be sure and one from which the nation recovered quickly. This kind of "correction" seemed to many the worst that could be expected, and it certainly bore little resemblance to those of the past. Corporate profits declined, but there were few dividend cuts, while late in the year both higher profits and dividends appeared likely. The advance from the recession did not end fears of a new depression but it did assuage some of the more pessimistic forecasters. At the same time, the acceptance of the Cold War and the uniting of the nation in a new moral crusade ended the period of doubt and uncertainty that had existed during the "great debate" in 1947–1948. Unpopular though he remained, Truman did achieve a degree of stature and respect as President of a nation that had become "the leader of the free world." Thus in 1949 and early 1950 there was a period of relative calm, a sense that the country had isolated its problems even though they were far from resolution. Communism —both external and internal—was the enemy, not depression and political division.

There was yet another problem, which in terms of public concern may have been a close second to communism. Ever since the war, inflation had troubled Americans, and after the fighting had ended, it became a major interest. This was a new concern for a generation of Americans who had lived through the 1920s and 1930s, decades during which prices tended to remain constant or even decline. The consumer price index was 85.7 in 1920 and by 1929 had fallen to 73.3, in the face of great prosperity and economic boom. The index went to 55.3 in the severe depression year of 1933 and by 1939 had risen only to 59.4. With the demands of war and in spite of wage and price controls, the index began to climb, so that in 1945 it stood at 76.9. Then followed the postwar inflationary spiral, and in 1948, the consumer price index peaked at 102.8. With federal spending on the rise—and promising to go higher—as a result of Cold War and social concerns, given mounting demand for consumer goods and the need for capital expansion, and adding a congressional unwillingness to pass controls legislation and an Administration determined to keep money rates low, the inflation appeared unstoppable.

But there was a pause, in 1949, when, due in part to the recession, the consumer price index actually declined for the first time since 1939. As recovery picked up, prices rose once more, and in early 1950 inflation was again a major threat.

The situation was different from what had existed in 1946–1947. Then it appeared the spiral would be ended with a recession or depression. By 1949–1950, it seemed inflation had become a permanent part of American life and would have to be dealt with on that basis. A people who had come of age fearing depression, and had stressed security in every aspect of their lives, putting their surpluses into government savings bonds and banks "to guard against a rainy day," now faced a situation where their wages bought less each month and the value of the dollar was declining. Conservative columnist Westbrook Pegler wrote that inflation was expropriation by a profligate government and that purchasers of war bonds in 1942 would, on redeeming them in 1952, receive less purchasing power than they had loaned the government. Liberal financial columnist Sylvia Porter protested. Pegler was unpatriotic, she said, and if all holders of government bonds cashed them in, there would be chaos. But she couldn't respond effectively to his argument.

Money rates were low that year. In August the prime rate—the amount of interest banks charged their most secure clients—was 2 percent. This was a time when savings accounts paid 3 percent, and 4 percent mortgages were not unheard of. The Federal Reserve's discount rate—the rate charged member banks for borrowings—was 1 percent, rose to 1¼ percent in January, and to 1½ percent in August amid protests from expansionists that the high cost of money would stifle growth. Such low rates could hardly compensate investors for their losses through inflation. A bank account made less sense each month, as inflation continued, and yet most Americans saw little else to do with their surplus funds. Thus, time deposits grew in this period, though not as rapidly as had been anticipated.

Then there was the stock market, depressed as it had been for several years even while dividends continued to rise. In 1946 the dividend return as calculated on Moody's Industrial Index was 3.75 percent. By 1948 the payout was at 5.86 percent, and in 1949, 6.82 percent. That year it was possible to purchase shares in leading industrial concerns—companies which had paid dividends through the

SELECTED COMMON STOCKS, 1949

Company	*Earnings Per Share*	*Dividend*	*Price Range*
Bethlehem Steel	$ 9.69	2.40	33⅞ – 23⅛
Chrysler	15.19	5.25	58 – 49⅛
Colgate-Palmolive	5.33	3.00	43⅞ – 29⅜
Firestone Tire & Rubber	2.21	1.00	14⅛ – 10¾
General Motors	14.64	8.00	73½ – 51¾
International Paper	7.13	2.50	37⅛ – 20⅞
National Cash Register	5.91	2.50	36⅜ – 30⅜
Safeway Stores	5.36	1.25	33½ – 16¼
Standard Oil (New Jersey)	8.94	4.00	75 – 60
United Fruit	6.25	4.00	55⅝ – 44¼
United States Steel	5.40	2.25	26½ – 20¼

SOURCE: *Moody's 1956 Handbook of Widely Held Common Stocks*

depression, many for over half a century—and receive a return of well over 7 percent.

During 1949 and for the next few years, stories about inflation and suggestions on how best to counter it appeared regularly in the nation's newspapers, and were prime subjects for syndicated columnists and radio and television commentators. Harvey Runner of the *New York Herald Tribune* wrote, on January 28, 1950, that "the purchasing power of the dollar—whether used by the public for personal or home needs or by businessmen to run their offices and factories—is at the lowest point in recent history," and he recommended the acquisition of common stocks as a hedge against inflation. So did Lewis Haney in the *Journal American*. "So it looks as if speculative momentum based on fear of inflation is the main steam behind the market's rise," he wrote the following month. The dominant force on Wall Street, added Sylvia Porter of the *New York Post*, is fear.

> It's fear that the value of cash in the bank and in U.S. bonds will dwindle even more, and an individual may "protect" his resources by owning stocks that may rise as the dollar goes down.
>
> It's fear that the men in the Administration and Congress won't have the nerve to hit hard at the inflation spiral, and, thus, an individual might as well do the best he can for himself.
>
> In short, fear of inflation is definitely catching hold. And it's useless to pretend this isn't so; it is.
>
> Since early January [1950] I've been asking stockholders, new and old, why they're in the market. Every one I've interviewed—every one!—has implied or mentioned this factor.
>
> For instance, from one: "Ordinarily, I'd never think of stocks. But today, I guess you have to have some for your own protection."
>
> From another: "I finally gave in and cashed my war bonds to buy these stocks. It'll give me a chance to recoup."
>
> From a third: "This salesman showed me in black and white how much better off I would have been if I had bought his fund [a nationally known investment trust] instead of keeping my cash in the bank."
>
> In the 1920s, it was a boom based on belief in the "new era" and the nonsense that the merry-go-round would go round forever.
>
> In the 1930s, it was a boom based on relief from the catastrophic depression that put an end to that merry-go-round nonsense.

In the 1940s, it was a boom based on war-created confidence in production and in attractive corporate profits.

Now it's a boom based in large part on doubt of the dollar.

"The stock market is sounding a warning bell as to inflation," added Leslie Gould. "The market is being put up by a flight from the dollar by people with surplus savings."

At such times in the past, many Americans sought the protection of gold and silver. But the gold price was pegged at $35 an ounce, and given the strong international position of the United States, there seemed little chance it would rise. In any event, Americans were forbidden by law to hold gold. As far as silver was concerned, its price was low; in 1949, the amount of silver in a dime was worth less than seven cents. Had the inflationary spiral gone higher—to over 10 percent per annum—fearful investors might well have turned to gold, either in the form of coins or stocks, and perhaps even illegal purchases of bullion. But this was not the case. At a time of high stock yields and cheap money, equities seemed a better way of mitigating the effects of inflation.

Given the increased earnings of American corporations, which were translated into higher dividends, stock prices may have risen gradually, while volume expanded slowly. As it was, the rush to equities which began in late 1949 and continued into 1950 was caused, in large part, by a small-scale buyers' panic. In this period trading volume advanced at a rapid rate, and prices rose at a steady pace.

The bull market began in the utilities, historically the safest of stocks, and then spilled over into the high-yield industrials. By early 1950 the railroads, predicting record earnings, started to inch upward. The Korean War began on June 25, and this precipitated a selling wave that threatened to put an end to the bull move. During the next week, 17.1 million shares were traded, the busiest since the panic that accompanied the outbreak of World War II in 1939, and the Dow Industrials fell from 224.35 to 209.11. Then recovery set in, and, led by the rails—expected to do well in a wartime atmosphere—prices moved upward once more. The year ended in a holiday mood on Wall Street, even though hostilities continued and Chinese troops had entered the battle. Almost 60 million shares changed hands in December, making it the most hectic month at the N.Y.S.E. in sixteen years. Average daily volume in 1950 was 2 million shares, also the best since 1934. There was no doubt the market was broadening and that new people were buying stocks and bonds. Also, minor setbacks, such as the beginning of the war and the entry of Chinese troops, were shrugged off after a few turbulent sessions, following which the upward march resumed. On the other hand, prices would leap ahead

MONTHLY VOLUME AND DOW-JONES CLOSING PRICES, 1949–1950

Month	*Volume* (millions of shares)	*Industrials* (price on last trading session of the month)	*Railroads*	*Utilities*
1949				
January	18.8	179.12	52.57	34.68
February	17.2	173.06	47.71	34.56
March	21.2	177.10	49.02	35.52
April	19.3	174.16	47.27	35.41
May	18.2	168.36	44.49	35.05
June	17.8	167.42	42.57	34.41
July	18.7	175.92	44.77	35.72
August	21.8	178.66	45.09	36.69
September	23.8	182.51	47.87	37.86
October	28.9	189.54	47.86	38.53
November	27.2	191.55	48.11	39.26
December	39.3	200.13	52.76	41.29
1950				
January	42.6	201.79	55.09	42.22
February	33.4	203.44	55.34	42.81
March	40.4	206.05	54.83	42.67
April	48.2	214.33	56.07	42.78
May	41.6	223.42	56.28	43.80
June	45.6	209.11	52.24	40.64
July	44.5	209.40	60.86	37.78
August	38.5	216.87	62.90	38.60
September	38.6	226.36	67.64	40.46
October	48.4	225.01	66.28	40.02
November	43.1	227.60	68.53	39.80
December	59.8	235.41	77.64	40.98

SOURCE: Maurice Farrell, *The Dow Jones Averages, 1885–1970.*

on good news, and even rumors were beginning to have a similar effect. By late 1950 the signs of a nascent bull market of major proportions were there to be viewed and pondered.

The N.Y.S.E. had done little to make all of this possible, or even to encourage the developments once they had begun. Emil Schram was tired and ill, and he spent a good deal of his time recuperating and away from the Exchange. The board was concerned with a new automation study then being prepared and for several months debated the wisdom of remaining closed on Saturdays throughout the year.

Internal matters, in particular a possible restructuring of the board, were of interest, as the power of the specialists grew, and so external business seemed more remote than before. The Exchange's leadership was concerned with encouraging companies to seek listing, hoping in this way to add to the volume of trading, and there was success in this area. In 1947 there were 1,334 stocks listed at the Exchange; for the first time the 1931 record of 1,308 was surpassed. By 1949 the figure was 1,419, and new listings were being approved at a near-record rate. In effect, this provided the store with additional merchandise, but it did not serve to attract customers. Whenever he was able, Schram made pronouncements on the subject of the virtues of stock ownership, usually before state chambers of commerce and the like, and other N.Y.S.E. leaders did the same. The special committee on public relations, established in June of 1949, did little more. The stress here was on institutional advertising, the kind that appeared in business magazines such as *Fortune* and *Dun's*. It would be promoted through *The Exchange*, the N.Y.S.E.'s own journal which, in the late 1940s, was still stodgy and curiously old-fashioned. Such campaigns had been conducted in the past, always without significant impact. In the absence of new ideas and approaches, the N.Y.S.E. continued along the established paths.

Charles Merrill, an outsider considered frivolous by most Wall Street leaders, capitalized on this situation and helped create a better mood for investment. Head of Merrill Lynch, Pierce, Fenner & Beane, the nation's largest commission house, Merrill was a significant figure. Still, he was far from the established sources of power. He showed little interest in the Exchange's management and the internal politics of the district, stating on several occasions that he found them boring and rather foolish. Nor did he have much to do with the established forces in investment banking, a closed community for several decades and one which, in the late 1940s, was under attack by the courts for violations of antitrust acts. Merrill was no crusader attempting to lead the commission houses in a counterattack against the specialists at the Exchange, a person who yearned for a political career, or a man of ambition hoping to remake institutions in his own image. Despite his hyperbole, he was no visionary, but rather a master opportunist in the best sense of the term, who, perhaps without always understanding his own role, was as revolutionary a figure for the N.Y.S.E. as any of the New Dealers, and who emerged in the late 1940s and early 1950s as the most influential Wall Streeter since World War I. Just as the elder Morgan had helped refashion investment banking and became the spokesman for the industry, so Merrill did the same for commission brokerage, with an even greater impact on the nation.

Commission brokerage had undergone many changes during the

previous half century. Before World War I, most brokers affiliated with N.Y.S.E. houses were conservative and prudent men, concerned with estate planning for the wealthy and the preservation of capital and production of annuities for those who sought their services. At times they would act as agents for trustees, and many of the most prominent and successful brokers were more at home with bankers than with private clients. Brokerage was a profession for gentlemen—at least, this was the ideal—who would act as a buffer between their wealthy customers and the harsh world of investment banking and the turmoil of the district. Large-scale speculators would act on their own, and often did so on the Exchange floor, in this way eliminating the need for brokers. Or if they did employ their services, plungers went to smaller and not very well known houses, since the major ones were not interested in speculation, nor the speculators with the attitude of the old-line brokers.

Of course, there were others, brokers for bucket shops and gamblers, who were on the periphery of the N.Y.S.E., or attached to marginal houses specializing in Curb and over-the-counter issues, or dealing at the outlaw Consolidated Stock Exchange, at the time the only major rival to the N.Y.S.E.

The situation changed dramatically in the 1920s, when for the first time since the end of the Civil War, mass speculation was realized. Just as brokerage expanded rapidly in the 1870s, so it did in the 1920s, drawing people who had no previous background, few connections, and little knowledge into the field. These men would only know a bull market, when it seemed that almost every stock was going up. They prospered, as did their clients, while the older men, still operating within the investment framework of the prewar era, did poorly, and lost many of their accounts. In 1909, the broker who recommended racy stocks was deemed irresponsible; the conservative broker who suggested government bonds in 1928 was considered out of tune with the times. Both judgments were justifiable.

Prudence became a virtue once more in the 1930s, when the daring young men of the previous decade were flushed out of the district. Given the temper of the time and the kinds of markets that existed throughout most of the Roosevelt years, brokerage was scarcely the field to attract aggressive, ambitious young men. Nor did the profession see the return of the respectable sons of old families, for the social changes of the New Deal and World War II era either helped eliminate those families or obliged them to adjust to the period through accepting the new dispensation. The brokers of the immediate postwar period were of a low level of ambition, promise, and imagination, as were the leaders at many of the brokerages. Given the situation in the industry, this was not surprising. Brokerage was not growing, and the conservatives of the 1930s were in positions of power, not likely to relinquish them willingly. Wall Street had a bad reputation, and its performance was just as sorrowful, while most American business was expanding. Individuals more noted for stamina and persistence than originality could be found at the major houses, while the marginal ones attracted hustlers and drifters, part-time workers seeking additional income and earning it on a percentage-of-the-take basis. The typical broker either resembled a life-insurance salesman or a carnival huckster, and he received the receptions those kinds of practitioners expected. In any case, brokerage could not be counted upon to increase interest in securities. Nor did there seem much of a chance for change.

Charles Merrill had survived all of this, and had maintained his own programs, making them acceptable by force of personality more than anything else. Although well known in the financial district, his name meant nothing to most of the country in the immediate postwar period. Merrill was sixty years old on V-J Day, head of a successful brokerage, but little more. He spent part of his time in New York, and much of the rest in his home at Palm Beach. He had few friends in the district, and didn't particularly care to have more. Throughout his life, Merrill had a rather low opinion of the intelligence and abilities of people in the business, although he prudently kept such sentiments to himself most of the time.

Like many important Wall Streeters of his age, Merrill came to the industry from the outside. He was born in 1885 in a small town near Jacksonville, Florida, the son of a local doctor who supplemented his income by running a drugstore as well. Charles attended the nearby schools and then went north to a preparatory academy. He entered Amherst in 1904, and in his two years there spent more time selling suits to undergraduates and helping manage a local boarding house than attending classes. Merrill then switched to Michigan Law School and liked it even less. He was at loose ends and engaged to be married, when his prospective father-in-law offered him a job as office boy in the Manhattan headquarters of the Patchogue-Plymouth Mills. While deciding, Merrill played professional baseball in the South, found he couldn't hope to make the major leagues, and in 1907 arrived in New York, in time for the financial panic of that year. Soon after, the engagement was broken and Merrill lost his job. He traveled to Michigan, considered his prospects, made a final stab at law, and in 1909 returned to New York seeking a position on Wall Street. While there he lived at the YMCA, where his roommate was Edmund C. Lynch, then a salesman for Liquid Carbonic Corp.

Merrill found a job at George H. Burr & Co., a brokerage

specializing in commercial paper. Burr's bond division manager fell ill, and Merrill was his replacement. It was a boom period, and Merrill did well. Shortly thereafter he hired Lynch as his assistant, and the two men worked harmoniously together. In 1913 Merrill moved to Eastman, Dillon & Co. as sales manager, and Lynch succeeded to the managership at Burr & Co. He left Eastman, Dillon in 1914 to form his own company, Charles E. Merrill & Co., starting with capital of less than $3,000. The following year Lynch left Burr to join the new firm, which then became Merrill Lynch & Co.

The company hoped to do a general brokerage business and at the same time seek underwritings of small concerns that were of little interest to the major investment bankers. Like most of the brokerages of the day, Merrill Lynch stressed conservative investment practices, preservation of capital, and dividend yield; unlike them, it also believed in advertising, and Merrill Lynch ads appeared regularly in the local newspapers, while it pioneered in the writing and distribution of sales brochures. Merrill felt the general public would buy stocks for investment if it realized that one did not need a great deal of capital to open an account and that it could do better in stocks than at savings banks. But his firm had to be cautious in dealing with neophytes, and this required a new kind of sales force. "I notice a very unfortunate tendency [on the part of our salesmen] to dwell upon the profits a customer is likely to make, instead of on the merit of an issue as an investment. . . . We try to be conservative and careful," he wrote in 1916. "Bear in mind that in every sale you are either destroying or building good will [for the next sale], which is our most valuable asset."

Merrill clearly had a talent for salesmanship, and the firm did moderately well. He was fascinated with selling as a profession, and this led him to attempt underwritings of retail establishments, the first of which was McCrory Stores, the initial Merrill Lynch offering, coming in 1916 and earning the firm $300,000.

By the time Merrill and Lynch entered the Army in 1917, they were millionaires. They left the firm in the hands of associates, most of whom began as salesmen. On their return in 1918, they picked up where they had left off and, after surviving the postwar slump, did well during the great bull market. Merrill Lynch was not a major underwriter during the 1920s, nor one of the larger houses. In fact, Merrill did much of his brokerage business through E. A. Pierce & Co., then the biggest wire house on the Street. A good deal of his time was spent in taking retail chain operations public and serving as their advisor. S. S. Kresge, Lane Bryant, Grand Union, Lerner Stores, and Western Auto Supply were among the more important Merrill Lynch undertakings. Merrill was also involved with Melville Shoe, J. C. Penney, and First National Stores; in 1926 he helped form Safeway Stores and remained a force in that firm for the rest of his life. He was not considered a major Wall Street figure, however, and certainly not one of the leaders of the bull market. Nor did he devote much time to promotion; in that period such encouragement was not needed, and, in any case, the newspaper columnists and speculators did a better job than any investment banker or broker. Rather, Merrill was considered a bright young man of no particular depth, a person with interesting ideas in the area of mass merchandising and, in the 1920s, something of a playboy. He also held conservative investment ideas, and his market letter, sent to clients, often stressed the dangers of speculation in a bull market. Because of his caution, Merrill Lynch's brokerage business suffered, but he more than made it up with underwritings.

By early 1928, Merrill had become convinced that stock prices were far too high and that a crash was imminent. He was not alone in this, but, still, his persistence bothered his colleagues, who suggested he see a psychiatrist. According to a company legend after a few sessions the doctor told Merrill he was perfectly sane and healthy, and then went out and liquidated his own portfolio. Whether or not this was true, Merrill mailed an investment advisory to clients on April 1, 1928, in which he wrote that his firm currently was underwriting only companies with small debts, because bad times were ahead. "We do not urge that you sell securities indiscriminately, but we do advise in no uncertain terms that you take advantage of present high prices and put your own financial house in order." He concluded: "We recommend that you sell enough securities to lighten your obligations, or, better yet, pay them off entirely."

Merrill later told of a visit to outgoing President Calvin Coolidge in which he urged him to issue some kind of statement warning speculators of coming dangers. Coolidge agreed the situation was bad but refused to act.

Merrill returned to Wall Street, and shortly after the crash transferred all his brokerage clients and employees to E. A. Pierce and invested $5 million in that house. For the next eight years, Merrill Lynch dealt only in underwritings, and since there were not many of these, Merrill concentrated on having a good time at his homes in Southampton, Palm Beach, and New York. He showed little interest in Pierce's reform efforts during the mid-1930s, although his sympathies were with the commission houses in their fight against the Old Guard.

Lynch died in 1938. The two men had had disagreements during the 1930s, and Lynch's death seemed to jar Merrill out of his semilethargy insofar as Wall Street was concerned. Then, in 1939, E. A. Pierce & Co. was in financial difficulty and, in fact, close to dissolution. Winthrop Smith, an old Merrill Lynch man who had gone over to Pierce in 1930 and had become a partner, asked for and received permission to invite Merrill to join the firm and help save it. Smith's invitation, combined with Merrill's $5 million investment and his desire to reenter the business, led him back to Wall Street. He merged his old firm with Pierce and another concern to form Merrill Lynch, E. A. Pierce & Cassatt in 1940. At first the company did poorly, losing $308,000 its initial year. Then, in 1941, Merrill negotiated a merger with Fenner & Beane, a New Orleans-based brokerage, to form Merrill Lynch, Pierce, Fenner & Beane.

This was a large operation, one of the biggest in the industry, but during the war progressed little. Then, in 1944, Merrill suffered a heart attack, and Smith took over much of the day-to-day operations. From that time until his death in 1956, Merrill devoted his efforts to public relations and a handful of accounts, Safeway in particular. But his most important work lay in the development of the firm's sales program.

Merrill made a valiant effort to "professionalize" brokerage. Realizing that the broker was the most significant person in the organization, since he represented the firm insofar as clients were concerned, Merrill scrapped the old ways and fashioned new ones that he hoped would create a feeling of confidence in investing. Merrill Lynch would charge no service fees, which were the rule at the time and so discouraged small investors from opening accounts. Other firms had training programs in the past, most of which were really orientations to essential operations. Merrill put forth a new program, in effect a school, which taught his personnel every aspect of the business. Particular stress was placed on the training and indoctrination of young securities salesmen—whom Merrill insisted be referred to as account executives. Most important, Merrill paid his account executives straight salaries, not commissions, as was the case in every other brokerage. And he made certain investors knew this, doing so through an intensive publicity campaign. The Merrill Lynch customer's man would not press clients to buy or sell stocks, or try to "churn" accounts to develop commissions. Instead, he was said to be there to offer a service. Of course, account executives who did not perform well were dismissed, and in practice the drive for turnover was as great at Merrill Lynch as elsewhere. But the atmosphere was different, and the public realized it. Finally, Merrill guaranteed his people would not suffer due to a loss of commissions. He instituted the first profit-sharing plan in the industry, one in which all employees participated.

As a result, Merrill Lynch attracted solid, substantial, and, for the most part, franker customers' men than most other brokerages. It was no place for the "go-getter" or "hot shot," who could earn larger commissions at other houses. This, too, was by design, for Merrill wanted average Americans, not speculators, to be comfortable at his brokerages and with his customers' men. His research facilities were also geared to this group. Merrill Lynch account executives were told to recommend only stocks suggested by the research arm, and these tended to be on the more conservative side. As Merrill put it in 1946, "Our business is people and their money; and we must draw the new capital required for industrial might and growth *not* from among a few large investors but from the savings of thousands of people of moderate incomes. We must bring Wall Street to Main Street—and we must use the efficient, mass-merchandising methods of the chain store to do it." Thus, Merrill combined the zeal of an evangelist with the experience he learned in the retail business. "We *owe* them this service for doing business with us, and they owe us nothing but the minimum commissions prescribed by the New York Stock Exchange. We must preach to all, 'Investigate, *then* Invest,' and we must practice what we preach."

Merrill understood that until the small investor believed Wall Street was an honest place, he would not return. Ever since the crash, the district had the reputation of shadiness, an area where honest people were in the minority. Just as the post–Civil War Republicans waved the bloody shirt for decades after Appomattox, so the Democrats recalled the Great Crash of 1929 and the depression that followed in subsequent political campaigns. Merrill, a liberal in most matters, denied that the Democrats had any right in maintaining that conditions in investing hadn't changed in the 1930s and 1940s. When President Truman condemned "the money changers" during the 1948 election, Merrill took out full-page advertisements in rebuttal.

> One campaign tactic did get us a little riled. That was when the moth-eaten bogey of a Wall Street tycoon was trotted out. . . . Mr. Truman knows as well as anybody that there isn't any Wall Street. That's just legend. Wall Street is Montgomery Street in San Francisco. Seventeenth Street in Denver. Marietta Street in Atlanta. Federal Street in Boston. Main Street in Waco, Texas. And it's any spot in Independence, Missouri, where thrifty people go to invest their money, to buy and sell securities.

By 1950 Merrill Lynch was the largest brokerage by far, grossing $45.7 million and numbering over 150,000 accounts. The firm spent upward of a million dollars a year on research and market letters, which were offered free to customers, and, for that matter, to prospective clients as well. The company's training program was a model for the industry, and the general success at Merrill Lynch led the other brokerages to imitate it, at least in part. More than any other postwar figure, Merrill had made investing respectable again.

His firm was in an excellent position to capitalize on the stock market boom caused by inflation, and in turn help draw still additional investors to the market. By 1956, when the bull market was solidly established, Merrill Lynch handled 10 percent of all round-lot purchases and sales at the N.Y.S.E. and 18 percent of the odd-lot business, the latter a most important statistic, since it represented transactions for small accounts, the kind that Merrill cultivated.

The firm was as much a symbol for Wall Street in the early 1950s as J. P. Morgan or Kuhn, Loeb had been for the district before World War I. Jokes were cracked on radio and television about "The Thundering Herd" and "We, the People," or "The Department Store of Finance," as ML, P, F & B came to be called. This was a sign of the firm's high visibility and national recognition at a time when few Americans knew the name of Emil Schram and fewer still those of John Coleman and Robert Stott. This too was an indication of the magnitude of Merrill's accomplishment. Most of the larger brokerages remade their operations in the Merrill Lynch mold. Bache; Francis I. Du Pont; E. F. Hutton; Paine, Webber, Jackson & Curtis; Dean Witter; Walston; Goodbody and other major firms imitated the new leader in their attitudes toward investors, training of account executives, and advertising—and the rest followed.

In the process, Merrill helped restore a measure of power to the commission houses as a group, thus undercutting the leadership of the N.Y.S.E.'s specialists. What the reformers of the mid-1930s had failed to accomplish through political pressures and legislative enactments, Merrill had done by salesmanship and promotion. Given additional business from the new investors, the Exchange could prosper. The specialists understood and appreciated this, but also knew that their power had its roots in a smaller, "clubbier" exchange. What would happen if the brokers turned their attention to the over-the-counter market makers and bought and sold shares—listed N.Y.S.E. shares at that—through the nonmember houses? Such activities would shatter the Big Board, and both the commission brokers and specialists understood this. The specialists could dominate the Exchange only so long as business was poor and little hope of large-scale public participation existed. Now this was changing, and the Exchange had to adjust to the new situation.

The commission houses were helped by another, nonrelated, development. In October 1947 the Justice Department initiated an antitrust action against seventeen major investment banking houses and the Investment Bankers Association, which they controlled. These firms—led by Morgan Stanley; First Boston; Dillon, Read; Kuhn, Loeb; and Lehman—had long dominated the investment banking industry, throwing occasional crumbs to the commission houses, who were allowed to participate in some underwritings as junior partners but only on the direct sufferance of the leading concerns. The trial opened on November 28, 1950, and lasted through May 19, 1953. In the end the defendants were completely exonerated, and in his scathing opinion, Judge Harold Medina not only dismissed the case "on the merits" but did so "with prejudice" against the government, charging the Justice Department with having drawn up a shoddy case that had little substantiation.

From 1947 to 1953, however, the issue was in doubt, and the major old-line investment banks were reluctant to offer the antitrusters additional ammunition. Thus, they held back and did not pursue underwritings with their customary aggressiveness. This was a period during which many new firms came to the market, and old ones refinanced obligations. In 1947, $779 million in common stock offerings came to Wall Street. The figure was $811 million in 1950, and in 1953, the year the Medina decision was handed down, $1.3 billion. Total securities offerings rose from $13.5 billion in 1950 to almost $20 billion in 1953. And increasingly the major commission houses competed with the old-line investment bankers for business and succeeded. By the end of the decade, First Boston, Morgan Stanley, Lehman, and Blyth were still the nation's major underwriters, but Merrill Lynch was larger than Kuhn, Loeb and Goldman, Sachs, and other commission houses were rising rapidly.

On the surface, this seemed simply another case in which an old organization was replaced by a new one. But it was more than that, and the rise of the commission houses had a far more significant impact, both on Wall Street and the nation. The old-line investment banks had little interest in the retail business, for the most part, and not since the 1920s had any of them offered leadership in bringing investors back to the markets. They appeared content to allow the situation to develop along the lines desired by the specialists. That is to say, the investment banks would dominate their end of the industry and the specialists control the floor and administration of the N.Y.S.E., with the former utilizing the latter whenever convenient and necessary. Now the larger commission houses, led by Merrill Lynch, posed a threat to both. More daring and perhaps less prudent and experienced than the older investment banks, they sought underwritings to enhance their profits, but also to provide "product" for their salesmen. Not all of this could be discerned toward the end of the Truman years, when the great bull market was still a calf. But the outlines were there to be seen, even though they were not analyzed as yet, and would not be until the bull market was almost over.

CHAPTER 10

People's Capitalism

Emil Schram was fifty-six years old in 1949, but he looked and acted older. Never an active or vigorous man, he had slowed down considerably during the previous few years. His speeches, which were neither fiery nor particularly memorable, at one time had been delivered with a Rotarian zeal that conservative audiences found comforting and even inspirational. Now that spark was gone. Increasingly, Schram gave signs of wanting to retire.

The Stock Exchange presidency involved less work than did the leadership of a large investment bank, commission house, or major specialist unit. But the man who filled the post had to be a supreme diplomat, using persuasion and guile to accomplish his goals; unlike many business leaders, he was not certain his orders would be obeyed. The president served at the pleasure of the board and was never allowed to forget it. Schram, who had been president longer than any of his predecessors, had come to understand and accept this. In any case, it wasn't too difficult a task, since his ideas and those of a majority of the board coincided.

Schram had spent a good deal of his time on the road, giving speeches, conducting public relations campaigns, and in general attempting to maintain the district's powers and enlarge upon them. He traveled regularly between New York and Washington, sometimes taking day trips to confer with lobbyists, offering testimony before congressional committees, and trying to influence old friends to support tax and related legislation beneficial to the Exchange. Often Schram would arrive in Pennsylvania Station past midnight, take a cab home, and rise a few hours later to attend a N.Y.S.E. meeting or travel several hundred miles to deliver a speech. The pace could be grueling, and by 1949 Schram was feeling its effects.

In early autumn, Schram indicated his intention to retire sometime during the next year, as soon as the board could find a suitable replacement. This was not unexpected, but the major specialists, who had worked well with him, regretted the departure. Would a new man fit their needs as well as Schram had come to do? Hopefully he would, but once in office such individuals often attempted to construct programs and reputations, either of which might be temporarily harmful to the specialists. While bandying about the names of possible successors, the new Old Guard considered institutional changes that would preserve their powers against the whims of any president.

Coleman still dominated the floor, with Stott a major figure. Benjamin Einhorn, of Astor & Rose, who supervised trading in several key issues, was a strong force for the specialist interest. William Meehan and James Crane Kellogg III, of M. J. Meehan & Co. and Leeds & Kellogg, respectively, were young men who would carry on the tradition. Together they handled some 10 percent of all listed issues, and more than twice that of the trading volume. That they would want to preserve their power and influence was understandable. Earlier they had done so through a man—Emil Schram. Now he was leaving, and they placed their reliance in constitutional safeguards.

The expected move came in the autumn of 1949, when the board approved and submitted to the membership three amendments. The first changed the eligibility for a governor's re-election following two consecutive terms from an interval of one year to two. This would not effect the specialist contingent, which tended to rotate positions among themselves. But it could be used to prevent re-elections of public members, commission brokers, and others who had accumulated board power.

The second amendment prevented limited or special partners of member firms from being eligible for election to the board and would further solidify specialist influence, since most major specialist firms had few such partners, while commission houses often had many.

The third amendment transferred the power to appoint special committees from the president to the chairman. This was the key amendment—one that enhanced the chairmanship at the expense of the presidency—which would give more powers to the members, drawing them from the professional staff.

The new amendments had been prepared and submitted without prior consultation with the S.E.C. Earlier, this might have resulted in a protest from Washington, threats of a fight, blast and counterblast and, in the end, some kind of compromise. Such was not the case in late 1949. By then the S.E.C. was a moribund operation, its members apparently more interested in a proposed move from Washington to Philadelphia than happenings on Wall Street. As late as 1940 the Commission had over 1,700 employees. By 1949 the number was below 1,000, falling rapidly (in 1954 the S.E.C. had only 770 employees, fewer than at any time since its founding, although the budget was a record $6 million). S.E.C. Chairman Edmond M. Hanrahan was an amiable man, not particularly concerned with enforcement problems, and few members showed more than passing interest in the matter, since they tended to be political appointees with limited knowledge. Even the conservative press recognized the agency was all but useless, the subject more of jokes than anger. "The S.E.C. may be moved from Washington back to Philadelphia," wrote the *World Telegram and Sun* the following year. "Its slumber will be as profound in one place as in another."

Thus, the N.Y.S.E.'s leaders could ignore some New Deal reforms, retake powers, and assure continued domination by the specialists. The amendments were approved on October 25, two weeks after having been submitted, and still the S.E.C. said nothing. Hanrahan resigned on the day after the amendments were submitted. His successor, Harry A. McDonald, also a man of no particular distinction and energy, took over on November 4, and he too seemed uninterested in reforms at the Big Board.

Nor was this the end of change in anticipation of Schram's retirement. On October 20—five days before the first three amendments were ratified—the board transmitted to the membership a petition signed by 422 members, requesting a new amendment that would increase the number of governors from twenty-five to thirty-two, to provide "adequate representation of active floor members." Six new floor members would be named, with the additional seat given to an out-of-town broker. Later on, the proposal was amended so that six would be from the floor, two from out of town, and the public member contingent was raised from two to three. The amendment was voted upon soon after New Years, and on January 13, Chairman Robert P. Boylan announced its passage by a margin of 686 to 400. Again, there was no comment from the S.E.C., which was more concerned with its moving problems than the revival of insider power at the Exchange.

That same day, Emil Schram told the board that, due to illness, he would ask for a leave of absence. It was common knowledge, however, that Schram would not return—that he was on "terminal leave," awaiting retirement plans. Boylan was immediately designated as president pro tem.

Boylan was a veteran of exchanges, although not of the N.Y.S.E. He had been born in Cincinnati in 1891, after which his family moved to Chicago, where he attended public schools. At the age of fourteen, Boylan took a job as clerk for a grain broker. Like Coleman and others of the new Old Guard in New York, he worked his way up, becoming a partner in 1912 and purchasing a seat on the Chicago Board of Trade three years later. Boylan was elected president of the Board of Trade in 1935, and the following year bought a seat on the N.Y.S.E. At the age of forty-five he moved to New York and tried to make a living at the Big Board. Uninterested in brokerage, and despite his career without significant contacts, he worked as a two-dollar broker—a person who executed orders for others, making a commission on each transaction. It was a difficult period, but Boylan survived and even prospered in the post-Whitney era, when a new face was not an altogether bad recommendation. He developed relationships at several brokerages, and was a particular favorite at E. F. Hutton & Co. Boylan worked out of Hutton and at the same time took committee assignments at the dispirited N.Y.S.E. In 1938 he was elected a governor, and two years later became vice-chairman. In 1947 Boylan succeeded Coleman as chairman. By then he was a solid member of the new Old Guard.

The new chairman became one of its leaders. Most members knew that he spoke for the floor and represented its wishes. In this capacity, Boylan helped organize the movement to revamp the constitution, always acting in close consultation with the leading specialists.

Schram thought the first three amendments unwise and, in a rare show of defiance, said so. This was surprising, since all at the Big Board knew that Schram hoped to obtain a consultantship of one kind or another after he left the Exchange—which would be soon—and that the decision on the matter rested with the very men he was opposing. Still, Schram's opinions carried little weight in 1949. He had been given the presidency in the hope that he would be able to exercise his influence in Washington in such ways as to benefit the N.Y.S.E., and for a while he did. Ironically, as Schram learned the intricacies of his job and came to perform it well, his contacts in Washington weakened. And when they went, so did whatever power Schram had at the Exchange.

By 1949 Franklin Roosevelt was dead and the New Deal consigned to memory; the S.E.C. was toothless and Jesse Jones in Texas, living out his few remaining years as a businessman. So the members listened respectfully to their outgoing president, in the knowledge that he soon would be gone and, in any case, was a redundancy, since Boylan had become the N.Y.S.E.'s true spokesman—and even he was more a figurehead than anything else.

At a general meeting of the members, Schram characterized the activities of those who sponsored the amendments as "a type of pressure-group operation which cannot be countenanced in a well-ordered organization," and he referred bitingly to the "old discredited committee system." Of course, the amendments passed. Schram would not be punished for his statements; he would receive his consultantship, and a large, well-publicized farewell party, complete with speeches and a testimonial. In one of these, Schram was referred to as a "monument to decency," but as was later remarked regarding another person at another time, people erect monuments to honor the dead, not respect the living. In terms of influence, Schram had been monumentalized long before 1949.

During the first eight months of 1950, Schram convalesced and planned his future, while Boylan assumed the duties of the office and helped direct the search for a new president. Schram's official resignation came on September 14, at which time the board announced his departure and also said he would remain as a full-time officer of the Exchange until May 1, 1951, receiving his usual salary but performing no stated duties. Thereafter, he would remain in the employ of the Exchange for eleven and a half more years, at reduced pay, although this too was not very clear. That same day, the board appointed a special committee to select a successor. Coleman, Stott, and others of their circle were named to it, with Boylan as an ex-officio member.

As had been the case previously, the search for a new N.Y.S.E. president was followed closely in the financial press which reported, correctly, that more than a hundred names were submitted and considered. It was not evident, however, what kind of a man the Exchange wanted and needed. The situation had been quite different with Martin and Schram; in the first instance, the members knew they had to have a reformer, while in the second, close connections with Washington were deemed important. Reform was no longer an issue, and while there was no doubt that the next president would have to perform lobbying duties, he need not have been a Washingtonian by profession or service. In 1950 the N.Y.S.E. was more free to select a person of its own persuasion than it had been on the two previous occasions.

What was that persuasion? The specialists controlled the administration and the commission brokers were gaining wealth and power. They had their differences, if only in terms of pecking orders and personalities and in approaches to common problems. On the other hand, they recognized that such problems did exist and would have to be met in a fairly unified fashion. The most important of these, in 1950 as before and since, was the volume of business. The specialists tended to think of increased business in terms of additional listings, while the commission brokers usually spoke about new investors and a greater public awareness of investments. The specialists could look to the slow, steady rise in the amount of listed stocks, which was accelerating by 1950, when the number reached 1,472. The commission brokers were enjoying a bonanza that year, with annual sales of almost 525 million shares and a daily average of close to 2 million shares, the best since 1933. The number of registered representatives, tickers in use, and new accounts was equally impressive, as was the coverage stocks were receiving in the newspapers.

Yet, the specialists and brokers still feared a downturn. The conventional wisdom had it that the bull market was fueled by a wartime economy—first the Cold War, then the Korean conflict. What would happen if "peace broke out," as it might when the Korean conflict ended? The Soviet-American antagonism was still young enough in 1950 for some Americans to believe it might have been caused by misunderstandings and mistrust. If the leaders could meet to iron out differences, in a way somewhat like the World War II summit meetings, perhaps harmony would develop and the arms budgets lowered. In that case, America might undergo a serious depression, and the new bull market would collapse, as would volume and interest in investment. Because of this, the price of a N.Y.S.E. seat fluctuated between $46,000 and $54,000 in 1950; as recently as 1946 a seat changed hands at $97,000, and in 1947, seats sold for between $50,000 and $70,000—when average daily volume was half that of 1950.

Commission brokers and specialists could agree that they wanted and needed a president who could cement the new prosperity into place. He should be on good terms with both government and business and be a harmonizer of differences at the Exchange. But his most important tasks would be those of salesmanship; he would have to attract new listings and be the kind of person who could devise and carry through a public relations program that would bring new investors and speculators to Wall Street. Such a person would accomplish this through native abilities, a knowledge of the industry, or personal stature—or a combination of the three. He could be a war hero, a prominent businessman, or a bureaucrat of some renown and influence. This, at least, was the Exchange's thinking in the autumn of 1950.

N.Y.S.E. special committees usually have had a better-than-average record at maintaining confidentiality, and so the newspaper reporters and columnists were obliged to circulate rumors, grasp at hunches, and print the names of men they believed would be accepted as plausible candidates. Francis Adams Truslow, head of the New York Curb Exchange, was a person of some prominence and ability and was viewed as a possibility. But the Big Board would hardly look to the Curb for its new symbol, and, in any event, Truslow had indicated an interest in leaving the district for a diplomatic career. Secretary of the Treasury John Snyder was another press-nominated candidate. He was well liked in Washington and considered very close to President Truman, on a personal as well as political basis. Snyder could use his influence in the Exchange's behalf during the next two years, and he could do worse than take the N.Y.S.E. presidency, if he was looking for a post–Truman job. Then the Secretary delivered several speeches in which he talked of the need for higher taxes, and, with these, the small boom collapsed. John Steelman, head of the Labor Department's Conciliation Service, was a man who possessed talents needed on Wall Street, but he lacked the stature for the position. Those who wanted a person with financial abilities and government connections spoke well of M. S. Szymczak, a Federal Reserve Board governor; when the Federal Reserve increased stock margins to 75 percent in early January 1951, the candidacy was aborted. John McCloy, then the High Commissioner to Germany, a man of great reputation who had good friends in both political parties, was put forth by several influential members. McCloy showed no interest, but in the atmosphere of the times the very suggestion caused reactions. Benjamin Buttenweiser, one of McCloy's aides, believed Alger Hiss innocent of having communist connections, and since he had not been fired, McCloy was deemed "soft on communism" by some.

The situation became complicated in mid-March. Several columnists reported that James W. McAffee would be offered the presidency. McAffee had been a St. Louis politician and judge and then went on to take the presidency of Union Electric Company. He was known as a reformer, a man who had helped clean up St. Louis politics and then had done the same with the scandal-ridden Union Electric. A young man of demonstrated skills in dealing with bureaucrats and businessmen, as well as an articulate speaker, McAffee appeared a fine choice. But he wasn't interested in the position; instead, he had political ambitions, and immediately indicated his disinterest before the rumors could develop further.

The search continued, and Boylan, whose term as chairman was coming to an end, announced he would step down. He had hoped to do so with McAffee or someone else installed as president. This was not to be, and so his successor, Richard M. Crooks, who had previously served as vice-chairman, was elected both chairman and president pro tem.

The committee looked to other candidates. There was talk that William Martin might return, but there was little chance of an offer and less of an acceptance. In any case, Thomas McCabe resigned as chairman of the Federal Reserve Board, and Martin was nominated by Truman to take his place. Then Truman dismissed General Douglas MacArthur, who had returned to a hero's welcome, and rumors developed of an offer of the N.Y.S.E. presidency as a stepping stone to the one in Washington. MacArthur showed no interest in this or any other position dangled in front of him.

* * *

In early May, Sidney Weinberg, of Goldman, Sachs & Co., one of the district's most influential men, put forth the name of George Keith Funston, then president of Trinity College. In many ways, Funston appeared a strong candidate. He was forty-one years old in 1951, a tall, handsome man, who tended to dominate a room when he entered. He had many of the proper credentials too. Funston was a midwesterner, who worked his way through high school then went to Trinity on a scholarship and on to Harvard Business School, from which he graduated cum laude. His first postgraduation position was in sales, at American Radiator. After a short stay there, he moved on to Sylvania as sales-planning director. Funston went to Washington in 1940 as a dollar-a-year man, and it was there he met Weinberg, who was establishing industry advisory committees for the War Production Board. Funston soon became the banker's protégé, and as such was named assistant to WPB Chairman Donald Nelson. He was asked to take the presidency of Trinity in 1944, accepted on condition that he be granted an immediate leave of absence to serve in the Navy, and arrived on campus in 1945. He found the school rundown and badly in debt. Given his sales background, Funston attacked the problem from the "image" point of view. "Gentlemen," he told the faculty, "in order to be successful you must look successful." He had the campus renovated and painted, so that it appeared on firm footing. Then he went out to raise funds from businessmen and foundations. Within six years, Trinity was solvent, thriving, and gaining in reputation. The faculty still considered him a huckster who knew little about education, and Funston was deemed a poor administrator. On the other hand, faculty salaries and status were higher than ever before, and there was no doubt he had succeeded in accomplishing what he set out to do.

Funston also maintained his business contacts. With Weinberg's help, he was named to the boards of directors of General Foods, B. F. Goodrich, Aetna Insurance, and other large corporations. Several medium-sized firms were considering him for their presidencies. Funston was known as "a man on the go." "Funston was a guy who had success on his mind, right from the start," said a friend. "I think he was thoroughly devoted to the idea that an awfully good place to start business was at the top."

The committee members approached Funston and meetings were scheduled, at which key brokers and specialists were impressed by the man and what he had to offer. Clearly, he was a person of abilities; his record indicated as much. Also, he had friends in the financial and business communities, among them the powerful and respected Weinberg. Funston's wartime experiences had enabled him to claim a certain entrée to Washington's power circles—Republican as well as Democrat. He was an all-American type, from his rugged good looks to his sincere manner, to his handsome family—an attractive wife, two daughters, and a son. Funston was professorial without being academic; he was no William Martin. He was businesslike but lacked the stigma that still clung in the faded aftermath of the great depression. And he was plausible at a time when this was a needed characteristic. Corporation executives considering listing their stocks on the N.Y.S.E. would be impressed by such a man, and so would middle-class investors seeking assurance from one of their own that stocks were not only safe but a wise holding.

Funston had one drawback. He knew next to nothing about Wall Street, and in his discussions showed an abysmal ignorance of the Exchange. When told one man was a specialist, another a two-dollar broker, and a third a commission broker, he had to have the terms explained, and later on would get them confused. But Funston was supposed to be a front man for the powerful individuals inside the building, just as Martin and Schram were to have been. Was experience really necessary for him to do the job? There were those who believed Funston's lack of knowledge regarding Wall Street and the N.Y.S.E. was a decided factor in his favor. Such a man would hardly interfere with the Exchange's operations.

The board announced Funston's appointment on May 24, adding that his salary would be $100,000 a year for a three-year contract. He took office on September 1, signaling the occasion by ringing the opening gong for trading. Funston's picture appeared in a large number of newspapers, and the event made the weekly news magazines as well. Prices were off more than a point that day, closing at 260.07. But volume was good; 1,657,000 shares were traded. The latter figure was of prime importance insofar as specialists and brokers were concerned. They were content. Funston's job was to keep them that way and perhaps even add to their joy. His prospects to accomplish both appeared bright.

Funston arrived at the Exchange as the bull market gathered steam, and he presided over the institution at a time when wilder speculation than any seen in previous eras—including the late 1920s—took place. He departed shortly before the denouement, leaving others to pick up the pieces and attempt needed reforms. Later on, his associates and members of the Exchange would credit him with helping create the optimistic markets of the 1950s and early 1960s, while absolving him of any responsibility for the harsh times that followed. Neither judgment is fair or complete. The N.Y.S.E. of 1951 was no longer the central focus of American capitalism—if indeed it had ever been that. Rather, the Exchange was the arena in which the drama was played. The real powers in the district were the men at the investment banks—Weinberg; John Schiff of Kuhn, Loeb; Robert Lehman of Lehman

Brothers; Alexander White of White, Weld; James Coggeshall of First Boston; and, of course, Charles Merrill and his vice-presidents at Merrill Lynch. Money managers at trust companies, banks, and pension funds were becoming increasingly important, as were the leaders of large mutual funds. These men and institutions utilized the Exchange when it suited their purposes, and if it did not, they would transact business elsewhere. Funston's task was to make certain the Exchange was an efficient, respected, and useful facility and to publicize it to potential clients and customers. He did this well—Funston was one of the most intelligent and able public relations men in the land—and in the process came to be considered a major force in American finance. This was not so; to believe it, would be to credit the manager of a motion picture theater for the production of *Gone with the Wind*.

Still, it was believed, and if Funston lacked the substance of power, the appearance of it often served as well. By force of personality and the wise use of press and television, he took advantage of the fact that most Americans knew little about the structure and operations of financial power in the nation and preferred a symbol to the reality in any event. The N.Y.S.E., which was more visible than any other institution in the financial district, as well as better known than any investment bank or brokerage, had often served as such a symbol in the past. The leading specialists were capable and, in the case of some, amiable men. Others, however, were blunt, somewhat crude, and certainly not the kinds of people the N.Y.S.E. could use as good-will ambassadors. Funston, the most public relations conscious of all N.Y.S.E. presidents, set out to become "the symbol of the symbol," as it were, and succeeded in this goal admirably. Unlike Martin, he was not shy and retiring, and he was more vibrant and dynamic than Schram or Gay. Merrill, old and ill in 1951, was the spokesman for commission brokers, not for an institution like the N.Y.S.E.

Still, there were some similarities between Merrill and Funston. Just as the broker geared his advertisements and campaigns at middle Americans—Merrill once spoke of the "thirty-three-year-old veteran with a wife and children, a small home and mortgage, and a $5,000 a year job"—Funston did the same. He glorified "People's Capitalism" and staked a claim as its most ardent booster. The term signified a free-enterprise system in which a large part of the population, including middle Americans, owned securities. Funston contrasted this with the situation in the late nineteenth and early twentieth centuries, when ownership was far more concentrated. Through the acquisition of stocks, Americans could become capitalists and share in the growth of the nation, even helping it along.

Perhaps without understanding at first the implications of this kind of an appeal, Funston managed to strike a vital nerve. The early 1950s was a period of intense patriotic zeal combined with fervent anticommunism, both of which were raised to the point of becoming quasi-religions. Schram and others had spoken of the virtues of America and the importance of securities, but they had done so in rather dry, often statistical fashion. When they talked of the need for preservation of free enterprise, they implied the dangers came more from radical New Dealers in Washington than communists in the Kremlin. Funston was more attuned to the anticommunist sentiments of the 1950s. People's Capitalism, he claimed, was a more revolutionary idea than Marxism. This was the theme he hammered away at in speeches throughout the nation during his first years in office. The ultimate aim of the N.Y.S.E., said Funston, was public ownership of the means of production, not through government but by an army of shareholders, "a nation in whose material wealth every citizen has a vested interest through equity ownership." Speaking before a New York audience in mid-1952, he indicated that "The way to fight communism is through American prosperity, which has proven it can accomplish more for more people than any other system in the world." Behind his desk at the Exchange was a picture of Independence Hall in Philadelphia. "I put that up to remind myself that freedom is the basis of everything in this country," he told a *New Yorker* reporter. "We're the epitome of free enterprise. Once that's lost, we're gone." He concluded that "We're trying to broaden the base of stock ownership and thus strengthen the basis of democracy." Or, as Big Board Vice-President Frank Coyle put it, "A regular dividend check is the best answer to communism."

Funston and others in the N.Y.S.E. administration made it appear as though the purchase of common stock was a vote for democracy against communism. Just as ownership of war bonds in 1944 was a sign of patriotism, so participation in securities investment was an indication of free-enterprise virtue in 1951. That year, 144,784 visitors came to the N.Y.S.E., to view floor trading, see exhibits, and listen to a short lecture about the way stocks were traded. This attendance was normal—in 1946, 145,897 had taken the tour. But in 1952, the number of visitors reached a record 187,645, and rose to 233,657 in 1953 and 270,354 in 1954. The exhibits, which stressed the history of the Exchange and a simplified version of stock flotation and trading, were presented with patriotic themes. The N.Y.S.E., which in the 1930s under Whitney had been the symbol of capitalist failure, became a citadel of capitalist—and American—success during the Funston years.

The early 1950s was a significant transitional period for the financial district, primarily because of changes taking place in the nation at large. The Cold War, entered into tentatively in the late 1940s, was compacted and annealed by the Korean conflict and hardened into ideology by the crusade best symbolized by Senator Joseph McCarthy. The New Deal–Fair Deal was rejected by the Eisenhower conservatives and moderates who came to power in 1953, but many of the practices and configurations of reformism were retained and, in some cases, even strengthened. Eisenhower would not turn the clock back, but he also would not goad the nation into new paths. The rhetoric was that of war, crusade, and conservatism, but during the Eisenhower years the reality was peace, stability, and genteel liberalism, presided over by one of the shrewdest and most popular chief executives in history. Eisenhower accepted deficit budgets, leading Senator Robert Taft, "Mr. Republican," to exclaim, "It's a repudiation of everything we promised in the campaign." He ended both the Korean War and most economic controls, instituted a tax cut, and presided over a recession in 1953–1954 which, though more painful than any since 1937, broke the back of inflation. Most importantly, Eisenhower inspired confidence, a key ingredient insofar as Wall Street was concerned.

It was a period for reiteration of old values by new men, and several such key figures appeared, some of whom affected the N.Y.S.E. William McChesney Martin, more political than before, was at the Federal Reserve, having taken office in 1951. He quickly established himself as an enemy of inflation who would operate independently of the Treasury, if necessary, to preserve fiscal integrity. The Securities and Exchange Commission remained weak and ineffectual. In the four years from 1952 to 1955 it had four chairmen—Harry McDonald, Donald Cook, Ralph Demmler, and J. Sinclair Armstrong—and all were either uninterested in reform or unwilling to create problems for themselves in Washington, where the atmosphere was decidedly pro-business. Francis Adams Truslow resigned from the presidency of the Curb Exchange to take a diplomatic post, and his place was taken by Edward T. McCormick, a former S.E.C. commissioner, who was even more of a booster and promoter of People's Capitalism than Funston. Observers at the time noted that the Commission might well become a breeding and training ground for future Wall Street leaders.

The climate was right for a revival of interest in securities, due to a new wave of investor enthusiasm, a hands-off policy by Washington, and a man of Funston's talents and proclivities to exploit the situation.

Funston spent his first two months in office in familiarizing himself with the Exchange, its personnel, and its problems. But there were signs of action as well. He announced the formation of an advisory committee, composed of representatives of the financial community, which would assist the N.Y.S.E. and the Brookings Institution in conducting a national census of stockholders, which would be useful in a campaign to attract people to Wall Street. There was some talk of closing the Exchange on Saturdays, and the president promised to gather information on the matter and submit it to the board as soon as possible. In all, Funston fortified the impression he had made earlier, that of a bright, aggressive, attractive young man who would help modernize the financial district.

It was not until November 29, when he delivered his first important speech to members of the Investment Bankers Association meeting in Hollywood, Florida, that Funston displayed his—to use that overworked word of the next generation—charisma. The talk itself contained no original ideas; in fact, a large part of it might have been delivered by Emil Schram the year before. But there were some new approaches. Borrowing perhaps from the thought if not the actual phrases of Franklin Roosevelt, Funston spoke of "the lost man," the person who works long hours and saves his money. "Agriculture, labor and manufacturing—the producers are organized; the consumer is protected by competition or, in its absence, by government regulation. It is the saver who has to take what is left."

Funston suggested no less than a "cooperative effort by the entire financial community to successfully represent the interests of the savers." The N.Y.S.E. would lead the way. "We are actively engaged in the preliminary steps of a program which, we hope, will lead to the broadest possible base of ownership of American industry by the American public." To further this objective, and to indicate the steps the Exchange would take in order to work for the investor, Funston came out against the capital gains tax and called for an income tax cut. This would provide savers with additional funds, which they should be encouraged to use to purchase common stocks. "One of the best ways for us to insure our productive enterprise system and, indeed, our democratic form of government, is to make certain all our people have a direct and tangible stake in that system and democracy." Of course, such individuals should not "gamble," and Funston opposed speculation. "However, a man should not buy stocks until he has protected his family with life insurance, has money in savings or government bonds, and perhaps an equity in a home." Then, he concluded, stocks should be seriously considered, not only as a good investment—"Common stocks in the N.Y.S.E. had an average yield of 6½ percent last year. Compare that yield to savings banks"—but as a sign of faith in democracy and capitalism.

Only three days before, the Chinese had entered the Korean

conflict, an act which to many seemed a vindication of earlier claims of a worldwide communist conspiracy. Funston had managed to combine a political and economic program with an emotional appeal for a union of savers to be led by the N.Y.S.E. and anticommunists, and did so with zest and apparent candor. "G. Keith Funston, president of the New York Stock Exchange, made a splendid impression," wrote Ralph Hendershot, the influential financial editor of the *New York World Telegram & Sun.* "In the opinion of this correspondent, we will hear great things from this tall, pleasant individual." Others echoed the thought. Within the next three months, Funston was the object of interviews in the leading magazines and was hailed as the new spokesman for American capitalism. Some called him a reformer, most recognized him as a conservative. His boosterism was evident to all. "To the Old Guarders on the Street, stocks are a way of making a living," wrote *Forbes* in a cover story on December 15. "To Funston, and the Young Turks, they are a means to a way of life."

Encouraged by this reception and buoyed by a natural enthusiasm, the new president took to the road to spread his message. In March he told the Economic Club of Chicago that stockholders could become the chief strength of the United States. The Big Board's goal, he said, was "the creation of a nation of share-owning capitalists—to maintain a strong equity market, to foster solidarity among our people, to assist in the spread of economic knowledge, and to enable our people to enjoy some of the satisfactions of ownership." In late April he told a large audience that the securities industry recognized two major dangers: virulent attacks on the American way of life from abroad and misinformation at home, and he strongly implied that there was some connection between the two. Funston compared communist and socialist dreams—often shattered by harsh realities—to the real growth in America made possible by businessmen, and he urged more Americans to become members of the capitalist brigades through the purchase of common stocks. In May, Funston was in San Francisco addressing the National Federation of Financial Analysts, and there he alluded to the power of millions of shareholders, who would be able to influence business and governmental decisions. The Exchange's report on stock owners would soon be ready for publication, he added, and then the country would realize how strong that group was.

The shareowner census was released on June 30, 1952. Entitled "Share Ownership in the United States" and published by the Brookings Institution, it revealed that there were slightly fewer than 6.5 million shareholders, and that of these, 1.3 million had purchased their first shares of common stock in the last three years, with 390,000 new accounts in 1951 alone. One out of every sixteen American adults owned stocks. The average age of the shareholder was fifty-one and his median income was $7,100.*

Funston hailed the report but stated that it demonstrated that there was no such person as the "average shareholder." On the other hand, he also noted that the survey showed that there were over 41.5 million individuals between the ages of thirty and forty-nine who owned no shares at all, and that many of them would be prime targets for a new public relations campaign. As Americans became wealthier and more aware of the rewards of investing, he said, they would come to the markets.

Four years later the N.Y.S.E. sponsored a second survey, very much like the first. It showed that there were some 8.6 million shareholders—2.1 million had been added since 1952. In 1956, one out of every twelve Americans owned stocks. The average age of the 1956 shareholder was forty-eight, three years below that of his 1952 counterpart, and his median salary was $6,200, $900 lower than it had been in 1952. It was an impressive performance, one for which Funston received congratulations from the press and the Wall Street community. In 1952, the annual volume had been 337,805,179 shares; in 1956, it was at 556,284,172 shares. That year, too, a N.Y.S.E seat changed hands at $113,000, or more than twice the high for 1952. The Exchange members had reason to be grateful, and Funston was the recipient of their gratitude. In September 1956 he was given the Sales Executive Club's "Applause Award" for his work in broadening share ownership. He pledged himself to still greater efforts in the future and later in the month took off for a European tour and series of meetings and speaking engagements. In Paris, Amsterdam, Stockholm, and London, he addressed large audiences on the subject of People's Capitalism. He urged bankers and political leaders in these cities to emulate the American experience, and his talks were given front-page coverage, both in Europe and America. If western Europeans would alter their orientations, away from socialism to free enterprise, they might expect significant American investments in their economies. In London, for example, Funston declared that Britain's industrial problems could be solved by automation, financed by large-scale investments. When told that such funds didn't exist, the N.Y.S.E. president responded that a more-confident British investing public would provide them, and Americans, eager for new opportunities,

* This was the first "scientific" study made of share ownership. Estimates vary as to the number of stockholders during previous bull markets. According to some, there were 20 million on the books of American corporations in 1929, but others indicate the amount was as low as 3 million. The latter figure seems more realistic. Robert Sobel, *The Big Board: A History of the New York Stock Market* (New York, 1965), pp. 252–54.

would follow, if and when the atmosphere improved for free enterprise.

It was a high point for America's world prestige and power, as well as the concept of People's Capitalism and national confidence. This was not Funston's doing—he was only one of many spokesmen and exemplars of the national and world mood. It was, after all, the Age of Eisenhower, not that of Keith Funston. But it was the height of his career—Funston was now not only a voice for the Exchange but for Wall Street and even the nation. Not since the turn of the century had a man of the district become so well known and admired. By then, too, there were rumors that Funston might not remain long at the Exchange—that he would be asked to accept a Cabinet post in Eisenhower's second administration and from there go on to become a candidate for the Presidency in 1960. All of this was the result of the success and confidence of the stock market boom of the previous four years—Funston's boom.

But was it? What, exactly, had Funston done to create this confidence, to help lift prices and volume, to attract new listings to the Exchange and, in the process, dissolve some of the tensions between reformer and new Old Guard, broker and specialist, that had been the heritage of harsher times? Very little, in fact. Rather, Keith Funston had arrived on Wall Street at a moment when the district was undergoing major institutional and psychological changes almost as important as those that took place in the early 1930s. Then and twenty years after, Wall Street and America needed symbols. Richard Whitney served as one for his time, Keith Funston filled the position for the later period.

CHAPTER 11

The New Investors

Funston excelled at shepherding groups of visiting dignitaries through the financial district, and such people took it for granted that he spoke for the larger American business community. He made favorable impressions on the presidents of corporations interested in Big Board listing; such men admired and even envied his grace and geniality. Senators and congressmen on committees considering legislation that might affect Wall Street found Funston articulate and reasonable. Brokers and specialists were grateful for his knack at projecting a pleasing image for their industry. Funston maintained excellent relations with the press, was good copy, and was always ready to cooperate with a journalist out for a story.

With few of these people, however, did Funston engage in detailed conversations or debates about the nature of the district or the rapidly evolving securities complex in the nation. To those who considered such problems, academics as well as businessmen, Funston appeared an intelligent and personable man, but one of limited interests—and the machinery of the financial district was not one of these. "Funston could have learned more about this place than any other president, before or since," was the view of one N.Y.S.E. veteran. "He certainly had the brains. But he was always busy with other things." Another said, "Funston was one of the most impressive people you would ever want to meet, especially the first time you met and talked with him. After a while, though, you came to understand that there was little depth to the man. It was all surface, but the surface was very, very impressive indeed."

Long after he left the presidency, Funston maintained friendly relations with old associates. Few had a harsh or even critical word to say about the man and his work. But when asked what he had accomplished during his tenure, they seemed at a loss for ideas, and few denied that Funston's knowledge of the district was rather poor and that as a result he had failed to direct the Exchange in meeting developing problems. In the end, however, a response would come, a defensive one delivered as though learned by rote. In one way or another, all replied, "He started the M.I.P."

It is significant, perhaps, that these individuals considered Funston's major accomplishment to be the Monthly Investment Plan, a program announced with great fanfare, one directed at the small investor, the amateur, and an effort to wean him away from the large institutions, such as the mutual funds. Professionals scoffed at the M.I.P., deeming it a gimmick and a faulty one that might increase brokerage commissions and floor activity but which would be abandoned once investors realized its deficiencies. Yet it was a success, one of the more important triumphs of the period, which saw the development of a new investing atmosphere that professionals capitalized upon but which was to a large extent molded for and by amateurs.

The ideas for the M.I.P. jelled in the early months of 1953, even though they had been bandied about for many years before. At the time Funston had established himself as a spokesman for the Exchange and the district, but his actual accomplishments in the area of reform had been minor. Trading volume had fallen in 1953, and like others in the district, Funston was under pressure to bring it back up to the 1950–1951 level. He had extended trading hours to 3:30 P.M. and announced that the Saturday closings would be continued throughout the year. This was not a N.Y.S.E. innovation, however. Rather, it had been initiated at the New York Curb by Ted McCormick. The Curb's new schedule went into effect in May 1952; Funston announced the N.Y.S.E.'s change two months later. It appeared as though McCormick, not Funston, was to be the major force for reform in the district. The Curb leader was trying to change the name of his market to the American Stock Exchange, talked of international listings, and, perhaps, in time, of evening trading on a once-a-week basis for a start. Curb volume and listings were doing better than those at the N.Y.S.E., and the junior market was receiving more favorable publicity than at any other time in its history. Funston could not have helped noting all of this. McCormick's success at the Curb may have provided impetus and served as a catalyst for his ideas.

Funston made his first allusions to a new program in early 1953, at a time when trading volume seemed to have leveled off and stock prices were declining. In a speech before the American Bankers Association on February 10, he noted that $37 billion worth of stock were owned by various trust funds. Private pension funds had risen from $475 million in securities in 1946 to $1.5 billion in 1952, while college and university endowments also held $1.5 billion, twice as much as in 1946. Personal trusts, only $13 billion in 1939, were $25 billion in 1952.

This was all well and good, said Funston, a sign of a vital interest in securities and a belief in the future of American capitalism. But what of the small investor? The N.Y.S.E. president regretted that more of them had not purchased stocks and bonds and, indeed, that they seemed fearful of doing so. He spoke of corporate democracy. "We can hope for a true democratic capitalism only when each and every share owner keeps closely informed about the affairs of his company and votes his proxy regularly."

This was a prelude to a Los Angeles speech on April 28, delivered to inaugurate "Invest in America Week." As expected, it was a patriotic exhortation. "We know the communist party line and can nail it cold when it comes out of the mud long enough to be nailed," said Funston. "But I wonder if we're equally as concerned about our—for lack of a better term—lukewarm friends at home?" He did not elaborate upon this, indicating instead his contempt for those who would "damn profits," calling them "extremists." It was one of Funston's best-received speeches:

> Capitalism will stand or fall in direct ratio to the support it gets from the public. That support will be fully forthcoming only when all the people share in capitalism and all the people know that they do share in capitalism. Invest in America Week is a reflection of this idea. The goal of the securities industry is to create a nation of shareholding capitalists; to make every man and woman a shareholder in our great corporations.
>
> I'm not trying to establish a cult of profit worship, for profits are only a means to an end. But let's not lose sight of the industrial progress which profits have made possible. Take away the profits and you destroy capitalism and substitute socialism or communism. . . .

Funston hammered away at this theme during the following month, always receiving good notices, and all the while preparing for a major address in which he would discuss a plan to implement his ideas. This came on June 25, at an Association of Stock Exchange Firms dinner in St. Louis. After delivering a few generalities about the need for additional stockholders, he disclosed that the Exchange had been conducting a "merchandising study," the conclusions of which would be revealed in a month or so. "Upon the results of this merchandising study may depend a momentous decision for the Stock Exchange—whether or not to establish a department in the exchange which would develop and coordinate merchandising techniques on behalf of our membership." Specifically, Funston suggested a new program. "Right at this time we are exploring the feasibility of making possible the purchase of listed stocks on a pay-as-you-go plan."

Funston did not elaborate upon the idea, but it certainly was not revolutionary or even new. For several years the so-called Quimby Plan had been in operation at a number of banks, through which customers could purchase stocks with the bank holding the shares. During the late 1930s, similar plans had been proposed at the Exchange itself, and as recently as 1946, one such proposal had received passing attention. Finally, the N.Y.S.E. had conducted several merchandising studies in the past, and the subject had been deemed significant by Martin and Schram, both of whom spoke and wrote of it during their tenures in office.

The speech received wide attention in the financial press and generally was misunderstood. All Funston was doing, said an Exchange spokesman later on, was floating a trial balloon, and because of this he kept his references to the plan deliberately vague. To the nation's reporters and columnists, however, it seemed the N.Y.S.E. was suggesting stock purchase on installment plans. If this were so, S.E.C. regulations would come to bear. Several thorny questions would have to be answered, and problems resolved. For example, how would margin requirements be satisfied in such a program? What would commissions be? Would the N.Y.S.E. permit all stocks to be purchased through installments, and if only a few were selected, what criteria would be employed?

In fact, Funston had no such plan in mind. Rather, he hoped that small investors would be able to open accounts at brokerages and purchase stocks on a regular basis, paying for them as would any ordinary client. During the next few months this was made clear, and the other aspects of the program—now called the Monthly Investment Plan—emerged. The name was a misnomer, however. A person would sign up with a brokerage, agreeing to purchase a fixed dollar amount of a selected security, the minimum being $40 worth every three months. The investor would mail his check, together with a sales slip, to M.I.P., which would then execute the order through the odd-lot dealer. The investor would pay the regular price plus commission, and the fractional shares would be credited to his account. Since the amounts of stock purchased by the small sums were minor, most columnists agreed that the N.Y.S.E. hoped the M.I.P. would draw investors—new ones at that—through the "thrift idea," and after these people became acclimated to the markets they would open regular accounts. "The M.I.P. is to the stock market what Christmas Club is to savings banks," was the comment of one reporter. Others observed that the commission rate structure was such that clients would have to pay very large fees for the service, as much as 12 percent on a transaction, while purchasers of large amounts of stock paid far less. M.I.P. was a gimmick, they said, one that was deceiving and even false. The N.Y.S.E. ignored this criticism, preferring instead to play upon the theme of "Own Your Share in America." As Funston put it:

> A nation of share owners is our strongest defense against the foreign "isms" that would sap our vitality and eventually turn us over to the evil enemy we know as communism. We can preach the virtues of capitalism until we are blue in the face, but one stock certificate in the name of Joe Public is a stronger argument than all the oratory of which we are capable. . . . There is no Stock Exchange in Moscow, nor is ownership in promising enterprises in Russia available to the public.

The M.I.P. was launched with great fanfare on January 25, 1954. Fifty-five member firms reported that 283 accounts were opened that day, representing $21,333 worth of orders—658 shares of 142 different stocks. By the end of twelve weeks there were 13,500 accounts, and of these, 90 percent had been opened by individuals who had never owned stock before. The leading M.I.P. stocks for 1954 were Radio Corporation of America, American Telephone & Telegraph, General Motors, Dow Chemical, and Standard Oil of New Jersey. The program continued to grow for the rest of the year, at the end of which there were almost 30,000 accounts, and by 1959 the number was around 170,000, although more than half were inactive.

Most surveys taken of M.I.P. participants revealed them to be middle-class, relatively unsophisticated in terms of investment knowledge, and interested in owning shares of large, solid corporations that were growing at a slightly more rapid rate than the economy as a whole. Clearly Funston had struck the proper note in spearheading the movement for an M.I.P., and perhaps his associates were justified in stating that its introduction was one of his major accomplishments. But although the program unquestionably resulted in new customers and additional commissions for brokerages, it also tarnished the credibility of the N.Y.S.E.—and Funston too—in the eyes of professionals. The unblinkingly conservative *Barron's* magazine launched a strong attack against the program, which it claimed was falsely advertised and contrary to the best interests of small investors due to its commission structure. M.I.P., said the journal, was an attempt "to lead the lamb back into Wall Street." Others noted that the program was appreciated by some brokerages, but not all; only those commission houses not involved in the management and promotion of mutual funds gave it much support, while even the Exchange had to admit that the average customer continued in his plan for only a half year or so. Indeed, at the time of its introduction, several columnists criticized the plan as makeshift, not as educational as Funston claimed it to be, and, worst of all, misleading. Several labeled M.I.P. as the Exchange's answer to the mutual funds, a poor one, perhaps, but a vehicle that was to have been anticipated. Without the mutuals, it is questionable whether many brokerages would have been as interested in the Monthly Investment Plan as they appeared to have been.

By stretching the point and the definition, it would be possible to trace the origin of mutual funds back as far as ancient Greece, where merchants banded together to take shares in commercial enterprises. Similar arrangements existed in Rome and Europe, and sedentary merchants in colonial America would take shares in voyages which, when completed, would be liquidated and the assets divided "according to shares." There are points of similarity between early corporations and present-day mutual funds, although they should not be carried too far.

Organizations quite like the mutual funds of the 1950s and 1960s appeared in Scotland in the 1880s organized, incidentally, to invest in American securities. The Scottish-American Investment Trust was formed in 1873 to hold a portfolio of American railroad bonds, and shares in the Trust were offered to interested citizens of Dundee. Other, similar trusts appeared both in Dundee and Aberdeen in the next few years, and some continue to this day. All were of the "closed-end" variety; they were capitalized at a fixed number of shares, which were bought and sold at the markets, with the prices set by supply and demand. Such funds appeared in America in the early twentieth century, and during the great bull market of the 1920s some of them, including Goldman Sachs Trading Corporation, United Founders, American Founders, and Lehman Fund, were among the darlings of the small investing public. Many of the closed-end trusts went under during the crash, but some survived, tainted and somehow mistrusted, into the postwar period.

Several management companies experimented with variations of the investment trust concept. The Massachusetts Investors Trust, State Street Investment Corporation, and Incorporated Investors were formed in 1924. Unlike the older trusts, these "open-ended" operations agreed to sell shares at net asset price, plus a small commission, and redeem them later on, also at net asset price. In effect, they offered investors shares in a package of stocks and bonds, with new money derived from sales utilized to purchase additional securities. Unlike the price of Goldman Sachs and the other closed-end trusts, that of Massachusetts Investors Trust could not be manipulated, since net asset value, not supply and demand, determined the price. Because of this, mutual funds, as they came to be called, did not attract the venturesome and speculative traders of the 1920s. Rather, they appealed to small investors who wanted "a part of the action," feared "putting all their eggs in one basket," and felt more secure with professional management than on their own.

The mutuals suffered along with the closed-end trusts in the market declines of 1920 and the early 1930s. Accounts were closed, and new units were hard to sell. Yet they were not tainted with speculation, as were the closed-end trusts, and throughout the depression investors continued to buy shares, though at a sluggish rate. In 1940, there were some 296,000 accounts in various mutuals, with net assets of under $500 million. Fund share sales grew in the 1940s, again among the small investors, so that by 1950 there were 939,000 accounts with assets of $2.5 billion. Still, the funds owned less than 1 percent of all listed securities on the N.Y.S.E., and their impacts were more potential than real.

It was then, when the bull market was gathering steam, that the sales of mutuals and the part they played in the investment picture began to change. By the end of 1951, there were over 1,110,000 accounts in force, and mutual funds owned 2.03 percent of all N.Y.S.E. stocks. The 5 million account mark was passed in early 1961, at which time the mutuals controlled assets of almost $23 billion and well over 4 percent of the Big Board's listed stocks.

Many factors contributed to the popularity of mutual funds in the 1950s, among them the same ones that drew small investors to common stocks and the M.I.P.: a prosperous economy, increased savings and discretionary income, and a bull market on Wall Street. As had been the case in the 1920s, a desire for a balanced portfolio and professional management were also important. To a person entering the stock market for the first time—who had been raised on stories of 1929—these were most reassuring. With a trifling amount of money, literally a few dollars a day, he could own parts of shares of I.B.M., General Motors, General Electric, Dow Chemical, and other corporate giants, and the professionals would make certain his investment grew steadily, or at least so it seemed.

Yet most studies concluded that mutual fund management was not exceptional in a majority of cases. A *Forbes* report in 1953 indicated that while the Standard & Poor's ninety-stock index had risen 151.2 percent from 1946 to 1952, the forty-one largest mutual funds had gone up by only 146.5 percent. Two years later *Business Week* compared the performance of forty-five large funds to the Standard &

Poor Index and found that in the first ten months of 1955 the Index had risen by 15 percent, the funds by 6.3 percent. A more scientific study, conducted by the Wharton School for the House Committee on Interstate and Foreign Commerce, begun in 1958 and completed in 1962, came to the same conclusion. "With respect to the performance of mutual funds, it was found that on the average it did not differ appreciably from what would have been achieved by an unmanaged portfolio consisting of the same proportions of common stocks, corporate bonds, government securities, and other assets as the composite portfolios of the funds."

The large majority of shares of mutual funds were not purchased, so the saying went, but sold. And it was here that the industry excelled and so was able to achieve far more than Keith Funston and the N.Y.S.E.'s publicity forces. With the exception of a handful of "no-load funds," mutuals carried a commission charge, usually around 8.5 percent of the purchase price, or 9.3 percent of the amount invested in shares. Thus, $1,000 put into such a fund would purchase $915 worth of shares. Furthermore, many of the funds were sold under contractual arrangements with heavy "front loads," which meant that a client who agreed to undertake a $10,000 plan, for example, would pay the bulk of the commissions out of the first $2,000 or so. Under some plans, almost a quarter of the initial payments went for commissions. Individuals who failed to complete the plans, then, paid heavy charges, usually far more than they would have had they opened M.I.P. accounts.

A large fraction of the commission went to pay the salesman, who was not only so encouraged to sell plans but particularly those of the front-load variety. Mutual fund salesmen were not as well trained as customers' men, at a time when the professionalism of the latter was under attack. Many mutual fund companies would give newcomers indoctrinations that lasted no more than a day, making them aware of the few restraints upon them as set forth by the Investment Company Act of 1940 and its 1954 amendments and offering tips as to how best sell the plans. Mutual funds were offered by a small army of part-timers who, after exhausting lists of friends and relatives, would leave the business. The salesman turnover was well known, and although the companies were criticized for this and for false advertising, little was done to correct the situation. It was far better to have ten part-time salesmen than five full-time ones, since the part-timers had that many more relatives to contact, and in either case each plan sold paid the same commission, whether placed by the part-timer or the full-timer. So it was that in 1950 the Hamilton Management Corporation had seventy-six salesmen, when the fund had assets of $7 million. By 1955 the organization had 624 salesmen, and the fund, assets of $31 million.

Hamilton's figures for 1961 were 7,800 salesmen and assets of $271 million.

The N.Y.S.E. had mixed feelings about mutual funds. On the one hand, they did attract individuals to investing who might otherwise have remained on the sidelines; today's purchaser of a mutual fund might open an M.I.P. tomorrow and later on a regular account. In addition, those brokerages that sold mutual fund shares found that the commissions on these nicely augmented the salaries of their customers' men and gave them another product to sell. Too, since most of the funds specialized in Big Board stocks, they helped swell trading volume. By 1962, $20.7 billion worth of listed stock were held by the various funds. Finally, some of them were notorious for "churning" their portfolios, especially just prior to the quarterly reporting periods. This meant that they would buy and sell more than they should, both in order to dress up their reports for the shareholders and to earn commissions for themselves and their affiliated houses. The Wharton Report indicated that in 1958 the funds turned their portfolios over at a rate of 16.9 percent, at a time when the N.Y.S.E.'s turnover rate on the whole was 12.9 percent, while some funds had a turnover of more than 50 percent.

On the other hand, the presence of the funds caused embarrassments for the N.Y.S.E.—the wide publicity given the Wharton Report being only one case of this. But even before the Report was released, thousands of investors and would-be investors who had been contacted by the part-time salesmen—either over the telephone or door-to-door—had come to distrust the sleaziness of the approach, while the industry made only feeble attempts to defend the front-load contracts. More important as far as the N.Y.S.E.'s immediate interests were concerned was the practice of "give-ups."

The Exchange's rule made no provision for volume discounts on large transactions, the kind the major funds usually engaged in. As might have been expected, the brokerages vied with one another for the business of leading mutuals. The funds, on their part, sought benefits from this competition and obtained them in the form of give-ups. Under this system, the fund would give its business to one or, as was more often the case, several brokerages, on the understanding that they would give up an agreed-upon portion of the commissions to specified third parties. In almost every instance the third parties would be commission houses whose customers' men sold a great many shares of the fund. In this way the organization offered an incentive to brokers who sold its shares, with the money coming from the houses that handled its business on the floor.

* * *

HOLDINGS OF CORPORATE STOCK BY FINANCIAL INSTITUTIONS, 1952–59
($billion)

		Insurance Organizations							
			Pension Funds						
	Total	Life Insurance Companies	Private	State and Local Governments	Other Insurance Companies	Open-End Investment Companies	Other Investment Companies	Mutual Savings Banks	Personal Trust Funds
1952	36.3	2.4	1.8	0.1	4.3	3.4	3.2	0.3	20.8
1953	37.2	2.6	2.4	0.1	4.5	3.6	3.3	0.4	20.3
1954	51.1	3.3	3.2	0.1	5.9	5.5	4.7	0.6	27.8
1955	63.4	3.6	6.1	0.1	6.9	7.1	5.7	0.7	33.2
1956	67.8	3.5	7.1	0.2	7.2	8.0	5.2	0.7	35.9
1957	63.3	3.4	7.5	0.2	6.7	7.5	4.8	0.8	32.4
1958	85.7	4.1	11.6	0.3	8.4	11.8	5.6	0.9	43.0
1959	97.1	4.6	14.5	0.3	9.1	14.4	5.9	0.8	47.5

SOURCE: Raymond W. Goldsmith, ed. *Institutional Investors and Corporate Stock—A Background Study* (New York, 1973), p. 144.

During the 1930s and 1940s, the N.Y.S.E. had grown accustomed to servicing small and occasional investors, along with a relative handful of speculators. Although there had been sporadic bursts of activity and interest during this period, they were generally short-lived and always followed by a new slump in volume and prices. Furthermore, large buyers and sellers were rarities throughout; a thousand-share order for a $20 stock was an event, something to be talked about for days afterward, while its satisfaction might strain the resources of the average specialist.

The situation was changing in the late 1940s and early 1950s, and the rise of the mutuals was one sign of it. New investment forces were in the process of formation, while old ones were being reinvigorated. This was due to several factors: the political confidence given the investing public by the Eisenhower Administration; the dawning sentiment that there would be no major recession after all; increases in the size of the middle class and its search for places to invest; and the growth of labor's economic power. If many Americans still viewed Wall Street as either a thieves' den or a playground for the wealthy, their union trust funds, or the company from which they purchased an insurance policy, thought otherwise. Throughout the decade, large institutions holding often enormous pools of liquid capital came to Wall Street seeking equities in which to invest. For the most part, they were interested in blue-chip stocks, which would be placed in trust portfolios and remain there indefinitely—what the industry then and later would call "one-decision investments." But as the market rose, with many of the smaller, more speculative stocks leading the rise, the large institutions became more venturesome and began purchasing and selling large blocks of stock on a regular basis.

The increase in institutional business could be detected as early as the late 1940s, when significant numbers of blocks appeared on the floor. At that time they were disposed of with little difficulty; the specialists were encouraged by the business and welcomed more of the same. Shortly thereafter, some of the blocks could not be "digested," and sharp drops in prices of leading issues were registered when one or another institution tried to sell, while rises on purchases were also common. This resulted in a congressional investigation of large investors, completed and released in 1956. Among other things, the study showed that in transactions in twenty-five leading issues in 1953–1955, large institutions—mutual funds, insurance companies, trust funds, and the like—accounted for little over 5 percent of all trading. But for some companies, the share was far higher—23 percent of Sears Roebuck and 22 percent of Southern California Edison, for example, were bought and sold by the institutions. By the end of the

NET PURCHASES OR SALES OF CORPORATE STOCK BY FINANCIAL INSTITUTIONS, 1952–59 (*$billion*)

				Pension Funds			
	Total	*Mutual Savings Banks*	*Life Insurance Companies*	*Private*	*State and Local Governments*	*Other Insurance Companies*	*Open-End Investment Companies*
				Annual Data			
1952	1.42	.11	0.16	0.48	0.02	0.18	0.47
1953	1.51	.10	0.09	0.55	0.02	0.19	0.56
1954	1.60	.14	0.27	0.71	0.02	0.16	0.30
1955	1.59	.08	0.07	0.74	0.03	0.16	0.51
1956	1.72	.05	−0.00	0.94	0.03	0.14	0.56
1957	2.24	.06	0.04	1.14	0.05	0.13	0.82
1958	2.74	.10	0.08	1.38	0.06	0.13	0.99
1959	3.53	−.05	0.19	1.74	0.08	0.27	1.30

SOURCE: Goldsmith, *Institutional Investors*, p. 137.

decade, dealings by large institutions accounted for about one-fifth of all transactions handled by the Exchange.*

The emergence of these new and revived investment forces did not catch the Exchange community unawares, and the transformation of the small investor's market of the 1940s into the large institutional one of the early 1960s took place gradually. Thus, the N.Y.S.E. had time to adjust to the situation and exploit it.

Some of the changes were made by the specialists themselves, without official prodding. As they became aware of the larger market opening before them, they increased their capital and inventories and expanded their operations, often taking on additional partners who brought new funds into the firms. The Exchange merged small specialists to form larger units, while a handful left that side of the business to enter others. On occasion a small specialist would relinquish an active stock he felt he could no longer service adequately, while major new listings were assigned to the more powerfully financed

* Surprisingly few studies of institutional activities in this period have been made. But see United States Congress, Joint Economic Committee, 84th Cong., 2nd session, *Institutional Investors and the Stock Market* (Washington, 1956), especially pp. 86 ff.

specialists. In addition, the Exchange itself kept a careful watch on the situation, making certain the specialist units were geared to handle the larger blocks that were appearing at that time. In all, these practices meant that in an evolutionary fashion, the larger specialists were obtaining increased influence and profits, while the smaller ones were obliged either to group together and become large or leave the field. Considering the nature of the business, this might have been expected.

This did not suffice to deal with the block business, however. Special offerings and secondaries were employed when large blocks were to be sold, in the same fashion as they had in the past. They were not popular, since a greater degree of management was needed for the large blocks of the 1950s. As a result, the Exchange sanctioned prearranged cross sales on the floor. Under this method, the broker hoping to dispose of a large block of XYZ stock would be brought together with one who wanted to purchase one. Often, but not always, the same broker would represent both buyer and seller, and the transaction would appear as though a normal one. But there was a significant difference: in effect, the transaction was negotiated as to volume and price, even though the latter had to be at the last recorded auction price. This was a variation from the pure auction market the N.Y.S.E. had always prided itself on being, and the difference was noted at the time. But it was necessary. Few specialists could handle a single order for $500,000 worth of stock without causing the price to rise or fall precipitously. Thus, another method had to be used. Cross sales indicated that the N.Y.S.E. was evolving, perhaps away from the auction principle, and was doing so slowly, apparently without a master plan of any kind.

The N.Y.S.E. approved of a variation on the cross sale in 1953, known as the Exchange distribution. In its essentials, this method was the same as the cross, but special selling efforts—the payment of bonuses and higher commissions—were made to move especially hard-to-liquidate blocks. The action would begin once approval was granted. Then the seller's brokers would enter the arena, lining up buyers. When all or most of the block had been taken, the sale would cross the tape at the agreed upon price, with the notation that it was an Exchange distribution. Like the cross, the Exchange distribution's price was negotiated rather than arrived at through the auction mechanism, and it provided yet another deviation from the old norm made necessary by the appearance of large blocks. In 1954, the first full year for Exchange distributions, fifty-four of them were made, involving 623,464 shares of stock offered and 602,881 taken, for a total market value of over $23 million. That same year, there were only twelve specials, for 168,309 shares worth $6 million. The aggressive selling of the Exchange distributions made them popular at a time of activity in the Street. The rather bland aspects of the specials, useful in a previous period but out of place in the hectic 1950s, seemed antique by then.

Increasingly, even Exchange distributions and crosses failed to service the block market, and the N.Y.S.E. found much of the business going to O-T-C dealers. In order to prevent commission houses from abandoning the floor for the telephones to the O-T-C firms, the specialists united to push through a new regulation, known as Rule 394. Perhaps the most contentious and debated regulation in Exchange history, Rule 394 forbade members from dealing as principals or agents in effecting off-board transactions in listed securities with nonmembers "except as otherwise specifically exempted by the Exchange." Rule 394 was ratified in 1955, when block trading was growing, but still was not considered a major problem or opportunity. On the surface, at least, it would appear a repudiation of the S.E.C., in particular of the Commission's position in the early 1940s regarding multiple trading. But the specialists deemed the risk worth taking, and the board passed the word down: enforcement would be strict and transgressors dealt with harshly.

Rule 394 did not create much of a stir in Washington, however, or, for that matter, at the O-T-C houses. Increasingly, even Exchange distributions and crosses did not suffice to liquidate and absorb large blocks, and the N.Y.S.E. was obliged to condone dealings with the over-the-counter brokers.

One such method was the specialist block purchase. If a specialist found himself short of shares in a particularly desirable stock and so unable to maintain an orderly market in the issue, he could request the approval of a floor governor to purchase the shares from an over-the-counter dealer. If the official decided that such indeed was the case, he could approve the request. Then the specialist contacted several over-the-counter houses, determining the amount of shares available and their prices. Finally, he would make his purchase on a negotiated rather than an auction basis, since such was the foundation of O-T-C dealings. Similarly, a specialist who found himself burdened with an excessive inventory could apply for permission to sell shares to over-the-counter dealers in what was known as specialist block sales.

In retrospect it is possible to see the movement away from the auction principle and in the direction of negotiated markets in the 1950s. This took place not through design or as a manifestation of ideology but rather as a result of pragmatic necessity. The changes in rules and procedures were accomplished in a tactical fashion, and intelligently, with alterations fashioned when desirable. The N.Y.S.E., which for over a century had proven capable of bending to the needs of the investment community, investors, and speculators, was once again making accommodations and adjustments in its procedures. In time, the old auction market might have been discarded, to be replaced by a dealer market which—as the Exchange itself appeared to be indicating through specialist block sales and purchases—was more attuned to the requirements of an institution-dominated market.

To accomplish this, however, the N.Y.S.E. would have to have bold leadership and a strategy, and neither existed in the 1950s. Rather, Funston and his staff spent most of their time attempting to influence Congress to pass legislation beneficial to small investors, promoting M.I.P., seeking additional listings, boosting People's Capitalism, and entertaining visiting dignitaries. Investment clubs, usually consisting of new investors, were becoming popular in this period. In October 1951, the National Association of Investment Clubs was organized, and soon after the Curb Exchange took a proprietary interest in the movement. Fearing perhaps that the clubs would draw clients from the M.I.P., Funston and the N.Y.S.E. stepped up the drive for new accounts. Matters such as these, not alterations in Exchange structure, dominated thinking at the N.Y.S.E.

This was to have been expected. Ever since the mid-1930s, the Exchange had geared itself to the needs of small investors and tried to lure them back to Wall Street. A second major concern had been Washington, and the desire to remain on good terms with the S.E.C. and Congress dictated a cautious policy. People's Capitalism was antithetical to some of the implications of institutional power, even though the institutions were only investing the savings of small members. Funston liked to portray the ideal American as one who could stand on his own; the idea of investing through intermediaries somehow smudged this image. Then there was Funston himself, a super-salesman, a fine representative of the ideology and drive of the N.Y.S.E. at mid-century—but at the same time, a man who knew little about the history of investments, the internal mechanisms of the N.Y.S.E., and the tensions of the district. Funston was intelligent; he could direct the Exchange in tactical maneuvers. But the strategic needs of the N.Y.S.E. were beyond him in the 1950s. Instead, he counterattacked rather than innovated, reacted rather than acted, and appeared to think more of form than content.

The major emerging problem of the 1950s was that of liquidity—the ability of the Exchange to provide an efficient marketplace for securities, to enable buyers and sellers to conduct business harmoniously, with a minimum of difficulty and certainly no panic. But strains were showing in this period, and these were alleviated in part by recourse to new methods and, significantly, those of the over-the-counter markets.

This situation created a paradox for customers' men and, more to the point, for the commission broker community as a whole. Under the law, the broker was obliged to seek the "best market" for his client. That is to say, he was supposed to canvas all markets where the stock could be found, to make certain he was obtaining the lowest price on a purchase and the highest on a sale. In practice, however, brokers handling small orders in listed stocks had them executed on the Exchange floor. By the mid-1950s it was evident that at some times, in some stocks bought and sold in quantities, over-the-counter dealers were making "better markets" than their N.Y.S.E. specialist counterparts. This meant little insofar as the small investors were concerned. If one of them wanted to purchase 100 shares of XYZ, and the N.Y.S.E. asking price was 50½, while an O-T-C dealer was offering a block at 50⅜, the Big Board would get the trade anyway.* But what should be done when the client was a large mutual fund, or a pension trust, and the order was for 3,000 shares? To execute such an order in that fashion would be to invite the loss of a customer at the least, and a law suit and scandal were distinct possibilities. Thus, the commission houses were drawn, increasingly, to the O-T-C market in listed stocks.

By so acting they were in violation of Rule 394—they were trading listed stocks at another market without first asking Exchange permission. In addition, they were angering powerful specialists, men who often were their allies in the district. At first, some large commission houses seemed willing to run that risk. After all, they could survive without the N.Y.S.E.—or any organized market, for that matter. So long as clients used their services to find a market for shares, and such existed—physically or over telephone lines, it made no difference—commission brokerage would survive and even prosper. And if this was all there was to it, the N.Y.S.E. might have declined, even though trading volume was rising, or, at the very least, the specialist system would have to be altered or scrapped.

But the specialists had a potential weapon, one that was discussed in the 1950s but not taken seriously until the following decade. Under the Exchange's rules, membership was limited to individuals, partnerships, and corporations whose primary concern was the securities business. Among other things, this meant that a bank, trust company, or insurance firm—or any other large institution whose interests were in buying and selling securities but whose major business was elsewhere

* Furthermore, while the N.Y.S.E. charged a fee for each transaction, the O-T-C dealers did not, thus lowering the net price even more than the quotes would indicate.

—could not purchase a N.Y.S.E. seat. If one of these institutions wished to buy or sell shares on the N.Y.S.E., it would have to employ the services of a broker. The same was true for mutual funds, all of which operated through commission houses. And as state and municipalities purchased stocks for various pension funds, they too used the services of commission brokers.

Yet the rule was cracking. During the 1940s, for example, only unincorporated partnerships and individuals could own seats. Members were forbidden to incorporate, the reasoning being that all firms should be completely responsible for their actions and so should have unlimited liabilities. In 1946, an amendment providing for permissive incorporation of member firms and the admission of corporations, under prescribed restrictions, was defeated. Its proponents argued that incorporation would allow member firms to raise additional capital and that, if passed, the amendment would attract nonmember brokerages to the Exchange and so enhance the value of seats as well as bring new clients to the market when they were needed. The amendment was revived in 1949 in a slightly different form. The old form was retained, but now incorporated members would have to engage exclusively in the securities business. This was added in order to capture the votes of some of the commission houses, which were wary of competition. And once again the amendment was defeated. A permissive incorporation amendment did pass in 1953, however, by a vote of 594 to 538. This was made possible by an alliance of specialists and large commission houses, interested in incorporating in order to raise more capital and, in the case of some, believing that in time, they might even sell shares in their operations to the public.

In the second half of the 1950s, some specialists spoke guardedly of a new amendment, one that would permit the admission of incorporated firms whose primary business was *not* in securities. If accepted, this would mean that mutual funds, for example, would be able to purchase seats and then deal directly with the specialists on their orders, by-passing the commission houses. And if this happened, the commission houses would soon lose a major portion of their business.

By the late 1950s, alliances and counteralliances were discussed on the Street. Commission houses were being attracted to the O-T-C, while some specialists talked openly of permitting financial corporations to purchase N.Y.S.E. seats. This was one of the more important Wall Street reactions to the emergence of institutional trading, the key development in the great bull market then taking shape. If the commission houses went one way and the specialists the other, the Big Board would be destroyed, at least in the shape it had been for the past century. The problem would grow, with Funston and the board paying it little heed, nor suggesting measures to heal the wounds or solve the problems.

The new investors created a different kind of talk too: rumors of a possible panic. In 1954, Professor John K. Galbraith of Harvard told the Committee on Banking and Currency that "another 1929" was a possibility, and the following year he wrote a popular work, *The Great Crash*, in which he appeared to be warning against excesses of speculation in the 1950s and comparing them to those of the 1920s. In part this comparison was political. Eisenhower was the first Republican to hold the Presidency since the 1920s, and his statements about restoring balanced budgets, along with a general feeling of conservatism in the land, disturbed liberals. What better weapon to use against conservatives and Republicans than memories of the Great Depression? The rise of a business-oriented Administration naturally led to the creation of an antibusiness rhetoric among its critics, one of whom was John Galbraith.

Yet the questions they asked were sincere and struck responsive chords among many. Was the stock market advance real? Would it last? How far would it go? Would it end in a crash? Such questions were often asked as the bull market gathered strength, and experts sometimes answered that on a price/earnings ratio basis, stocks could still move higher.

What would happen, however, if many small investors—people who owned shares in mutual funds—decided to liquidate their holdings? Or if the economy took a minor dip, which some large pension funds interpreted as a signal to sell? Would the market be able to absorb, say, ten 1,000-share blocks of General Motors in a single session? Or even in a week? The answer clearly was "no" in the late 1950s.

The investors who came to Wall Street in the 1950s provided the N.Y.S.E. with a source of strength and opened new opportunities to its members. Interest in investment was rising rapidly, so that by the end of the decade the district was in the midst of what was conceded to be a general prosperity, the first since the 1920s. And this parallelism bothered some observers. The Street had institutional difficulties in the 1920s that had been overlooked and later proved disastrous. A new set of problems evolved in the 1950s, and the leadership of the N.Y.S.E. appeared to be ignoring them, behaving as though the reforms of the 1930s had obviated any crisis. Funston and other Big Board leaders did not respond to the challenges of the institutional investors, except to say that prices were low, the economy sound, and that they were purchasing shares for their own portfolios. For a generation and more, the N.Y.S.E. had tried to draw new money to the Street. Now that it had arrived, in greater amounts than believed possible, the Exchange could hardly be expected to frighten it away.

CHAPTER 12

The Euphoric Decade

Dwight Eisenhower confounded his critics and baffled his friends during his first year and a half in the White House. The rhythm of American politics seemed to dictate the alteration of periods of reform with those of consolidation, of movement with stability, imagination with prudence. After sixteen years of New Deal–Fair Deal, the general sentiment was that the nation could expect eight of retrenchment, in which the reforms of the past would be subjected to scrutiny and debate, and, afterward, either rejected or altered. Such might have been the case had a true conservative—Robert Taft, for instance—been elected in 1952. But Eisenhower was no conservative. Indeed, analyzing his performance in this period, commentators seemed uncertain as to his political ideology, and Washingtonians began to suspect he lacked one. The view of Eisenhower as a political innocent, born during the campaign of 1952, became part of the lore in 1953–1954. At various times he characterized his stance as "modern Republicanism," "dynamic conservatism," and "progressive moderation." "When it comes down to dealing with the relationships between the human in this country and his government, the people in this Administration believe in being what I think we would normally call liberal," said the President in January 1953, "and when we deal with the economic affairs of this country, we believe in being conservative."

What did this mean in the area of economic policy? Eisenhower had inherited the Korean conflict and inflation from the Truman Administration. He had ended the war in July 1953, but inflation was a more prickly problem. The classical method was to balance the budget, tighten up on the money supply, increase taxes, and support a policy of high interest rates. His influential Secretary of the Treasury, George Humphrey, believed in these measures, along with the rapid repayment of the national debt and programs faintly reminiscent of the Coolidge years. Yet such policies, which if pursued diligently would have stifled inflation, also would result in higher unemployment and a lower rate of economic growth.

The new Administration was willing to pay the political and economic price that came with a deflationary policy. Almost all wartime economic controls were dropped soon after Eisenhower took office, a sign to business that government would adopt a hands-off policy in the future, and that such restrictions would no longer be needed. Government spending programs were cut drastically, as Eisenhower announced his intention to balance the budget. The Federal Reserve stopped pegging the prices of government bonds, which then fell. At the same time, the central bank increased the discount rate from 1¾ percent to 2 percent, the highest since 1933. The prime rate responded, rising slowly through 1953, as the tight money strategy took hold. These policies, together with decreased military spending in the aftermath of the Korean conflict, caused the recession of 1953–1954, what Democrats called a prelude to another 1929 and Republicans termed a "rolling readjustment." In 1954 the unemployment rate reached 5.5 percent, a sharp jump from the 2.9 percent figure of 1953. That same year, the Consumer Price Index was 114.8, an increase of only .4 from the previous year, the lowest such rise since the recession year of 1949.

With this, the Administration relaxed its tight-money policy, reduced taxes, and incurred a budget deficit. The recession slowed in the summer of 1954 and recovery began in the final quarter. Economic growth resumed and unemployment dropped. Inflation slowed to a crawl. If the economy did not expand as rapidly as many Democrats thought it could, and unemployment fell to the 1952 level, at least Eisenhower managed to keep inflation in check. The nation would suffer through two more recessions in the Eisenhower Presidency, but even then there seemed no doubt that the Administration would do little that might result in a new spurt of inflation. Although the Federal Reserve lowered the discount rate in 1954 in order to stimulate the economy, and the prime rate followed suit, for most of the Eisenhower years money rates were higher than they had been under Roosevelt and Truman. In 1956 the President utilized a new slogan—Peace and Prosperity. But the Cold War intensified and the economy performed below capacity during his Administration.

In terms of the conventional wisdom, many of the Eisenhower programs and attitudes should have had a bearish impact on stock prices. High interest rates, tight money, and a low level of economic growth could be expected to result in lower quotations and decreased activity at the N.Y.S.E. At the time, inflation was considered a stimulant to stock prices, as individuals and institutions rushed to put their money into instruments that would rise with the cost of living.

Eisenhower was dedicated to halting inflation and accepted recessions in order to do so; this too should have put an end to the stock boom.

On the other hand, Eisenhower did contribute three significant factors which more than compensated for his bearish programs. First of all, his was a pro-business administration, dedicated to halting, if not reversing, the drift of power to Washington. True, this did not occur, and toward the end of his Presidency, Eisenhower warned of the growth of the "military-industrial complex" in Washington. The federal budget increased while he was President, as did the national debt. Time and again Eisenhower was obliged to accept the contents of liberal programs, if not their forms. Yet his rhetoric throughout remained that of a free-enterpriser, and this was a tonic for the Street.

Next, Eisenhower provided a sense of stability in these years, something that had been lacking in the country since the mid-1920s. Events and leaders since 1929 had imparted a sense of dynamism—often an unwelcome one—to the nation and the world. Uncertainties usually result in bearish movements on Wall Street, the sole exceptions being upward sweeps based on fear of inflation and sporadic "buyers' panics." All major bull markets, including those of the early twentieth century and the 1920s, had taken place during periods when investors felt the underlying institutions of the nation were sound. This sentiment existed in the mid-1950s, after the end of the Korean conflict and the crippling of the inflationary spiral.

Finally, the new President inspired confidence in his person, not quite the same emotion as stability but closely allied to it in this case. Few men have been so trusted and admired for so long by so many Americans. Eisenhower had a grip upon the nation that was at times compared with that of Franklin Roosevelt. But Roosevelt was a partisan and an advocate of change, with more in common with Wilson and Lincoln than most great leaders. Eisenhower, on the other hand, appeared as a nonpartisan leader (a source of great anguish to dedicated Republicans, who claimed he had done more to harm their party than could any Democrat). In his public image, at least, he was more in the mold of a Washington, a person who avoided dichotomies and ameliorated differences. To activists he seemed stodgy and somewhat dull; in 1959, one newspaper called him the closest America had developed to a Queen Victoria. Perhaps this was so, but Victoria too was respected and helped provide a sense of stability for a changing nation.

Although Eisenhower's popularity was evident during the 1952 campaign, stock prices and trading volume did not rise in this period. On November 3, the day before Election Day, the Dow closed at

270.23, with 1,670,000 shares traded; at that, it was less than one point higher than its price on January 2. The Eisenhower victory resulted in a point advance on November 5, with volume at only 2,030,000 shares. On Inauguration Day, January 20, 1953, the Dow closed at 288.00 on 1,490,000 shares. Prices had risen on peace rumors and the general euphoria that usually accompany a new beginning in politics in America, but the rise was smaller than had been anticipated, and trading volume had not expanded during the interregnum.

After rising 22.67 points in November and December of 1952, stock prices declined 23.64 in the first half of 1953. Two of the reasons for the unexpected fall came from developments overseas. Joseph Stalin died on March 14, and his successor, the seemingly benign Georgi Malenkov, began a "peace offensive," leading to talk of an end to the Cold War. At the same time, the Korean conflict was clearly in its last stage. What would happen if "peace broke out"? Every American war had been followed by a period of dislocation, and most by recessions. Eisenhower seemed intent on cutting the budget to the bone, and this surely would exacerbate the situation. The Great Depression was considered to have been signaled by the Stock Market Crash of October 1929, which took place little more than six months after Herbert Hoover assumed the Presidency. Eisenhower was the first Republican Chief Executive since Hoover. Was history repeating itself? Wall Streeters, who are usually fascinated with such parallels—especially when they spell boom and bust—began making them in April. Lewis Haney of the *New York Journal-American*, a perennial pessimist, thought "an important decline in the market lies somewhere ahead," but conceded that "no decline as great as that in 1929 seems probable." "We are not going to have a depression in America" said Secretary of the Treasury Humphrey on April 21, by which time he was obliged to try to calm fears. "There will be readjustments, of course. But depression, no. We cannot preserve our way of life through another long, deep depression and we must never permit it to occur." Prices rallied slightly in July and then declined again in August, losing 14.16 points that month, the worst showing since the beginning of the Korean conflict.

In mid-September, as prices declined steadily on low volume, talk of "another 1929" intensified. Yet, the country was prosperous. Inflationary pressures were loosening, and although the economy was in a recession, it bore no resemblance to the situation in the 1930s. The market bottomed out at Dow 255.49 on September 14, and then began to rise slowly, with volume remaining poor. Prices shot up by more than 11 points in October and 5 in November, but declined slightly in December, closing 1953 at 280.90. In all, the Dow Industrials lost 11 points in 1953, a year in which the turnover rate of listed N.Y.S.E.

stocks was 12 percent, the worst showing since 1942. Toward the end of the year, a Stock Exchange seat changed hands at $38,000; at the conclusion of World War II, the price was close to $100,000, while in early 1953, a high of $60,000 was reported.

In this fashion, Wall Street reflected the national mood during the depth of the first Eisenhower recession. V-J Day had been followed by inflation, boom, and uncertainties. The winding down of the Korean conflict and the short hiatus in the Cold War had taken place during a man-made recession and an attempt to introduce a measure of stability into the economy that had been lacking earlier. All things considered, said Eisenhower critic Sylvia Porter, "the price wasn't that high." By no stretch of the imagination could 1953 be compared with 1929. Whatever else he was, Eisenhower would not be a carbon copy of Herbert Hoover.

There was another difference between the markets of 1929–1930 and those of 1953. While there was little in the way of bullish market news in the earlier period, a small but significant rally began in 1953.

As early as 1948, low-priced petroleum issues had boomed on the Toronto Stock Exchange and other Canadian markets. In 1953, news of a large uranium find in the Athabascan region of Saskatchewan appeared in American newspapers, followed by other mineral strikes in New Brunswick. Then came announcements of major investments by American steel companies in Canada's ore fields, and multimillion-dollar opportunities in a new transportation network, utilities, retailing, and almost every other area of the economy. Newspapers carried stories of the boom, and in them the situation in Canada was compared favorably to those that had existed in America in the late nineteenth century.

The boom attracted speculative capital from all parts of the world, and leading the way were Americans seeking "action." "The speculative craze in Canada, aided in no small part by those on this side of the border, who think they can get rich quickly, goes on apace," wrote C. Norman Stabler in the *New York Herald Tribune* on March 13, 1953, at a time when American stock prices and volume were falling. "Most of it is based on sound considerations of the Dominion's unquestioned wealth in natural resources, but there is evidence that part of it stems from the gambling spirit usually associated with horse races."

Advertisements in Canadian newspapers, offering information on "special situations" and all but guaranteeing results, were reported in American journals. *The Penny Stock Special*, one of the leading advisory services, received thousands of subscriptions from Americans. In

February trading volume on the Toronto Stock Exchange reached 144.4 million shares, a new record, and late that month 12 million share days became the norm. Of course, much of this was in shares costing a few cents each, and so the volume figures could not be compared with those of the N.Y.S.E. Still, in March seats on the Toronto Exchange were selling for $90,000, while Montreal Exchange memberships went for over $40,000, and Canadian brokers and dealers were doing better financially than many of their American counterparts.

So were their customers. Such stocks as Gunnar Gold Mines, Chimo Gold Mines, New Larder Uranium, and the like were quadrupling in price in a matter of a handful of trading sessions, when American Telephone & Telegraph was standing still and General Motors and General Electric were declining. Ted McCormick of the Amex* saw in the Canadian boom the opportunity to attract new listings, and he traveled regularly between New York and leading northern cities seeking them. In 1951, the Amex had 75 Canadian stocks; by 1953, the number was 93. At mid-year, the Wall Street press seemed to believe that speculation would be concentrated in foreign issues for the time being; American stocks were for the stodgy.

But not for long, or for all American issues. The boom had demonstrated that many individuals, wealthier and more secure than ever before, were interested in speculation. Those who had been burned by the 1929 crash and its aftermath were wary of securities, but their children, who had no memories of the disaster, were now adults and ready to try their hand at the game. A new generation of speculators came of age in this period, and their appetites were whetted by the news from Canada. Financial columnists warned of unwise speculation, but for the most part these were people who still remembered the 1929 crash, and so were to be ignored. In less than a month, New Larder Uranium went from 12½¢ a share to $2.76. The boom might not continue, but while it was on, fortunes could be made. Canadian brokers purchased "sucker lists" consisting of Americans and began selling shares over the telephone. Soon after, American brokers joined in the game. And the suckers more often than not lost their investments. Some did not, however; seemingly worthless Canadian properties rose in price, in large part due to sales pressures. But whatever the reason, money was made in Canadian markets, and interest in securities spilled over into Wall Street in late 1953.

By then, the recession seemed about to end, while confidence in Eisenhower's abilities was high. Investors—the kinds of people who had purchased sound stocks in the late 1940s, primarily for income—began to return to the market. At the same time, speculators played

* The Curb Exchange changed its name to the American Stock Exchange on January 5, 1953, and was soon called "Amex" by the press and public.

with low-priced stocks. As a result, both varieties of securities rose in early 1954, giving the appearance of a solidly based, unitary market going to the upside in strength.

At first it was not certain whether the speculators or investors would dominate interest, even though Wall Street veterans knew that speculation would become rampant only if the bull market continued for more than a season or so. The answer seemed to come in March, when Walter Winchell began offering stock tips during his Sunday evening broadcasts. At the time, Winchell was easily the most influential radio personality in America, as well as a popular newspaper columnist. His listeners believed he had inside information regarding practically every aspect of American life, and so when Winchell reported good corporate news at a company and recommended the purchase of its stock, the price would rise the next day, on heavy volume. Most of the stocks he discussed were low-priced—Eastern Air Lines, Western Union, Bell Aircraft, Twentieth-Century Fox, Amerada Petroleum were among them. When Winchell said that Amurex Oil Development would soon report "the biggest oil strike in North American history," the security rose from 14⅞ to 20⅞ in a day. Missouri Pacific was supposed to "make market news"; the stock rose 5½ points the next day. Universal Consolidated, American Bosch, Webb & Knapp—all did the same. In January 1955, Winchell claimed that had a person purchased round lots in all the forty or so stocks he had mentioned in the previous year, he would have a paper profit of around a quarter of a million dollars. This was not so; in fact, most of the Winchell stocks declined soon after the initial buyers' panic ended. Still, Winchell drew many thousands of speculators into the markets, and in his own way was a more effective agent for the exchanges than either Funston or McCormick.

Amex prices and volume began to rise in early 1954, and then they took off at the N.Y.S.E. Increasingly, low-priced stocks appeared on the most active list. Brokers spoke of a new kind of customer appearing in the offices, people who were more gamblers than investors, and didn't know how to handle them. Old-timers recognized some as being similar to the clients of the 1920s, people who wanted action more than security. To such individuals, the M.I.P. and investment clubs were almost antique concepts, while the mutual funds were vehicles for the aged and overly cautious. Later on it would be claimed that Wall Street's brokers lured clients into speculation. This was not the case. In 1954 the brokerages were manned by old-line personnel who believed in investment, who were accustomed to poor markets, and who were schooled in conservative practices. The new speculator obliged the brokerages to take on additional personnel, while high volume and commissions assured that they would be aggressive individuals, often young people like many of their clients. To such customers and brokers, Wall Street history began in the postwar period. The Great Crash was a historic event, in somewhat the same category as the Civil War.

The great bull market of the 1950s can be traced to the reaction to inflation in 1949. Prices began to rise, in what may be viewed as the return of some old investors along with the new, all of whom appeared to stress safety of principle and return on investment. The people and ideologies of 1954 were different; it was then that social and structural changes began that would become the hallmarks of the bull era, among which were optimism, unbounded faith in the future, security in the fundamental virtue of America, and an unbridled belief in progress. In short, in some surface manifestations, the speculators of the 1950s would resemble their kin of the 1920s. But there were differences. The old laissez-faire attitude had been replaced by acceptance of government regulation, which investors believed was effective and a guarantee against chicanery. Through his dealings with the 1953–1954 recession, Eisenhower had proven a flexible, eclectic politician, one who would incorporate aspects of the New Deal into his Modern Republicanism. It was a blend that many investors thought wise, which would result in greater confidence in stocks, and stimulate business to ever greater performances.

Such was the case in 1954, as the recession ended and peace and prosperity appeared to have arrived. The Dow Industrials began climbing in early January and scarcely paused thereafter. From 282.72 on January 2, it reached past the 300 mark on March 5. This was deemed a newsworthy event; the last time the Dow had been at that level was October 26, 1929. Secretary of Commerce Sinclair Weeks, charged with major responsibilities in handling the recession, considered the Wall Street activities significant, as he hailed "Eisenhower Prosperity." "I don't care what others think," he said. "I believe the stock market is still one of the best barometers of business this country has."

Stocks were front-page news in early summer, as the average neared the 1929 bull market high of 381.37. In July, clients followed the Dow as they might baseball scores, cheering it on. Prices dipped briefly in August, responding to reports of the Soviet development of a hydrogen bomb. During the late 1940s such adverse foreign policy news could kill a boom. This did not happen in 1954. Rather, stocks rose in September and October, discounting the bomb, and in response to evidence that large institutional investors were shifting from bonds to stocks. The only weak spot was in mutual funds, whose sales remained constant even though appreciations of portfolios resulted in a rise of fund assets to the $4 billion mark, a record, in the fourth quarter. Even this was deemed bullish by some Wall Street analysts, who claimed "the little guy is always wrong."

The Dow passed the 1929 high on November 17, an event marked by loud cheering and celebrations on the Street and in brokerage back offices. Without pausing, it rose to 400 on December 29 and closed 1954 at 404.39. Stock prices had advanced more than 120 points for the year, an increase of 44 percent. It was the greatest year in terms of prices since the late 1920s. Trading volume in December was 76,455,000 shares, the best since June 1933. Over 573 million shares were traded in 1954, the largest amount since 1931. Average daily volume exceeded 2.2 million shares; it was the first time the 2 million mark had been bettered since 1933. On the next to the last trading day of the year, a Big Board seat changed hands at $88,000—almost twice the price of December, 1953. Little wonder, then, that the Wall Street community was euphoric by Christmas.

Stock analysts discussed the great advance of 1954 during the holiday season, and most agreed that the Eisenhower Administration deserved a good deal of the credit. Inflation control and a restoration of confidence in government-business relations were given as major factors. In other words, it appeared to them that the 1954 boom was based on changes in the economy and a reversal of national psychology. The seeds were planted in 1953; they bloomed the following year. This, at least, was the conventional wisdom, and if it were true, then continued confidence and stable prices should have resulted in a steady rise in stock quotations, perhaps in a direct ratio to advances in the gross national product, corporate profits, or some statistics.

This was not the case. During the Eisenhower years the Dow Industrials rose from 289.16 to 637.15, more than doubling. When Eisenhower came to office the unemployment rate was 2.9 percent; when he left, it was 6.7 percent. He assumed the Presidency at a time when the economy was booming and retired at a time when the nation was in a recession. The gross national product went from $347 billion to $507.3 billion in the Eisenhower era, and corporate profits from $38.5 billion to $49.7 billion—hardly as impressive a performance as stock prices. Nor did dividend yields keep pace with the rise in stocks. In 1952 the return on the Dow Industrials was 5.8 percent; in 1960, it was 3.1 percent. Indeed, by any statistical measure, securities prices outran the economy during the Eisenhower Presidency. Secretary

Weeks's comments to the contrary notwithstanding, insofar as the Eisenhower Administration was concerned, stock prices were a poor barometer.

The reasons for this unusual situation may best be understood by a comparison of the market's performance during the Eisenhower Administration with its record through the Truman years. When Roosevelt died, the nation was still at war, even though victory was in sight. Most economists were predicting a major recession—perhaps even a depression—when peace arrived. Some went so far as to say that American prosperity had been based on military spending, and once that ended, the economy would undergo a slump of the proportions of 1929–1933. Stock prices were still depressed in 1945, despite the minor bull move of the wartime years, and trading volume was low. Thus, Harry Truman entered the White House when the economy was strong but fears great, and when a majority of Americans were uncertain as to his abilities.

The Dow Industrials stood at 159.17 that day. When Truman left the Presidency, the average was at 289.16. This would appear a great achievement on its face, but considering the performance of the economy, the market lagged. There was no depression after the war, but instead a major economic boom, one of the most spectacular in American history. Inflation, not recession, troubled Americans, and inflation had always been good for stock prices in the past and should have been the same in the late 1940s. The gross national product in 1945, when the nation was at war and operating at full steam, was $213.6 billion. In 1952 it reached $347 billion. Corporate profits in this same period went from $21.2 billion to $38.5 billion. Considering the problems of 1945 vis-à-vis those of 1952, the economic record of this period was most impressive and should have been reflected in stock prices. It was not, and a major reason for this was the unpopularity of the national Administration and uncertainties as to its actions, which were summed up in a Republican slogan of 1952—the Democrats stood for "Communism, Corruption, and Korea."

Whatever the costs, and whatever else the Truman Administration did, it helped create a booming economy. Yet this was not reflected in stock prices until 1949, and then it was inflation, not trust in the President, that propelled the market upward. In 1949 the gross national product was $45 billion more than it had been in 1945, and corporate profits stood almost $7 billion higher than they did in the last year of the war. Dividends in 1945 had been $6 billion; in 1949, they were $9.5 billion. In the summer of 1949 the Dow Industrials were where they had been on the day Roosevelt died.

During the period from 1945 to 1949, the economy outran the stock market. The two were neck and neck in 1950, and in 1951–1952 stocks were rising at a slightly more rapid rate than corporate earnings and dividend increases. Clearly the Eisenhower bull market was solidly based upon the Truman prosperity. In 1953 the market resembled a coiled spring. Trust in the new President helped release the coil. Large and small institutions came to the market in greater numbers and with a degree of confidence not seen in a generation. Trust companies, wary of common stocks during the early Truman years, were more certain that values would increase with a moderate Republican in the White House, and they added to the boom. Old investors who had stayed away from the brokerages since the early 1930s returned; their children, now adults, purchased stocks for the first time, many through mutual funds, others through M.I.P. and investment clubs. It was the kind of climate that encouraged a Keith Funston and a Ted McCormick in their work. Eisenhower provided a secure umbrella for a Wall Street surge. Truman had not. Soon after leaving the White House in 1961, Eisenhower said, "When I came to the Presidency the country was rather in an unhappy state. There was bitterness and there was quarreling . . . in Washington and around the country. I tried to create an atmosphere of greater serenity and mutual confidence, and I think that it . . . was noticeable over those eight years that that was brought about." * Even allowing for the self-congratulatory tone of the statement, it was one that Wall Streeters would certainly accept.

The spectacular advance in stock prices in 1954, in the face of the first Eisenhower recession, led to talk of manipulation and increased speculation. Were stock prices too high? And if they were, why did the situation develop? Were any federal laws broken by "operators" during the advance? Would the rapid rise in quotations be followed by an equally sharp collapse? Parallels between 1929 and 1954 abounded. The last era of Republican prosperity had ended in a bust and so, claimed Democratic critics, would this one. That autumn John K. Galbraith and others in the academic community said speculation was rampant and that a major crash was on its way. Even the most sanguine analysts and financial writers seemed to agree that a "correction" would soon take place. It did not. Instead, the market continued to rise in January and February of 1955.

This seeming defiance of the laws of financial gravity resulted in the first major investigations of the securities industry since the late 1930s. A subcommittee of the House Committee on Interstate and Foreign

* Emmet John Hughes, *Ordeal of Power: A Political Memoir of the Eisenhower Years* (New York, 1963), p. 331.

Commerce came to Wall Street to take testimony from exchange and banking leaders, as well as several professors, and then returned to Washington to complete its work. It was followed by the Senate Banking and Currency Committee, headed by J. William Fulbright of Arkansas, a group which received the bulk of the publicity. Prior to the first sessions, Wall Streeters feared an inquisition-like probe, somewhat similar to those the industry had experienced during the New Deal. Such was not the case, one of the clearest indications of a new era in Washington and New York.

During the 1930s, the regulation of business was a "hot issue," upon which ambitious and hard-working legislators could erect reputations. By 1954, talk was of the Cold War and internal subversion. Foreign policy, not economics and business, was the stuff from which important careers were fashioned. Furthermore, there was little public interest in the matters under investigation, a surprising situation considering the growing popularity of investing and speculating. Finally, few senators knew much about the subjects being discussed. One of them, Paul Douglas of Illinois, a distinguished economist, subjected several Exchange figures to examinations on matters involving registration and operation of securities markets and securities. It was clear that some of those he questioned did not understand his comments, or if they did, know how to respond. Herbert Lehman of New York, who had been a member of a major investment banking concern in the 1920s, hadn't given the industry much attention since then, and his questions—and reminiscences—showed it. Senator Mike Monroney of Oklahoma had to be told what a specialist did. Fulbright was intent on demonstrating that the nation still faced serious economic problems, but he was unsure of the role stock markets played in it and appeared to believe that the financial industry, in some way he did not explain, pegged stock prices. Homer Capehart of Indiana, the ranking Republican, was certain the chairman had initiated the investigation to throw mud at the President, and after a while the two senators began engaging in partisan shouting matches, while the Exchange leaders watched, some in amazement, others in amusement.

McCormick, whose S.E.C. experience had prepared him for some of this, cheerfully conceded that a few of the stocks on the Amex were "cats and dogs," and the senators didn't know what to make of it. Funston told the committee that he had purchased stocks for his own account in January and February, "and as soon as I get some more savings, I'm going to buy some more." The market was rising, he said, because the supply of stocks was limited and the demand was expanding; this appeared to impress the committee. Also, changes in the capital gains tax encouraged investment, as did the growing influence of institutional investors.

The last factor, which would appear to have been the kind of material that should have interested the more reform-minded senators, was allowed to pass without question or comment. The reformers were seeking examples of 1920s-type speculation and could not appreciate that a different kind of market, with a new group of large investors, had grown up after the war. Not for another decade would they realize this; not until the older legislators were replaced by individuals more in tune with the postwar economy would congressional probes turn up significant evidence or even ask the proper questions. By then, all the senators involved in the 1955 investigation had moved on to new areas—foreign policy for Fulbright, for example—or retired. As it was, they listened carefully and with interest to Galbraith, who seemed less concerned with imparting information than in constructing several hypotheses that clearly were not grounded in an empirical knowledge of the workings of the district, and to Bernard Baruch, who had entered Wall Street in the late nineteenth century, had gone on to a distinguished career in public life, indicated that he had kept up with events in the district, and was in touch with recent changes. After Galbraith's testimony, during which he repeated beliefs that America might undergo another great crash, one newspaper ran the headline, "Egghead Scrambles Market."

In the end, the Senate Committee could find no significant chicanery. "One striking characteristic of the recent boom in stock prices," it reported, "is that the increase in common stock values was unusually persistent and did not suffer from the recurring setbacks which took place during the other extended advances that have occurred since 1915."

Stock prices continued to rise that spring, adding almost 42 points to the Dow Industrials in April–June, and then proceeding at a slower pace thereafter. On September 24, when the Dow was at 487.45, Eisenhower suffered a heart attack. It was a Saturday and the exchanges were closed, as they were on Sunday. Prices opened lower and on heavy volume on Monday, September 26, when the Dow fell 32 points on a volume of 7,720,000 shares. They recovered the following session, but for the next few days prices were skittish, so that by October 11, the average stood at 438.59, having lost 10 percent of its value in less than a month, the first major correction of the Eisenhower bull market. Then, when it appeared the President was recovering and would soon return to work, prices advanced, closing the year at 488.40. Although 1955 had not been as strong a period on Wall Street as 1954, market analysts noted that without the heart attack, it might have been. At the same time, the importance of Eisenhower to the market became clear during this episode. In contrast, stock prices rose after Roosevelt's death in 1945.

By the end of 1955, there seemed little doubt that the bull market was no fluke, a minor flurry that would be dissolved in a bearish correction, after which stocks would regroup for yet another small upward move. Trading volume in 1955 was 649,602,000 shares, the best since 1933, and given the strength of the market that December, an even better performance was expected in 1956. N.Y.S.E. seats were selling for $90,000 that Christmas, the high for the year. Perhaps reflecting the mood of the period, *Time* named Harlowe Curtice, president of General Motors, as its Man of the Year. The last such prominent businessman to be so honored had been Walter Chrysler, and he appeared on the magazine's cover, noted one critic of Wall Street's boom, in 1929.

With all the talk of prosperity the economy was not as strong as the market appeared to indicate. True to his campaign pledge, Eisenhower had cut government spending. He was convinced that there was a good deal of waste in the bureaucracy, that small government was better than large, and that fiscal virtue rested in a balanced budget. In addition, he believed that only through restraints could inflation, which persisted at a low rate in 1955, be resolved. In Truman's last full year in office, 1952, federal expenditures were $65.4 billion. They rose to $74.3 billion in 1953, but in 1955 were down to $64.6 billion, in part due to budgetary slicing, but more to the end of the Korean conflict spending programs. Still, Eisenhower had reported deficits in each of his three years in office, and he was determined to reverse the trend. Additional spending cuts were planned for 1956, and the Federal Reserve instituted a tighter money policy. The discount rate, which had been 1½ percent in early 1954, rose to 1¾ percent in April 1955, to 2 percent in August, 2¼ percent in September, and 2½ percent in November, in the sharpest escalation of rates since 1931—at which time they had further depressed the economy. The discount rate went to 2¾ percent in April 1956, 3 percent in August, and there was talk of a further increase, perhaps to 3½ percent, by Christmas.

This did not transpire. Still, the discount rate of 3 percent was the highest since 1933, and a certain sign that the Federal Reserve was cooperating with the Administration's deflationary programs. Furthermore, the central bank slowed the growth in the money supply, and through open market operations and public comments by Chairman Martin indicated that the policies would continue until inflation was ended.

The Administration's economic programs, combined with Federal Reserve actions, dampened the economic boom while doing little to slow inflation. Toward summer, Eisenhower eased his policies somewhat. It was an election year, and the President didn't wish to campaign in the midst of a recession. He didn't. The gross national product was $419.2 billion, a record, in 1956. Unemployment stood at 4.1 percent, down from 4.4 percent in 1955. Still, Eisenhower's policies were auguries of what could be expected in his second term. To obtain stable prices, the President would accept sluggish economic growth and even deflation and recession.

Eisenhower and the world underwent a stormy summer and autumn. In June the President had an ileitis operation which, together with his heart attack, led to rumors he wouldn't run for another term. In late October the USSR sent its tanks into Hungary to put down anti-Soviet forces that had assumed power there, and this was followed by an Israeli attack on Egypt and a French-British paratroop landing at the Suez Canal. On the eve of the American Presidential election, it appeared a third world war might begin as a result of any or all of these conflicts.

In the light of these problems—economic and military—the market performed well in 1956. It declined in January in the face of the business slowdown, but then rose strongly, crossing the 500 mark in mid-March and proceeding upward until the meaning of the poor economic news in the first quarter sunk in. Prices fell sharply but orderly in May, and there was no panic as a result of the Eisenhower operation the following month. By the end of July, the Dow was at 517.81. Then it collapsed once more in August and September, again primarily because of forecasts of further economic problems and possible war in the Middle East. The Hungarian and Suez fighting did not depress prices, however, or lead to an unusually high amount of trading. "The market has lost upside momentum," reported analyst Edmund Tabell, "but this is not a bear market. It is just a selective market."

Tabell proved correct. There was no major war either in the Middle East or central Europe. Eisenhower won a smashing electoral victory. Prices rose in December, closing the year slightly below Dow 500, for an 11 point advance over the 1955 closing.

In their year-end reports and forecasts for 1957, many analysts predicted new records for Wall Street and stock prices. On the other hand, some noted that with the election behind him, Eisenhower would be free to renew his deflationary programs, balancing the budget and ending inflation at the same time. The President indicated such would be the case. In January he came out in favor of limitations on federal spending, and he presented a balanced budget to the Congress for consideration. Secretary of Defense Charles Wilson imposed a $38 billion ceiling on defense spending and instituted a "stretch-out" in procurement in order to obtain compliance. "I would deplore the day that we thought we couldn't ever reduce expenditures of this terrific amount, and the terrific tax we are taking out of the country," said Treasury Secretary Humphrey in mid-January, speaking of the need for "fiscal responsibility." "If we don't," he added, "over a long period of time, I will predict that you will have a depression that will curl your hair." The Humphrey statement was misreported, however, and the nation read that its Treasury chief was predicting "a depression which will curl your hair." Former President Herbert Hoover was asked his opinion and replied: "Mine has already been curled once, and I think I can detect the signs."

Humphrey protested he had been misquoted, and other Administration figures made optimistic forecasts. By midsummer, however, it appeared that the economy was slowing down, that the nation was perhaps entering the second Eisenhower recession, and by early autumn it was evident that such was indeed the case. Unemployment began to rise, steadily; in 1958 it would reach 6.8 percent, a postwar high. Administration economists claimed the decline was due in large part to a "resting phase" after the spectacular performance of 1955–1956, to which critics responded that growth had been sluggish during the Eisenhower years and called for strong counter-cyclical policies. The Administration made it clear that none would be forthcoming and that the economy would be encouraged to "right itself." Eisenhower would not ask for a tax cut until and unless conditions became far worse than they were. Nor would he increase federal spending, even on defense, which some critics charged had become weakened during his Administration. Instead, the President delivered encouraging speeches, spoke at press conferences of an imminent upturn, and was echoed by others in his Cabinet.

The stock market declined on the bad economic news. The Dow was at 456.30 at the end of September and headed downward. Ford Motors had recently announced the release of a new auto, the Edsel, which was supposed to boost sales in the popular middle range. Then, on October 4, the USSR shocked the world by orbiting its first "sputnik." The United States was made aware of Soviet advances in science and technology, and earlier reports of the size and effectiveness of the Red Army now took on more ominous meanings. To many it seemed that while Americans had been pampering themselves, the communists were winning the Cold War. A period of questioning of nation purpose commenced, with the Administration attempting to assure the public that all was well. Defense Secretary Charles Wilson called sputnik "a nice technological trick," while Presidential aide

Sherman Adams scoffed at those who claimed it was a brilliant achievement; sputnik was "an outer-space basketball game" as far as he was concerned. But Democrats in Congress, many of whom had been critical of Eisenhower's economic performance and to whom sputnik offered an opportunity to mount an attack, thought otherwise. "It is not very reassuring to be told that next year we will put a 'better' satellite into the air," said Senate Majority Leader Lyndon Johnson. "Perhaps it will even have chrome trim—and automatic windshield wipers."

The Edsel had become the symbol of a nation gone wrong. In mid-October, the Dow Industrials slumped to 419.79.

Sputnik sparked a brief but effective puritanical wave in America. Large, flashy autos became unfashionable, while small "sensible" cars were eagerly sought after and purchased. There was talk of the virtues of hard work and self-denial, or trimming fat and putting on more muscle. And to some, this seemed to indicate less consumption and a deeper recession.

But consumer purchases remained constant in October and November, and even rose in many areas. Meanwhile, the Administration rushed to assure the public that America was prepared militarily for any and all threats, and this required an increase in spending on defense and related supplies. By entering the space race in late 1957 and early 1958, the President was able to escape from his promises of a balanced budget and a tighter spending posture. In 1957, Eisenhower reported a budgetary surplus of $1.6 billion. The budget showed a deficit in 1958 of $2.8 billion, and in 1959, the deficit was $12.4 billion, the largest the nation ever had in peacetime. It may well have been that even without the increase in federal spending, America would have emerged from the recession in 1958. The fact of the matter was, however, that increased spending showed the way to recovery in the summer of 1958.

Anticipating economic revival and also indicating that an increase in government defense expenditures was inevitable, the stock market began to rally in October 1957, beginning with a jump of 17.34 points on October 23, when the average closed at 437.13. By the end of November the Dow was a fraction from 450, and it closed the year at 435.69, after a technical reaction in December. Some stocks did far better, however. Lorillard, Polaroid, and American Motors, all of which were "special situations," had good years, but the newest glamor industry, created out of the sputnik fear, was the "space-age group," which performed in a spectacular fashion in the month and a half after the Soviet satellite was orbited. Aerojet-General, a manufacturer of rocket engines, rose by a third. Douglas Aircraft, General Dynamics, Lockheed, Marquardt, Martin, Thiokol, Reaction Motors, and others whose prices had been depressed after the end of the Korean conflict came to life and showed large price increases in expectation of Department of Defense contracts for missile and space work.

In early 1958 the Eisenhower Administration and the central bank added monetary policy to the fiscal efforts employed in late 1957 in their drive to end the recession. The discount rate was lowered from 3 percent to 2¾ percent in January, and by April it was at 1¾ percent. Meanwhile, the Federal Reserve pumped additional money into the economy through open-market operations, while the Treasury floated record bond issues that served to depress the bond market and nudge investors toward stocks. In January, too, the Federal Reserve lowered margin requirements from 70 percent to 50 percent. The stock market responded, as a new rally began in late February, one of the longest and most sustained since the late 1920s. From a low of 436.89 on February 25, 1958, the Dow advanced to 678.10 on August 1, 1959; it rose 141.21 points in little more than seventeen months.

This third leg of the bull market was different from the two that had preceded it. Income stocks had been popular in 1949, as investors sought a means to achieve a higher rate of return on their investments and cared little about capital gains. Old-fashioned gamblers plunged in uranium and oil issues in 1954, and were joined by investors looking for bargains among the blue chips, stocks whose prices had been depressed while earnings had risen. Like those who had entered the market in 1949, they too were interested in value, security, and an increase in prices that would reflect the realities of their time. As such, they bore little resemblance to the speculators of the 1920s, and despite fears of another 1929, stock prices in the mid-1950s were hardly excessive. As has been indicated, they either made up for lost time or reflected true economic growth in the present.

The bull move of 1958–1959 featured a new group of stocks, a different attitude toward the markets, and a fresh group of investors. It was the age of the glamor stocks and the high rollers, of people who were less interested in past performance and present activities than they were with prospects for the future. Furthermore, the American advance spread to Europe and Japan, as almost all the world's exchange indices moved upward together. "The whole world seemed to be caught by a frenzy of speculation," said a Swiss banker in June. "If this goes on something serious is bound to happen soon." But the rise continued, drawing growing numbers of investors to the district. N.Y.S.E. volume rose from 560 million shares in 1957 to 747 million in 1958, and 820 million in 1959, which was the second best trading year—after 1929—in history. In this same period, the price of a seat rose from a low of $65,000 to a peak of $157,000. Warnings of an impending crash were heard and, after so many false alarms, ignored. "It is stupid, after years of a publicity campaign to get people to buy stocks, to come out now and blow the whistle," said Charles Schwartz, the senior partner of the brokerage house of Bache & Co. When the Federal Reserve took note of increased speculative activities, and raised the margin requirement from 50 percent to 70 percent in August 1958, and then to 90 percent in October, Funston objected mildly. To be sure, member borrowings were at a twenty-eight-year high. "There is no evidence of excessive use of credit in this market," he said.

Almost all stock groups participated in the bull market of 1958–1959, but the electronics and "high technology" issues featured the advance. This was to have been expected, at a time when investors and speculators alike were more concerned with the future than the present or past. It also meant that elaborate "scenarios" as to what the nation, industry, and company might be expected to do in the next five to ten years had to be drawn up and examined, with impressive statistics and charts on yet-unrealized goals taken as hard evidence to support purchase and sale decisions. In this way, investors discounted the future, pricing stocks not on current earnings or past performance but on projections. A stock that might be fully valued at $50 a share could be made to appear underpriced if you really believed the company's earnings would double by 1962. Thus, the price would rise, and then the buyer would begin discounting 1966, and purchase additional shares. By the summer of 1959, when stock prices seemed stratospheric, the Wall Street joke was that the market had not only discounted the future but the hereafter as well.

Annual Trading Volume and Prices of N.Y.S.E. Seats, 1952–1960

Year	*Volume*	*Range of Seat Prices* *High*	*Low*
1952	337,805,179	$ 55,000	$ 39,000
1953	354,851,325	60,000	38,000
1954	573,374,622	88,000	40,000
1955	649,602,291	90,000	80,000
1956	556,284,172	113,000	75,000
1957	559,946,890	89,000	65,000
1958	747,058,306	127,000	69,000
1959	820,296,279	157,000	110,000
1960	766,693,818	162,000	135,000

Source: *The New York Stock Exchange Fact Book, 1962*

Wall Street brokerages busily sold the vision of a scientifically oriented future to eager buyers. At night the customers' men would pour over physics texts so as to understand the terminology of the newly glamorous industries. People who only a few years before had been concerned with railroads and automobiles, utilities and grocery chains, now spoke knowingly of transistors, klystron tubes, space travel, and the like. Texas Instruments, a premier company in the field, rose from $15\frac{7}{8}$ in 1957 to $193\frac{1}{2}$ in 1959, paying no dividend and with an increase in earnings from $1.11 a share to $3.59. This, perhaps, could be digested. But what of the rapid rise in Hewlett-Packard, an instrument manufacturer, whose stock went from $18\frac{1}{8}$ to $46\frac{7}{8}$ in the same period, on an earnings' advance from $1.92 a share to $2.40? Or Beckman Instruments, which rose from 21 to $74\frac{3}{4}$, with earnings of $0.16 in 1957, a deficit the following year, and then a rise to $1.30 in 1959, made possible in part by tax write-offs?

Such firms as Texas Instruments, Beckman, Ampex, Thiokol, Varian, and Hoffman, hardly seasoned corporations, were selling for well over fifty times earnings by mid-1959. Companies like these were in the vanguard of the space-age bull market. And new ones joined them—usually with prefixes like "electro" and suffixes like "tron" tacked on. Astron, Dutron, Transitron and many more were taken up by investors and speculators eager for action and glamor, excited at the possibilities of participating in romantic ventures. Jack Dreyfus, head of the brokerage house of Dreyfus & Co., commented upon the mania after it had peaked in 1960:

> Take a nice little company that's been making shoelaces for forty years and sells at a respectable six times earnings ratio. Change the name from Shoelaces, Inc. to Electronics and Silicon Furth-Burners. In today's market, the words "electronic" and "silicon" are worth fifteen times earnings. However, the real play comes from the word "furth-burners," which no one understands. A word that no one understands entitles you to double your entire score. Therefore, we have six times earnings for the shoelace business and fifteen times earnings for electronic and silicon, or a total of twenty-one times earnings. Multiply this by two for furth-burners, and we now have a score of forty-two times earnings for the new company.

In this kind of market, the business-machine manufacturers became the backbone of the new "information industry," and National Cash Register, Pitney Bowes, Sperry Rand, Addressograph and, of course, I.B.M. shot ahead in a manner pleasing to their shareholders. Drug firms—Bristol-Myers, American Home Products, Pfizer—did the same, as did science-oriented specialty firms—Eastman Kodak, Rohm & Haas, Corning Glass. A bowling craze led Brunswick and American Machine & Foundry to new heights. Even the normally slow-moving utilities joined in, jumping from a 1957 low of 62.10 on the Dow to close at 91.00 on the last trading day in 1958.

The rapid increase in stock prices—across the board, as it were—worried many securities analysts. It had been a case of too much, too soon. To be sure, firms like I.B.M. and Eastman Kodak had sparkling futures, and the same might be said of some of the newer corporations—Texas Instruments, Polaroid, and Litton Industries among them. By 1959, however, companies with deficits and no performance records were selling for astronomical prices. Underwood, a badly mismanaged maker of business machines, received some of the spillover from the information-processing craze. In the four years from 1957 to 1960 the company lost a total of $36 a share. But it had been taken over by Olivetti of Italy, was the subject of optimistic rumors, and rose from a low of 12⅛ in 1957 to 57 in 1960. Farrington Manufacturing, a maker of handbags and credit-card machines, obtained a patent on a new electronic device. The firm had consistently lost money and yet went from 3 to 57½ before plummeting to below 2. Developments such as these concerned many of the more conservative analysts and reporters, and increasingly warnings of a downturn were heard in the district.

The long-awaited decline came in the summer of 1959, when due to strikes, minor economic setbacks, and, more important, a technical correction in securities quotations, the average fell almost 62 points in a month and a half. The end of a long steel-workers' strike and completion of the correction in September led prices upward once more, and the Dow closed the year at 679.36 in the midst of a new rally.

Despite this, the spirit was gone from the Eisenhower bull market. Fear of a possible conflict with China in January 1960, added to talk of a series of strikes, caused prices to collapse 56.74 points in a month. Not since October 1929 had stocks fallen by so great an absolute figure, and they declined on heavy volume and rumors of a coming panic and depression. Prices recovered slightly in February, however, but they fell again in March and April.

On May 1, the Soviets shot down an American U-2 surveillance plane which had been taking pictures of military installations. The episode, together with inept Administration handling of it, destroyed all thought of success at the Paris Summit Conference that month, one Eisenhower hoped would cap his Presidential career with a softening of Cold War tensions. This was followed by the seizure of American assets in Cuba by that country's new leader, Fidel Castro, and a subsequent decay in Cuban-American relations. On the economic front there was fear of a new recession, and this, capping the general malaise, led to a flight from the dollar. For the first time since the end of World War II, gold speculation became pronounced, with the price of an ounce of the metal reaching $\$35.25\frac{1}{2}$ in September, a six-year high. In all, it was the worst loss of confidence in America's future, as reflected in speculative activity, since 1937. Finally, 1960 was an election year, and Democratic candidate John F. Kennedy warned of coming economic problems as a result of inept Presidential leadership, and a "missile lag" that had made America second to the USSR in military might.

Stocks fell in a near-panic atmosphere in early autumn, when the Dow lost almost 50 points and bottomed out at 569.08 on September 29. Then the market rallied, but declined again in late October, reaching the year's low of 566.95 on October 25. Prices were where they had been in November 1958, when the bull market was still gathering steam. Although they rallied in November and December, closing the year at 615.89, the recovery was due more to the election of John Kennedy and promise of change than to confidence in Eisenhower and the economy.

The Euphoric Decade had come to an end, as most such periods do, in a hangover. Eisenhower, who had been so popular throughout most of his Administration, was still beloved by the nation, and he would never lose the affection of the people. By late 1960, however, he seemed tired, worn-out, and not a little ineffectual. He had been the last Chief Executive to have been born in the nineteenth century; Kennedy was the first to be born in the twentieth. In January 1961, Presidential power would pass from the hands of the oldest man to hold it to those of the youngest to be elected. This symbolism was important to a nation where such things had become more significant than reality, on Wall Street as much as any other place.

The Republican bull market of the 1960s ended, just as the Great Bull Market of the 1920s came to a close, at the end of a decade. Some reporters compared Eisenhower to Hoover and Kennedy to Franklin Roosevelt. As always, such comparisons were tortured and exaggerated, and nowhere was this more evident than in the financial district. Ever since the first stirrings of the bull market, the nation had been warned by a variety of critics of another 1929. In January 1960, and later on in September, such a debacle appeared possible. But it didn't arrive. There were no bank failures, no reports of brokers jumping out of windows, no bread lines—in short, none of the accouterments Americans had been led to believe would accompany a major stock market collapse. Instead, prices had rallied, and in early 1961 there was

MONTHLY CLOSING PRICES OF THE DOW INDUSTRIALS, 1952–1960

Month	*1952*	*1953*	*1954*	*1955*	*1956*	*1957*	*1958*	*1959*	*1960*
January	270.69	289.77	292.39	408.83	470.74	479.16	450.02	593.96	622.62
February	260.08	284.27	294.54	411.87	483.65	464.62	439.92	603.50	630.12
March	269.46	279.87	303.51	409.70	511.79	474.81	446.76	601.71	616.59
April	257.63	274.75	319.33	425.65	516.12	494.36	455.86	623.75	601.70
May	262.94	272.28	327.49	424.86	478.05	504.92	462.70	643.79	625.50
June	274.26	268.26	333.53	451.38	492.78	503.29	478.18	643.60	640.62
July	279.56	275.38	347.92	465.85	517.81	508.52	502.99	674.88	616.73
August	275.04	261.22	335.80	468.18	502.04	484.35	508.63	664.41	625.99
September	270.61	264.04	360.47	466.62	475.25	456.30	532.09	631.68	580.14
October	269.23	275.81	352.14	454.87	479.85	441.04	543.22	646.60	580.36
November	283.66	281.37	386.77	483.26	472.78	449.87	557.46	659.18	597.22
December	291.90	280.90	404.39	488.40	499.47	435.69	583.65	679.36	615.89

SOURCE: *The Dow Jones Averages, 1885–1970*

MONTHLY CLOSING PRICES OF THE DOW UTILITIES, 1952–1960

Month	*1952*	*1953*	*1954*	*1955*	*1956*	*1957*	*1958*	*1959*	*1960*
January	48.63	52.68	54.09	62.02	63.88	70.93	72.27	90.88	85.56
February	48.43	52.50	54.67	64.05	65.09	70.40	72.49	92.05	86.76
March	50.21	52.25	55.99	63.57	67.37	71.47	74.00	93.43	88.30
April	48.43	51.07	56.49	64.79	65.24	73.01	77.37	91.33	88.71
May	49.94	50.83	58.07	63.63	65.24	74.03	78.19	89.80	88.10
June	49.66	48.54	58.20	64.34	67.37	69.84	78.19	87.30	93.39
July	50.55	49.45	60.10	66.59	71.15	69.88	79.58	89.99	92.83
August	50.79	49.60	60.11	66.10	68.63	67.84	77.97	91.11	95.70
September	50.17	49.48	61.04	63.14	65.57	66.67	80.71	87.91	91.29
October	49.94	51.14	57.81	63.37	66.20	65.75	83.22	87.47	92.54
November	51.60	52.33	60.75	65.92	66.42	67.73	85.25	86.56	95.19
December	52.60	52.04	62.47	64.16	68.54	68.58	91.00	87.83	100.02

SOURCE: *The Dow Jones Averages, 1885–1970*

much talk of the forthcoming "Soaring Sixties," led by a dynamic and attractive young President who would "get the country moving again."

This is not to say that confidence was fully restored. Stock prices had fallen 9.3 percent in 1960, and although this did not match 1957's 12.8 percent, the decline did leave a residue of fear. "As the year develops," wrote one cautious stock analyst in January, "the business climate may be either much better or much worse than now expected," while another, no less cagey and addicted to the district's double-talk, opined, "We are entering the New Year with a mixture of apprehension and anticipation." It was a time when "guarded hope" and "clouded future" were common Wall Street phrases.

> In conclusion, we think that while near-term uncertainties exist and no one can really say the decline in stock prices has gone as far as it will, we believe we are beginning to form a base which will be both fundamentally and technically sound and from which—given the anticipated improvement of business in 1961—we could get a stock market rise of worthwhile proportions.

Underneath it all was a strong spurt of optimism. The community—brokers, analysts, specialists, investment bankers—had gone through a major correction and survived. During the 1950s, stock prices had risen by 257.1 percent, the best record for a decade in the district's history. The post–World War II generation had come through the fire in good shape. This was the general belief in early 1961, when prices began to rise on heavy volume, attracting the timid to Wall Street along with those who were now convinced that in the future the economy might catch a cold, but pneumonia was out of the question. It would be more of the same, said brokers to their clients, as both looked at the record of the 1950s and sought new glamor and new opportunities for large capital gains. Dividend return, once the *sine qua non* of a "prudent" investment, was forgotten; the yield on the Dow-Jones Industrials declined from 8.1 percent in 1950 to 3.1 percent in 1960, as stock prices far outran increases in dividends. In fact, such concern marked a person as stodgy in this new kind of market, one in which the last vestiges of fear seemed to have fled by 1961.

PERFORMANCE OF THE DOW-JONES INDUSTRIAL INDEX, 1950–1960

Year	*Closing Price*	*Percentage Change in the Year*	*Percentage Dividend Yield*
1950	235.41	plus 17.6	8.1
1951	269.23	plus 14.4	6.9
1952	291.90	plus 8.4	5.8
1953	280.90	minus 3.8	5.6
1954	404.39	plus 44.0	6.2
1955	488.44	plus 20.8	5.3
1956	499.47	plus 2.3	4.7
1957	435.69	minus 12.8	4.3
1958	583.65	plus 34.0	4.6
1959	679.36	plus 16.4	3.6
1960	615.89	minus 9.3	3.1

SOURCE: *Moody's Investors Service*

Keith Funston and his retinue were in the mood for celebration, and so they did with the resumption of bullish sentiment, in what already was being called the "Kennedy Bull Market." The N.Y.S.E. had prospered in the Eisenhower years, and more of the same was anticipated under the new President. But Wall Street was different in 1961 from what it had been a decade before, and the changes were qualitative as well as quantitative. The bull market had brought prosperity to a new generation of Stock Exchange members and the people they serviced. No longer did the brokers and specialists question whether they were needed in the economy and nation; the flood of orders provided the answer every working day. The Eisenhower prosperity had also given birth to new investment forces, enlarged old ones, encouraged rivals, and did so in ways the Big Board's leaders could scarcely contain or control. These factors, as much as increasing business and higher prices, would dominate talk in the board rooms in the 1960s.

CHAPTER 13

Flaws in the Design

The Dow Industrials closed at 678.73 on Tuesday, April 4, 1961, up slightly more than a point for the session. Trading volume was over 7 million shares, hectic by the standards of the time. In January, 4 million share days had been normal, and even then the back offices were becoming jammed by paperwork. By March, volume was averaging well over 5 million shares. Then, on Monday, April 3, volume hit 6.5 million, a high for the year, which was topped by Tuesday's 7 million. Clerks throughout the district had been told by noon that they would have to work overtime, a practice that was becoming standard. The Dow had risen more than 62 points since the first of the year; apparently the bulls could do no wrong. Wall Street was feeling the strain.

Within a decade the district's mood had gone from investment to speculation to gambling. Stocks were purchased on margin, held for a few days, and then sold to buy others that were "hot." The Exchange reported that margin credit in March was over $4.6 billion. In April the figure topped $5 billion for the first time in twenty years.

Funston and others at the N.Y.S.E. were concerned. There was talk of a government investigation. A special S.E.C. team, headed by Ralph Saul of the Division of Trading and Exchanges, was probing conditions at the Amex and had already charged prominent figures there with wrongdoing. There were signs the Big Board would be next on the list. Funston had no skeletons in his closet, but such an inquiry might be embarrassing.

The N.Y.S.E staff was feeling the pressure, as was the membership. Specialists and floor brokers missed lunches or grabbed fast hot dogs from street vendors during ten-minute breaks and then remained in the district after dark, trying to prepare for the next day while straightening out accounts for the session that just ended. Not since the 1920s had business been so good, they told one another—and then, someone would recall 1929.

The comparison worried Funston, who spoke to the issue on April 4. He noted "disquieting evidence that some people have not yet discovered that it is impossible to get something for nothing, and they are attempting to make improper use of the facilities of the investment community." Then he offered examples. Reports had reached him indicating that "some would-be investors are attempting to purchase shares of companies whose names they cannot identify, whose products are unknown to them, and whose prospects are, at best, highly uncertain." He realized, however, that "an overwhelming majority of investors" used the markets wisely.

Funston knew better than that. Slightly more than a year before, in late 1959, the Exchange had released the results of a survey that showed that two out of every five investors could not define the term "common stock." More than half of another sample, described as "being on the threshold of investing," were in the same state of ignorance, while three out of four of a much larger population that was interested in investment did not know the meaning of the term. Finally, almost a quarter of this last group thought the chief reason for purchasing stock was an "opportunity for quick profit."

And they were right. The Dow rose sharply after Funston's warning speech, hitting the 700 mark for the first time in intraday trading on April 11. Prices consolidated at that level and were close to 700 when Funston spoke on the subject again, on May 16. "It is clear . . . some people are feverishly substituting rumor, hearsay, and a desire to get rich quick for sound investment judgment," he warned. Prices stabilized somewhat, but volume remained high. In 1961, for the first time since 1929, volume crossed the billion share mark.

Participation in the great bull market had increased at a geometric rate during the previous decade as excitement replaced caution and in turn was displaced by frenzy. In 1952, the N.Y.S.E. estimated that there were 6.5 million shareholders in the country. By 1956, the figure was 8.6 million, and in 1959, 12.5 million. As Funston spoke in the spring of 1961, the number of shareholders was estimated at 15 million. Two million more would be added to the rolls by the end of the year. In 1952, one out of every sixteen American adults owned common stock. In late 1961, the figure was one in six.

Necessarily, this meant that an army of amateurs had become stockholders. People who found themselves with extra funds sought security, excitement, and wealth on Wall Street. Many, of course, looked to mutual funds. There were only 2.6 million shareholder accounts as late as 1958; in 1961, the amount had swollen to 5.2 million. In 1951, the industry sold $674 million worth of funds, and that year American mutuals had $3.1 billion in assets. Fund sales in 1961 matched fund assets a decade earlier, and at the end of the year, $22.8 billion was invested in the mutuals.

While the prudent purchased their shares, the venturesome looked to the new-issue market for action.

In the spring of 1961, a spate of new stock offerings appeared, many from marginal brokerages who handled shaky companies. The flotations complied to the letter of the Securities Act, even when they violated its spirit. In 1934, a speculator remarked that if you planned to organize a company to encourage people to jump off the Brooklyn Bridge, and said so in your prospectus, it would be accepted by the S.E.C. Some of the new issues of 1961 were of this variety—Mother's Cookies, Polychrome, Wyle Laboratories, and others. Most did well, jumping by 50 percent and more in the first hours of trading, making those fortunate enough to "get in on the ground floor" rich, providing bonanzas for the underwriters, and instant millions for company insiders.

Mutual fund owners grew wealthy slowly, while speculators did so in a matter of days. Everyone seemed to be winning; the game had no losers. The only questions seemed to be "How long will it take you to make your pile?" and "How much do you want to make?"

Battalions of clerks, managers, investment advisors, and brokers were needed to service the growing army of investors, speculators, and gamblers that came to cause and profit from the bull market. Both workers and clients were of a different breed than those of the previous generation. Then the district had attracted a conservative work force, and employers prized devotion and dependability more than ambition and imagination. In that period investors wanted "sound" securities, considering quality more desirable than growth or quick profits, a not unexpected reaction to the 1929 crash and its aftermath. Similarly, the workers received low but secure salaries and wages. To be sure, the top echelons at the investment banks and some brokerages did quite well, even during the depression. Most who were employed in Wall Street, however, received poorer financial compensations than their counterparts in other industries.

The situation began to change in the early 1950s, in a way that paralleled the arrival of new clients. When investors seeking dividend payers looked for investment advice, they found it in modestly expanded brokerages and were serviced by men and women who were newly arrived in finance, just as dedicated as their elders (in part because they still feared the return of depression and the loss of work) but far more ambitious. To both investors and workers of the early 1950s, the depression was a scar, no longer a wound. Then the scar too began to fade. Speculation increased, and the hoards began to descend upon the financial world—investors seeking quick profits, workers looking for fortunes of their own. To the old-timers, it seemed a distorted replay of the 1920s, with the descendants of the uninformed investors/speculators, the inexperienced work force, and the leading gamblers all on the scene by the late 1950s.

There were major differences, to be sure. In the 1920s men like Jesse Livermore, Arthur Cutten, Percy Rockefeller, and, later on, Joe Kennedy, were master manipulators and also performers with panache and imagination. Their counterparts of the late 1950s operated in a far more complex market, one regulated—albeit inefficiently—by government and increasingly dominated by large investment trusts, two forces of less importance in the 1920s. Thus, they appeared smudged carbon copies of their predecessors at best, sleazy operators at worst. Lowell Birrell conducted clever manipulations of minor stocks—Claude Neon, United Dye & Chemical, and Fidelio Breweries. He had been on Wall Street since the late 1930s, attracting little attention. Now that the climate for speculation was more favorable, he expanded operations. Alexander Guterma, who had replaced Serge Rubinstein as "the mystery man of Wall Street," controlled United Dye, F. L. Jacobs, Bon Ami, and other issues. Earle Belle sold shares in Cornucopia Gold Mines to the citizens of the small town of Saltsburg, Pennsylvania, and in the end all but wrecked the community financially. After making his fortune in that and other manipulations he fled to Brazil to avoid prosecution and was joined there by others who, like him, had specialized in over-the-counter and Amex issues. At one time, Livermore controlled the prices of R.C.A., General Motors, and Westinghouse, while Cutten contested him for domination of these and other Big Board issues. Compared to them, Guterma and Birrell were sideshow attractions. In the 1950s, at least, there appeared little danger of rigging N.Y.S.E. stocks.

The situations regarding the work forces were more complex. During the 1920s and 1930s, the back offices put in long hours and worked weekends during bull and bear raids and panics and on other occasions when volume expanded. The same condition prevailed in the 1950s and early 1960s. The staffs of both periods used similar technologies at their tasks. The clerks of the earlier era had typewriters and adding machines; those of the 1950s utilized electric typewriters rather than manuals and learned to use calculators. By the late 1950s, however, top executives in the district recognized that just as office machinery stocks were star performers on the markets, so their products would become increasingly important in their operations. Automation, a new word and one that was heard increasingly at the brokerages, investment banks, and trust companies, would end the "paper jam" that was beginning to develop in the back offices.

But would it? Wall Street executives of the period noted that the generation of office workers that had utilized pen and ink made the transition to typewriters without undue difficulties. They seemed to believe the change from calculators to computers was not very much more complex. During the late 1950s and early 1960s an increasing number of brokerages invited representatives from I.B.M., N.C.R., Univac, and other office-machine firms to provide estimates as to costs and savings of automation. They were impressive. So the transformation of Wall Street from the electric to the electronic age began—while the personnel of the mechanical era managed the offices and were charged with responsibilities in the area of conversion. The public knew little of this situation, and what it did know came from business journals that were uniformly optimistic about the changes, claiming they would "modernize" the district's operations. New problems and unexpected opportunities would appear later on, for, as much as anything else, technology would alter the face and framework of American finance in the 1960s.

If customers were interested in the Wall Street work force, it was in the district's account executives, mutual fund salesmen, and others in the "distribution" end of the industry. As volume rose along with prices, this became a major concern, as brokerages advertised for trainees, and experienced personnel were at a premium, with salaries and wages rising steadily.

In 1945, there were 7,261 registered representatives employed by member firms, and as late as 1950, the amount was only 10,608. Then, as activity and profits increased, along with remunerations, the expansion began in earnest. By 1955, the number was 14,388, and in 1962, 31,435. Between 1950 and 1961, branch offices of N.Y.S.E. brokerages increased by over 100 percent. By then, too, more than a few brokers who handled large accounts were earning more than $100,000 a year, while those who made less than $30,000 were considered either "on their way up" or lacking in some essential ingredient.

Money and glamor attracted the battalions to high finance, even more so in the late 1950s and early 1960s than during the boom years of the 1920s. Young, aggressive people came, joining retreads from other occupations and brokers who had left the Street decades before in order to seek better employment and now hoped for their old positions. Research branches of large brokerages, investment advisory services, and trust departments scoured the business schools, seeking bright M.B.A.'s to add to their staffs. Small armies of part-time workers began selling mutual funds, if only to close friends and relations.

They found entry into the field relatively painless. In order to become a registered representative, candidates had to pass an examination conducted by the National Association of Security Dealers. It was a simple test—prospective brokers would receive a booklet containing questions and answers which they could memorize prior to the test. In 1961, more than 30,000 people took the examination, and less than 100 failed. Since not all states required registered representatives to pass, some of those who failed were hired anyway. The quality of brokerage in the early 1960s was at its lowest point in more than three decades, while research was not far behind. Prices were rising, however, and seemingly headed for the stratosphere. In such a market, informed brokerage and research was not important. Indeed, lack of information may have been a blessing for many speculators, since veteran brokers would have shied from some of the highly speculative issues then in vogue.

A generation of brokers, analysts, and clients were enthusiastic about the market in this period. They had survived the 1960 correction and were convinced that such was the worst that could happen to them. There was an old Wall Street saying that originated in the late nineteenth century to the effect that "No one is more certain to undergo a bear market than people who have never seen one."

This was the view held by S.E.C. Chairman William L. Cary, who had been appointed to his post by President Kennedy in late January 1961. The agency had done little to investigate Wall Street during the bull market. In the early 1950s, New York office chief Paul Windels campaigned against boiler-room operations that sold questionable securities to inexperienced investors. Ralph Saul's investigation of the Amex began after that market had initiated one of its own, and was limited in scope and budget. An activist in the Douglas tradition, Cary promised to breathe new life into the agency. In the late spring of 1961, shortly after the S.E.C. charged Amex specialists with serious violations of rules, Cary testified before a congressional subcommittee conducting hearings preliminary to a full-scale investigation of the financial district.

The chairman was critical of many aspects of the bull market, especially the quality of the registered representatives. "Many securities salesmen work on a part-time basis; many have no particular qualifications to sell securities; and most important, many are not subject to the kind of supervision which insures high ethical standards," said Cary. "The possibility exists that these factors may have led to questionable merchandising techniques. They have also undermined the important personal relationship between broker and customer in which the broker seeks to ascertain whether the security is suitable for a particular customer."

Still, no laws had been broken. The legislation of the 1930s, written to safeguard investors against unscrupulous Wall Streeters, had been enforced by a vigorous S.E.C. In the 1950s, customers had been ill-served by brokers who were often inept, and even had the S.E.C. the desire to act, it lacked the will and the tools. Cary hoped to change the situation. In the past, Congress had refused to pass new regulatory legislation or even increase the S.E.C.'s budget so it could perform its tasks, while President Eisenhower never showed much interest in the matter, and his chairmen were ciphers. Given the prodding of a new investigation, encouragement from an activist chairman, and a President believed unfriendly to the industry, conditions might well change, especially if the Amex probes turned up additional evidence of wrongdoing.

For the moment at least, the N.Y.S.E. took no action. Funston made no reference to the situation except to note that the S.E.C. had not accused the Big Board of violations, either in letter or spirit, and that he and his staff stood ready to cooperate with the Commission. But the N.A.S.D. did make its examinations more difficult, resulting in an increase in the failure rate from 3 percent in 1961 to 10 percent in 1962.

The Exchange felt in a strong position politically. Given the large investor population, combined with the bull market, President Kennedy would scarcely do anything that might precipitate a collapse or loss of confidence. Funston's mild reactions were appropriate under the circumstances. He would await Cary's next move before committing himself to actions.

While defending itself well against Washington and reaping benefits from the bull market, the Exchange confronted a threat from the investment community. The bull market had all the hallmarks of previous periods of wild activity on the Street—rank speculation, unbridled optimism, high volume, quick fortunes—and the creation of significant competition for the N.Y.S.E.'s business. The outlines of the danger could be discerned in the 1950s, but at the time little was made of it at Wall and Broad. It would come to fruition in the next decade and prove one of the most vexing and challenging problems in the Exchange's history, one that many felt would lead, eventually, to the end of the Big Board itself.

The origins of the problem were complex. Stated simply, the Big Board had never lacked competitors. When trading was slack, the Exchange would contest with them for available business; during bull periods, new rivals entered the field while old ones grew stronger and bolder. The challenges were met by the use of political leverage, law suits, threats, concessions, accommodations, and whatever else seemed appropriate at the time. Such had been the case for more than a century and a half.

The twenty-four securities dealers who gathered in 1792 to organize the ancestor of today's N.Y.S.E. included some of the city's most powerful businessmen, but the group itself was a minority of those who purchased and sold such instruments. The so-called Corre's Hotel Pact bound the signatories to charge one another fixed commissions on purchases and sales, and this would remain a key Exchange rule until recently. But the twenty-four were not forbidden from dealing with nonmembers, on whatever terms both sides found acceptable. Indeed, such a regulation would have been rejected out of hand, and was unenforceable in any event. In that period, nonmembers made up a larger group than members and probably transacted a larger volume of business. So relations between the two factions were maintained.

This remained the case until 1817 when, in an attempt to crush or at least cripple the nonmembers and take some of their business, the Exchange passed two resolutions. The first forbade dealings with outsiders at commissions lower than those charged members, and the second stated that members were not to inform outsiders as to the prices of stocks bid and asked at the auctions (an attempt to prevent nonmembers from pegging their prices to those at the inside market, where the president of the Exchange auctioned shares once a day).

Wall Street enjoyed its biggest bull market to that time in the mid-1830s, as canal shares, government bonds, and the newly arrived rails boomed ahead on heavy volume. The auction method proved incapable of handling the volume of business, and so Exchange members would spill over into the Street "between calls" and trade among themselves, or seek out nonmembers for bids and asks. Some of the outside brokers banded together to form an organization called the New Board, to distinguish itself from the Exchange—then called the New York Stock and Exchange Board—and for a while transacted a larger share of the business than the old. As a countermeasure, the Exchange passed a resolution in 1836 forbidding members from dealing with nonmembers, with violators subject to suspension. The rule, like the other two, was unenforceable, and, in any case, the panic of 1837 ended the short life of the New Board.

The outside dealers and traders—called curbstone brokers by the newspapers of the day—prospered in the bull market that followed the discovery of gold in California in 1848. Several rival exchanges were organized in the early 1850s, some as auctions, most as places where brokers would seek one another out on a continuous basis. Once again,

Exchange members traded there, in violation of rules, because to do otherwise would be bad business. On a busy day in 1856, the Stock and Exchange Board might transact 6,000 shares, while outside as many as 70,000 could be traded. A group of mining exchanges in particular drew trades from the older inside market, and although most of these dissolved after the panic of 1857, a few remained. They were joined by others during the Civil War, when trading was an around-the-clock business in New York, with at least twenty organized markets in operation, some of which drew business from the Stock and Exchange Board. One of these, the Open Board of Stock Brokers, was organized in 1863 as a continuous market, and charged lower fees than did the Stock and Exchange Board. After the war, important traders and brokers gravitated to the Open Board, so that by 1868 the Exchange had become a secondary market, lacking customers, but possessing tradition and status. Clearly the continuous method of trading was superior to the auctions, more in keeping with the large-volume days that had become the norm in post–Civil War America. Unable to defeat its rival, the Stock and Exchange Board came to terms with it, and in 1869 the two were merged to form the New York Stock Exchange.

Other small exchanges survived, most of them specializing in low-grade mining issues. In addition, private auctions of securities took place daily in the offices of some brokers who were not affiliated with the N.Y.S.E. Finally, some Exchange members, noting an interest on the part of investors in "odd lots" of stock (less than 100 shares) began selling them, contrary to Exchange rules.

By 1885 several of the operations, together with dissident N.Y.S.E. members who had started specializing in odd lots, had united to form the Consolidated Stock and Petroleum Exchange. Most of the Consolidated's own issues were marginal, as were its brokers. But the "Little Board" had Western Union tickers on its floor, which printed the transactions at the N.Y.S.E. The C.S.E. brokers would trade off the ticker and buy and sell odd lots for their clients. On occasion, they would do the same in round lots, thus drawing business from the Big Board. On the one hand, the Consolidated was clearly a gaming operation, servicing the nation's bucket shops. On the other, it pioneered in organizing the first workable clearing house and appealing to small investors.

Whatever else it was, however, the C.S.E. was a rival to the N.Y.S.E., and from its opening, the senior exchange tried to destroy it. N.Y.S.E. brokers and specialists were warned that dealings with the Consolidated could lead to expulsion. Many attempts were made to force Western Union to withdraw its tickers from the Consolidated's floor. Exchange lobbyists in Albany called for investigations of the district, which they anticipated would lead to the closing of all markets but the N.Y.S.E. The Big Board formed an "Unlisted Trading Department," where its members could deal in C.S.E.–listed stocks, in a clear attempt at retaliation. It came to terms with leaders of the Curb Market, agreeing to recognize the association so long as N.Y.S.E.–listed stocks were not traded out of doors. And in the end, the C.S.E. was crushed. A series of investigations, beginning in 1903, together with poor leadership and proven chicanery, followed by removal of the tickers, resulted in the decline of the Little Board. In 1901, the C.S.E. claimed to have done a larger business than the senior exchange. By 1921, it was a minor force in securities; it closed down completely in 1928.

The struggle with the Consolidated, and the N.Y.S.E. victory, convinced potential rivals to remain on the periphery during the bull market of the 1920s. In this period, the Exchange dominated New York, with the Curb as a satellite. But the regional exchanges did well, and for a while the Chicago Stock Exchange tried to mount an attack against the Big Board, one that was short-lived and never had a chance of success. Most of the regionals concentrated on stocks of local firms which, if they became popular, often sought N.Y.S.E. listing. In addition, they traded shares of large companies already listed on the Big Board, though rarely in amounts considered significant by New York standards.

The regionals suffered a major decline in business throughout the 1930s, as did the N.Y.S.E. Some minuscule markets closed down, while others combined so as to save money. All tried to garner as many trades as they could, and even the Big Board entered the contest. This was why President Martin, in 1939, banned N.Y.S.E. members from trading in listed issues on regional exchanges. At the time the Big Board was transacting more than 89 percent of the dollar volume of all stock exchanges, a record high, while even the larger regionals were in dire straits. The S.E.C. attempted to induce the Exchange to rescind the ban, but Martin refused to do so. In any case, N.Y.S.E. brokerages regularly ignored it, for they too sought savings, and on occasion these could be had at the regionals. For his part, Martin did not insist on compliance, looking the other way even when some specialists complained to him of violations.

The S.E.C. took action against the N.Y.S.E. in 1940, and the following year the so-called *Multiple Trading Case* was decided in favor of the regionals. In its brief, the Commission pledged support to the out-of-town exchanges, citing the important services they provided to local businesses and noting that the regionals prevented the N.Y.S.E. from completing its monopoly over trading in its listed shares. As the Commission put it:

If the regional markets in dually traded issues are destroyed or materially decreased, the public investor who wishes to buy or sell such securities will have to trade on the N.Y.S.E. and pay the higher costs attending such transactions. Even if the issues affected by the rule continue to be traded on the regional exchanges, the customer can expect slower deliveries and poorer service in many cases. The debilitation of regional exchange services in dually traded issues will also permeate their trading services in local issues as well. The investor may therefore be faced with the alternative of trading only in the centralized market located in New York or in the over-the-counter market.*

Partly as a result of the decision, but due more to the increased business on all exchanges that made such tactics unnecessary, the N.Y.S.E. ceased attempts at curbing the regionals, whose share of the market remained fairly constant during the next few years. To consolidate their positions and offer a stronger front against the N.Y.S.E., the larger regionals began to unite with one another. In 1948 the Philadelphia and Baltimore exchanges came together, and Washington joined five years later, to form the Philadelphia-Baltimore-Washington Stock Exchange. The Chicago, Cleveland, and St. Louis markets united to form the Midwest Stock Exchange in 1949, with New Orleans added in 1959. The Pacific Coast Stock Exchange was organized in 1956 through a merger of the San Francisco and Los Angeles markets. None of the new organizations garnered a great deal of business until the bull period, and then their volumes tended to rise along with that of the N.Y.S.E. During the 1945–1961 period, the best the regionals could do as a group was 7.96 percent of total dollar volume on organized exchanges, and that in 1953, while the lowest dollar percentage year was 6.44 percent, in 1945. Still, internal reforms and efficient management made the Pacific Coast and Midwest exchanges viable alternatives for brokers seeking markets in Big Board securities.

As the S.E.C. had indicated in the *Multiple Trading Case*, the O-T-C market was an important competitor for the N.Y.S.E. William Martin had noted this threat when, in 1940, he attempted to unite the exchange community against it. The rivalry was not new; ever since the Stock and Exchange Board had been founded, nonmembers had dealt in its stocks, buying at the lowest price and selling at the highest obtainable. They continued to function on a dealer basis, even when the N.Y.S.E. adopted the specialist system in the 1880s. Their clients

* 10 S.E.C. 270, pp. 283–84, as quoted in United States, 88th Congress, 1st session. House Document No. 95, Pt. 2, *Report of the Special Study of Securities Markets of the Securities and Exchange Commission* (Washington, 1965), p. 924.

knew that O-T-C dealers would pay them a slightly lower price for their stocks than that obtainable at the Big Board, while purchase prices were similarly higher. On the other hand, one did not pay commissions to O-T-C dealers, since they were not performing a public service (as the specialists were supposed to be doing) but instead were acting for their own accounts.

The N.Y.S.E. would have liked to rid the nation of those over-the-counter dealers who conducted transactions in listed stocks, but did not know how to proceed. Since the dealers tended to operate separately from one another in the nineteenth century, they did not provide a single target, but rather hundreds of them. This situation continued through the 1920s. At the height of the bull market, some over-the-counter dealers transacted larger volumes of business in key listed securities than did the specialist in the issue. Not only were their net prices better than those of the specialists but since the operations were essentially private, and did not appear on the ticker tape, manipulators preferred to use them when amassing large blocks of stock or disposing of them.* In 1929, when sales on all of the nation's exchanges totaled $135 billion, it was estimated that the over-the-counter dealers did a volume of $22 billion. Of course, this amount included stocks not listed on exchanges as well as those that were, and dealings in them far outnumbered those in listed stocks. There is no way of knowing by how much, or the accuracy of such figures, since at the time the O-T-C lacked a central statistical bureau.

Still, the dealers did form a community, one which recognized common interests and concerns. One of these was the "segregation issue" of 1935–1936. As has been indicated, the N.Y.S.E. saw it as an attempt on the part of New Deal reformers to separate broker and dealer functions in the work of specialists. If the government had its way, specialists would buy and sell their securities to service the public but would not be able to conduct transactions for their own accounts which, the specialists had claimed, was often necessary to provide cushions against sudden upward and downward movements. The New Dealers thought in terms of ending speculation on the Exchange floor; the N.Y.S.E. viewed the issue as pertaining to its institutional structure and the work of specialists in particular. But the O-T-C traders realized that if the functions were separated, it would only be a matter of time until the Exchange's specialists became virtually indistinguishable from the over-the-counter "market makers." Since the N.Y.S.E. would continue to charge commissions, while there were none at the

* In addition, the O-T-C traders had no restrictions regarding short sales, which helped make it more appealing for speculators.

O-T-C market, the latter would be able to compete with organized exchanges on a favorable basis. In effect, they could make the exchange system obsolete. Given the mood of the period—the height of the New Deal—there was significant public support for proposals to close the N.Y.S.E. for good. But the segregation issue was resolved in favor of the exchanges, and the O-T-C leaders had to bide their time.

Although business was bad at the over-the-counter market during the 1930s, it did better than the N.Y.S.E. or the regionals. Sales of stock at all exchanges was $11.4 billion, while the over-the-counter dealers transacted $3.4 billion in common stock. In 1929, the O-T-C market's sales had been 16 percent of those of the organized exchanges; ten years later, the figure was 30 percent. The over-the-counter market lacked an expensive building and staff, was more flexible than the exchanges, and its market makers aggressive and imaginative in securing the bulk of the sale of American securities owned by Europeans. To some, it must have appeared a replay of the situation of the late 1860s, when the Stock and Exchange Board contested with the Open Board, a struggle that ended in a merger. As has been indicated, several N.Y.S.E. commission brokers, led by Amyas Ames, suggested cooperation between the N.Y.S.E. and the O-T-C market, perhaps a sharing of business, while the Curb's management went even further. Stott and others of the new Old Guard would not hear of it, and whatever small chance existed for merger, consolidation, or amalgamation passed quickly.

This is not to say the O-T-C leaders were eager for such an accommodation. Under the terms of the Maloney Act of 1938, the market was regulated for the first time, albeit in a minor fashion, and the National Association of Security Dealers, whose function it was to provide self-regulation, was established. In 1939, the N.A.S.D. had some 1,500 members, and by 1941, over 2,000 had joined, more than 30 percent of the nation's O-T-C dealers. Leaders of such a vigorous and growing organization were in no mood to discuss cooperation with the stagnant N.Y.S.E., especially when Stott and others indicated, through word and deed, that they considered the over-the-counter traders second-class citizens, if that.

Was a clash between the two kinds of markets inevitable? If the N.Y.S.E. remained interested only in listed issues, while the O-T-C dealers did not seek additional business in such stocks and stressed wholesale rather than retail operations, perhaps one could have been avoided. If this occurred, their relationship might have become similar to that between the N.Y.S.E. and the Amex, and in time personal and institutional relationships could have grown in such a way that both markets could accept coexistence. This was not the case, however.

If this was war, then the O-T-C market was the aggressor. The

N.Y.S.E. could not, by its own regulations and S.E.C. law, invade the O-T-C market and trade in unlisted securities. It could and did encourage companies whose stocks qualified for listing to apply, but the N.Y.S.E. was not very good at this and "raided" the O-T-C list infrequently, preferring to leave that task to the Amex. Then, after the stock was "seasoned" at the A.S.E., the N.Y.S.E. would take it for its own, usually without complaint but with muffled resentment. The O-T-C dealers had a long tradition of trading in N.Y.S.E.–listed stocks, and they hoped to expand upon this business. The change would have to come slowly, with quantum leaps possible only when investment conditions were altered in America. In 1941, the O-T-C houses transacted only $84 million worth of business in listed issues, and most of these were inactive securities, often preferred stocks, usually in the real estate, financial, and utilities industries. The owner of a large block of stock would learn that the specialist could not take all of it at the last quote, or all at once. He would then learn that the O-T-C dealer would purchase the block but at a net price below the last N.Y.S.E. sale or the current quote. After comparing the two situations, he might conclude that he could do better for himself with the O-T-C dealer than the N.Y.S.E. specialist. And so the sale would be made.

Little was thought of such business in the 1940s, but the very fact they did occur indicated a flaw in the specialist system—or at least, the system as advertised. The N.Y.S.E. prided itself on having "orderly markets," which is to say that price changes on transactions in a given stock tended to be small, that the specialist's function was to purchase stock for his own account when a selling wave developed and sell it from inventory when a large demand existed. This was the rationale used to oppose the S.E.C.'s attempt to segregate broker and dealer functions in the 1930s, and it still existed as a bedrock belief of the exchange system a decade later.

But it didn't work in the case of transactions in inactive stocks. As might have been expected, brokers kept small inventories of such issues, not wanting to tie up funds. So when they were offered comparatively large blocks, they would lower the price to discourage the sale, and when sudden demand developed, they would raise the price. On such occasions they might deal with an O-T-C market maker, a practice against N.Y.S.E. regulations in the 1940s, but done anyway, and accepted in the 1950s. Thus, the specialist system did not function well in thin markets, at which time the specialist tended to operate in his self-interest rather than that of market continuity. And he would utilize the services of the O-T-C market when necessary.

If this were the case in thin markets, what would happen if specialists were deluged with orders to buy or sell large amounts of a given stock? This question was discussed in the late 1940s, and the answer seemed to be that the specialist was supposed to do all in his power to assure an orderly market. This was the theory; the practice was otherwise. Increasingly in the late 1940s and early 1950s, specialists allowed large gaps in prices to develop. Additional dealings by specialists in the O-T-C market might have mitigated the situation, but to the Exchange, this was tantamount to working with the enemy. So in 1948, the N.Y.S.E. issued Circular 52, which required prior Exchange approval before a member could transact business off the floor.

The issuance of the circular and the debate preceding and following its promulgation indicated a division of opinion at the Exchange. Some specialists argued that they could not maintain orderly markets without easy access to the O-T-C dealers, while others regarded any relationship with such people as akin to treason. The debate was somewhat reminiscent of that between the reformers and the standpatters of the 1930s, with one side arguing for accommodation to outside forces and institutional requirements, while the other appeared to believe that weakness in the face of challenges would lead to downfall.

There was more to the matter than that, however. In 1948, market pressures on the buy or sell side, when they developed, came from an increase in the number of relatively small orders. During the 1950s, as the institutions entered the market in force, large blocks of stock were offered for sale and were purchased. The specialist system had not performed well the last time this had happened, when the Europeans disposed of American shares in 1939–1940. Once again it cracked. Indeed, it was becoming evident that the specialist system had many drawbacks which might not be correctable. The "soft-liners" won their point; in 1952, the Exchange reverted to its earlier position, allowing off-the-floor transactions by members if they operated to the advantage of the customer.

Who was this customer? More often than not an official at a major institution, and not a small purchaser, be he investor or speculator. If the manager of a large trust placed an order for 1,000 shares of General Motors at a brokerage, he might pay the going price—in 1952, around 60, or for the 1,000 shares, $60,000—plus commission. The commission on a 1,000 share purchase was ten times that for 100 shares—there were no volume discounts. And the specialist and the floor representative of the brokerages did not do ten times the work for their fee. Such business was quite lucrative, and eagerly sought. The major purchaser knew this, and he also realized that increasingly the specialist was using the services of the O-T-C market to obtain large blocks, thus performing as a middleman, not a principal, and assuming few risks for sizable profits.

Why not go directly to the O-T-C? By eliminating the middleman, substantial savings might be had. To this, defenders of the exchange system responded that the O-T-C market was a chancy place, unregulated, with untrustworthy quotations that did not appear on a ticker tape, as did the N.Y.S.E.'s. This was the case; historically, the O-T-C market makers felt little in the way of public responsibility and were quite candid about admitting it. When asked by an S.E.C. official in 1962 of his obligation to the public, one dealer replied, "I don't believe I have a duty to the general public." While the specialist was expected, and indeed required, to stay at his post to deal in his stock, the O-T-C market maker would remain only if a profit were possible. "If there is too much competition and I can't make any money, I am going to drop out of a stock," one such person told the S.E.C. "If it got too competitive you might drop it?" "That is right," he replied. "We try to make the best market, but we are not going to make the best market on every stock at all times." "Do you think you have any obligation or duty with respect to your own profit-making activities to that customer of, say, Merrill Lynch who is buying through Merrill Lynch?" "None whatsoever," replied the O-T-C market maker. "You expect that selling broker who comes to you, or the buying broker, to act for his customer?" "That is right. That is what he is getting his commission for."

The O-T-C market had always been more a wholesale than a retail operation, and its members were accustomed to dealing with professionals, not the small investor. This attitude, then, was to be expected. But the manager of a large trust was hardly an amateur. He did not require the protection the specialist system afforded him; in the words of the O-T-C dealer, "That is what he is getting his commission for." In effect, the trust manager's client would be paying two fees—one to the manager, the other to the Exchange—if the manager transacted business on the Exchange when the net price was lower at the O-T-C market.

Such was the situation in the 1950s. While Keith Funston extolled the small investor, created the M.I.P. to serve him, and contrasted People's Capitalism with Soviet communism, the system was evolving. Increasingly, it was becoming evident that the future of the securities industry rested not with small investors but with large institutions. Despite the development of such devices as specials, secondaries, specialist block sales, and the like, the N.Y.S.E. had not come to grips with the situation. How could it, given the ideology Funston had fastened upon it so firmly and so well? Not until the Exchange was willing to abandon its dreams and visions and come to terms with reality would the situation change. What was needed in the early 1960s was a market geared to the requirements of institutions that might also accommodate those small investors who wanted to trade on their own. Instead, the N.Y.S.E. was designed for small investors, with institutions receiving few of the benefits they felt they merited. The O-T-C market makers thought otherwise, and set about constructing just such a market. By 1961, they were transacting an estimated $2 billion in listed stocks, up from the $84 million of twenty years earlier. Even then, the Exchange was not prepared to act; with the exception of Rule 394, it had done little either to counter the O-T-C market or reform its own house. The situation bore some surface resemblance to that of the early years of the century, when the N.Y.S.E faced the C.S.E. At that time, the Little Board had been destroyed by its own internal problems and exposure by government agencies. There was no sign in the late 1950s and early 1960s that the O-T-C market had such problems, while the government was not prepared to move against it, or prodded by the N.Y.S.E. to do so.

During the 1930s and 1940s, the Exchange had been obliged to adjust to low volume, stagnant prices, and political attacks, and it had done well, while at the same time preserving its pre-eminent position. What hardship could not accomplish, prosperity might. Volume, prices, and profits were all excellent throughout most of the 1950s. These in turn caused internal strains at the Exchange and encouraged a rival to attack the N.Y.S.E. directly. Not only was Funston unable to meet the threats and challenges, he gave no sign of even recognizing they were there. But as overworked clerks, harried brokers, and benumbed specialists participated in the bull market of 1961, the flaws in the design were beginning to show.

Part Three

DECAY AND RESPONSE

1961 - 1975

CHAPTER 14

The Shape of Things to Come

The headlines commented on the national mania. "The market moved ahead yesterday on heavy volume." "Stocks advanced along a broad front, with the glamors leading the way." "Once again the market discounted bad news to close at record highs."

News such as this was commonplace in 1961. To one who did not know what was happening, it might have appeared that an army of equities was advancing or retreating, as though at war with some unnamed, evil force. The enemy did have names, however—bears, pessimists, cranks, fogeys, and the like. Those who had faith in the market's advance—bulls, optimists, boosters—had become enthusiasts, expecting upward moves and further bear defeats as a matter of course and helping to create them through their purchases. Brokers served as combination reporters-artillerymen. They would telephone clients to communicate the latest news and then receive buy orders, which they aimed at the enemy, and, in the process, rallied the faithful to new victories. A decline in a major glamor issue—Control Data, Litton, Polaroid—was seen as both a buying opportunity and as a rebuff; if the price fell below the point at which the investor/speculator had purchased it, the purchaser would interpret the move as an affront, an insult to his good judgment, and rush to buy additional shares, both to indicate his faith in the stock and help it move upward. More often than not the issue would rally, at which point the investor/speculator would bring in his heavy artillery—additional orders—and put the enemy to rout.

The participant in the market mania of 1961 was often a zealot and didn't mind being labeled as one. A half century earlier, William James had written of "the moral equivalent of war." The new speculators of the early 1960s seemed to have discovered its financial equivalent. It took the edge off aggressive instincts, was exciting, and, as the market moved upward, was a battle with no real losers.

This was how it seemed. New issues became the prime topic of conversation at cocktail parties, and even neighborhood saloons, in 1961. For the first time since the late 1920s, brokers and investors became the subject of friendly, not bitter jokes. A *New Yorker* cartoonist drew several businessmen discussing the market on a commuter train. "I had the weirdest dream about my mother last night," mused one. "She said I should sell my A.T. & T. when it hits 132." Another portrayed an upper-class gathering with two groups of men in animated conversation, and in the foreground one woman remarked to a friend, "It's like last time. All the brokers are talking about art, and all the artists are talking about stocks." A third cartoon showed two skid-row derelicts sharing a bottle. One turned to the other and asked, "How's I.B.M. doing?"

Stocks had become a national pastime, or, at least, so it appeared. In 1961, the turnover ratio of listed N.Y.S.E. shares was 15 percent, with 1 billion shares traded, against 1960's 12 percent and 767 million. New York Attorney General Louis Lefkowitz announced an investigation of Nicholas Darvas, a dancer who claimed to have made a fortune in the stock market and whose book on the subject was a best-seller. Investment advisory newspapers and newsletters did record businesses. In an attempt to capitalize on the craze, a group of dealers advertised that huge profits could be made in the art market, and they put together the AMG 500–Painters Average, which they promised to explain and analyze for subscribers. The typical market letter might spotlight, "Fifty Stock Split Candidates." The AMG group's ad screamed, "32 Artists to Triple in Price." "We all know it is ridiculous," said broker Sidney Lurie, who had seen such crazes in the past. "But the stock market reflects every human frailty, and the big one now is greed. Others are fear and stupidity. They'll come a little later." Bernard Baruch spoke to his biographer of the tulip mania, and helped promote a new edition of Charles Mackay's *Extraordinary Popular Delusions and the Madness of Crowds*, a century-old classic that usually enjoyed revivals during incipient bear periods. Market technician Hamilton Bolton warned, "We are well entranced in the fifth and final upward wave—the last in a bull market." Lurie agreed and then, in late 1961, wrote, "The market will perform better." For a while, Data Control, a small, marginal firm whose shares were listed on the Amex, moved ahead briskly. There was no reason for this, and one analyst, in studying the situation, concluded the stock had been purchased mistakenly by individuals who confused it with Control Data.

The market fed on stories such as these. Reflecting the drive for youth and vigor in Washington under the Kennedy Administration, Wall Street firms sought young people for their staffs. In particular, they wanted them in research and portfolio positions. A new investment world was being born, the theory went, and men and women who were too attached to the old would be unable to function efficiently in it. Experience was a detriment; novelty was prized.

This was the market the public saw, read about on the pages of the newsmagazines, viewed in special television programs about Wall Street, and learned of from friends at social gatherings. But it was not the new era they perceived but rather a pale reflection of the old—that of the 1920s—and one that had grown to maturity in the 1950s. This is not to say there was nothing unique about this market, or that forces unknown or barely recognized in previous bull markets were not at work. The investment population was changing in ways that some Wall Street professionals understood but which were hidden from view insofar as most investors were concerned. This was not the result of a conspiracy of silence but rather due to the disinterest of most amateur investors in the inner workings of the district.

As this market developed and flourished, marked by ever-higher quotations, glamor stocks, new issues, and newer personnel, a powerful professional market grew even more rapidly, one that remained somewhat separate from the amateur, even though they shared interests in some of the same securities.

There were, in fact, four levels of sophistication in the market during the early Kennedy period. The least knowledgeable were those who obtained the name of a broker, opened an account, and bought and sold on the basis of overheard conversations, rumors, talk of new issues, and the like. Such individuals might have difficulties understanding parts of the financial sections of most newspapers, but in any case, this was not necessary to operate in the market. Their information came from friends, and if they read a book on the subject, it was likely to be Darvas's *How I Made Two Million Dollars in the Stock Market* or some similar work.

Other investors could and did follow the market through their newspapers, and perhaps had a favorite columnist or two. They would read investment market letters sent out by their brokers, and even might subscribe to such magazines as *Barron's* and *Forbes*, both of which enjoyed large increases in circulation.

A third, more sophisticated group, learned the techniques of analysis and tried to apply them in making investment decisions. Such terms as "triple tops," "false breakouts," and "resistance points" were featured in their conversations, and they tried to master the intricacies of the Dow Theory and the Elliott Wave Theory, and understand the convolutions of point-and-figure charts. Skeptics called these market watchers "the astrologers of Wall Street," but adult education courses in charting techniques flourished throughout the country.

Finally, there were those who operated under different terms than the first three. Unlike them, they did not invest thousands of dollars, or even tens of thousands, but rather tens of millions, often in a single day. They were the institutional investors, the men who headed the major trusts and mutual funds, whose names were hardly recognized by those who fell into the first three levels of sophistication. Dwight Robinson, Joseph Fitzsimmons, Walter Morgan, and Cameron Reed, all of whom were presidents of large mutual fund organizations, made the kinds of investment decisions that affected the fortunes of the Street and caused prices of leading issues to move one way or the other. In 1962, the large trusts and other institutional investors owned some $70.5 billion worth of stock listed on the N.Y.S.E., 20.4 percent of the total. Spot checks indicated that large institutions accounted for approximately one-fifth of all share volume at the Big Board in the early 1950s. By 1962, the amount was closer to one-fourth, and growing rapidly.

Each of the four groups appeared to have a primary interest in one large category of stocks and subsidiary ones in others. For instance, the least knowledgeable speculators traded eagerly in new issues; shares in small companies that were listed at the Amex or traded over-the-counter; and penny stocks that were sold by pitchmen over the telephone. On the next level of sophistication were to be found investors who were interested in "emerging growth companies," "the I.B.M. of 1970," and the like. The technicians were involved with all stocks, so long as their charts showed the proper forms. As for the institutions, they concentrated on the "favorite fifty," blue-chip growth issues for the most part. These were "one-decision" stocks; the only question was when to buy the stock and at what price. Once purchased, they were rarely sold.

In the bull market of 1961, profits were being made in an inverse proportion to knowledge and power. That is to say, the new issue prices soared, and rank amateurs were able to double their money quickly, and then redouble. The small companies with relatively little stock outstanding saw their quotations rise rapidly, as investors and speculators on the second level of sophistication bid for the available shares. A similar situation occurred when a major stock signaled a breakout and the technicians rushed to buy. Since many of these firms had large capitalizations, the advances were not as impressive. The institutional favorites, with the most outstanding shares of all, often were among the slowest movers. But advance they did.

Everyone seemed to be making money. As might have been expected, the most spectacular performers received the most attention. Thus, it appeared a market of amateurs. To the N.Y.S.E. and O-T-C leaders, however, the institutional investors were the most important of the four.

One reason for this interest was a theory then popular that the markets would soon have to face a shortage of common stocks. Available statistics seemed to support this hypothesis. Despite the rush of new companies to sell shares, there was no significant change in the rate of increase in the 1950s.

NET NEW ISSUES OF CORPORATE STOCK, 1952–1960
(millions of dollars)

Year	*New Issues*	*Retirements*	*Net Change*
1952	2,586	145	2,441
1953	2,216	284	1,932
1954	2,999	1,196	1,802
1955	3,619	1,725	1,893
1956	3,920	1,373	2,548
1957	3,309	596	2,713
1958	3,070	943	2,127
1959	3,378	1,002	2,376
1960	2,725	1,029	1,696

SOURCE: Goldsmith, *Institutional Investors and Common Stock*, pp. 170–7

There were further indications that small firms were floating new issues, while the larger ones were repurchasing their own shares so as to enhance their earnings-per-share. Furthermore, well-established concerns financed their operations out of retained earnings and the flotation of bonds more than through the issuance of additional equity.

According to this theory, since most of the nation's major companies were listed on the N.Y.S.E., that exchange would suffer a loss of listings and total shares traded, or at the best, stand still or advance at a sluggish pace. In 1954, N.Y.S.E.–listed firms repurchased $273.9 million of their own stock; in 1960, the figure was $598.4 million. The number of shares listed on the Big Board increased in the late 1950s but hardly as rapidly as did trading volume.

What did this mean? In 1961, it appeared that the large institutions, hungry for one-decision stocks, were gobbling them up at a record pace, so that in time, there would be little remaining for the average investor. The implication could easily be drawn: buy shares of I.B.M., Eastman Kodak, Sears Roebuck, Coca-Cola, Minnesota Mining, and other favorite fifty issues, before the institutions had them all. This resulted in a second contest: try to guess which stocks will be added to the list from which the large institutions drew their purchases. Among the leading candidates were Xerox, Polaroid, Control Data, Fairchild Camera, Litton Industries, and Texas Instruments.

It was, then, a complicated market, one in which theories, rumors, and outright lies competed with one another, were elaborated upon, and in the end, led prices to move—usually upward. The speculators

N.Y.S.E. Listing and Trading Statistics, 1956–1961
(millions of shares)

Year	*Number of Issues Listed*	*Shares Listed*	*Shares Traded*
1956	1,502	4,462.1	556.3
1957	1,522	4,803.8	559.9
1958	1,507	5,016.7	747.1
1959	1,507	5,847.3	820.3
1960	1,528	6,458.4	766.7
1961	1,541	7,088.0	1,021.3

Source: *N.Y.S.E. Fact Book, 1973*

caused volume to soar at the O-T-C market, while the Amex, which reported sales of 488 million shares in 1961, up from 286 million the year before, eclipsed its 1929 record for the first time.

In the fourth quarter of the year, mutual fund sales were $813.1 million, another record, and twice that of the corresponding quarter of 1957. Thus, the small investor was making his presence felt. And the representatives of the small investors, the large trusts, were coming to dominate the market for the leading N.Y.S.E shares, trading in thousands of shares at a time. In 1960, the N.Y.S.E. reported 410,000 shares sold through Exchange Distributions; in 1961, there were 1,186,000 shares disposed of in this increasingly popular vehicle of the large trusts. Total sales by special methods came to 17,415,000 shares that year; in 1957, the amount had been 7,196,000 shares.

On the surface it appeared the N.Y.S.E. had adjusted to the growth of institutional power and would prove responsive to whatever changes might develop in the future. Some troublesome matters remained, however. If institutional purchases could drive the price of a blue chip upwards, what might they do to quotations of more thinly capitalized issues? What would occur if several large institutions decided, about the same time, to sell their holdings in a stock? Might not the small investors be whipsawed in such situations? Could specialists function efficiently under these circumstances? Statistics on block purchases and sales at the N.Y.S.E. were encouraging, but indications were that the O-T-C market was handling an increasing amount of business in listed stocks. In 1961, then, structural forces in the market appeared about to change, in qualitative as well as quantitative ways.

On December 13, the Dow Industrials reached a peak of 734.91, and on the last day of trading in 1961 closed at 731.14, having gained 115.25 points for the year. It was an impressive showing, and the fact that the market ended 1961 on such a high note, and had discounted the failure of the Bay of Pigs invasion, the erection of the Berlin Wall, and other apparent setbacks in foreign relations, added to the optimism of the times.

Strong though it was, the 1961 stock rise was not as great as recoveries during the Eisenhower years. In 1953, for example, the Dow Industrials Index lost 4.7 percent of its value and recovered to rise by 50.1 percent in 1954. The 17.4 percent decline in 1957 had been followed by a 38.5 percent advance in 1958. Stocks had fallen 10.3 percent in 1960; in 1961, they added 23.7 percent to their prices. On each occasion, the recovery had been less forceful than the previous one.

The postwar bull market had started when investors sought bargains in stocks, in particular securities that paid high dividends and were safe. In 1949, the market price of a dollar in dividends, as measured by the Dow Industrials, was 12.67, meaning that the dividend yield of the Dow was slightly below 8 percent. In 1959, the price of a dollar in dividends was 32.74 at its high, or little more than a 3 percent yield. The high for 1960 was 32.74, and for 1961, 32.36. It would appear the Dow Industrials had peaked, at least insofar as those who purchased stocks for income were concerned. During the 1950s, these securities had risen more rapidly than their dividends, as the prices made up for lost time in the 1940s. By the early 1960s, the process was completed. Indeed, some believed it had gone too far and that a retreat was in order. At the very least, such stocks would rise in line with increases in dividends. Investors concerned with yields could do better in bonds and even in savings accounts.

The response to this kind of argument was that growth, not yield, was the primary interest of investors, and so it was. A generation earlier, a decent growth stock was supposed to sell for around ten times earnings. This measurement had been discarded in the 1950s, and was deemed antique by 1961, when some stocks were selling for over 100 times earnings and still continued to climb. As far as the glamors were concerned, however, the advance had been impressive, and Wall Street analysts, concerned that such a rise could only lead to a fall, thought that a correction was overdue.

The economic news during the President's first year in office was encouraging. Kennedy prodded business into reinvesting in new plants through a system of tax incentives. This in turn led to additional jobs and increases in the gross national product. Similar policies had been tried in the past and usually resulted in inflation. In order to prevent price boosts this time, Kennedy relied upon a combination of moral suasion and reciprocal pledges. Labor would be asked to keep wage demands to a minimum, to tie them to increases in productivity. In return, industry was to make every effort to hold down prices. This policy was not signaled by the signing of pacts. Indeed, prominent labor and business leaders opposed the idea as an intrusion. Kennedy hoped that public opinion, channeled through his office, would accomplish his ends.

There was doubt on Wall Street that this policy would succeed. Little that Kennedy had done during his first year in office had inspired the district's confidence. The nation's financial establishment, which had been so comfortable with Eisenhower, was disturbed by the styles of some of the men in power in Washington in 1961–1962. To this were added the institutional problems on Wall Street, at the securities markets in particular, and the growing belief that stock prices were getting out of hand. The result was an erratic market in the first quarter of 1962. Prices fell steadily in early January, and on January 17, declined by 7.88 points on heavy volume to close at below 700 for the first time since September 26, 1961. The financial press published stories about a slowdown in corporate stock purchases, and a switch to bonds, where yields were good and prices reasonable—far more so, it would appear, than those of stocks. Prices rallied late in the month, but recovered only slightly in February. There was another rally in early March, and then a further collapse. The Dow Industrials fell from 723.54 on March 15 to under 700 once again on April 6. Volume was below normal—only 2,730,000 shares traded on April 6. It appeared to some that the market was awaiting a news item, an excuse to move one way or the other.

The anticipated signal was given on Tuesday, April 10, when United States Steel announced price increases averaging six dollars a ton. The Steelworkers Union had signed a new contract with the companies less than two weeks before, under which it accepted minimum wage boosts in return for an apparent industry agreement to maintain prices at current levels. To the President and the workers, the United States Steel action was a violation of faith. Furthermore, it ran contrary to the anti-inflationary program of the Kennedy Administration. "My father always told me that all businessmen were sons of bitches," the President exclaimed to his aides, "but I never believed it until now!"

Within hours, most of the other large companies fell in behind the industry leader, lifting their prices by the same amount. Then Kennedy attacked the companies (excluding Kaiser and Inland Steel, which had maintained prices). "The simultaneous and identical actions . . . constitute a wholly unjustifiable and irresponsible defiance of the public interest," he told a television audience. The full weight of government was brought to bear against the companies. Cabinet members and the President threatened a boycott of all steel companies that had raised their prices, announced grand jury investigations of the increases for evidence of collusion and violations of antitrust laws, and

Internal Revenue Service probes of the companies' books. It was the most massive federal attack against business since the early days of the New Deal. To some, it appeared the prelude for an antibusiness crusade. Others thought the actions unwarranted. "Should a President of the United States use the enormous powers of the federal government to blackjack any segment of our free society into line with his personal judgment without regard to law?" asked the Senate Republican Leadership Committee. Contrasting Kennedy's firmness in dealing with the steel companies to his indecision in the face of foreign policy dangers—the Bay of Pigs and the Berlin Wall, for instance—the *New York Herald Tribune* commented, "We do respect decisiveness in an executive and so do the people. We can only wish it had been displayed in a better cause."

The pressure continued for three days. Kaiser and Inland held firm, and the government announced new contracts would be given to them. Then the industry conceded defeat and rescinded the price increases. The President's supporters hailed his quick action and victory over the companies.

The episode had bearish effects on investments and was a further sign that lightening of portfolios should commence. Soon after came an announcement of an S.E.C. investigation of the district, the first since the war, and this added to the skittish feelings. Stock prices began to fall, though on light volume and in an orderly fashion. On April 10, the Dow Industrials had closed at 695.46. A week later, the index was at 688.43. But block activity picked up, indicating selling by institutions. There were 124 new lows on April 13, the largest since October 24, 1960. By the end of the month there was talk of strikes that autumn and a further testing of the Kennedy wage-price program, this time by the unions. The Dow closed the month at 665.33, for a loss of almost 42 points in April. By then, price declines of 10 to 20 percent a day for individual stocks were not uncommon. I.B.M. lost 31½ points on April 30, and other sudden declines frightened professionals and amateurs alike.

The erratic price movements to the downside and the quantum leaps in prices indicated the arrival of both a crisis and testing period.

The crisis was the anticipated correction in market prices. By late April and early May, the bears were in the decided majority and their only important area of disagreement lay in the extent of the anticipated decline. Optimists thought prices would fall slowly and settle around the 650 level, after which consolidation would occur in preparation for the next upward movement. Some of the pessimists believed the Dow could decline to the mid-300s. Both agreed that prices had already fallen considerably, far more than the Dow indicated. The vending-machine issues, which had led the market upward in late 1961, lost over

50 percent of their value in the first quarter of 1962. Transitron and Sparton Industries, two sought-after stocks that had risen on heavy volume, were down by more than 40 percent in the same period. I.B.M., Rohm & Haas, Litton, Beckman, and other pivotal high-technology issues were scraping the bottom. The new issue craze ended abruptly, as did booms in small business investment corporations. None of these declines and collapses were reflected in the Dow, which consisted, for the most part, of seasoned, conservative stocks. The crisis had arrived—some said it appeared even before the steel confrontation, which had served to dramatize and broaden the decline.

The testing period was at hand as well, and this was of considerable interest to the district's professionals. Ever since the beginning of the bull market, there had been some question as to the viability of the specialist system. It had performed well in the quiet markets of the 1940s and continued to do so during the early 1950s. Then, as prices rose sharply, "gaps" had appeared in heavily traded and desirable stocks. Jumps of several points were not uncommon, and were accepted with gratification by the bulls who, after all, had no quarrel with higher prices. Yet the specialists—and the Exchange itself—had always claimed that the system acted to stabilize prices. Statistics bore out the contention. Still, the fears remained. Investors might not complain about jumps upward, but what would they say and do if prices fell in the same fashion? If the pessimists were correct, and a major decline was in the works, then the viability of the system would be tested. Should the specialists use their funds to shore up prices and insure orderly declines, then all would be well. If, on the other hand, they did not assume the risks of such operations, then reformers might call for changes in the system.

On May 1, the Dow closed at 671.24, up almost six points from the previous close. It had traded in a range of 673.59–655.44, however, and the gyrations, combined with a heavy volume—5,100,000 shares traded—indicated the time of testing had arrived. If the blue chips that made up the Dow Industrials followed the glamors, it might be said that a full-fledged bear market had begun.

The churning continued through the first sessions in May, with prices declining irregularly on moderately high volume. On Friday, May 11, the average closed at 640.63. Prices rose on Monday, May 13, and then stabilized. Trading slowed. It appeared as though investors and speculators were testing the bottom. The Dow was at 650.70 on May 18, up 10.07 points for the week. Given a period of calm, the crisis might have been ended.

Volume was low on May 21; at 2,260,000 shares traded, it was the most sluggish day in over nine months. The Dow fluctuated in a narrow range and closed down 2.11 points. The public had withdrawn to the sidelines. So had the specialists, who appeared somewhat awed and excited by the situation, torn between the need to save their own skins, the hope for profit, the responsibilities of their positions, and an awareness that the S.E.C. and N.Y.S.E. leadership was watching their actions with more care than usual.

Prices were lower from the start on Tuesday, and volume was up. The Dow closed the day with a loss of 12.25 points on 3,640,000 shares. Wednesday saw more of the same—the Dow was down 9.82 points on a volume of 5,450,000 shares, and toward the end some panic selling commenced, with gaps in prices common. Additional declines came on Thursday and Friday. The Dow stood at 611.88 Friday afternoon, down by 38.82 points for the week. The entire advance of the Kennedy bull market had been wiped out.

What did it all mean? Keith Funston told reporters there was no slump in sight. Edwin Posner, the veteran specialist who had assumed the presidency of the Amex, added that "this definitely is not panic selling. We have had a ten-year bull market, and this evidently is the time for an adjustment." Still, in a single week, stocks on the N.Y.S.E. had lost $30 billion in value, more than the combined gross national products of Australia, Sweden and Ireland. Posner's statement to the contrary notwithstanding, there was a sense of panic in the air. Furthermore, the N.Y.S.E. was showing signs of strain. The tape fell behind by thirty-two minutes at the close on Friday, and the week's record in terms of gaps in trades was poor. Popular stocks gyrated in spectacular fashion, as though abandoned by their specialists. I.B.M. fell 15 points on Tuesday, 20 on Wednesday, 17 on Thursday, and rose a point on Friday. Afterward, the S.E.C. asked the I.B.M. specialist about his actions that week and the following, and the ways he prepared for contingencies such as a bear market.

Q. Did you attempt to reduce your positions during the last part of last year or the first three months of this year?

A. . . . There were times when our position was probably a little on the small side, yes.

Q. When would that have been?

A. Well, that was during the end of May, when the break was strenuous in IBM . . .

Q. How did you end up with a small position in a period of a break?

A. Well, self-preservation . . .

Other popular stocks were stabilized by their specialists, but large gaps in Polaroid, Xerox, and Texas Instruments, among others, indicated that the attitude of the I.B.M. specialist was not unusual.

Later on, O-T-C leaders would point to prices in the May 21–25 period as a sign that the specialist system would not work well in crisis situations. True, the O-T-C market makers did not stabilize prices either in this period, but they never claimed they would, or indeed that it was a proper function to do so. "There is something worse than no cop on the corner," said one market maker, "and that's a cop without a gun who is blind. Then you think you have protection, but you really don't. That to me is the specialist system."

Newspaper stories that weekend were ominous, as were the jokes and stories about the market. One advisory service flatly predicted a crash of the magnitude of 1929. Wall Streeters generally blamed Kennedy for the decline, forgetting or ignoring the fact that it had begun before the steel confrontation and that the dramatic collapse had taken place a month after the companies had capitulated. There was agreement, however, that Monday, May 28, would be a bad day.

The bears were not disappointed. The Dow opened at 609.11, down more than two points from the Friday close, and sank throughout the day on extraordinarily heavy volume. Many technicians had claimed that 610 would be a "major support level." When they saw the early prices they began to sell heavily. Beginning at 10:20 the ticker was behind floor transactions, and "flash prices" for thirty key issues were sent at regular intervals. At noon these were dispensed with, since each time they were flashed, the operators fell that much more behind. There was no way for customers' men and their clients to learn the latest quotes. The N.Y.S.E. had always prided itself on "operating in a fishbowl," with the ticker a window for outsiders; unlike the O-T-C, brokers and investors could find the last sale with ease. This was not the case on May 28, and added to the failure of specialists to maintain the market—to do so would be tantamount to shaking a fist at a hurricane. The crisis appeared to substantiate O-T-C claims that a dealer market was preferable to, and more realistic than, an auction one.

By 1:00 many orders simply were not being filled; frantic brokers stuffed new ones into their pockets, hoping to take care of them during a lull, which never came. A week and a half later the Board of Governors ruled that those firms which had not filled orders would not be punished under the negligence rule—still another round of ammunition for the O-T-C dealers. It was, in effect, the most benumbing experience the Street had witnessed in more than a generation. At last, "another 1929" had arrived.

(It wasn't as bad as had been anticipated. Participants on the floor, interviewed on television that evening, were calm, and some were even in good humor. They had lived through a horrible event and congratulated themselves on the fact. "It was though some great natural calamity had occurred to some far-distant people," said one such individual, "and we watched with fascination, but not fear.")

A great cheer rose from the floor at 3:30, when the closing bell sounded. But the ticker kept working, catching up with the unreported sales. The last of these was punched out at 5:58. Then it was learned that the Exchange had recorded its fifth most active day—9,350,000 shares were traded. The Dow had fallen by 34.95 points, to close at 576.93. The Big Board was a shambles. The same was true at the Amex, where 2,980,000 shares changed hands. A different kind of situation prevailed at the O-T-C, where some market makers simply had refused to deal, turned down sales, or didn't answer telephones. If the crash of May 28 had demonstrated the weaknesses of the auction system in a time of crisis, it also showed that under such circumstances, the dealer market was even less functional.

What did it all mean? Funston blamed the crash on the President. "There has been a growing disquiet among investors because of Kennedy's steel action," he said. Furthermore, "The Securities and Exchange Commission hearings hurt the market." The *New York Times* thought "Something resembling an earthquake hit the stock market," and noted that despite the crash, the current economic situation was "cheering." Some of his advisors urged Kennedy to speak to the nation that evening, but he refused; perhaps he recalled that Hoover had done so in 1929 and he wanted to avoid further comparisons. Henry Ford II also declined comment, as did Thomas Watson of I.B.M. and most other leading industrialists. Secretary of Commerce Luther Hodges, when asked about comparisons of 1962 and 1929, observed that most modern large corporations were more self-financing than they had been thirty-three years before. Even if the market continued to decline, he implied, business would remain strong.

The most important bullish rumors that evening emanated from the large institutions, the mutual funds in particular. Many were in a highly liquid position and seeking a good buying opportunity. Fund sales in the first quarter of the year had been $922 million and redemptions, $282.4 million. In contrast, sales in the corresponding quarter of 1961 were $719.9 million and redemptions, $331.1 million. Apparently, as the market fell, mutual fund holders increased their purchases, thus providing a countercyclical force to stabilize prices. The Massachusetts Investment Trust, with over a billion dollars in assets, was 10 percent in cash and ready to buy. "While we're not jumping in with both feet," said a senior vice-president of Wellington Fund, "we are investing selectively." "We came into the market with a 20 percent cash position and we have been buying recently," added a spokesman for Dreyfus Fund. Walter Benedict of Investors Planning Corporation, an industry giant, announced that his funds had purchased some $20 million worth of stock in the last two sessions and would buy more on Tuesday.

News that the giant funds were in a buying mood provided what little cheer the market could muster Tuesday morning. The initial trend was a continuation of the previous day's decline. By the end of the first hour, the Dow Industrials had fallen 11 points on heavy volume. At noon the average was at 554—or at least, this was the guess, since the ticker was too far behind to really know. By 1:00 the ticker showed a loss for the day of 13.61 points. But a spot check on last sales on the floor indicated that, in reality, the average was up by 7.72 points. In other words, brokers knew that prices were rallying, but the clients and customers' men in brokerages throughout the nation thought the decline was in full swing. Then, as fund purchases provided an underpinning for the bulls, a major rally began. From a bottom of 553.75, the Dow rose in the greatest upward surge since the 1920s, to close at 603.96. The specialists and floor brokers were triumphant at the 3:30 closing. It was eight hours before the last sale was recorded on the ticker. Volume had been 14,750,000 shares, the second highest day in Exchange history—first place still belonged to October 29, 1929.

Wednesday was Memorial Day, and trading was suspended. Thursday was relatively calm, considering what had transpired on Monday and Tuesday. The Dow rose to 613.36—9.4 points—on a volume of 10,700,000 shares. There was a slight decline on Friday, to 611.05, with volume at 5,760,000 shares.

The scare was over. And the question was repeated: what did it mean?

Stock prices stabilized in July. The economic news indeed was good, with auto sales at a post-1955 record. In August, President Kennedy promised reductions in taxes for 1963, and the market began to move upward. The fears of June were being quickly dispelled. Even the report that mutual fund sales were declining while redemptions rose was deemed bullish; the Wall Street explanation was "the little guy is always wrong." The Cuban missile crisis in October resulted in selling and lower prices for two days. Then, when it appeared to have been resolved in America's favor, the market moved upward, gaining almost a hundred points in a month and a half. The Dow closed December at 652.10, off 79.04 points for the year, but well above the May lows.

During this time the S.E.C. and the exchanges investigated the crash in greater detail than they had any similar phenomenon, not excluding the crisis of 1929. The tape was pored over for clues, its story fed into computers to discern patterns, and floor and office personnel questioned as to their activities in that hectic period. Fortuitously, the S.E.C. investigation of the district had been in full swing when the crisis developed, so there was a small army of trained officials on the scene.

The results of the S.E.C. investigation were released in a series of documents, beginning in April and ending in September of 1963. Its official title was: *Report of the Special Study of Securities Markets of the Securities and Exchange Commission.* More commonly known as simply *The Special Study*, it became the bible for the district in a matter of days, with thousands of copies ordered by firms and individuals, who pored over them, extracted sections, passed them on to friends and associates, and debated their contents. Indeed, so significant was the report that a commercial publisher put out a one-volume condensation of it the following year, which also proved popular.*

As might have been expected, the newspapers considered the analysis of the crash to be the centerpiece of the study. The section of *The Special Study* dealing with the market in late May was released on August 8, 1964. Its conclusions were not very enlightening.

> Neither this study nor that of the New York Stock Exchange was able to isolate and identify the "cause" of the market events of May 28, 29, and 31. There was some speculation at the time that these events might be the result of some conspiracy or deliberate misconduct. Upon the basis of the study's inquiry, there is no evidence whatsoever that the break was deliberately precipitated by any person or group or that there was any manipulation or illegal conduct in the functioning of the market.
>
> The avalanche of orders which came into the market during this period subjected the market mechanisms to extraordinary strain, and in many respects they did not function in a normal way. Particularly significant was the lateness of the tape and the consequent inability of investors to predict accurately the prices at which market orders would be executed. . . .**

Having said this, the S.E.C.'s recommendation was rather mild. It believed the exchanges "should make a joint study [with the S.E.C.] of possible intermediate measures, short of suspending trading, that might be invoked to assure minimum disruption of the fair and orderly functioning of the securities markets in times of severe market stress."

This section barely skimmed the surface of specialist activities prior to and during the break, however. Detailed analyses were made of trading in eight stocks—American Telephone & Telegraph, Avco, Brunswick, General Motors, I.B.M., E. J. Korvette, Standard Oil Co.

* John W. Hazard and Milton Christie, *The Investment Business: A Condensation of the SEC Report* (New York, 1964).

** *Special Study*, Part 4, Chapter XIII, p. 859.

(New Jersey), and U.S. Steel. These showed a variety of responses, from specialist units which reacted valiantly to difficult situations to others which performed badly. The S.E.C. discovered that from the end of December 1961 to May 25, 1962, the specialists as a group had reduced their inventories by about one-third. "The extent to which this net selling contributed to the deterioration of the market prior to the actual break cannot be determined." On the day of the break itself, May 28, the specialists purchased 1,649,810 shares and sold 1,443,410, for a net purchase balance of 206,400 shares, indicating at least an attempt to fulfill their functions (although the S.E.C. did not ask the dollar amounts on either side, an even more significant set of figures). Still, "it was found that as the day progressed and the decline continued, the net purchases of specialists in these thirty stocks tended to decrease. Toward the latter part of the day balances shifted to the sale side." The S.E.C. drew no implication from this, but it would appear that as the panic psychology grew and as men in the midst of that wild market looked about them and saw values toppling—like their fathers had told them had occurred in 1929—they put their own fortunes above those of their functions on the floor.*

To what extent was the specialist supposed to act in the public interest and against his own? Did the Exchange want the specialist to sacrifice himself, to risk his financial solvency in order to maintain orderly markets? And if he did so, what possible good would be served, since to stand against the mob would be to invite certain destruction?

Given the nature of the marketplace in 1962, was it realistic to expect the specialist system to continue to function unchanged? In the late nineteenth century, when trades were for a few hundred shares at a time, and when specialists were not charged with stabilizing the market, the system performed well. In the post–S.E.C. period, when institutional forces were growing and the specialists were saddled with responsibilities in the area of stabilization, could anything short of abandonment in time of stress or utter destruction be anticipated?

The N.Y.S.E. conducted its own study of events on May 28 and May 29 and learned that on the 28th, large institutions were net purchasers by 1.2 million shares, and the following day, their purchases exceeded sales by 1.4 million shares. The trust managers thought prices were too low, and their willingness to back that opinion with purchase orders proved to have a greater impact on prices than the activities of specialists, even when attempting to create an orderly market.

If the part of *The Special Study* that dealt with the 1962 market break was relatively uncritical of the specialists, an earlier section, on

* The specialists might have argued that toward the close of trading they noted their cash positions low, and concerned with meeting their net capital requirements, they sold stock into a declining market. This explanation was not offered at the time, however.

the exchange markets, took a different point of view—leading to suspicions that the two sections had been put together by separate teams and not harmonized due to haste in releasing the document. In it, the specialist in Ford recounted his activities prior to the break, in the period from August 1961 to early May 1962.

> Not that I am any student of charts, but I took a look at the Ford chart and it looked very dangerous to me. . . . I liquidated our whole position and went short, and we have maintained a short position, actually in only three of our stocks, all the way through, practically, during this whole period. During the day, we have become long, but almost every night, we were short stock.

There were two ways to interpret this statement. If a specialist felt a stock could soon be subjected to selling waves, he would be prudent to lighten his inventory in advance so as to have cash with which to "eat stock" when the time to do so arrived. Thus, he would sell into a strong market and buy when the market weakened. This was the textbook definition of the way specialists provided for orderly markets. Perhaps this was what the Ford specialist was saying.

The action could be viewed differently, however. If a person found himself with a large inventory of stock and he felt the issue was due for a decline, he might sell so as to avoid what would amount to an "inventory loss." In this way, he would be abandoning the stock before the hoards did, relying upon his "feel" for the stock, his proximity to the trading center, and even his position as a specialist to get out while the getting was good. And such an action would be against Exchange rules. But it would be difficult to prove intent.

The situation recalled the debates on the segregation issue in the mid-1930s, when the S.E.C. attempted to separate the functions of broker and dealer. At the time the agency claimed that the same person could not serve his clients (and the public interest) while dealing for his own account, and the N.Y.S.E. responded that specialists had to do both in order to fulfill their functions efficiently. In 1962, specialists were accused of looking to their own interests first and those of the public afterward. Some of them, in discussions with S.E.C. personnel, helped reinforce the suspicions.

> We had been accumulating, accumulating and in April [1962]—I don't remember the date, but we had as large a debit balance as we had ever had.
>
> I decided to clear shop.
>
> I didn't like the market. I didn't like the fact that you bought

> 500 and sold 200 and then you were buying 500 more and you were selling 300, but you were always buying on balance.

Another specialist noted that he began to have doubts about the market in 1961, at which time he reduced his holdings. When asked, "To what would you attribute the reduction of inventory over this period?" he replied, "I don't know. I can't answer the question. I don't know how to answer it." His conclusion was illuminating. "Specialists are like all people. They get frightened."

This part of *The Special Study* concluded:

> Obviously, no one person has the capital to stem a selling wave such as that of May 28, but with his central location, the specialist is in a position to cushion the public's selling by giving depth to the markets, and some specialists undertook this function. Other specialists, however, confined their activity to providing technical price continuity and a few specialists seemed to contribute to the "pounding" down of prices by their selling.
>
> Whatever other lessons may be drawn from the May 1962 market break, the results of this study indicate that both the tests of specialists' performance and public presentations of the test results are in need of revision.*

How could the situation be improved? Greater surveillance, stronger specialist units, and Exchange backups during crisis periods were mentioned. The S.E.C. noted, in passing, that automation might bring some changes as well. In 1962, however, there seemed no doubt that as far as the Commission was concerned the specialist system would remain at the heart of the securities markets.

In yet a third part of *The Special Study*, the S.E.C. discussed the over-the-counter market in N.Y.S.E.–listed securities. On a selected day, January 18, 1962, over-the-counter purchases and sales of such stock amounted to $19.5 million, or 5.2 percent of the amount traded at the Big Board that day. The S.E.C. estimated that for the year as a whole, the O-T-C dealers accounted for approximately 4 percent of the N.Y.S.E. total. "Dollar volume of over-the-counter trading in listed securities increased 185 percent from 1955 to 1961, some 10 percent more than the increase in over-the-counter trading generally, and three times as much as the 60-percent increase in volume for the same period reported by the Exchange."

Increasingly members of the National Association of Securities Dealers were drawn to the market in listed stocks. There had been

* *Special Study*, Part 2, Chapter VI, pp. 110–21.

only three such dealers in the early 1940s. Nine more began specializing in listed stock in the 1950s. An additional five joined in 1961 and 1962. Clearly, this was a significant part of the industry.

The O-T-C houses were still formulating programs and approaches. Dealers in listed securities were involved with institutional sales; none had attempted to obtain a following among small investors, to advertise, or to seek parity with the commission houses that transacted business at the N.Y.S.E., the Amex, and the regionals. In almost every respect, the O-T-C houses were wholesalers to professionals. What might occur if they entered the retail end of the business, if they challenged the N.Y.S.E. across the board, and established a telephone network that would seek to replace the trading floor? The question was not moot in 1963. Astute Wall Streeters thought the challenge would arrive in less than a decade.

The Special Study was poorly organized, often contradictory, and repetitive. It offered conclusions based upon insufficient evidence and, in places, evidence with no conclusion. It was a rambling document that failed to present an overall view of the securities markets or an agenda for reform. The volumes would be cited by contending forces in the years that followed, each finding sections to support its view. In these respects, it was a flawed report.

If the document lacked coherence, it possessed a wealth of basic research, segments and fragments that could be put together, like a mosaic, to form alternate views of reality, to illuminate corners and bring to light problems and ideas not previously considered. *The Special Study* was a seminal set of volumes, but for the moment more so for a relative handful of people in Wall Street and Washington than for the nation. The bull market resumed in late 1962, and was wilder and, on the surface at least, as vigorous and healthy as that of the 1950s. By May 1963, the crash was considered only a temporary setback, one that could be discounted or, if recalled, viewed as the worst that could possibly happen. The country and the bulls had survived 1962. They could survive anything. On May 29, 1962, the market had closed at 576.93. On the first anniversary of the crash the Dow was at 717.95.

The fact remained that the specialist system had been challenged during the crisis and had performed questionably. Reformers thought the situation could be improved through automation, more the magic word and salve than ever before. Financial columnists wrote of automating the specialist system, not really knowing what that meant or would entail. Soon there would be talk of an automated specialist book, one that would make decisions on its own, with the human being there as an override in a period of crisis. (The suggestion seemed strange, since it was only during a crisis that automation might be completely desirable.) But discussions and debates on the issue were meaningless. The specialists still controlled the N.Y.S.E. They could scarcely accede to reforms that would, in effect, put them out of business by making them obsolete.

The Special Study had little to say about the reactions of the O-T-C market makers during the crisis. Later on, some would report that they acted to protect their positions. This was to have been expected, since, as before, these men had never claimed a public responsibility to maintain the market. The events of May indicated that perhaps this approach was best, since it removed the sham of responsibility, one the N.Y.S.E. still insisted was there but which in fact was, at the very least, questionable. The crisis had also demonstrated the powers of the institutional traders, and clearly some of them considered the O-T-C market a viable alternative to the N.Y.S.E. All indications were that the institutions would continue to grow at a faster rate than would the number of small investors, and that O-T-C trading in listed stocks would increase more rapidly than volume at the N.Y.S.E. Still, so many unexpected events had occurred in the early 1960s—both on Wall Street and in the nation as a whole—that such projections were of dubious value. What if the O-T-C market makers won a major share of the institutional business? What then might become of the N.Y.S.E.? The questions should have been asked and answered in the 1950s, for the outlines of change could be perceived during the Eisenhower years. With the exception of developing new techniques for dealing in blocks, the Exchange had done little to meet the threat. Wedded to the system as it existed, how could it do otherwise?

The problem was discussed in 1963. The O-T-C traders had challenged the N.Y.S.E. and had found a structure to contain their attack. *The Special Study* was the first significant document to describe it—*The Third Market.* It was still more a new name for an old way of trading, but given additional problems on the Street, it could pose a serious threat to the survival of the securities industry as it had existed for as long as most Wall Streeters could remember.

CHAPTER 15

Belshazzar's Feast

Surveying the decade just past in early 1970, James Reston wrote that the 1960s began as realism, slipped into surrealism along the way, and ended as abstract expressionism. Even those readers who knew little of art understood what he meant. It had been a stressful, frightening, explosive, and frustrating period. Economic growth had been strong, and there had been significant social advances as well. At the same time, the nation seemed to be coming apart at its seams.

Historians compared the decade with the 1850s, a time of disorder, reformism, economic progress, and high tension. Then, too, there were the dissolutions of old political and social coalitions and the formations of new ones. The antagonists of the earlier Jacksonian era, enemies though they were, shared a belief in antique patriotism and the nation's shining future. This had been dissolved by 1860. The Civil War followed soon after.

In much the same way, what publisher Henry Luce had called "the American Century" ended sometime in the 1960s. Domestic and foreign problems and entanglements that appeared incapable of resolution rent the national fabric. In the process, those shared truths that a generation of statesmen from Franklin Roosevelt to Dwight Eisenhower had held forth as unifying themes were destroyed or made to appear irrelevant. The value of work, of accepting direction from those in authority, the benefits of the family, the dictates of Puritan morality—all were questioned and, by some at least, discarded.

Capitalism was no exception. Indeed, for some critics it represented all that was wrong with the society and nation. At a time when much of the rest of the world was trying to imitate America's economic successes, the institutions that made it possible were under attack domestically. To antiwar activists, businessmen had finagled to get America into the Vietnam struggle in order to obtain profits. Ecology-minded reformers drew attention to the destruction of the landscape and blamed it on rapacious business interests. Ralph Nader and related critics condemned the profit drive for the creation of a shabby, sensate civilization. Capitalism was labeled dehumanizing, contrary to the Christian ethic, and simply evil. Many thought "the system" was in its death throes and would soon be replaced by a better, humane method of structuring economic activities. And more than a few, in some ways the most disturbing of the lot, ignored business completely, seeking "alternate life-styles."

There was little that was new in such indictments, predictions, and reactions. Businessmen and the press and television afforded those who made them a great deal of attention. In the end, however, all proved more than a little hysterical, exaggerated, or simply false or wrong. Critics and criticisms would hold center stage for a season, to be replaced by new attackers and charges, and then these too would go. American capitalism was concerned with external threats, but none of them had much of an effect on the essentials of the system in the 1960s.

More important by far were the internal stresses felt by corporations and industries during this period. The largest merger movement in the nation's history changed the face of American capitalism. An old kind of firm with a different twist—the conglomerate—puzzled and then troubled conventional businessmen. A "new breed" of entrepreneur attracted a good deal of attention, one who was brash, unconcerned with tradition, almost rapacious, and apparently rootless. Manipulations that men of the 1920s would have considered audacious were planned over lunch, put into effect by dinnertime, and completed a few weeks later, with a blithe spirit and apparently little forethought—and they often worked, creating centimillionaires in the process. Deals that would have occupied the attention of a James Hill, E. H. Harriman, or Andrew Carnegie for a decade were carried out in months by men who had been in graduate schools of business or laboratories only a few years before. President Kennedy had spoken glowingly of the new generation of Americans in his Inaugural Address in 1961. Five years later, a protest leader proclaimed, "Never trust anyone over the age of thirty." Meanwhile, in business, new men, industries, and forms were appearing regularly, confusing experienced executives, frightening those in power, and creating turmoil in the corporate world.

The financial district had long been the symbol of American capitalism, and it was attacked as such by critics in the 1960s, some of whom appeared to believe the Vietnam War had been hatched at the investment banking houses and that racism was somehow encouraged by the trust companies. The preachers of the 1950s, who had appeared in the vicinity of Wall and Broad to warn of the coming Armageddon, were still there in the 1960s. Now antiwar protestors, young people concerned with racism and other social injustices, and individuals interested simply in advertising different "life-styles" joined them. On occasion, too, one could find hawkers for land in the Poconos or franchise businesses that promised to make onlookers millionaires in their spare time.

The N.Y.S.E. not only survived through all of this but—on the surface, at least—appeared more prosperous than ever before during the immediate post-1962 period and the years that followed. Those who knew the district and the Exchange recognized that both would have to face challenges soon, and that the problems exposed in the 1962 crash, documented in part by *The Special Study*, had not vanished.

One would not have believed this was so by watching and listening to Keith Funston. The N.Y.S.E. president, heavier, grayer, but as ebullient as he had been upon taking office in 1951, promised to make those changes necessary to prevent a recurrence of the chaos of May 1962. He spoke often of the value of self-regulation, knowing that the Exchange's reforms would be watched carefully by the S.E.C. and other government agencies, as well as the White House.

There was a whiff of antibusiness sentiment in the air in the aftermath of the crash. Fresh from his victories against the steel companies, President Kennedy found that his actions had been applauded, even by opponents, as a sign of strength. More self-confident than at any time since entering office, he appeared to have located his natural constituency in the reform wing of his party, and he began moving to the left, a journey that would include attacks against the business community. That autumn Chairman Cary criticized the exchange structure in stronger terms than those employed by any S.E.C. spokesman since Jerome Frank. Using data gathered for *The Special Study* as his text, he spoke out on the subject before a meeting of bankers in November. "Every member of the New York Stock Exchange will concede," he told his audience, that the N.Y.S.E. "still seems to have certain characteristics of a private club—a very good club, I might say." The implication could not be missed: there would have to be changes. Self-regulation would not suffice, and the S.E.C. would make its move soon after the final release of *The Special Study*.

On April 3, 1963, when Cary submitted the first part of the report to the Speaker of the House, he did so with far more circumspection than his public addresses the previous winter would have indicated. "The report demonstrates that neither the fundamental structure of the securities markets nor of the regulatory pattern of the Securities Acts requires dramatic reconstruction," he wrote. "The report should not impair public confidence in the securities markets, but should strengthen it as suggestions for raising standards are put into practice."

Cary had two excellent reasons for employing moderate language. The first, and less important, was that the market was skittish prior to release of the document. Wall Street gossip had it that Cary would recommend a drastic overhaul of the entire industry, one that might upset the bull market that was clearly forming. An unwillingness to be labeled the cause of a new decline might have figured in his thinking in late March.

More significant, however, were the actions of the various markets during the post-crash period. Amex President Edwin Posner had shuttled back and forth between Washington and New York in the summer of 1962, attempting to restore his exchange's independence after internal scandals placed it, effectively, in the hands of the S.E.C. Some of the Amex specialists were making book on whether or not their market would be nationalized and operated under government control. The more pessimistic believed the exchange might go out of business. The Amex had a talent for survival, however; by April 3, 1963, it had a new constitution and a new president—Edwin Etherington—and both were approved by the S.E.C. That exchange and the N.Y.S.E. promised to review specialist procedures and finances, while Funston explored the possibility of installing a faster ticker at the Big Board so that transactions during peak periods could be more rapidly reported. The N.A.S.D., too, under attack for ignoring the public interest, made efforts to provide for greater surveillance of its members in the future.

Cary noted these changes and developments with approval in his letter of submission. "It would go too far to assert that all of these, and other numerous changes, are the direct products of the Special Study and of the initiating legislation," he concluded. "Yet it would be difficult to deny that their existence has at least produced a reevaluation of existing practices and procedures by the industry, as well as the Commission, which can only be beneficial. In other words," said Cary, "the financial community has taken the opportunity to make its own special study, with valuable consequences."

Little was accomplished in the way of reform that summer and autumn, as the market paused in its tracks, retreated, and then moved ahead smartly, as though in preparation for a year-end push to the 800 level. At the Amex, Etherington had organized his administration, given life to the new constitution, and dominated the floor. Several committees were formed at the N.Y.S.E. and the N.A.S.D., charged with exploring reform suggestions but operating more with an eye toward Washington than to trading methods and procedures. If Congress seemed about to pass a strict law, then the markets would act swiftly in the direction of self-regulation. Otherwise, little would happen.

The moment of testing came without warning, but the N.Y.S.E.'s reaction was quickly overshadowed by more important events. On Tuesday, November 19, it was learned that Allied Crude Vegetable

Oil Refining Corporation had filed a bankruptcy petition. A relative handful of Wall Streeters knew that Tino De Angelis, head of the company, had used the N.Y.S.E. brokerage house of Ira Haupt & Co. to finance some of his receivables and to trade futures in the oil. If De Angelis fell, Haupt might not be far behind. Furthermore another Big Board house, Williston & Beane, was involved with Allied and might also be obliged to close.

Members of the N.Y.S.E. board explored the situation the following morning and found both Haupt and Williston & Beane in dire straits. Accordingly, the firms were suspended pending reviews of their conditions. The exact meaning of the action was unclear, since this was only the second time in Exchange history that suspension had been applied. Vitally interested were Haupt's almost 21,000 clients, most of whom had securities and/or cash on deposit at the firm, and Williston & Beane's 9,000 clients, in the same circumstance. Funston had spent his career assuring small investors that Wall Street was no casino. If they suffered in any way, or if the crisis continued for long, action from Washington, either in the form of S.E.C. intervention or new legislation, could be expected.

The public relations men at the two brokerages issued press releases, assuring all that the firms were in good shape and that the suspension would soon be lifted. Meanwhile, partners made hurried telephone calls to colleagues, attempting to arrange credits or even mergers or takeovers. On a lower level of power, researchers and customers' men began looking for new jobs.

Haupt's checks began to bounce on Thursday, when it was also learned that American Express, which had guaranteed De Angelis's warehouse certificates, might be liable for losses and, if so, could collapse. A brokerage panic—a rarity at the time—began on the Street, as clients called their brokers to demand their certificates and cash balances. This was somewhat akin to a run on a bank; if it continued long enough, the companies might have to close their doors. The entire brokerage community, as well as the N.Y.S.E., had a stake in the salvaging of Haupt and Williston & Beane.

On Friday morning, November 22, officials at Williston & Beane reported that two other brokerages, Walston & Co. and Merrill Lynch, had offered it a $500,000 loan, which would enable it to meet the N.Y.S.E.'s net capital requirements: Rumors on the Street had it that if the situation at the firm worsened, Merrill Lynch was prepared to take it over. Shortly after noon, Williston & Beane was reinstated, while upstairs at the Exchange, Funston and his staff pored over the books of Haupt & Co. There was little doubt the firm had been destroyed; the only question was the extent of its problems. It appeared, on initial investigation, that Haupt owed ten American and

British banks more than $37 million. The brokerage held customers' stocks worth $450 million, of which $90 million had been purchased on margin. In order to obtain margin money, Haupt had pledged these stocks to banks for loans, and these were in danger of being lost. In addition, Haupt's customers had some $5.5 million in cash on deposit at the company.

Under law, the N.Y.S.E. had no obligation to these people, so that on the face of it they could lose a good deal of their funds and stocks held by the brokerage.* If this happened, the public uproar would have been such as to cause new investigations of Wall Street, perhaps the passage of the most punitive legislation in its history. The situation was showing up in stock prices, which fell more than 9 points on Thursday and declined early Friday on heavy volume.

Funston was at a loss as how to act. Even had he desired to put the Exchange behind Haupt and to guarantee losses, the N.Y.S.E. lacked the funds for such a large rescue mission. He could call upon other brokerages for assistance, but he was doubtful as to their responses. Perhaps Haupt's creditors could be put off for a while—at least over the weekend—so that he and the board would have time to consider a proper course of action. Funston decided to meet with the bankers, who were asked to come to the Exchange for a conference.

Before they arrived, news of President Kennedy's death flashed on the ticker.

Now the Exchange faced the possibility of a panic on top of a crisis. The Dow Industrials fell by more than 24 points in a half hour, when more than 2.6 million shares were traded. Prudence might have dictated closing the Exchange; later on Funston would be criticized for not doing so immediately. But he could not have done so without the concurrence of a majority of the board, and most members were out to lunch and could not be reached. In any case the leadership was in a state of shock, as were the floor members. All had been deeply troubled by the Haupt situation. Then, superimposed upon it, came the initial news of the assassination. Was it a Soviet or Cuban plot? Did it mean World War III? No one knew in those first minutes after the news broke. As it was, the board met at 2:00 and seven minutes later the Exchange was closed.

Fortunately, the next day was Saturday. While the rest of the country pondered the meaning of the assassination and remained close by their television sets to learn what had transpired, Funston and the board attempted to devise a satisfactory solution to the Haupt problem. Gustave Levy, the senior partner at Goldman, Sachs and a growing power in the district, flew to London to obtain agreements from the

* In 1960, however, the Exchange did reimburse the customers of DuPont, Homsey & Co., to the extent of $690,000. The Haupt failure was much larger, of course.

British banks, while Funston and others worked out procedures with American creditors.

The Exchange remained closed on Monday in observance of a national day of mourning. That afternoon, Funston presented the Exchange's plan to the bankers and the Haupt officers. The N.Y.S.E. would raise $12 million through assessments of the members and use the money to pay the brokerage's debts to clients. The banks would defer up to twice that amount of money due them. Haupt would be liquidated, its assets used to pay off the banks and the Exchange. Whatever was left would go to the partners. All agreed—the partners reluctantly, the others with satisfaction. In effect, the Exchange had assumed responsibility for the failure of a member firm. The event was certainly minor compared with what was happening then on the broader national and international canvas. But it was an important action for Funston and the Exchange to take, the most significant in the president's career on Wall Street.

The news was released Tuesday morning. Resolution of the Haupt situation, together with evidence that President Johnson had a firm grip on affairs, affected stocks from the opening. The Dow rose 32.03 points that day, the largest one-session leap in Exchange history. Gratified, Johnson called Funston to congratulate him. The next phase of the bull market seemed about to begin.

The Exchange's actions in the Haupt affair helped end criticisms in Washington. The N.Y.S.E. would use $9.5 million of its assessment, and a year later, Funston announced the creation of a Special Trust Fund consisting of $10 million in cash backed by $15 million in bank credit to be used in similar circumstances should they arise. In January, Funston established higher capital requirements for specialists; if the S.E.C. had criticisms of the group's actions, this would answer them. Lyndon Johnson seemed pleased. In those days he often measured the extent of his popularity by the status of the stock averages, which he liked to quote. The Dow was above 800 for the first time on February 28. Volume was high. Everyone seemed to be making money. The nation had survived the Kennedy assassination, and although it continued to mourn the dead President, his successor was at the height of his power. The N.Y.S.E. had come through the Kennedy reform wave intact, and it too appreciated Lyndon Johnson.

Such was the situation in mid-1964. After long debate, Congress finally passed legislation based on the findings of the S.E.C. The Securities Act Amendment of 1964 extended the Commission's powers to include most of the over-the-counter issues, and the government was given the authority to set standards for the securities firms. That was all. Nothing significant had been done to end abuses in the mutual fund industry, to change what Cary, as William O.

Douglas before him, had called "the private club atmosphere of the Stock Exchange," or to rationalize the various markets for listed securities. Congress was in no mood to consider such questions in an election year. Neither was the new President, who, in late 1963, had told regulatory agency chiefs, "We are challenged . . . to concern ourselves with new areas of cooperation before we concern ourselves with new areas of control."

The message was clear. Johnson already had the support of labor for 1964; an end to the antibusiness atmosphere in the White House would bring him the votes of business as well. Cary resigned as S.E.C. Chairman on August 20. He was succeeded by Manuel F. Cohen, an able, intelligent bureaucrat but one who would not rock the boat.

Yet the N.Y.S.E., and the securities industry in general, might better have been served by a restructuring than a policy of neglect. On the surface, it seemed the N.Y.S.E. was as secure as ever. The Dow closed 1964 on a strong note—874.13—having gained 111.18 points for the year. A seat sold for $230,000, the highest since 1933. Volume had been 1,236,600,000 shares, an all-time record. On December 1, the Exchange unveiled its new 900-character-a-minute ticker, designed to handle 10 million shares a day. With the exception of the 14,746,000 share session on May 29, 1962, volume hadn't been so high since 1929. Wall Streeters confidently expected 10-million-share days regularly by the late 1960s, and Funston proclaimed that efforts to develop an even faster ticker would continue. Not comprehending fully what such volume would do to the Exchange, the community cheered the news.

There was much to celebrate that Christmas season. The economy was in fine shape, having achieved a balance between growth and inflation. There was a lull in the Cold War, as Khrushchev was overthrown and his successors were busy with internal political matters. The massive Johnson victory over Barry Goldwater in November gave the President a mandate for almost anything he wished to do. Vietnam was still a troublesome minor conflict which many believed would be ended in a matter of months.

That the country faced difficult times in the next four years may be comprehended today, but such retrospective vision was obviously not available to Washingtonians in early 1965. Similarly, Wall Street and the N.Y.S.E. were about to enter a period of testing more severe than any since the late 1920s and early 1930s, and in some respects even more dangerous than that dark age. It was there to be seen in 1965, but the outlines would not come into sharp focus until later on.

N.Y.S.E. leaders knew that high trading volume could be a problem, but they believed it could be overcome through technology; the computer and the high speed ticker could solve almost any difficulty that came along. They did not take into account two elements that would lead to chaos: human failings and the rapidity of the change. Trading volume in 1965 was 1,556,300,000 shares. Although a fully automated quotation service was introduced in March and other developments to speed floor operations came later in the year, the tape and transactions were slower than volume dictated. There was one 11-million-share day in December, two with 10 million shares, eight in which more than 9 million shares were transacted, and four with more than 8 million shares. The slowest day of the month, when 5,950,000 shares changed hands, would have been considered hectic only three years earlier.

The average daily trading volume in 1965 was 6,176,000 shares. The following year, when trading volume was 1,899,500,000 shares, the average was 7,538,000. In 1964, the N.Y.S.E. had prepared for periods when volume would peak at around 10 million shares. Three years later, the average day saw 10,080,000 shares change hands, while annual volume was 2,530,000,000 shares. In March of 1967, when volume was 267,658,000 shares, there was a 14-million-share day and one when over 12 million shares traded. More trading took place on the floor that month than in all of 1944. The slowest day in 1967 saw 5,998,000 shares traded, 695,000 more than on the busiest day in 1960. Nor was this the end of it. In 1968, average daily volume reached 12,971,000 shares.

If the floors were hectic and specialists harried, the brokerages were in a state of chaos. Customers' men had little time to talk with even their better clients, while suburban brokerages, usually quiet and rather subdued, took on the aspects of a miniature exchange, with customers shouting to one another and to their brokers, who themselves were talking on three or more telephones simultaneously. Time was at a premium, though money was abundant. So the investment houses hired large numbers of relatively unskilled workers to take care of clerical, secretarial, and back office chores. Since there was more business than most customers' men could handle, new ones were taken on, often through lures offered successful or promising individuals at rival houses. The number of registered representatives doubled from 1965 to 1968.

It was the problem of the 1950s all over again, this time greatly magnified. A large number of inexperienced and often inept workers were required to handle a great deal of money and certificates, and in the process, serious mistakes were made. For a while these were considered departures from the norm, for which brokers would apologize and then correct in an embarrassed fashion. By 1967, however, errors had become commonplace. Clerks either didn't have the time to check them out or lacked the knowledge. Often, when they received notification of the mistake, they would mark the slip, "D.K.," for "don't know," and pass it on to someone else, who might do the same with it. In 1967, the S.E.C. received 2,934 complaints from customers about processing errors. In 1968, the Commission handled 7,551 of them, and in 1969, 14,211.

An old Wall Street term became familiar to millions of clients and readers of financial pages in this period. "Fails" referred to the back offices' inability to deliver certificates or complete transactions within the required time. Most fails prior to 1968 had been caused by understandable human errors and could be rectified with a telephone call. Indeed, until 1968, Wall Street hadn't bothered keeping statistics on fails, considering them a minor problem. Then, as snafus appeared with newly installed electronic data systems and were compounded by mistakes made by inexperienced personnel, the fails began to multiply, so that by December 1968 more than $4.1 billion in certificates could not be accounted for. At the time there was talk of Mafia infiltration of Wall Street and theft on a massive scale, and there was some small truth to this. Later on, some observers noted that drugs were used by Wall Street office personnel, and that this clouded their judgments. This was to be expected, since drugs, both hard and soft, were becoming more popular in many parts of American society in that period. Still, no hard evidence exists that the situation was worse in the financial district than anywhere else, while a large majority of observers indicate that, as far as they could tell, drugs had little impact on the work of the community.

FAILS TO DELIVER BY N.Y.S.E. BROKERAGES
APRIL 1968–APRIL 1969
(millions of dollars)

	Month	*Total Fails*	*Aged Fails*
1968	April	2,670	478
	May	3,466	535
	June	3,769	715
	July	3,675	837
	August	3,095	724
	September	3,082	751
	October	3,358	586
	November	3,274	556
	December	4,127	620
1969	January	3,300	596
	February	2,969	529
	March	2,477	433
	April	2,319	352

SOURCE: *N.Y.S.E. Fact Book*

Significantly, although the number of fails increased dramatically throughout 1968, the amount of "aged fails"—those that were thirty days old or more—peaked in July and then declined. When the situation became serious that spring, the Exchange's leaders met to consider action. It was decided that the floor would be closed on Wednesdays so that the back offices would have an opportunity to clean up the mess. In addition, brokerages were prohibited from advertising for new business, hiring additional customers' men, or opening branch offices. The bans remained in effect for the rest of the year, but had no appreciable effect on trading, which continued to expand. Still, the easing of the situation in aged fails went unnoticed as total fails rose, capturing the attention of Wall Street columnists and S.E.C. officials.

The back offices had begun to catch up on their business by October 1968. Then volume rose at year-end, and the army of clerks fell behind once more. There was a decline in trading in early 1969, and this afforded the office personnel a breather of sorts. Trading returned to a five-day schedule on January 2, 1969, but the hours were shortened—the N.Y.S.E. was open from 10:00 to 2:00. Additions of thirty minutes a day were made in July and September, and on May 4, 1970, the hours returned to normal.

The hectic trading sessions of this period gave the impression that an entire nation was rushing to buy and sell securities. Indeed, the shareholder population did rise rapidly. From 12.5 million in 1959 it had gone to 20.1 million in 1965. In the years between "playing the market" had become what seemed to be a national pastime. Still, the so-called small investor accounted for an ever-decreasing share of the trading volume in the 1960s, as the large institutions came to dominate the markets.

By any quantitative measure or qualitative judgment, the institutions came of age in the late 1960s. Not only were hundreds of millions of dollars pouring into the trusts, pension funds, and the like—mutual fund assets went from $15.3 billion in 1960 to $52.7 billion in late 1968—but the managers of these huge pools of capital increasingly were drawn to common stocks. More important, as far as Wall Street was concerned, they were engaged in trading rather than holding. In 1961, 26.2 percent of all N.Y.S.E. volume came from institutions, with 22.4 percent accounted for by members and 51.4 percent by individual investors. The institutions took 42.4 percent of volume in 1969, while the outside individuals' share came to 33.4 percent, with the rest being traded by members for their own accounts.

All the institutions increased their activities sharply in the 1960s, but the mutual funds advanced more than the rest. As late as 1955, the

Estimated Holdings of N.Y.S.E.-Listed Stocks by Selected Institutional Investors

Type of Institution	*Year End*								
	1949	*1955*	*1962*	*1963*	*1969*	*1970*	*1971*	*1972*	*1973*[p]
	Billions of Dollars								
Insurance Companies:									
Life	$ 1.1	$ 2.2	$ 4.1	$ 4.6	$ 10.2	$ 11.7	$ 16.1	$ 21.2	$ 21.1
Non-Life	1.7	4.2	7.1	8.2	11.7	12.2	15.6	18.6	16.9
Investment Companies:									
Open-End	1.4	6.3	15.4	18.6	39.0	39.0	46.7	51.4	37.2
Closed-End	1.6	4.6	5.3	5.7	4.1	4.1	5.6	6.4	5.0
Noninsured Pension Funds:									
Corporate	0.5	3.2	17.9	22.6	52.4	57.2	75.6	98.6	82.2
Other Private	**	0.2	1.0	1.3	3.1	3.5	4.6	5.9	4.9
State & Local Government	**	0.1	0.6	0.8	5.6	7.6	10.7	13.6	15.5
Nonprofit Institutions:									
Foundations	2.5	6.9	8.5	13.1	16.0	17.0	19.3	23.9	19.2
Educational Endowments	1.1	2.3	3.5	4.2	6.4	6.6	7.4	8.8	7.5
Other	1.0	2.5	5.0	5.9	8.9	9.0	10.1	11.8	9.5
Common Trust Funds	**	0.9	1.7	2.2	4.1	4.1	5.5	6.8	5.5
Mutual Savings Banks	0.2	0.2	0.4	0.4	1.0	1.2	1.5	1.5	1.7
TOTAL	$11.1	$33.6	$70.5	$87.6	$162.5	$173.2	$218.7	$268.5	$226.2

Market Value of All N.Y.S.E.-Listed Stock	$76.3	$207.7	$345.8	$411.3	$629.5	$636.4	$741.8	$871.5	$721.0
Estimated % Held by Selected Institutional Investors	14.5%	16.2%	20.4%	21.3%	25.8%	27.2%	29.5%	30.8%	31.4%

** Less than $50 million.
p Preliminary estimates.
SOURCE: *New York Stock Exchange*

funds turned over less than one-sixth of their portfolios a year, and by 1965 the amount had risen to only one-fifth. In 1968 and 1969, however, that average velocity was one-half.

Transactions by Institutions at the N.Y.S.E., 1961–1969
(millions of dollars)

Year	*Pension Funds (private)*	*Life Insurance Companies*	*Non-Life Insurance Companies*	*Mutual Funds*	*Total*
1961	4,610	975	n.a	6,710	12,295
1962	4,200	790	1,150	6,415	12,555
1963	5,315	940	1,310	7,240	14,805
1964	6,480	1,215	1,545	8,655	17,895
1965	8,145	1,585	1,735	11,695	23,160
1966	9,755	1,935	1,725	19,685	33,120
1967	15,690	2,560	2,145	28,250	48,645
1968	20,100	4,655	3,890	38,595	67,245
1969	25,500	5,890	6,660	41,910	79,960

Source: *N.Y.S.E. Fact Book*

The 1920s had had its lone wolf speculators and manipulators, men who twisted and prodded stock prices from the decks of yachts, palatial estates on Long Island's North Shore, or secret back offices in the district. The press called them "Mystery Men of Wall Street," although by the time the stories were printed and read, there were few mysteries left. In the late nineteenth century such men were known as "Young Napoleons of Finance," as they had been during every bull market since the 1830s. The press looked for their counterparts in the 1950s and 1960s and found only Serge Rubinstein, Guterma, and others of their ilk, men whose actions were often bold but whose impacts, individually and collectively, were close to nothing. The market was simply too big for a single person, or even a combine, to control or influence significantly. For a while it appeared the great bull market of the postwar era would lack hero-speculators.

Then, in the mid-1960s, they arrived. They were not operators for their own accounts, however, but rather managers of mutual funds, who were as different from the old-line leaders of M.I.T. and Wellington as the jet airplane was from the Model T. Most were young, almost all were brash and cocky, and their records were excellent during the bull market. Fred Carr, manager of Enterprise

Fund, said in 1968, "Essentially we are traditional, conservative, long-term investors." In fact, Carr was a master trader, and his billion-dollar fund gained over 117 percent in 1967, while the Dow advanced 15 percent. Fred Mates, the leader in the drive to form funds dealing with "letter stock," manipulated prices in such a way that Mates Fund showed phenomenal results, rising 153 percent in 1968, when the Dow rose 4.3 percent. When Gerald Tsai left Fidelity Capital in 1966 to form Manhattan Fund, thousands of small stockholders rushed to give him their money. Tsai had planned to sell $25 million worth of shares in the initial offering; he wound up with $270 million instead. Tsai, Carr, Mates—and John Hartwell, Howard Stein, George Chestnutt, Fred Alger and other fund managers—were the logical successors of Jesse Livermore, Arthur Cutten, and Joe Kennedy. The age of the individual investor and speculator had been replaced by that of the institutional force; what Jesse Livermore had been to 1929, Gerry Tsai would be to 1969.

The new breed of fund managers operated in a context that was far removed from that of small investors whose funds they handled. Their methods of trading and the kinds of securities they were interested in were discussed in business magazines and the financial pages of large newspapers. Some of the more colorful managers made the Sunday supplements, or were interviewed for television. Books were written about them, and one of the most informative magazines in the district—*The Institutional Investor*—was dedicated to their activities, and not for sale to the general public.*

Few of the new breed were interested in "old faces," such as I.B.M., Eastman Kodak, or even Xerox and Polaroid. Instead, they sought out "growth companies of the future"—National Student Marketing, Equity Funding, Cameo Parkway, Riker Video, Guerdon Industries, and the like, names that would have nostalgic rings to them later on, or bring back bitter memories, but which for a while seemed very intriguing. Alger liked Applied Logic, a computer software company. Carr went into Kewanee Scientific which, despite the name, made laboratory furniture for schools. Fred Mates dabbled in Technical Tape, a firm that tried to take a share of the transparent tape market from Minnesota Mining's Scotch Tape and was not technical at all. Indeed, most of the really big money made by the fund managers was in stocks such as these—relatively obscure, with small capitalizations, which were held for short periods and then sold.

Some of the reasons for this were obvious—in an age of glamor, the

* The best example is Gilbert Edmund Kaplan and Chris Welles, eds., *The Money Managers* (New York, 1969), which was drawn from *The Institutional Investor.*

unknown is usually more attractive than the familiar—but others were not. The idea that had been propounded a decade earlier regarding a shortage of blue chips was forgotten by the late 1960s, when the new issue craze was going once more. Nevertheless, it was so. Large, well-managed firms rarely sold additional common shares. Instead, they obtained funds through the issuance of bonds and the plowing back of earnings into operations, while some borrowed from insurance companies and other financial firms. New securities had been a backbone for the bull market of the 1920s. At the time new securities issues had accounted for a quarter of the nation's capital requirements. The situation was markedly different after World War II, when many large corporations were able to finance their expansions through their reserves and cash flows. Less than 20 percent of capital needs in the 1950s had been provided by additional issues of securities, and the percentage declined to below 15 in the early 1960s and under 10 percent later in the decade. According to one estimate, from the turn of the century to 1929, common stock issues provided between 10 and 20 percent of external and internal funds raised by nonfinancial corporations. In contrast, between 1950 and 1962, such issues accounted for about 5 percent of capital needs.*

A shortage of blue-chip stocks at a time when demand for them was growing helped turn the attention of fund managers to issues of newer companies. The "floats" of such firms as Coca-Cola, Sears Roebuck, Minnesota Mining, Proctor & Gamble and, of course, I.B.M. did not increase as rapidly as did the bids from trust funds, and so they became "fully priced." The search for fresh glamor issues probably would have occurred anyway. On the other hand, the changes in the structure of American capitalism did help mold investment decisions, whether the managers realized it or not.

The mutual fund industry was only one of several that appeared new and fresh in this period. Conglomerate corporations, often headed by young outlanders, dominated business news for several years, their leaders attaining celebrity status. James Ling, Charles Bluhdorn, Tex Thornton, and other conglomerateurs bid for companies with hundreds of millions of dollars and made complicated tender offers that resulted in speculation in the shares of firms that were takeover candidates, while I.T.&T.'s Harold Geneen was deemed an authentic genius at the game. Old-line investment banks—Lehman, Goldman, Sachs, and Morgan itself—became the handmaidens of the new men, and searched for their counterparts in banking to give them jobs of power and status. A bright day had dawned, but at the same time the balance wheel of the financial machine appeared wobbly, and warnings of denouement were becoming louder and more convincing.

* Irwin Friend, *et al.*, *Investment Banking and the New Issues Market* (Philadelphia, 1965).

As might have been anticipated, the business press played up the fact that the fortieth anniversary of the Great Crash would soon be marked. Instead of debating the possibilities of another 1929, however, much of the nation was more worried about the parallels between 1969 and 1775 or 1861. After years of internal conflict, debate, assassinations, cultural divisions, and violence, serious people questioned whether the country would survive in its present form to celebrate its two hundredth birthday in 1976.

Wall Street was troubled. Speculators and specialists wondered if theirs would be the last generation to know good times, even while stock prices continued to climb. Considering the state of the nation, it may have appeared only a minor point, but at the time, as a result of internal stresses and external pressures, the Big Board was concerned about its own future.

Difficulties in handling volume and chronic problems in back offices continued to worry the leadership. There wasn't much the Exchange could do about the brokerages, but pressures on the floor could be lifted. With this in mind, the board planned for a new building, one that would contain the latest in electronic gear, a huge trading floor, and facilities to handle 20-million-share days with ease. It would be erected on landfill on the East River end of Wall Street. Already funds were being assigned for the project, which was to be the Exchange's token of belief in the future of American capitalism and of the district. The specialist contingent also received a vote of confidence. As before, it would handle all floor transactions.

It was a bold move and a dramatic one, and even then, when the irrational and unusual were becoming commonplace, was quixotic. The Exchange's methods of operation hadn't been altered in more than a half century; they had merely been mechanized. If one were to create an exchange system *de novo* in 1969, based on existing and anticipated technology, it would not resemble the N.Y.S.E. The proposed new building was being compared to a white elephant and the N.Y.S.E. to the dinosaur.

Three kinds of people spoke in this fashion, with each using a different rationale for drawing conclusions. Wall Streeters could tick off a list of the Exchange's problems, reciting them as though a litany, going from archaic procedures to ill-trained personnel and ending with demonstrated weaknesses in time of stress and a vague, formless leadership. The N.Y.S.E. would fall, they said, as a result of internal contradictions.

This was a period when gloom permeated the nation and uncertainty was commonplace. The universities were under siege, defense industries were being attacked, and assassination and rebellion were in the air. The conglomerates were deemed only the latest manifestation of the evils of capitalism, and reformers called for their control. "The Military-Industrial Complex," a term that was never satisfactorily defined by any who used it but seemed to be understood as an evil nexus of politicians and businessmen, was blamed for a variety of ills, from Vietnam to racism to pollution. As before, the Big Board was a prime symbol of capitalist power. And so, said the protestors, it must be destroyed, or at the very least defanged.

Another group, smaller than the others but just as vocal, claimed the N.Y.S.E. would crumble because it was obsolete. At one time the auction performed its function well, but it had not adapted itself to the new kinds of markets that had appeared in the 1950s and 1960s, especially the ones required by large institutions. It was an amateur market that filled the needs of amateur investors; the professionals—the trust managers, the fund leaders, portfolio directors at insurance companies—would be better served by a dealer market, such as that which existed at the O-T-C. The idea was bandied about in the universities and law schools, and received support from a mixed group of liberals and conservatives, the former because it would take power from the "Establishment," the latter as a vindication of the benefits of free enterprise and competition in the marketplace. Pragmatists liked the idea because it seemed more rational on the surface than the construction of a new Exchange building.

As might have been expected, those O-T-C dealers already trading in listed stocks were the most vocal advocates of such a transformation, and they invited comparisons between their methods of transacting business and those employed at the exchanges. There was even a name for their alternate trading mechanism—the Third Market.

Although the term began to crop up on the financial pages in mid-decade, and appeared more regularly thereafter, not many casual readers knew what it was, or recognized the significance of the name it had been given. One student wrote: "In simplified terms the Third Market consists of broker-dealers, nonmembers of either large stock exchange, who actively engage as principals in buying and selling listed securities over the counter on a continuous basis and who themselves make the markets in such listed securities." * Why was it a *third* market? Conflicting stories about the origin of the term exist, arising from the fact that it signified different things to different people. According to *The Special Study*, where it was first discussed in any detail:

> The rapid growth in recent years of an off-board market for the trading of listed common stock has made this an increasingly

* Anthony D. Schlesinger, "The Third Market—Challenge to the New York Stock Exchange," *Southwestern Law Journal* (Vol. 20, 1966), p. 640.

important segment of the national securities markets. Although the stocks are listed on the exchanges, the market operates as a part of the over-the-counter markets. It thus has elements of each market but is distinguishable in important respects from both [and for this reason has been designated in this part as the "third market"].*

This leaves the impression that the Third Market was a hybrid—a mixture of the exchange system (first market) and O-T-C (second market). This was not what most people in the investment industry meant by the term a few years later, however, and the difference was significant.

Textbooks on finance defined the primary market as one where new stock and bond issues were sold, with the central factor being the Wall Street investment banks. The secondary market, then, was the organized exchange structure, with the N.Y.S.E. its key element. Under this system of categorization, the Third Market was the O-T-C operation in listed securities.

More than a few journalists, and most on the Street, used a different set of definitions. To them, the primary market was the Big Board, the secondary consisted of the regionals, and the Third Market was the O-T-C structure. It was possible, and indeed common, for people in conversations on the subject to confuse the definitions of primary and secondary markets. But all meant the same thing by the term, Third Market.

The N.Y.S.E., the regionals, and the Third Market competed with one another in the mid-1960s in a struggle that received little attention at the time due to the rampaging bull market. Eager for additional business, the regionals adopted the techniques of give-ups formerly associated with the mutual funds. They permitted members to share commissions among themselves and also with nonmembers who brought business to them. Thus, members of regional exchanges were permitted to utilize the services of O-T-C dealers when it suited their interests.

The N.Y.S.E. firms lacked this right. As a result, some Big Board firms purchased seats at regional exchanges and dealt with O-T-C traders there. Furthermore, the Big Board had rules against institutional memberships, obliging the institutions to deal through the commission houses. The regionals abandoned such rules in the late 1960s and so obtained an increasing share of institutional business. This situation attracted the attention of the S.E.C. in 1966, which feared that the give-ups might lead to further churning in mutual fund

* *Special Study*, Pt. 2, Chapter VIII, p. 910.

accounts, and the Commission received strong N.Y.S.E. support in this. "If not quite the life blood of the regional exchanges," wrote *Business Week* in January 1967, give-ups were "at least the cream that makes them fat."

It was a good simile. Much of the institutional business was in large blocks, which required only slightly more effort than small ones to transact, and which, even after give-ups, earned much more in profits.

The Big Board enjoyed excellent business in 1967, but despite this was concerned about rivals. That year the N.Y.S.E. and Amex together transacted almost 92 percent of the dollar volume at all American exchanges, a figure that was consistent with past performance. But the A.S.E.'s share had risen sharply since its reorganization and the advent of the bull market in lower-quality shares. In 1962, the junior market did less than 7 percent of the dollar volume at all exchanges; in 1967, the figure was over 14 percent, a record. This meant that the Big Board's share was below 78 percent, likewise a record—but this one on the low side. The Midwest and Pacific Coast exchanges were prospering, grabbing a good deal of institutional business. Every time a big block was reported at either of these exchanges, Big Board brokers felt it had been at their expense. In order to regain the business, the N.Y.S.E. began consideration of volume discounts in May of 1967, and by autumn Wall Street rumors had it that a plan to that effect would be presented early in 1968.

"We won't be worried until they go to zero commissions, and that will never happen." This was the reaction of one O-T-C market maker to discussions of volume discounts. As one who regularly bought and sold listed stocks without commissions, he realized that the N.Y.S.E. was being prodded into change by the regionals, but could not go all the way. The Big Board was the main rival for the Third Market, to be sure, but as long as it retained its mid-decade form, the market makers felt they had little to fear. If and when the N.Y.S.E. innovated as the regionals had, and in the process moved closer to O-T-C trading methods, problems might develop. This was not in sight, however.

Unencumbered by traditions, structures that could dictate rules, a dominant elite, or even a central building whose form might influence functions, the Third Market operators were relatively free to innovate. The nature of the market, the desires of clients, the capitalization of the trader, and the state of technology relating to trading—these were the prime considerations. N.Y.S.E. specialists were bound by literally hundreds of regulations and folkways of the district. They operated, as Funston liked to say, in a goldfish bowl, with the public and the S.E.C. ever present. The specialist was responsible for several stocks, and he knew the meaning of the term, "responsibility." Among other things, he was supposed to stabilize the issue when necessary and possible. Specialists understood that their "stabilization rates" and "participation rates" would be taken into consideration when the time came to allocate desirable new listings.

Third Market dealers had few such problems. A dealer whose net capitalization was comparable to that of a specialist might deal in a hundred or so listed issues at various times, concentrating on one or another when profits and opportunities were present. According to *The Special Study*, in 1961, 712 Third Market firms made markets in 270 listed securities, although, as previously indicated, only a handful of firms concentrated on such business. Stabilization and participation did not trouble these dealers; nor did other considerations which made for "good markets." They said so, openly, in ways that surprised neophytes in the industry. After all, they were dealing with professionals, men as experienced as themselves. They were offering merchandise at a net price lower than that to be had at the N.Y.S.E. "The same people who wanted to put the discount retail stores out of business are after us," said one Third Market leader. "If you prevent Korvette from selling an air conditioner for $150, when a department store offers the same machine for $180, who is the loser? The customer. And it's the same thing with stocks. A share of General Motors is the same as all the others, whether it is purchased at the N.Y.S.E. or here."

As it had done when challenged by the Consolidated a half century earlier, the Big Board reacted against the Third Market by indicating that it was operating contrary to the public interest and threatened its own members with reprisals if they consorted with the market makers.

At first the N.Y.S.E. attempted to create the impression that the O-T-C market makers were not as responsible as their specialist counterparts. To the degree that the specialists were bound by rules and were more carefully watched, this was certainly true. On the other hand, several of the larger members of the Third Market were as well-financed and as powerful as most of the specialist units. Weeden & Co., headed by Frank Weeden, an O-T-C veteran, regularly maintained an inventory of between $10 million and $15 million in stocks in the late 1950s and bought and sold large blocks with as much ease as any N.Y.S.E. specialist. In 1961, Weeden & Co. did a business of almost $900 million and was expanding rapidly. One of Frank Weeden's sons, Donald, was emerging as the spokesman of the Third Market, apparently acting for it as Charles Merrill had for the commission houses after World War II. When the market makers were charged with being in some way marginal, Weeden responded by citing the specialists' record in the 1962 crash and noting that the Big Board was in no position to talk of irresponsibility.

Funston often spoke of the N.Y.S.E.'s commitment to the principle of liquidity, that without it, security capitalism as it then existed would hardly be possible. As though retreating from the earlier position that the N.Y.S.E. was a superior market for stocks than the O-T-C, he argued, in November 1962, that maintenance of a strong Exchange was necessary for the public interest.

> The success of the Exchange's auction market depends to a large degree upon the presence of enough buyers' and sellers' orders on the floor so that the prices reflect the composite opinions of the greatest number of investors. However we are informed that over the past few years our listed issues and shares are being traded in increasing numbers on the nation's regional exchanges and the over-the-counter market. We believe this erosion of the primary market is not in the public interest. It tends to undermine the purpose and usefulness of publicizing transactions in the primary market and may impair the liquidity which all investors rightly expect when investing in securities listed on this exchange.

The president went on to say that "there is no assurance of obtaining the best price available in the primary market at the time the order was executed."

> These diversions may bring about insufficient supply and demand on the primary market necessary to appropriately reflect the public's evaluation of the prices of these securities. This might result in the Exchange becoming merely a quotation board furnishing prices for the bulk of the transactions in listed securities being made off the Exchange floor.*

Without the N.Y.S.E. ticker, Funston was saying, the Third Market could not function. (Although he probably knew little about the N.Y.S.E.'s position against the Consolidated, the same argument had been used when calling for that exchange's closing.) There was force to this argument; it was certainly true that in most cases the Third Market traders worked with an eye to Big Board prices. Some claimed the reason was technological, that if and when electronic displays and other devices were available to create an "electronic stock exchange," they would purchase them, and at that time, would have a true alternate market to the N.Y.S.E. Such was not the situation in the 1960s, however.

At a significant point in its history, the Consolidated Stock Exchange had been crippled by the removal of N.Y.S.E. tickers from

* *Special Study*, Pt. 2, Chapter VIII, pp. 955–56.

its floor. Here, too, the Big Board behaved in a similar fashion against the Third Market, though with different results.

Two Dallas O-T-C houses that dealt in listed stocks had private wires connecting them with several N.Y.S.E. members as well as tickers from the Exchange. The tickers had been installed pending a N.Y.S.E. investigation of the firms' business status and repute. After seven months, the Exchange removed the tickers and wires without giving the O-T-C dealers reasons for the action. One of the firms, Silver & Co., sued the N.Y.S.E. for damages, charging violations of the Sherman Anti-Trust Act.

The case was decided by the Supreme Court in 1962, and the verdict was against the Big Board. In the words of Justice Arthur Goldberg, the Exchange's rules had to be "just and adequate to ensure fair dealing and to protect investors." Justice Potter Stewart added, "The purpose of the self-regulation provisions of the Securities Exchange Act was to delegate governmental power to working institutions which would undertake, at their own initiative, to enforce compliance with ethical as well as legal standards in a complex and changing industry."

What did Goldberg mean by "just and adequate" and "to protect investors"? Did Stewart want to permit the S.E.C. to decide the issue? According to the Department of Justice, there was a "fundamental antitrust interest in assuring broker-dealers equitable and nondiscriminatory access to the 'important business advantages' which flow from access to N.Y.S.E. as the Nation's dominant securities market." Under *Silver v. New York Stock Exchange*, "such access can be denied only on the ground that the restriction is necessary to make the Exchange Act work." Generally speaking, the decision was interpreted as requiring procedural safeguards against arbitrary actions; had the N.Y.S.E. removed the tickers according to its own rules, it might have won the case. Nevertheless, the N.Y.S.E. was not to enjoy the status of a protected monopoly. The Big Board was put on notice that it could not proceed against the Third Market as it had against the Consolidated.*

The Third Market continued to grow and prosper, as did the regionals and the New York exchanges. A heightened awareness of the situation may have served the Exchange well. Member firms were encouraged to establish "block departments," and the specialists competed aggressively with the market makers for business. In 1965, there were, on the average, only nine block transactions on the floor each trading day.** By 1969, the number was sixty-one, and it

* A clear presentation of the case and its ramifications is "N.Y.S.E. Rules and the Antitrust Laws—Rule 394—Necessary Restrictions or Illegal Refusal to Deal?" *St. John's Law Review* (Vol. 45, 1971), pp. 812–64.

** Then and now, a block is defined as 10,000 or more shares of a given security.

appeared the specialists had fought the Third Market dealers to at least a draw. Volume at the Third Market was approximately 5 percent of that at the N.Y.S.E., and block trading at the Big Board was still only 14 percent of total volume that year.

Did this mean the Exchange had successfully thrown back its major rival? Not necessarily, for the Third Market was still vigorous and developing. Its leaders were ambitious and, more important, recognized the nature of their problems and the continuing weaknesses at the Big Board. The N.Y.S.E. had expanded its capacities for handling blocks, and new techniques were bound to be introduced in the future. Alterations in the commission structure, even the adoption of give-ups, was possible in the fight to retain clients. The Exchange would automate procedures so as to handle increased trading, and the new building might be erected as well. But nothing would be done to change the specialist system, which remained the very heart of the Exchange. Given another crisis like that of 1962—this time with perhaps twice the volume—the system might bend, crack, and fall apart.

Meanwhile, the Third Market would work to improve its procedures, to prepare in its own ways for additional business. In many of its externals, the Third Market resembled the old O-T-C. To be sure, the offices had computers to store data and other paraphernalia of the electronic age, but the heart of the operation was still the trader on the telephone and the teletype.

Unlike the specialists, the traders were prepared, even eager, for change. As early as 1961, William Claflin, chairman of the board of the N.A.S.D., told a meeting that "other electronic devices, as they became available, will make pushbutton execution feasible and were they here today there would be no problem in handling trading volume." According to the board minutes:

> Growing trading volume subject to electronic handling will bring about a form of revolution in the execution of over-the-counter orders, Mr. Claflin said, and "this will present new problems for the N.A.S.D." The board, he advised, "should attempt to steer this period of change, not only to promote the advancement and modernization of our industry but also to predetermine that the end result is controllable. Otherwise, we may well see leadership fall into the wrong hands and thereby lose our ability to supervise." *

"The relevance of automation to standards of performance and

* *Special Study*, Pt. 2, Chapter VII, p. 658.

conduct and to the quality of over-the-counter markets generally is the point of ultimate significance," concluded *The Special Study*. "Despite inertia or even resistance, the industry must ultimately take advantage of technological progress where considerations of efficiency and economy so dictate, as in other fields of endeavor."

To the N.Y.S.E. specialists, whose existences as viable businessmen were threatened by "technological progress," the computer and all it signified was anathema. They claimed that an automated market operating without the human aspect would fail during times of stress, to which Third Market defenders responded by noting that it was in just such periods that the specialists tended to run for cover. To the O-T-C market makers, the specialists were old fogeys, reactionaries, and foolish antiques whose stubborn insistence on salvaging their own egos stood in the way of progress. On their part, the specialists looked upon the Third Market operators as dangerous freebooters, rootless men who were taking rash and unconsidered actions that would harm all investors. They accused some of them, in private conversations, of taking drugs and consorting with radicals. Meanwhile, the market makers whispered that some specialists were secret drinkers and others open lushes, whose idea of a sane foreign policy was to destroy whole civilizations with atomic bombs.

Caricature replaced fact, as baseless charges that could have been disproven by a telephone call were repeated and enlarged upon. It was fashionable to hate opponents, to attempt to destroy them, in America in the late 1960s. The men at the top would behave responsibly; there would be no war between the N.Y.S.E. and N.A.S.D. But the troops were restless. The financial district was a bitter place in which to work at that time. For that matter, so was much of the rest of the country.

Still, personal animosities would not determine the shape of the marketplace. Nor would government dictates and investigations and reports. Rather, the answers would be found in technology.

The Big Board's leaders did not reject technological advances. Indeed, throughout the early 1960s, Funston and others had spoken of the need for automation, more efficient methods of handling orders and certificates, and almost any change that might facilitate trading. Already there was talk of 20-million-share days; one student of the subject believed that by 1975 more than 100 million shares a day would be traded at the N.Y.S.E. Preparations had to be made for all eventualities. The Exchange had miscalculated volume for the early 1960s; it did not want to make the same mistake for the 1970s.

There were areas that were sacrosanct, however. Funston would not agree to any change that would result in the transformation of the auction market into a dealer market—given the nature of the membership, he could hardly do otherwise. When asked if some kind of accommodation was possible on the matter of N.Y.S.E. members dealing on the O-T-C market, Funston said there was not. "Rule 394 is one of the pillars of the Exchange and we cannot, and will not, budge on the issue."

The matter was out of his hands. The S.E.C. prodded the Exchange into altering the rule, charging it with being contrary to the public interest. In 1965 an over-the-counter dealer, Morris A. Schapiro, announced he would sue the Exchange unless 394 was repealed. Schapiro had made a market in the stock of Chase Manhattan Bank, and when the issue was listed, N.Y.S.E. members could no longer deal with him and at the same time follow the rule. Schapiro's threat bore fruit. In September 1966, prodded by the S.E.C., the Exchange amended the rule to permit members to deal with O-T-C traders in listed securities under certain specified circumstances, thus creating Rule 394(b). The Big Board did budge after all, embarrassing Funston and making his position at the Exchange somewhat strained. Further changes seemed in the works.

The rate structure and relations with institutions and the Third Market were the crucial issues of 1966–1967. The public was interested in prices of securities at a time when it was believed the Exchange was enjoying its most prosperous period in history. Profits were high, to be sure, but so were risks and problems. The 1960s had been a period of lost opportunities, mistakes, and miscalculations as well as high prices and volume. Many of these were in the areas of attitudes toward rivals, responses to challenges, and relations with Washington. Nor had the administration been successful in altering trading conditions on the floor, a most difficult task to be sure. Funston had led the N.Y.S.E. to the promised land, but having arrived, the members didn't seem to know what to do, how to proceed, and more than a few wondered whether the journey had been wisely undertaken.

Here, too, Wall Street reflected the nation. It was a time when Senator Fulbright and columnist Walter Lippmann were saying that America's foreign policy successes in the 1940s and 1950s had resulted in an "arrogance of power," which in turn led to unwise commitments in Vietnam. The moment had come, they and others like them said, for a serious reconsideration of national goals. In Paris, President Charles de Gaulle told an interviewer that the United States had won the Cold War without realizing it and that the nation should alter its foreign policies accordingly. If this was so, and given the nature of America in 1966–1967, had the prize been worth the race, and were the new problems of success better or more easy to handle than the old ones?

At the Exchange, Keith Funston had been the symbol of People's Capitalism. He had been appointed to lead the members to a period of prosperity. Funston had assumed office in 1951, a year when average daily volume was barely 2 million shares, when only 6.5 million Americans owned stock, and specialists and customers' men complained that business was bad. But the members were generally well-off, their operations efficiently managed, and there was no question—as there had been a decade earlier—that the Exchange filled an important economic function.

"I'll try to be the salesman of shares in America," said Funston in 1951. Whether he was responsible for the expansion in volume was questionable, but Funston accepted the plaudits that came with it. In 1966, average daily volume was 7.5 million shares and rising rapidly. There were 21.5 million shareholders in the land. The N.Y.S.E. members were prosperous beyond their hopes of 1951. The price of an Exchange seat had risen from $52,000 to $270,000. Those who had been on Wall Street in 1951 were overjoyed a decade and a half later. Two years after, in 1968, average daily volume was almost 13 million shares, and the price of a seat, a half-million dollars.

By then, however, the men of the Exchange were no longer certain they controlled their own destinies or even their individual operations. They were harried and distracted, and certainly inefficient. Large gaps opened in trading, a sign that the specialist system was not functioning as claimed. Although the back offices of brokerages were in somewhat better shape than before, several were suspected of being in shaky financial circumstances, and a repeat of the Ira Haupt affair appeared possible. The Third Market's defenders claimed the Exchange was obsolete, that the new kind of market would soon take its place. Some of the specialists and many more at the brokerages were coming to believe this too. Ironically, the failures of the 1930s had led to an accommodation and a measure of success in the 1940s and 1950s: the tight ship of Robert Stott and John Coleman. Then came the bull market, one almost all had conceded was not really possible. Volume ballooned, activity soared, fantasy replaced hard realism, the Exchange system sputtered and choked, and acted irregularly. There was apprehension in 1966, and fear and discontent in 1968. Even as volume and prices rose, an increasingly large number of members sensed the bonanza years created more problems than they solved. Perhaps there wouldn't be another 1929 after all, but was the present situation any better? Were the problems of Keith Funston more desirable than those of Charles Gay and William Martin?

CHAPTER 16

Another 1929?

On September 12, 1966, Keith Funston announced his intention to resign from the N.Y.S.E. presidency as soon as a suitable successor could be found. His term had another year to run, and Funston wanted to give the members ample time to select such a person. He assured reporters he was not leaving due to any difference of opinion with the members or pressures from a clique of dissidents, and there was no reason to doubt this was so. Funston had served in office for fifteen years, a record, and he had accumulated a reservoir of good will. Even those who questioned his abilities liked the man. As might have been expected, they told each other that the next president would have to be very much in the Funston mold. On reflection, however, they would concede that perhaps the moment was right for a new man with a different approach.

"I think I deserve a rest," said Funston. He would travel, pursue his hobby of archaeology, and spend more time with his family. Still, he was only fifty-five years old, too young to retire for long. After a while, so it was believed, Funston would re-enter the business world, and in early October rumors had it that he would accept the chairmanship of a large industrial corporation. There was no talk of a political career, as there certainly would have been had Funston stepped down in the late 1950s. The time for that had long passed, and a new kind of politics had evolved, one in which a person like Funston would have appeared out of place.

Always a man of tact, and with a fine sense of timing, Funston was leaving the Exchange at just the right moment. Now he would select the proper niche for a man of his talents, reputation, and abilities. He would take that vacation, and then accept the chairmanship of Olin Mathieson Corporation.

He was gone from the Street, then, during the troubled years that followed. Funston was praised for the positive accomplishments of his tenure, even when he had little to do with them, and was credited for the general prosperity enjoyed by the district in 1966. His successor would suffer the consequences of the errors and omissions of the 1950s and early 1960s and would become the scapegoat for the disasters the community suffered through later on.

Hours after the announcement the rumor mill began to grind. Immediately interest centered on Edwin Etherington, the personable and intelligent president of the American Stock Exchange, who could have had the post had he so desired. But Etherington had earlier indicated his intention of leaving Wall Street to accept the presidency of Wesleyan University in Connecticut, the first step, so it was believed, to a Senate seat from that state. Once it was clear Etherington was firm in his commitment to Wesleyan, the rumors began in earnest. As might have been expected, they centered on politicians believed ready for a change. For a while, Robert Wagner of New York was deemed a prime candidate, but the city's former mayor was still interested in politics, and said as much. Douglas Dillon, who had been Secretary of the Treasury in the Kennedy Cabinet and continued under Johnson, was also mentioned, and he quickly squashed the talk. Secretary of State Dean Rusk and Secretary of Defense Robert McNamara had supporters; neither wanted the job. Then there was a flurry of interest in S.E.C. Chairman Manuel Cohen, who laughed it off. Then–Wall Street lawyer Richard Nixon was believed intrigued with the post, but this proved not to be the case. And so it went.

As had become the custom, the board named a committee to put forth recommendations, interview candidates, and make the selection. Although confidentiality held, there seemed little doubt that the members did not want a "front man." The duties of the president were twofold—to represent the Exchange to the outside world, including Washington, and to help direct its internal operations. William Martin had done well at both tasks. Emil Schram and Keith Funston had been selected for other reasons, the former for his political position, Funston for his flair at public relations. The next president would have to know his way around Washington and have the proper connections at the S.E.C.—indeed, these would be prime considerations for the presidency of any stock exchange—but he would also have to understand the problems of the district, have a comprehension of the situation at the N.Y.S.E., and an ability to make needed changes in a tactful manner. In other words, the new man would be charged with responsibilities in the area of internal reform; his value as a symbol for Washington and Main Street was a secondary consideration.

The task would be more difficult than it appeared, for over the past two decades—and especially during the Funston period—power had become centered in the Board of Governors, the chairman in particular. Contrary to popular belief but well known to Wall

Streeters, Funston had little influence within the Exchange building. During his last years in office, John Coleman and Robert Stott, together with others of their group, continued to rule the floor, and at times acted as though Funston was merely their messenger boy. Walter N. Frank, an Exchange veteran, a senior partner of Marcus & Co., and board chairman, was deemed one of the district's most influential men, and yet was unknown outside of the Wall Street area and content to allow things to remain that way. There was a brief attempt to make Frank the new president, but he quickly rejected the notion which, in reality, would have been a step downward. In any case, Frank wanted to return to his company full time, and was ready to turn power over to Gustave Levy of Goldman, Sachs, the first investment banker to hold the post.

Levy had chaired the committee that had restructured the Amex, had been one of Edwin Etherington's early sponsors, was a leading figure in behind-the-scenes national politics, and a banker of international reputation. No president could hope to become a dominant figure so long as a man like Levy was chairman; the next president would have to have his good will, and accept a secondary role even while serving as the N.Y.S.E.'s public face. He would have status without power. Funston had accepted this, knowing he would handle public relations while the chairman would have primary responsibility for internal matters, many of which did not interest him anyway. It would be different with his successor.

In early 1967 the committee believed it had found its man: Donald C. Cook, president of American Electric Power Co. and an S.E.C. chairman in the Eisenhower Administration. He had all the requisites —ability, interest, and connections among them. The Exchange drew up a contract, signed it, and sent the document to Cook for signature. The announcement of his appointment was prepared; it was an open secret in the district.

Cook balked, for reasons that were not disclosed. One story had it that the board at American Electric Power made a counteroffer that was too good to reject, and that he felt he had an obligation to the company. Another was that Cook had asked the board for verbal assurances that he would receive the authority to make internal changes, and that this was refused. In any case, the search went on.

Robert W. Haack was the next choice. He was fifty years old in 1967—just the right age—and had the proper background for the position. Haack was born in Milwaukee, went to local schools, and then to Harvard for an M.B.A. After wartime duty in the Navy he took a position at a local brokerage, and in 1950 joined Robert A. Baird & Co., a midwestern securities firm. Interested more in administration than sales, Haack became involved in N.A.S.D. affairs in the early

1960s, and in 1961 was named a governor. When the S.E.C. asked the N.A.S.D. to reform itself as a result of the findings of *The Special Study*, the Association wrote a new constitution providing for a paid president as chief operating officer. Haack was the first choice for that job.

The N.A.S.D. was being restructured, both at the direction of the S.E.C. and because of the needs of its members, including the contingent that was promoting the Third Market. Haack performed creditably in his post. He clashed with S.E.C. Chairman Cohen—"Once in a while you get the feeling that in some areas the S.E.C. may be overly zealous," he said—but the two became friends and even played golf together regularly. Several major commission houses, Merrill Lynch among them, thought he was an outstanding candidate, and the big brokerages were gaining strength and influence in Exchange politics. But some board members had doubts. After all, Haack was the leader of a market that increasingly challenged the Big Board. He was a Democrat, a liberal one at that, and a man who had spoken out in favor of social reforms at a time when a large majority of the board consisted of conservative Republicans becoming increasingly disturbed by violence and change. On the other hand, wouldn't it be intelligent to hire the one man who, more than any other, understood the operations of the enemy? And if Haack could be credited with making the N.A.S.D. so strong as to rival the N.Y.S.E., couldn't he lead in the rehabilitation of the Big Board just as well? As for his political ideas, these could be ignored if all else went as hoped. This, at least, was the reasoning of the committee in early April, when serious negotiations began.

Haack knew that Cook had turned down the job. Funston had already announced he would join Olin Mathieson in September; the story about the need for rest and recreation had been forgotten—Funston simply wanted to leave the district. Stock prices were booming, it was almost expected that the tape would be late, and there was talk of a "volume panic" and fails in the district. Would Haack be given the power to make changes to accommodate such a market? "In my negotiations with the selection committee I asked certain questions, and the things that I can do at the Exchange were settled in a way that is satisfactory to me," he later told reporters. At the time this was taken to mean that Haack would be permitted to select his own staff. But real power would remain on the floor and in the board; the chairman, not the president, would rule the institution. Despite this, Haack accepted the offer of the presidency. He received a five-year contract at $125,000 a year plus perquisites and expenses.

Why did Haack take the position under these circumstances? A simple answer would be that he had no choice; had he demanded a free hand on the floor it would have been refused, and the committee would have looked elsewhere. Being an ambitious person, Haack wanted the top job in the American securities exchange structure and so accepted in the belief that he could accomplish his ends anyway; in fact, the lack of authority only increased the challenge and made it more inviting.

Powerful specialists, eager to retain their positions, were unhappy with the Third Market, angry at criticism, and disturbed with the ever-closer relations between the large commission houses and the O-T-C traders. The brokerages were saying, openly, that the Big Board was becoming a ramshackle operation—and at the same time appeared unable to solve the situation regarding fails. "One of my biggest jobs will be reconciling the interests of the floor people and the big brokerage houses," Haack told reporters. "At the risk of sounding like a Boy Scout, I think it eventually can be done. After all, everybody has the same interest in bringing more business to this Exchange." He said this at a press conference announcing his appointment on April 25. That week over 10 million shares were traded each day, and the ticker was chronically late. Clearly the N.Y.S.E. didn't need additional volume. Haack was saying, as diplomatically as he could, that he would attempt to stanch the flow of business to the O-T-C traders, his old employers. "I'm no great stranger to conflict. After all, as you know, I had a few problems at the N.A.S.D." None, however, were of the magnitude of those to be faced—without proper weapons—at the N.Y.S.E.

Haack was a popular choice. By then, most members conceded that Funston's time had passed and that a new man with different credentials was needed. The outgoing president was great at selling the idea of investing, said one member. "But a few years back the character of our problems began to change. They got more technical and more involved with the way this business works. Bob Haack is ideal for this kind of environment. He grew up in this business, and he knows it inside out. For the problems we've got now, there couldn't be a better man."

The Exchange was about to enter a long period of testing, and Haack indeed seemed the proper leader. He was intelligent and experienced and proved an articulate spokesman for the district. Quieter and less flamboyant than Funston, but exuding confidence, Haack was able to speak before large audiences without prepared notes and did so with a fine sense of humor and a clearly defined set of values. In addition, he possessed stronger nerves and diplomatic skills than were recognized at the time of his appointment in 1967.

But he lacked authority and united support. His situation was strange to those who had little contact with business and the financial district in particular. Haack was not the first choice for the position. He knew this. The board and the members on the floor understood that Haack realized that the committee had come to him after others had rejected the post. And Haack understood that his position was weak from the start because they knew he had taken the post anyway. Clearly, such a situation was not promising.

Haack was interested in reforms, in transforming the N.Y.S.E. into a more efficient market, and this would mean acceptance of change. The membership and the board wanted to retrench, to maintain the *status quo.* The prognosis for success was not good.

Being a realist, Haack recognized this to be so. Significantly, he retained his residence in Potomac, Maryland, spending working evenings in New York but weekends with his family. This too appeared unusual to outsiders but had a special meaning to business executives. The board knew that Haack still considered himself a resident of Maryland. He wanted the members to know this. In turn, they realized what that meant. Haack would not break Funston's record for longevity, or that of David Clarkson or even Emil Schram. For the first time since William Martin had left Wall Street more than a quarter of a century before, the N.Y.S.E. had a president who not only understood the market but was committed to changing it.

Keith Funston took his official leave of the Exchange on September 9, a Friday, and Haack assumed office the following Monday. In fact, however, Funston had initiated the transfer of power a month before, while Haack spent as much time as he could at the Exchange prior to taking his position. He would not enter the Exchange as an unknown quantity. Instead, it would be "something like an old home week," he said. "I know most of these people personally."

The Dow Industrials closed at 909.62 on September 11, 1967, with the volume at 9,300,000 shares. The ticker ran late on occasion, and yet it was a below-average day for that year. Already there were signs of a breakdown on the floor, a precursor to the shortened trading sessions of 1968–1969. Record volume in May, a slight turndown in June, and then new highs in July, when more than 10 million shares were traded on sixteen of the twenty sessions, led to a crisis in the back offices in August. In his last significant act as president, Funston ordered the trading floor closed at 2:00 for nine days in August, both to keep volume down and permit brokerages to catch up with paper work. Volume at the Exchange was somewhat lower on those days, but the difference was made up by additional trades on the Amex and O-T-C markets. Funston, who had come to the Exchange promising to increase volume and who, toward the end, was committed to preventing rivals from taking N.Y.S.E. business, left after attempting to hold trading down. It was that kind of period.

The nation and world were troubled that September. Hopes that the

Vietnam War would end had existed in early 1967 but were shattered that summer when a peace offensive proved more a public relations gimmick than anything else. Now there was talk of a "credibility gap" in Washington. In May, American troops had invaded the demilitarized zone between North and South Vietnam, leading to fears of an expanded conflict, perhaps with the Chinese entering on the side of their North Vietnamese allies. Then in June, Israel attacked Egypt after repeated provocations, and once again it appeared a major confrontation might develop between the United States and the USSR.

The economy was overheating. In January, President Johnson asked for a 6 percent surcharge on corporate and most individual income taxes, a measure that most conservative critics argued had been long overdue, both to help pay for the war and prevent runaway inflation. Antiwar forces opposed the surcharge, on the grounds that to pass it would be to support the Administration's Vietnam policies. The measure was bottled up in the Ways and Means Committee of the House, where Chairman Wilbur Mills refused to permit it out. Prices were rising, and inflation accelerating. Clearly the economy was in trouble, and for a while it seemed Johnson might be obliged to withdraw from Vietnam in order to salvage domestic order. Chairman William Martin of the Federal Reserve warned against fiscal irresponsibility and called for support of the surcharge. If it did not pass, he intimated, the Federal Reserve would utilize monetary policies—including much higher interest rates—to curb inflation. And that, so it was believed, might trigger a recession. As he had so often in the past, economist John K. Galbraith talked of the possibilities of another 1929, but the market continued to roll on. Martin noted that speculation on the Street reminded him of the pool operations of the 1920s, and this had only a temporary effect. The stock market had risen in the face of poor economic news during the summer of 1929. Was the same kind of development taking place in 1967?

There was a subtle psychological change on Wall Street that autumn. In the early stages of the war, prices would decline on rumors of an end to the fighting. Ever since 1947, stocks had risen on war talk and had fallen when investors and speculators feared "peace would break out." The conventional wisdom had it that the economic boom was fueled by war-related orders, and that without them, the nation would sink into a recession, perhaps a depression. This attitude was changing in 1967, as inflation, caused by war spending, was becoming more of a problem than recession, and as the Vietnam War became increasingly unpopular. Late in the year there were rumors of a new "peace offensive," to be mounted in January or February. Having failed to win the war militarily, so it was believed, President Johnson would seek a negotiated peace, without which he could not achieve re-election. Stocks moved upward on such rumors. Peace had become bullish, just as inflation was bearish, the opposite of what they had been earlier in the decade. It was another indication that Haack's Wall Street would be different from that of Keith Funston.

Economists predicted that the autumn Presidential election would take place in an atmosphere of prosperity. Conditions appeared bright in early January, as prices moved upward on Wall Street. But 1968 was a year in which festering wounds erupted, the unexpected changed projections, and the bizarre became the norm. It could be seen in politics, economics, and in social relations, and at the N.Y.S.E. it resulted in confusion and uncertainties.

Late in the month the Vietcong initiated an offensive which took them into Saigon itself. There was no more talk of peace negotiations. Instead, it seemed the war might be broadened through an invasion of the North. At the same time, as a result of a North Korean seizure of the U.S.S. *Pueblo*, conflict threatened there as well. The Tet offensive killed the last hopes of any easy withdrawal from Vietnam, and the Korean outbreak only complicated what was an already tense situation.

There were economic troubles too. In Europe there was a rush to get rid of paper money and buy gold, which was only indirectly associated with the American difficulties. In early March the United States Treasury reported heavy foreign buying into the American reserves. On March 18, the price of gold was permitted to float in an attempt to stave off a financial panic.

The cost of living was soaring, and the position in Vietnam was bleak. On March 29, the Dow closed at 840.67, having lost more than 60 points since New Year's Day.

That weekend, President Johnson declared he would not seek re-election. He ended the bombing of North Vietnam and announced the beginning of a new search for peace. The deep gloom of late March was replaced by soaring hopes on the next trading session on April 1. Prices rose from the opening, and volume was high, with the ticker running late throughout the day. In all, 17,730,000 shares were traded, almost double the March average, while the Dow Industrials rose by more than 20 points.

Volume would not fall below the 11-million-share level until late July. It was the most hectic period the Street had known since the late 1920s, but in terms of confusion, it was probably worst. During this time Martin Luther King and Robert Kennedy were assassinated, there were riots throughout western Europe and a near revolution in France, and the Bank of England appeared shaky. The Soviets would shortly invade Czechoslovakia. The Democratic Convention in Chicago ended in violence and despair. The world monetary crisis worsened. The hopes for peace in Vietnam were frustrated. And at the

N.Y.S.E., these events caused sharp reactions, both up and down, on superheated activity. Prices rose sharply in April and early May, declined later in the month, and then rose again, peaking at 923.72 on July 15. Then they cracked downward, collapsing to 869.65 in fifteen trading sessions, only to rise again, to 967.49 on October 18. By then, only the brave and foolish would predict future movements—and even they would hedge. Columnist Reston's age of abstract expressionism had arrived, in the nation and on the Street.

It is a truism that Wall Street dislikes uncertainty, and on the surface at least, it would appear that this was the cause for the downward move in July and August. How could one account for the upward drives in May and early July, however, and the spiraling market in the autumn? This was not an uncertain market but rather one in which there were all too many certainties, each shattered by an unanticipated event. The Johnson abdication, the assassinations, the violence in America and Europe—none of these could have been predicted in the spring of 1968.

War and inflation were the overriding issues in the Presidential campaign that year, as Hubert Humphrey and Richard Nixon offered solutions to problems, while a sizable part of the electorate rejected both men and their arguments. Stability and the methods by which it could be achieved were on the minds of many that year. A nation which had welcomed the Soaring Sixties with a measure of self-assurance, and had been captivated by the dynamism and grandiose plans of John Kennedy, yearned for a respite from action and change, for peace and an end to sudden transformations in their lives. The bedrock seemed gone; none could be found.

On Wall Street, Robert Haack struggled with his problems. Still viewed as a newcomer to the Exchange—a place with a tradition of distrusting outsiders—he had to face a major crisis during his first year in office, and he lacked the authority to impose his will upon the members. Long-range reforms would involve the floor, but for the moment, the commission houses needed attention. In January the S.E.C. wrote to the N.Y.S.E. and Amex as well as to the N.A.S.D., expressing concern about "accounting, record keeping and back office problems and their effects on the prompt transfer and delivery of securities." Fails were increasing, and yet the commission houses continued to look for new business, while the churning of accounts to earn commissions was becoming scandalous. Nor would the specialists speak out on the subject, fearing perhaps they would lose trades to other markets. In February, Haack urged members to curtail their operations and refrain from seeking additional clients. This was done in an informal fashion, for Haack lacked the authority to act under existing regulations. In March, however, prodded by the S.E.C., the

Exchange sent member firms a letter in which "serious operations problems" were discussed.

> Firms with serious problems may be asked to take steps to limit the growth of business or to reduce business when an organization's operations capacity falls seriously short of handling it. In the absence of voluntary action, restraints may be imposed by the Exchange on the conduct and growth of business of member organizations which appear to be in danger of losing control of their records and consequently of being unable to properly supervise customer accounts and registered representatives.

The Exchange could act against a firm if its capital fell below requirements or if it was not performing as well as standards dictated. Otherwise, it could do nothing but urge and prompt.

Then came the first clear sign of distress. Pickard & Co., a small firm that had been in trouble in the past, was forced to liquidate as a result of an inability to keep up with volume and maintain proper records. In the investigation that followed, it was learned that Pickard had churned accounts, manipulated issues, sold unregistered stocks, and in other ways violated S.E.C. regulations and laws as well as N.Y.S.E. rules. Yet none of this would have been known had it not been for the volume crush, something other firms were also undergoing.

It was the first liquidation since the demise of Ira Haupt in 1963, and so the first time the Special Trust Fund was utilized. Pickard's 3,500 clients were paid more than $400,000 from the fund, of which all but $160,000 was recovered afterward. The Exchange boasted that no client lost a cent because of the bankruptcy.

But the Pickard collapse aroused fears of additional, more serious failures. Haack and others attempted to assure the public that all was well, but several financial reporters began investigations of their own. In early August, 1968, *Fortune* magazine reported that thirty-five member firms were under special restrictions "designed to prevent the sort of overload that did in Pickard." The clear implication was that these firms were mismanaged, "although no one at the Exchange cares to put it that way." These included some of the district's most prestigious houses. Lehman Brothers, the oldest in the district, was one which, among other things, was forbidden from hiring new salesmen and establishing additional branches. Immediately other brokerages voluntarily curtailed operations. Paine, Webber, Jackson & Curtis, which was not one of the thirty-five, declared a moratorium on advertising, increased minimums needed to open margin accounts, and discouraged trading in low-priced issues. Merrill Lynch declared that it had long exceeded the Exchange's basic requirements and refused to deal in low-priced stocks. Neither firm, of course, was considered in danger of failure. Nor was Hayden, Stone & Co., one of the fastest-growing commission houses, which now announced it would stop planning new offices.

Political uncertainties and sheer investor exhaustion, as well as the imposed and voluntary curbs on trading, gave the Exchange a breather in August, when on ten out of eighteen trading days volume fell below 10 million shares. Then, in September, volume and prices rose once more, as did speculation. At this point, S.E.C. Chairman Cohen began speaking of the need for a new study of Wall Street. He was disturbed by the breakdowns at the commission houses, tales of manipulations, and rank speculation in the new issues market. Earlier the Federal Trade Commission had announced a plan to investigate conglomerate corporations, and now Cohen would do the same for that other group of "gunslingers," the young men who had come to the Street in the early 1960s and appeared to be directing the wildest market in memory.

An S.E.C. probe of the district, directed by a person with Cohen's knowledge and political bent, was bound to uncover serious problems and areas for reform. Clearly something drastic would have to be done regarding the commission houses, their ways of transacting business, and techniques utilized in churning accounts. The entire matter of institutional membership on exchanges would be raised, as the mutual funds showed increased irritation at having to deal through brokerages and pay for services they really didn't want or need. But the real issue was bound to be the floor, and the necessity for the specialist system in the light of technological and procedural advances. Already several private companies were preparing to introduce automated trading in large blocks, while the N.A.S.D. worked on its own program. The Big Board's response, of course, was the new building. An S.E.C. investigation of all of these, concluding with recommendations for action, might prove unsettling to those in power at the Exchange.

Haack recognized this and did not appear displeased with reports of S.E.C. activism. He knew that Cohen's ideas were similar to his own. Haack wanted to reform the Exchange, to introduce some of the methods he had helped develop at the N.A.S.D., change them to meet the essential structure of the N.Y.S.E., and in the process create a viable market, one that would contain the best elements of both the Exchange and the O-T-C. If this were done, then the Third Market would no longer be an alternative to the Big Board, which would now offer investors all of the O-T-C's benefits and none of its liabilities. Already he had scrapped one of the Exchange's haphazard automation plans, on which $3.5 million had been spent and which was obsolete before being placed into operation. For decades the Exchange had talked about a central depository for certificates, one that would relieve back offices of heavy paper work and mark the beginning of the end for an outworn practice; Haack named John Cunningham of the Midwest Stock Exchange as his executive vice-president and charged him with bringing it about. Most important, Haack was known to be in favor of volume discounts, by which purchasers and sellers of large blocks would not be obliged to pay the same commission per share as those who traded small amounts. (In December 1969 Haack convinced the board to accept volume discounts on trades of 1,000 shares or more, despite grave misgivings, fears it would lead to a price war with the O-T-C, and end with discount operations at the Exchange itself. If extended, the discounts would eliminate the need for give-ups, a practice already under S.E.C. fire.)

Given the paper work mess and Pickard failure, the much-discussed S.E.C. probe, and the support of a relatively small group of commission houses and investment banks, Haack was able to make progress in the summer and autumn of 1968. His was not the only possible response to these problems, however. Bernard J. Lasker had another.

Gustave Levy was chairman in 1968 and so occupied a position of great power and eminence at the Exchange. Both meant less to him than they did to his predecessors, however. Years before taking the post, Levy had been considered one of the most influential and respected individuals in the district, and the N.Y.S.E. was only a part of the financial complex, while Levy was close to its heart as head of Goldman, Sachs. He appeared bored at many N.Y.S.E. meetings but, always the gentleman, played his part well.

It was different with Bernard Lasker, whom almost all called "Bunny." Lasker had taken the old-fashioned road to power and position. He had begun as a runner in 1927, worked his way up the brokerage ladder, and purchased his seat in 1939. Lasker, Stone and Stern, his company, was involved in trading and two-dollar brokerage, and Lasker was a familiar figure on the floor, which he came to love. He joined the board in 1965 and immediately became one of its mainstays, serving on many committees, accepting assignments even when it meant ignoring his business, and generally earning a reputation for loyalty to N.Y.S.E. traditions and interests. Thus, he was a perfect complement to Levy. In 1967, Lasker was selected vice-chairman, which meant, in the course of events, he would accede to the chairmanship in 1969. Given Levy's attitude toward Exchange business, Lasker would have a good deal of power for at least four years.

Like many self-made men, Lasker had an affinity for those who rose to the top through work and effort. He opposed most New Frontier and New Society welfare programs, and increasingly was drawn to the free-enterprise wing of the G.O.P. Lasker saw in the riots and disorders of 1968 a threat to American freedoms. He was angered by what he deemed anti-American statements and actions of opponents of the Vietnam War. The threats to his beloved N.Y.S.E. seemed of a piece with the rest. So it was not unusual that Lasker became a major fund raiser for the Republicans, or that his candidate for the Presidency was Richard Nixon, an old friend who had become prominent through hard work and represented old-fashioned virtues in his campaign.

In late September, candidate Nixon sent a letter to a group of prominent Wall Streeters, which was then released to the press. In it he criticized the S.E.C. for its "regulatory schemes." If the Commission's campaign continued, he warned, confidence in the market would be eroded and panic would follow. Nixon went on to say that if elected he would enforce existing laws. In contrast, said Nixon, the Johnson Administration had taken the view that "disclosure alone is not enough, and that the government can make decisions for the investor better than he can make them for himself. This philosophy I reject."

The meaning was clear. Once in office, Nixon would cut short any plans for investigations. There would be no further warnings against speculation, or threats of government action if reforms were not made. Lasker rejoiced. Together with Peter Flanigan of Dillon, Read, he found donations relatively easy to obtain once potential donors read the letter. At the same time, small investors and speculators were assured that, if elected, Nixon would do nothing to throw doubt on the bull market. This might have been translated into votes.

Thus, Lasker was able to point to an alternative to the Haack program. To be sure, he said, the Exchange had to move with the times, but this did not mean drastic alterations in the specialist system, higher standards at the commission houses, or the introduction of untried techniques. Lasker staunchly believed the N.Y.S.E. was superior to any other market in the world and that with good faith and the right men in command it would demonstrate this superiority. Never enthusiastic about the Haack candidacy, and increasingly wary of the new president, Lasker had come to view the political contest that autumn not only as being between Nixon and Humphrey but also himself and Haack.

Peace talks in Paris seemed promising in October, and political columnists speculated that some sort of cease-fire could be agreed upon before Election Day—Lyndon Johnson's final gesture and one that would help Humphrey at the polls. There was no peace, but prices and volume rose at the Exchange. The Dow was above the 950 mark, having advanced more than 100 points since February. More than 20 million shares were traded during two sessions in October. It was unusual, but no longer remarkable.

Nixon was elected by a slim margin, and the market continued upward, peaking at 985.21 on December 3, before closing the year at 943.75. Then prices began to fall. On Inauguration Day, January 20, 1969, the Dow was at 920.13. It slipped below 900, briefly, on February 25. Then it began to rise once more, reaching 968.85 on May 14, only to fall to 801.96 on July 29, in the most disastrous decline since the early 1960s.

The reasons were there to be seen and analyzed. The new Administration continued the tight-money policy that had been initiated in the last months of the Johnson Administration, viewing it as a major effort at stemming inflation. The discount rate, which had been 4 percent in October, 1967, was 5½ percent in early 1969 and went to 6 percent in April, a mark not seen since 1929. The prime rate was 7½ percent by then, an all-time high. The continuation of the war, fears of new conflicts in Korea and the Middle East, an antitrust campaign against the conglomerates, talk of a coming recession—all led the market downward. The Nixon victory had not been viewed as the beginning of a bright new era—as had been the case with those of Eisenhower and Kennedy—and the world was not very much different in the summer of 1969 from what it had been the year before. To be sure, the violence of 1968 had ended, but the war continued, with no conclusion in sight, and Nixon had not been able to bring the nation together as he had hoped to do.

Stock prices fell, not out of fear or even because the levels were deemed unreasonable. Rather, the nation's small investors and speculators were enervated and exhausted, while the institutions were wary of new commitments in the face of economic and political uncertainties. Volume declined at the Big Board, not to the pre-boom levels, to be sure, but to a pace that was moderate by 1968 standards. Trading fell below the 10 million mark on three days in February, twelve in March, and six in April before rising again in May. Then trading slowed again in July, when there were nine days below the 10 million mark, while in August there were fifteen. Only 6,680,000 shares traded on August 11, the slowest session in two years. The volume crisis appeared ended. Three days later, William Martin spoke out in favor of Nixon's tight-money policies. There was "less inflationary momentum in the economy than there was three months ago," he said. But unemployment was rising and there was talk of recession in the air. The President's defenders argued that a minor recession would be a small price to pay for economic stability, while his attackers observed that unemployment was increasing at a faster rate than the advance in prices was slowing. Optimists saw this as a replay of 1953, when another Republican President accepted a recession to end inflation; pessimists spoke instead of 1929.

The situation at the brokerages was confused. For months the commission house leaders had realized that they could not sustain operations at such high volume. Now that trading had slowed, they discovered their deficits mounting. The concomitant decline in prices hurt their inventory positions. By early October, several were in serious financial difficulties. Then, on October 22, Gregory & Co. was suspended from membership. Shortly thereafter it was learned that the small brokerage had deficiencies of more than $4 million. Haack moved quickly to make funds from the Special Trust Fund available, and as in the case of Pickard, the public did not suffer. There was no panic nor more than a hint of additional failures to come. In December, Amott, Baker & Co., a small brokerage, was liquidated and its clients reimbursed by the Special Trust Fund. The Dow was below 770 by then, having seen the entire last stage of the Johnson Bull Market wiped out. Even though prices rallied to close the year a fraction above 800, friends chided Lasker and other Administration supporters about the "Nixon Market" and wondered when the next rally would begin.

While investors and speculators were concerned about falling quotations, Wall Street was distressed regarding the situation at McDonnell & Co., a large and rapidly expanding brokerage. In late 1969, however, in a sudden reversal of policy, the company began closing its offices and firing personnel. The news broke in the *Wall Street Journal*. The company, which at one time hoped to challenge Merrill Lynch and for a while had been directed by Larry O'Brien, chief strategist for the Kennedy family, was in a shambles. The firm's spokesman denied the stories, swearing all was well.

In March, with stock prices declining rapidly, McDonnell closed its doors, in effect conceding the stories to have been true. In April, the S.E.C. investigated and found that the firm had engaged in fraudulent practices and failed to maintain adequate records. Clients' accounts had been churned. T. Murray McDonnell, one of the district's rising stars and a close friend of Henry Ford, had personally engaged in illegal sales. It was the biggest collapse since the Ira Haupt failure, and the news had been broken by a reporter. Did this mean that there were other, similar problems in the brokerage community that neither the Exchange nor the S.E.C. knew of? Or if the Commission and the N.Y.S.E. had knowledge of difficulties, were these kept secret? Exchange and S.E.C. leaders said this was not so. Haack told reporters that the top twenty-five commission houses were all in compliance with capital requirements. But this was not the case, and readers of the financial press soon learned otherwise.

Led by reporters from the *Journal, Fortune*, and the *New York Times*, a contingent of newsmen descended upon the district in the spring of 1970. Difficulties and shortages were uncovered at more than a dozen brokerages, most of them small to medium in size. Bache & Co., one of the largest, volunteered the information that it had lost almost $9 million in 1969 and that its troubles had not ended. Hayden, Stone, with some 90,000 clients, had been fined for infractions of rules in late 1969, and was still in difficulty. Dempsey-Tegeler, a major brokerage in the Midwest, was short of capital. There were rumors of shortages at Goodbody, and scarcely a house was spared from such talk. Clearly the Special Fund would be inadequate if a major brokerage collapsed. Additional capital was needed. (Ironically, this might have been obtained by selling stock in the commission houses, and the previous year one brokerage, Donaldson, Lufkin & Jenrette, did so. In the spring of 1970, however, stock prices were low, and even then there was no market for shares in troubled brokerages.)

MONTHLY CLOSING PRICES OF THE DOW INDUSTRIALS, 1964–1969

Month	*1964*	*1965*	*1966*	*1967*	*1968*	*1969*
January	785.34	902.86	983.51	849.89	855.47	946.05
February	800.14	903.48	951.89	839.37	840.50	905.21
March	813.29	889.05	924.77	865.98	840.67	935.48
April	810.77	922.31	933.68	897.05	912.22	950.18
May	820.56	918.04	884.07	852.56	899.00	937.56
June	831.50	868.03	870.10	860.26	897.80	873.19
July	841.10	881.74	847.38	904.24	883.00	815.47
August	838.48	893.10	788.41	901.29	896.01	836.72
September	875.37	930.58	774.22	926.66	935.79	813.09
October	873.03	960.82	807.07	879.74	952.39	855.99
November	875.43	946.71	791.59	875.81	985.08	863.05
December	874.13	969.26	785.69	905.11	943.75	800.36

SOURCE: *The Dow Jones Averages, 1885–1970*

Several small N.Y.S.E. firms and many nonmember commission houses closed down in the spring and early summer. Both Dempsey-Tegeler and Hayden, Stone were in violation of the capital rule. They had been rescued earlier by loans of securities from outside, but with the decline in stock prices, they still fell short of what the N.Y.S.E. considered safe. Haack responded, increasing the size of the Special Fund by transferring to it $30 million the Exchange had been saving for its new building. With that, the two companies were saved and the plans for the facility scrapped. As one reporter noted, "They could have gone ahead and built the thing, but who would have been there to trade if Hayden, Stone went under?" That firm and Dempsey-Tegeler were still in shaky circumstances, while the Exchange busily arranged the final liquidations of McDonnell and three other firms. "If someone had told me a year ago that we could have four New York Stock Exchange firms in liquidation at one time and not have suffered a complete loss in confidence among investors, I wouldn't have believed it," said a prominent Wall Streeter.

The frightening news from the brokerages must have had an effect on stock prices, as distressed clients sold out and went to cash. Prices fell, with the high technology issues being hardest hit. But given the standards of the day, volume was not high. There were five sessions in April when trading was below 9 million shares, and two consecutive days in May when less than 7 million were traded. Nor was there a correlation between front-page news of troubles at the brokerages and the movement of the Dow or the size of volume. On May 26 the Dow fell by 10.20 points, closing at 631.16, below where it had been when Kennedy was inaugurated seven years earlier. The volume that day was 17 million shares. Prices rose sharply the next session, with the Dow up by 32.04 points, and volume was 17.4 million shares. If this was a panic, there had never been one like it.

For the most part, it appears clients maintained their accounts in April and May—even at those commission houses known to be in trouble. The reasons for this were not clear, then or later. It certainly wasn't due to confidence in Haack or Hamer Budge, who had become S.E.C. chairman in 1969, since most investors didn't know who they were. Nor was it the result of a belief in the integrity of the district's leaders, the Special Fund, willingness on the part of the Nixon Administration to save investors, or any other rational factor that could be isolated. Investors who understood the implications of the distress at the brokerages and realized they could lose their securities seemed reluctant to remove them, even then.

One theory which gained wide acceptance afterward was that this generation of investors had never known a real panic before, had become used to the idea that protection was at hand from the government and so didn't give the matter serious thought. In other words, the average investor did not trust Nixon, Budge, or Haack, but had an unspoken confidence in the institutions they represented—at least insofar as protecting their capital was concerned. The same phenomenon was witnessed when a bank was rumored to be in difficulty. In 1920, such news would have caused a run to develop immediately; such was not the case in 1970.

If this theory is valid—and it is one of the very few that has any plausibility—then it must be viewed as a vindication of the Wall Street reforms of the 1930s and beyond. Whatever their failures, in conception and execution, they did instill a confidence in the investing public that no other generation had.

This situation had two implications. First, it would be difficult to shake investor confidence, and a true panic would require more difficulties than earlier ones to trigger. This could be seen in late June, when the Penn Central conceded that it was bankrupt. In previous times, such news would have resulted in a selling wave. This was not the case in 1970, when stocks declined but then stabilized and rallied. The second implication was less gratifying. What would happen if that confidence was finally shaken? If the blow was so great as to shatter the trust that had been built up over two generations? Then the nation might witness a crash of monumental proportions indeed. Would one occur in 1970? That summer, as it once again appeared peace was in sight in Vietnam, stocks rallied, so that on August 28 the Dow closed at 765.81, having risen more than 130 points in three months. It was an "on-off market," with investor moods switching from extreme bullishness to gloomy bearishness suddenly, without stopping in between, and in each case ignoring contrary evidence on the other side. For the moment, the market was bullish.

Additional brokerages went under. Orvis Brothers, two years shy of its hundredth anniversary, failed in June, followed by Blair & Co. and Dempsey-Tegeler. Fearful that investor confidence was being shaken —despite the surprising lack of evidence that this was so—Haack announced the names of ten brokerages in bankruptcy or liquidation and the steps being taken to assure the safety of their accounts. Haack informed Chairman Budge of the situation, and the actions were noted. Additional safeguards would be needed, however. Budge stated, "We also believe the Exchange must accept responsibility for any other firms who may be permitted by the Exchange to operate in violation of such requirements. . . ." Lasker, who had succeeded Levy as chairman, joined with Haack in assurances that this was so. The new vice-chairman, Ralph DeNunzio, told Senator Edmund Muskie, "As I indicated, if any member of the Exchange gets into trouble from here on out, the Exchange is going to have to cope with that problem at that time." Clearly, the Special Fund would be inadequate, especially if, as suspected, other firms were in trouble. Additional capital, or an entirely new kind of rescue operation, would be needed. And to maintain investor confidence, some form of insurance program, similar to Federal Deposit Insurance—funded either by the N.Y.S.E. or the government—might have to be considered.

The Exchange suspended First Devonshire Corporation and Charles Plohn & Co. on August 18. Robinson & Co., which had sold its N.Y.S.E. seat in July, fell later in the month, but since it was no longer a member, was not covered by the Special Fund.

With this, attention turned to Hayden, Stone. The firm might have gone under in March had it not been for an infusion of capital from a group of Oklahoma businessmen who, in effect, loaned the firm $12.4

million in securities in return for collateral and interest at 7 percent. Much of this was gone by August, and once more, Hayden, Stone needed funds. Now the Exchange stepped in with plans of its own. It purchased some nonliquid assets owned by the brokerage for $6 million. Preparations were made to divide Hayden, Stone's branches between two other member firms, Walston & Co. and Cogan, Berlind, Weill & Levitt, Inc. Negotiations were almost completed when, on September 2, it was learned that the Chicago Board of Trade had announced it would suspend Hayden, Stone for insolvency. If this occurred, the N.Y.S.E. would be obliged to do the same, in which case the deal would fall through. Lasker and Haack contacted associates in Chicago to ask for a reconsideration of the suspension order. Felix Rohatyn of Lazard, Frères, considered a genius at working out mergers and soon to be known as "Felix the Fixer," was called in to help in the work. And their efforts were rewarded; the Chicago Board of Trade would withdraw the suspension in return for the deposit of $500,000 in escrow money.

All that remained was to obtain the agreement of Hayden, Stone's creditors for the deal. The N.Y.S.E. leadership dropped all business to concentrate on this. As Levy had done in the Ira Haupt crisis, Haack flew to London to get approval of creditors there, while Rohatyn, Lasker, and others telephoned across the country, pleading, arguing, and even threatening in order to obtain the necessary approval. They succeeded. The last to agree was an Oklahoma creditor, Jack Golsen, who indicated acceptance on September 11. The mergers went through, as CBWL-Hayden, Stone was born, Walston was enlarged, and the old Hayden, Stone was completely liquidated.*

Other brokerage crises followed. Goodbody & Co., the nation's fifth largest firm, with 225,000 accounts, was taken over by Merrill Lynch. Francis I. du Pont & Co. was merged with Glore, Forgan & Staats and Hirsch & Co. to form F. I. du Pont–Glore, Forgan & Co., which was backed by Texas millionaire H. Ross Perot. In late November, after the last merger was arranged, Lasker announced, "This is the first time

* The best studies of the brokerage crisis may be found in *Fortune*'s series of articles on the subject, especially those by Carol J. Loomis, which appeared in May and August of 1969, July and December of 1970, and January and March of 1971. Hurd Baruch, ***Wall Street: Security Risk*** (Washington, 1971), is a detailed study by the then-special counsel in the Division of Trading and Markets of the S.E.C. All subsequent accounts appear to be based, in large part, on the works of Loomis and Baruch. For a dramatic and lively overview of the entire period, see John Brooks, ***The Go-Go Years*** (New York, 1973). Also, Charles D. Ellis, ***The Second Crash*** (New York, 1973). Both attempt to compare 1970 with 1929, and Ellis claims that if Golsen hadn't agreed to the Hayden, Stone merger, the market would have crashed the next day. This does not take into account the powers of the government, especially with Nixon-friend Lasker on the telephones. Nor does it consider that there was hardly a panic atmosphere on Wall Street that September. On the other hand, one can never know about these things, and the question is certainly debatable—but incapable of resolution.

since August that we haven't had some kind of crisis facing us." Of course, Lasker was referring to ailing brokerage firms. The crisis in the industry itself was not over; the events of 1970 had served to dramatize them, and now the difficulties had to be confronted and reforms considered. Additionally, the brokerage crisis of 1970 had drawn attention away from the challenge of the Third Market, which continued into the new year and promised to be a long, difficult one for the Exchange.

WEEKLY CLOSING PRICES OF THE DOW INDUSTRIALS, 1970

January	2	809.20	*May*	1	733.63	*September*	4	771.15
	9	798.11		8	717.73		11	761.84
	16	782.60		15	702.22		18	758.49
	23	775.54		22	662.17		25	761.77
	30	744.06		29	700.44	*October*	2	766.16
February	6	752.77	*June*	5	695.03		9	768.69
	13	753.30		12	684.21		16	763.35
	20	757.47		19	720.43		23	759.38
	27	777.59		26	687.84		30	755.61
March	6	784.12	*July*	2	689.14	*November*	6	771.97
	13	772.11		10	700.10		13	759.79
	20	763.60		17	735.08		20	761.57
	26	791.05		24	730.22		27	781.35
April	3	791.18		31	734.12	*December*	4	816.06
	10	790.43	*August*	7	725.70		11	825.92
	17	775.94		14	710.84		18	822.77
	24	747.29		21	745.41		24	828.38
				28	765.81		31	838.92

SOURCE: *The Dow Jones Averages, 1885–1970*

It had been a traumatic experience. Never before had the leadership labored so long and as hard as it did in 1969–1970. Rarely had stock prices gyrated as wildly. The antiquated operations at the brokerage firms, which had been evident in the late 1960s, surfaced. As though in a gigantic whipsaw, volume increased and prices rose, forcing the houses to expand rapidly and unwisely. Then prices and volume fell, eroding reserves, piling inventory losses upon capital losses, and forcing many brokerages out of business. In the two years the Exchange intervened directly in the affairs of 200 member firms—more than half the number that dealt with the public—and indirectly in others. A total of 129 went out of business, merged, or were acquired. Through its various rescue operations, the N.Y.S.E. committed $75 million to protect customers and facilitate liquidations (an additional $15 million was set aside for possible use in the du Pont situation and $20 million for the Goodbody merger).

It was an impressive accomplishment and commitment, one in which Haack and Lasker could take pride. They had led the N.Y.S.E. through a period as difficult and significant as that of the early 1930s.

Had it been "another 1929"? Was this the long-feared crisis that would plunge the nation into an economic dark ages? Statistically, it would appear that it was. From May 26, 1970 to April 28, 1971, the Dow Industrials fell 319.66 points. At the peak of the bull market in 1929, the Dow was only 381.17. In other words, the bear market decline of the early 1970s was not far below the entire average after the bonanza years of the 1920s. Still, America was not in a panic situation in 1969 or 1970—nor would it be in 1971. Nor did depression stalk the land. Rather, there was a recession—a man-made one, created to combat inflation. Stocks plummeted in May 1970, brokerages failed in the autumn, and there was no sign of panic on either occasion. Indeed, the Dow actually gained close to 30 points for the year. Trading volume and daily activity were slightly higher in 1970 than they had been in 1969. In this respect, at least, there had been no crisis.

There were casualties, however. Glamor was gone from the market. The new issue mania had ended. No longer were amateur speculators rewarded for purchases of small electronics and space firms. Several high-flyers went bankrupt. Others would follow. The postwar generation's taste for adventure had been slaked. Brokerages were no longer crowded with the idle and curious, who watched the tape with zest and anticipation. In the words of George Goodman, who under the pseudonym of Adam Smith wrote the best-seller *The Money Game*, millions of investors and speculators learned that "The world is not the way they tell you it is." Mutual fund sales, which had been a record $2.1 billion in the first quarter of 1969 and had netted $6.7 billion for the year as a whole, declined to below $1 billion in the third quarter of 1970 and $4.6 billion for the year. Still, the institutions remained in the market as the "little guy" began to exit. In 1969, they accounted for 34.2 percent of the value of stocks traded at the Big Board and 22.4 percent of the volume. In 1971, as the debris was being cleared, institutions took 44.1 percent of stocks by value and 28.4 percent of the volume.

The growth of the institutions, their persistence in the face of difficulties, obliged the N.Y.S.E. to deal with such vexing problems as additional volume discounts, institutional memberships, and cooperation with other markets. These issues had to be faced, along with other difficulties that had been by-passed in the mid-1960s. The signs were there to see, in the kind of language N.Y.S.E. members understood. Brokerages had made profits in 1969, even when the back offices were clogged. They lost badly in 1970, when through mistakes and miscalculations they had expanded rather than contracted and guessed wrong on market movements. The specialists too were in difficulties, for their behavior during the May decline had been poor; as had been the case in 1962 and 1963, many had run for cover instead of stabilizing the market in their stocks. Specialists still made money—how much was a guarded secret, but the "informed guess" often quoted was around 20 percent on their investments—but not as much as before. It showed in the price of a N.Y.S.E. seat, which declined from a high of over a half million dollars in 1969 to $130,000 a year later.

The period of drift and bonanza had ended, to be replaced by one that featured harsh debate and questioning. The Big Board would be pushed and pulled, and obliged to come to terms with the new kinds of markets that were emerging and indeed already existed. Of course, it could have been worse. It could have been another 1929.

CHAPTER 17

NASDAQ

The differences between Haack and Lasker had been both masked and exacerbated during the crisis months of 1970. When it had appeared survival was in doubt, the two could and did cooperate with one another, and together were able to bring the Exchange to safety. At the same time, they had arrived at differing conclusions regarding the disease and its cure. Lasker still felt the Exchange was fundamentally sound and that only minor alterations in its structure were needed. These, along with good men and close rapport with Washington, would suffice to prevent a recurrence of the problems. Lasker wanted some form of federal insurance for clients, better surveillance, and higher standards, both at the commission houses and on the floor. Given these, all would be well. The Third Market and the regional exchanges would continue to exist, but the essential superiority of the N.Y.S.E. structure would show in the end. Even if it didn't, the Exchange could lobby for legislation against rival markets—not for its own sake, but in the public interest.

This was not an unreasonable or unusual position at the time. It was shared by a large majority of N.Y.S.E. members and had been expounded upon and enunciated by boards of governors, by Funston, and various N.Y.S.E. spokesmen before congressional committees and in public speeches for a decade. By late 1970, Lasker and others who thought like him felt vindicated. The N.Y.S.E. had, after all, survived. Member firm clients had either been reimbursed or would be in the future. When it had appeared panic would develop in May, President Nixon invited businessmen to Washington, spoke well of economic conditions, and prices recovered. The Federal Reserve had lowered both margin requirements and the discount rate afterward, and the prime rate followed. Then came recovery. Already legislation for a stockholders' protective insurance plan had been prepared, and the Exchange itself was moving ahead rapidly with reforms of its own. These and related matters, thought Lasker, would suffice.

Haack agreed that the commission firms would be stronger as a result of the mergers and other salvage operations. Higher standards, together with some form of insurance, would protect investors and go a long way toward restoring confidence. The specialist system would require strengthening; even Lasker conceded it had performed badly on occasion. As far as Haack was concerned, however, these were peripheral matters, made to appear more significant than they really were as a result of the crises. Of primary importance was the answer to a question, the same one thoughtful N.Y.S.E. members and students of Wall Street had asked in the late 1930s. Did the N.Y.S.E. fill a valid economic role? Mere survival was no answer, for if the Exchange continued to exist primarily to serve the interests of its members, then perhaps it indeed had become obsolete, as some of its critics maintained.

During the postwar period, as new kinds of investors had appeared and large institutions came to dominate trading, the Big Board had responded through various plans to handle large blocks on the floor. The regional exchanges had gone further, wooing the institutions even to the point of permitting them to purchase seats and trade for their own accounts. The appearance and growth of the Third Market was the clearest sign that there was, perhaps, a better way than the N.Y.S.E.'s auction method for institutional trading. Already there were plans to seek the business of small investors as well, and if this were done, could it still be said that the N.Y.S.E. was a vital organization, one which, if it vanished, would have to be replaced? Critics of the Third Market spoke of legislation to curb its activities. To Haack this kind of suggestion was a concession of defeat, an admission that without federal intervention the Third Market would continue to take N.Y.S.E. business—perhaps because it served the needs of its clients better.

The Big Board's defenders replied that this was not so, the proof being the loyalty of the commission houses. If the regionals and the Third Market sufficed, then the brokerages would have sold their N.Y.S.E. seats and transacted their business there. Clearly this had not happened. In response, critics noted that ties of custom, habit, and tradition, as well as personal friendship, worked in the Big Board's favor. So did the fact that the Third Market still lacked the technology to go with its techniques in trading large blocks. But the technological barrier was being overcome, and the ties could be rended. Given a lack of outside interference, they believed the N.Y.S.E. would decline and, perhaps, disappear, or at least no longer be the nation's primary marketplace for securities.

There was, however, one other factor which, even more than friendship and technology, bound the brokerage houses to the

N.Y.S.E.—fixed commissions. Although the Exchange had accepted volume discounts, the commission rates remained fixed, and at a point so as to assure decent profits for member firms. This served as an umbrella for marginal firms, and as an incentive for brokerages to trade at the Big Board rather than the Third Market. It also encouraged churning, commission splitting, and similar practices forbidden by the N.Y.S.E. but which took place nonetheless. Fixed commissions, of course, had been a hallmark of the N.Y.S.E. since its founding. Indeed, the organization's ancestor had begun in 1792 when a group of brokers, fearful of the effects of competition in commissions, banded together and agreed to fix rates in dealing among themselves. Do away with fixed commissions, said some students of the subject, and the costs of buying and selling stocks would come down, clients would be encouraged to trade more than they did, and the brokerages would make up the losses in volume. In addition, lower commissions would enable the Exchange to strengthen its position against the Third Market. Others, however, looked upon the idea as one which, if put into practice, would destroy the Exchange. Competition between commission houses would result in a raft of new failures, chaos, and switching of accounts as clients shopped for the best deals. Competitive commissions would decrease the value of Exchange membership, since with lower rates the brokerage houses' earnings would decline. In time they might even sell their seats and patronize rival markets. This, at least, was the N.Y.S.E. position during Department of Justice hearings on the subject in 1968. "Without some effective rate differential between members and nonmembers, the incentive to join the N.Y.S.E. —thus bringing trades to the N.Y.S.E. floor, and thereby contributing to the liquidity of the market—would quickly disappear. The entire complexion of the marketplace would change." *

For some, then, competitive commissions would mean the regeneration of the Exchange, while others believed that under such a system the market would be destroyed. Behind the scenes, it was known that Lasker and most of the board would not budge on the issue and that the chairman viewed fixed commissions as the *sine qua non* of the N.Y.S.E. When he arrived at the Big Board in 1967, Haack too believed in fixed commissions; indeed, had he not, the post would have gone to someone else. By 1969, however, he had begun having doubts, and these crystallized during the 1970 crises. Toward the end of the year, he appeared willing to precipitate a confrontation on all of these issues.

Perhaps it was the strain of the period, one in which the Exchange's leaders were under constant pressures from several sides and had to make decisions without concern for protocol. There had been

* New York Stock Exchange, *Economic Effects of Negotiated Rates on the Brokerage Industry, the Market for Corporate Securities and the Investing Public* (New York, 1968).

occasions when rules were broken and bent—the Special Fund had been used to save brokerage firms without going through the motions set down in the rules simply because there wasn't time to do so. Tension was an expected part of life, surprise and shock not at all unusual, and slack periods rare.

In early November, after having helped arrange the Goodbody takeover, Haack spoke publicly about the operation. Had it not succeeded, he told critics, "we would have had a panic the likes of which we have never seen."

Goodbody was the Exchange's fifth-largest commission house, and its collapse would have been a severe blow. The commitment of N.Y.S.E. reserves to guarantee a member firm was an unusual step and an issue that Haack might have felt uncomfortable with. But the crisis at Goodbody had occurred after the Exchange had rescued dozens of other firms, and one such operation—Hayden, Stone—had offered an even greater threat to the stability of the district at the time it surfaced.

The worst was over by early November. The situation was settling down. Stock prices had stabilized and were headed upward. Volume was good and there were signs of restored investor confidence. Mutual fund sales were up for the first time in a year, and portfolio managers were stirring. At the Exchange, board members and administrators congratulated one another on their performances; for the moment, at least, the divisions between Lasker and Haack were not evident in an atmosphere of relaxation and anticipation of Christmas bonuses.

Of course, the failure of a firm of the magnitude of Goodbody would have ended all this, but why speculate on the matter—especially at a time when the S.E.C. and the press were praising the Exchange and Merrill Lynch for their prompt and effective actions? What possible purpose could be served by Haack's statement? At the Exchange, it was said that the president had been under great stress and needed a vacation. Otherwise, he would not have spoken to reporters as he had. For although the Exchange would tolerate differences of opinion, discussions of touchy and basic problems, and even philosophical disputes such as those between Lasker and Haack, they were to be kept private. As far as the public was concerned, the Exchange would have one face, one voice, and one set of goals. Squabbles among the family were not to be aired in public. As president, Haack was to be that face and voice; he understood and accepted this, as had Funston, Schram, Martin, and Gay.

Haack had delivered several public addresses during the 1970 crises as well as published articles on the Exchange and its problems. In all of these he had defended current programs, giving little indication of differences with other members. There was, however, an undertone of impatience, of mild criticism, in some of them. "It has been said that the real purpose of self-regulation is to protect brokerage firms against themselves—and there is more than a grain of truth in that," he wrote in September. "But a side affect that cannot be overlooked is that self-regulation also helps firms to help themselves in ways that can earn and keep the confidence of their customers."

There had been a time when Haack might have awaited a blast from Manuel Cohen's office and then used it as a prod to move recalcitrant members to action. Hamer Budge was different, more placid. But the S.E.C. could block N.Y.S.E. plans even if it wouldn't insist upon reforms. In October, the Commission rejected the Big Board's proposal for increased rates, suggesting the moment had come to consider negotiated commissions and that further study of the subject would be made. This set the stage for Haack's confrontation with Lasker—and indeed most of the floor contingent. The commission question was important in itself, but it was also a symbol of significant philosophical differences at the Exchange.

Despite protestations to the contrary, most N.Y.S.E. specialists preferred to function in a protected monopoly, one in which rivals were eliminated, more often than not by a sympathetic government. True competition, they claimed, was not in the public interest. It would lead to chaos in the community, cut-throat tactics and the like, an end to liquidity in primary markets, and attract unsavory characters to the industry. The Exchange's critics responded that it was rather paradoxical for a citadel of free-enterprise ideology to demand an end to competition, and noted that the objections could be seen as a sign of weakness, an admission the N.Y.S.E. was an inferior market.

Haack took a third point of view. With modifications, the N.Y.S.E. would be a market superior to all others and so would triumph without federal intervention. He had hoped the membership would accept reforms. In late 1970, however, there was little chance of this. Perhaps due to fatigue, a sense of frustration, or reaction to S.E.C. attitudes, he decided to speak openly on the matter. The occasion was an address before the Economic Club of New York on November 17. It was rumored the president would toss a few "bombshells" in his speech and that they would be concerned, directly or indirectly, with the S.E.C.'s action. But few expected his speech to be as bold as it was. Later on, Haack was compared to Patrick Henry asking for liberty or death—but he knew all the while the latter would be his fate.

The speech was entitled "Competition and the Future." It was anticipated that Haack would offer the Exchange's views on the subject. This was not to be. "There is an old forensic principle that speeches should never begin with a disclaimer," he said. "At the risk of violating that counsel, let me say that the concerns, assertions and questions which I will pose are expressed by me as an individual and do not necessarily represent the views of the Board of Governors. The policies of the New York Stock Exchange can be made only by the board."

After a short defense of the Exchange's past, Haack noted that it had been losing its business to rival markets. "As recently as 1967, the regional exchanges and the Third Market combined to account for just over 10 percent of all trading in our listed stocks. Today they account for almost 20 percent. . . . Available data indicate a significant loss of block trades, with an estimated 35 percent to 45 percent of 10,000 shares or more traded away from the New York Stock Exchange." The reasons for this were evident, and the most important was "the presence of antiquated and unequal rules and the emergence of a new environment for trading in securities."

> The New York Stock Exchange, to put it crassly, no longer has the only game in town. The result has been a break in the similarity of interests between people engaged in floor activities, whose profitability depends on the share of business brought to our Exchange, and firms doing business with the public, who have become willing partners to fragmentation. For the fact is that most business is taken to regional exchanges by our own members.

This "fragmentation" of markets had been accelerated by reciprocal deals among brokers and dealers, and as had others, including Lasker, Haack spoke out against proliferation of markets which crippled liquidity, made for thin markets, and so caused prices to jump in untoward fashion. In so doing, he attacked directly those N.Y.S.E. members who engaged in such practices. "Our members, who will trade one New York commission for one and one-half or two commissions on another exchange, as well as people on the other side of the transaction, detract from the efficacy and liquidity of the central marketplace. The auction market functions best when it brings together the greatest number of buyers and sellers, enabling them to seek out the best price and the quickest execution." Yet this did not exist. Instead, "the securities industry, more than any other industry in America, engages in mazes of blatant gimmickry, all of which have been disclosed under oath at commission rate hearings. Deals are frequently involved, complicated, and bizarre and do no credit to the donor or beneficiary of the reciprocation."

How could the situation be rectified? At the hearings to which Haack referred, the S.E.C. suggested that commission rates on orders of more than $100,000 be negotiated. The Big Board was strongly opposed to the idea. It was here that Haack threw his bombshell, not only accepting the S.E.C. view but going beyond it.

> Notwithstanding my own previous personal and strong support of fixed minimum commissions, I believe that it now behooves our industry leaders to rethink their personal judgments on negotiated rates. While I question whether or not the industry is presently sufficiently strong financially to completely disregard fixed minimum rates, I personally think it might well consider *fully negotiated commissions as an ultimate objective* [emphasis added]. The initial emphasis might be placed on larger transactions, and certainly larger than amounts stipulated by the S.E.C. for a specified trial period. The results could be monitored and evaluated and subsequent action could then be determined. I have altered my own personal thinking as a result of the commission rate proceedings of the last two years and the fragmentation of markets that has simultaneously been increasing.

With understandable hyperbole, one of the audience called it "the most radical statement ever made by a N.Y.S.E. president," and afterward, another said that non–Wall Streeters would not comprehend its meaning. "It's as though Lyndon Johnson, sometime in 1969, came out against the decision to go into Vietnam."

Had Haack stopped at this point, his speech would have been deemed not only unusual but bold and adventuresome. But he went on, suggesting that negotiated commissions would resolve the problems of institutional memberships on stock exchanges and end a large amount of hypocrisy in the district. Haack next criticized members of his own organization, though at first in a mild fashion.

> I realize that opposition from some of my constituents can be expected because as members of the New York Stock Exchange, and under the present industry structure, they have the best of both worlds in that they are afforded the protection of the minimum commission schedule on trades on the New York Stock Exchange while they possess the ability to negotiate commissions in other marketplaces, and to trade with institutional members on regional stock exchanges to facilitate their recapture of commissions.

"Unless the New York Stock Exchange is willing to compete effectively with markets where commission fees are presently negotiated," he warned, "it faces a continued reduction in its share of overall trading, and at an accelerated pace." Thus, Haack indicated his belief that the Lasker approach lacked merit. Most of those in the audience understood this. But for those who did not, and for non–Wall Streeters, Haack pointed the finger at the board.

> Restructuring of the Exchange as an organization needs to go deeper than simplifying rules and regulations. The policy-making body of the Exchange, its Board of Governors, as well as the Exchange's voting and election procedures, should also be examined and restructured as necessary to meet the changing times in our industry. Whatever vestiges of a private club atmosphere remain at the New York Stock Exchange must be discarded. Understandable economic biases and fears of dislocation must not impede necessary changes, as they so often do, but must be fused and melded to accomplish desired objectives.

The term "private club" had of course been first used extensively by William O. Douglas and had been referred to by other New Deal critics of the N.Y.S.E. William Cary and Manuel Cohen had revived the term in the 1960s. Always it had been utilized to indicate scorn and criticism of a deep variety. Haack must have known this. Yet, he used it in his speech, as though throwing a red cape in front of a bull. He had given the board no option. Through word and deed, it would have to respond to the speech.

Clifford Mitchell, head of the Association of Stock Exchange Firms, told reporters, "Ninety-nine percent of the people I talk to are against [negotiated rates]." A member of the Association wondered whether Haack was guilty of treason or mutiny—or both. It was recalled that the president was a liberal Democrat and so was probably against big business anyway. William Salomon, managing partner of Salomon Brothers & Hutzler, a leading block-positioning firm, took another view. "Many of his suggestions would be good for the Street." Howard Stein, president of the Dreyfus Fund, remarked favorably on aspects of the address, though couching his comments in Wall Street banalities. "I don't necessarily agree with those suggestions, but they open the way for a meaningful dialogue on the issues." Lasker, the person at whom the address had been aimed, put an end to such talk. There would be no dialogue. For that matter, as far as he was concerned, Haack was finished at the Exchange. "The policy of the N.Y.S.E. is made by the Board of Governors, not the president," he told reporters. Robert Stott had said as much to Emil Schram, and John Coleman made certain Keith Funston understood. So did Haack. He knew what he had done.

Would there be an open confrontation between the two? Some

thought the speech would spark a debate, or at least a contest of wills. There was reason to believe Haack had some support on the board, and only a few days prior to his speech, Amex President Ralph Saul had said that methods of transacting business "conceived in other times and under other circumstances may no longer be adequate." A weaker statement than Haack's, to be sure, but one that was supportive of the N.Y.S.E. president. But Saul was master in his own house, the result of reforms made during the early 1960s and precedents set down by Etherington. Haack lacked power at the N.Y.S.E., and no board member spoke out in his favor. Even his sympathizers agreed that the president was the agent of the board.

There would be no doubt as to the outcome of a contest between Lasker and Haack. The president had lost the battle before entering the lists, and he knew it. The only matter to be decided was if he would be fired, resign, or serve out his term. The Exchange would not discard Haack—to do so would be to create a nasty situation. Nor would he resign, although Haack did spend more time at his Maryland home after the speech than before, and must have been glad he hadn't sold it. Rather, he would remain and, after his five-year contract was completed in 1972, announce his departure. The board would accept it with regret, give him a farewell dinner, and then find another, more amenable leader. Such was the decision. This was the way matters were handled on the Street. It was another thing upon which Lasker and Haack could agree.

Those sympathetic to Haack's position later claimed that he had sacrificed himself in order to precipitate an open debate on several key issues, believing that the membership would discuss such matters as negotiated commissions and, in the end, come to the same conclusions he had. If this were true, he failed, for the N.Y.S.E.'s leaders rejected his proposals outright, and with such vehemence as to discourage further talks. These men believed Haack was incorrect in his assessment of the market's structure and future and in any case wrong to have presented his views in so open a forum. It became fashionable to play down all of Haack's accomplishments, and in the process Keith Funston seemed to look better than ever. Comparing the Exchange's actions in two crises—1963 and 1970—Haack's detractors concluded he lacked nerve and judgment, and his Economic Club speech appeared to vindicate this.

Such conclusions were based more on emotional reactions than thoughtful reflection. The Ira Haupt scandal was a minor episode compared to the market collapse in May and the brokerage failures thereafter. Haack had led the Exchange into many areas of reform which even his critics conceded had been well planned and executed. The Central Certificate Service, initiated in 1969, had climaxed forty years of discussion but little action; Haack had made it possible. Together with Ralph Saul and others, he had been instrumental in the creation of the Banking and Securities Industry Committee (BASIC), among whose goals was the organization of an industry-wide clearing-house operation and the automation of back offices. Haack had not been the first to speak of the need for additional protection for investors; the Securities Investor Protection Act of 1970, signed into law in December, had been designed and pushed through Congress by Senator Edmund Muskie. But the Securities Investor Protection Corporation (SIPC) created under the act was endorsed by the N.Y.S.E., with Haack candidly admitting that the community had been remiss in its duties in the past, and in so acting made the best of a bad situation. Under his leadership and direction, the Exchange expanded its coverage of clients' accounts and established new surveillance procedures. Together with board members, Haack introduced and pushed through a series of rules that raised capital requirements for member firms, and when several could not comply with them, he helped arrange for mergers into larger, more viable companies.

There was no massive loss of confidence in Wall Street in 1970–1971, a further indication that the crisis of 1969–1970 had indeed not been another 1929. Part of the credit for this belonged to Haack. He remained the symbol of the N.Y.S.E. to the outside world and proved a good one for the period, demonstrating that the Exchange was not in the hands of the spiritual heirs of Richard Whitney. Thus, through his discussions of vital issues and apparent willingness to accept change, Haack helped fend off critics of the institution.

The president had participated in and at times led the Exchange in the creation of a stronger market. Paradoxically, this may have hastened his downfall. An unreconstructed N.Y.S.E. might have fallen to the enemy—both its rivals and reformers would have had ammunition to mount an attack. But a reformed market, which appeared to be emerging in the early 1970s, could maintain the battle and for a while at least repel the invaders. The N.Y.S.E. was strong enough to indicate that Haack's intimations of gloom and doom were untoward. At the same time, in the matters of the specialist system and negotiated commissions, it was sufficiently vulnerable to encourage its rivals.

Those who challenged the Exchange for its business increased in number and power. By 1970, the Big Board had to face not only the regional exchanges and the Third Market but a growing "Fourth Market," consisting of two new operations already in existence and others in the planning stage.

The oldest of these was AutEx, which began servicing clients in 1969 and within a year had 140 subscribers, 75 of which were institutions. Under this system, a subscriber might receive an order for a block of shares from one of its clients. He might then go to his AutEx keyboard and punch in the information, in effect asking other subscribers if they were interested in selling a specified amount of stock in the company. The message would be read on a television display, and then one or more of the clients might contact the broker, by telephone, through the network, or through a third broker so as to assure anonymity. From that point on, the deal would be transacted in much the same way as it was on the Third Market. By late 1970, AutEx claimed to be handling fifteen trades a day for an average of $5.2 million in business.

Institutional Networks Corporation, which began operations in March 1970, went a step further. Headed by a former stockbroker and a director of a computer time-sharing firm, it offered institutions an electronic network—known as Instanet—through which they could deal with one another on a partially automated basis. The first subscriber would punch his needs into the terminal—the stock he wished to buy or sell, the number of shares, and his code number. This information would be flashed to other subscribers who, if interested, would make their counteroffer in the same way. All the different parts of the transaction could be accomplished over the wire, with confidentiality assured. During its first half year in business, Instanet obtained thirty subscribers and claimed to have completed more than $75 million in business.

The N.Y.S.E. argued that Fourth Market firms like Instanet and AutEx would be harmful to the securities business. Not only would they drain business from the central market and so lessen liquidity but the operations were transacted under cover of anonymity and not in the open atmosphere the Exchange prided itself upon. Yet the appeal of such automated systems could not be denied; nor could the needs of large institutions be ignored. Because of this, the Exchange created the Block Automation System (BAS) which functioned in a manner similar to AutEx. BAS had 175 members—59 of which were institutions—by the end of 1970 and claimed an average of between eighteen and nineteen transactions a day. The fact that the N.Y.S.E. could present BAS at a time when it was fighting against institutional memberships indicated the difficulties it was facing in maintaining old forms in the light of a different kind of market.

Perhaps, given time, the Exchange could have expanded upon BAS, making it the focal point for the institutional market and in the end develop a hybrid specialist-dealer exchange that would satisfy most, if not all, of its member firms. Even then, however, the district knew that the Big Board lacked both time and determination to make such a commitment. And given the state of its finances, the money might not be available. In 1969, as part of its attempt to modernize, the Exchange appropriated $7.5 million for future automation projects, including expansion of the market-data system then in operation. At that time Bunker Ramo Corporation was spending more than $25 million on hardware and programming for NASDAQ, the major challenger to the N.Y.S.E.

As in the case of Instanet, NASDAQ (National Association of Securities Dealers Automated Quotation System) was the product of collaboration between stock market and technological personnel. The system, work on which had begun in the late 1960s, went into initial operation on February 5, 1971, providing information on 2,400 unlisted securities to more than 800 dealers. Some thought it was a variety of automated stock exchange for over-the-counter stocks, one which would eliminate the human factor, while others believed it was only a replacement for the telephone and typewriter. Even some of the managers in O-T-C houses installing NASDAQ were uncertain about its capabilities and future.

There were three "levels" to NASDAQ, and three different kinds of subscribers to the service. Level I enabled broker-dealers to obtain median bid and ask prices, which usually came through older systems such as Quotron. Level II subscribers received all bids and asks and were free to act upon them through the normal channels—the familiar telephone networks. Level III terminals received all the information in the system—bids and asks, the amounts of stock offered and requested, and the houses involved, as well as price and volume statistics for the day.

NASDAQ, which operated with few technological problems even in its shakedown period, was the classic example of how technology could change both the content and structure of an industry. Prior to NASDAQ, many commission brokers were somewhat reluctant to deal in over-the-counter issues. That market, they claimed, was unreliable. They would receive orders for stocks, call several broker-dealers for quotes, and then when they placed the orders discover the quotes had been withdrawn or changed. In most instances this was due to the time lag between the gathering of information and the placing of the order, but whatever the reason, the commission brokers preferred to deal in listed securities, which were easier to follow. Additionally, the brokers found that the "spreads"—the difference between the bid and ask price—of many issues were unusually large. They would be told that they could buy a stock at 20, and sell it at 19, a difference of a point, while the spread for a N.Y.S.E. stock in that price range would be a quarter of a point. Finally, a conscientious broker would call several market makers to get the best price for his client. This meant that he would have to spend more time on O-T-C trades than those at the N.Y.S.E.

NASDAQ changed this. The spreads became smaller as rival market makers competed with one another on the display. Information was easily obtained and reliable since records were kept. Significantly, the S.E.C. would be able to monitor NASDAQ through the displays, thus eliminating the N.Y.S.E. complaint that the O-T-C market was unmanageable, while the Big Board operated in full view of all. The system was fast, efficient, relatively inexpensive, flexible, and controllable. It did not function in such a manner as to replace the human element. A broker-dealer at the terminal, not a machine, made decisions to buy and sell.

N.Y.S.E. specialists who learned about NASDAQ through word of mouth were both impressed and scornful of the devices and the system and were not certain what to make of it. Some looked upon the new system as only a first step in eliminating the human factor, although they did not know how this would be done. The more optimistic spoke of not fighting technological advances but rather utilizing them to improve upon, and even strengthen, the specialist system. For example, the specialist in a stock would enter into his "book" all orders to buy and sell if they were above or below current quotations, along with the prices at which the trades were to be executed. His operations would then be based upon his "feel" for the market and the status of the book. Critics of the system argued that some specialists utilized their inside information regarding orders in an unfair fashion. If they saw a large number of sell orders at a certain price, for example, and they realized that the market was declining, they would sell from their inventory in order to avoid being hurt once the lower-priced orders were "set off." In this way, the specialist could actually manipulate the market to his own advantage.

With the exception of reneging on one's word, this was viewed as the most serious breach of conduct at the Exchange. Proof would be difficult, if not impossible, to assemble. But the introduction of an "electronic book" would end such charges, and NASDAQ sparked talk of this innovation. All orders would be placed in a computer, which would match bids and asks and perhaps even execute orders for limited amounts of stock. If and when trading threatened to get out of hand and go beyond prefixed limits, the specialist could step in and handle it on his own. Some thought an electronic book would be the salvation of the specialist system, while others were convinced that if developed and adopted, it would be the first step toward the system's elimination. The members were undecided on the issue, lacked information, could not even formulate limits for debate, and in the end deferred the concept, as NASDAQ's successes became apparent and its implications became clearer.

Among other things, NASDAQ made possible the collection of better and more complete data in shorter periods. The N.A.S.D. was able to provide newspapers with statistical information in time for early editions. In the spring of 1971, more newspapers carried O-T-C tables than ever before, and that market received a larger share of the financial page. By summer, the columns carrying news of Amex and O-T-C dealings would often have a headline indicating O-T-C activities, much to the chagrin of the Amex and trepidation at the Big Board. Then, on April 15, NASDAQ began carrying information and facilitating trades in a limited number of N.Y.S.E. issues, and the list expanded rapidly.

On November 1, NASDAQ began releasing volume figures, and the general public learned that the O-T-C market—in NASDAQ stocks alone—was larger than the Amex but far smaller than the N.Y.S.E. The National Clearing Corporation, the O-T-C's counterpart to the Exchange's clearing firm, went into operation at this time, and N.A.S.D. President Gordon S. Macklin announced plans for an upgrading of member firms. Within a year, average daily volume on NASDAQ was 8 million shares, more than the total for the Amex and regionals combined, though still far below the N.Y.S.E. figure. Given a few more years, however, and the continued expansion of the block market, the Third Market might yet surpass the Big Board. Already there were days when more shares in certain N.Y.S.E.–listed issues were traded at NASDAQ than at the Exchange. The Third Market had captured the imagination of the district—and the financial press corps—while the N.Y.S.E. appeared to be foundering, its leadership in transition and incapable of unified, effective response.

Many specialists spoke of government curbs on NASDAQ and, in any case, still did not think the O-T-C system better than their own. On their part, O-T-C leaders believed they would live to see the demise of the N.Y.S.E. as the central market. Large and powerful Third Market houses—Carl Marks & Co., First Boston Corp., New York Hanseatic, M.A. Schapiro, and Allen & Co.—had thrown down the gauntlet. Led by Weeden & Co., and Donald Weeden in particular, they became increasingly aggressive, and certain of the superiority of their way of trading. In 1970, Weeden and Schapiro challenged N.Y.S.E. Rule 394 (b) (the modification of Rule 394), charging that it "prevents a member firm from obtaining the best execution for its customer." Weeden was certain that if the customer's well-being were the sole criterion, the Third Market would triumph. He and others at the Third Market would litigate and lobby in their efforts to achieve victory. So would the leaders of the N.Y.S.E.

The struggle was waged in Washington, headquarters of both the S.E.C. and N.A.S.D., as well as Congress. Chairman Budge didn't seem to know how to handle the issue. But in 1971 he stepped down, to be replaced by William J. Casey, a colorful and erratic lawyer, businessman, and speculator—he described himself as a "venture capitalist." Once he had been charged with violations of the securities laws, and at the time of his selection he was still a contestant in a civil action. Casey was believed friendly to Big Board interests, but his movements were so rapid, and his ideas changed so often, that neither side could count upon him for long. As the N.Y.S.E. and the Third Market jockeyed for position at the S.E.C., the Commission was investigated by Congress to determine whether it had helped cause the 1968–1970 crises due to failures in enforcing laws and regulations. "Who cares about the financial crisis and all that stuff?" asked Casey. "That's all in the past. We've got more important things to think about." Still, the S.E.C. was not particularly effective in this period.

The issue at stake was both vital and complex: would the N.Y.S.E. or the Third Market be the leader in the exchange structure in America? There were those who believed the question was poorly formulated and that there was room for both organizations. But Weeden and Lasker would have disagreed; each was convinced his place of business was superior. Neither had the power to defeat the other without strong help from outside forces, and given the state of the S.E.C., allies would have to be found elsewhere. Congress, of course, was a key element in the struggle. Through legislation, the N.Y.S.E. could be obliged to accept competition, end specified practices and introduce new ones, and even come to terms with the Third Market. Or, under different circumstances, the Third Market could be legislated out of existence. If Congress refused to accept the responsibility for deciding the issue, it might be determined in the board rooms of the major commission firms, which belonged to both the N.Y.S.E. and NASDAQ. It might be said that Bache & Co.'s views were as important as those of Budge or Casey, while Donald Regan, chairman of Merrill Lynch, would have more to say about the determination of the issue than any senator or representative. Weeden understood this and based his campaign on it. Lasker, the chairman who felt most at home on the trading floor, also recognized that its power had faded during the 1950s and 1960s, while the commission houses grew stronger. NASDAQ merely confirmed the fact, topped it off, as it were.

There were men on the floor—Coleman and Stott, for example—who had lived through and adjusted to such changes in the past. During the 1920s, the real power was in the investment banks, where it had been since the days of J.P. Morgan. Major bankers, like Morgan, associated with emperors and Presidents; they would not deign to go to the floor, even for nonbusiness reasons, and certainly not to trade. Rather, they sent their associates there—highly paid employees—with the understanding that they were to make certain a good market existed for the new issues floated in the primary market, and the realization that no matter what the public view, the N.Y.S.E. was an exile from the main theater of operations. The bankers—Thomas Lamont of Morgan, Albert Wiggin of Chase, William Potter of Guaranty Trust, Seward Prosser of Bankers Trust, and others—were in control in 1929, while Richard Whitney and his kind, though far more famous, carried out their wishes, often as messenger boys.

The situation changed in the 1930s, one of the darkest periods in the history of investment banking. As the N.Y.S.E. lost business and was obliged to retrench, the power vacuum was filled by the specialists. The trading floor remained the symbol of finance capitalism, recognized as such by the mass of American people, but most of the securities legislation passed during the New Deal affected the commission firms and investment banks and not the specialist.

The inability of the S.E.C. to resolve the segregation issue in the mid-1930s was the crux of the matter. The Commission had hoped to separate the specialist's functions as a broker from his work as a dealer. When this effort collapsed, the specialists, as a group, emerged as the most powerful influence at the Exchange. The private traders had either fled due to losses or were circumscribed in their activities by the S.E.C. Similarly, the investment banks were restricted in their actions, both by economic circumstance and government.

But the specialists were relatively unscathed. After the reform effort had waned, they assumed power, cut back on waste and inefficiency, and dominated the floor. Though the members were no longer prosperous, they survived. In the process, the Exchange became more of a private club than it had been during the 1920s, since it existed to serve the interests of the members more than those of the public. How could it have been otherwise, given the low level of activity in the primary market and the increasing power of government in financing industry through such agencies as the R.F.C.?

This was the kind of Exchange that had to respond to the bull market of the 1950s, when volume expanded and prices rose. The great revival in business had occurred when many old-timers had despaired of ever again seeing another period of excitement and high profits. At first, the N.Y.S.E. did not know what to do. Then, under Funston, it sought new business. But the real power remained on the floor; just as Lamont and the others had utilized Whitney, so Coleman, Stott, and the major specialists viewed Funston as a spokesman, never a policy maker. Of course, he did his job well, but increasingly, the key element was the commission firm, through which the large institutions funneled their trades. Charles Merrill, the most important leader at the commission firms, often sounded like Funston, but in fact he represented a different constituency. Merrill traded at the Big Board because at the time it was the best place to transact business. Given a superior market, he might well go there. Funston encouraged Americans to invest, feeling certain that their trades would be executed at the Big Board. And for a while they did, with the specialists prospering.

By the late 1960s, however, the commission firms had found that on occasion they could obtain better prices at the regionals and the O-T-C than at the N.Y.S.E. The large institutional investors, increasingly important, pressured them to seek the lowest net price on buys and the highest on sells, threatening to purchase seats on the regionals and trade for themselves unless they did so. The N.Y.S.E. offered fixed commissions, which provided the brokerages with large profits on block sales—a margin big enough to enable the brokerages to make concessions of various kinds to clients and provide them with services that otherwise could not be afforded. Without fixed commissions, it was believed, the brokerages would leave the N.Y.S.E., selling their seats to trade at other markets. The fixed commission, then, was the glue that bound the brokerages to the specialists at the N.Y.S.E.—or at least, this was the accepted wisdom on the floor. This was why the N.Y.S.E. petitioned the S.E.C. for increased rates in 1970, and why the specialists viewed Haack as a traitor when he suggested the end of fixed rates.

What did the brokerages think about this? It depended upon whom you asked, for by that time the brokerage community was dividing into factions and specialties. Regan of Merrill Lynch was believed to be a key figure. He was chairman of the largest firm in the business, one that was entering other fields, as diverse as land development and the management of mutual funds, and on its way to becoming a multinational financial conglomerate. As such, it felt no particular loyalty to the N.Y.S.E. Merrill Lynch would trade in those markets where its interests were best served, as well as those of its large variety of customers. Some clients' needs would be met by the specialist system, and Regan wanted it to remain at the N.Y.S.E. "I think the notion that a battery of computers in Omaha, Nebraska, perhaps vaguely resembling the computers that now constitute the Strategic Air Command, replacing the floor of the Exchange, is a bit far out. The specialist on some floor somewhere, despite his current fears, will in my judgment still have an essential role to play in the transaction process." Regan also believed in the virtues of competition—because, as cynics observed, Merrill Lynch could destroy its rivals in the brokerage business if allowed to do so. In his 1971 book *A View from the Street*,

Regan wrote that "the most important regulator of all is competition. At present, Wall Street is hiding behind a protective pricing system, while it preaches free competition and free markets. . . . We live as exceptions to our own rules." And two years later, in February 1973, Regan explained that "Fixed commissions are one of the causes of trades leaving the N.Y.S.E. and going to the Third Market. . . . [C]ontinuing fixed rates will make it more difficult for member firms to compete with Third Market makers." This did not mean, however, that Merrill Lynch would shift business to the N.Y.S.E. if it went to negotiated commissions. Then, as before, it would trade in the market where its interests would best be served—in effect, continually playing one off against the others. He did not claim to know what the end result would be. "Two separate systems, especially when they deal in the same securities, cannot exist side by side unless the regulatory hand is equal for both," he wrote, and so the S.E.C. would have to take a stronger role in the district than it had in the past, and the N.Y.S.E. cooperate with the regulators. Would this solve the matter? Regan still had no programmatic suggestions to make. "There is no assurance that all else will fall into place if it does come; but it is certain that nothing will fall into place without it." *

In 1969, chairman of the N.Y.S.E. Gustave Levy was strongly opposed to negotiated commissions. Speaking before a congressional committee, he said that Goldman, Sachs would leave the Exchange if and when they came about. Two years later he felt differently. "We'll go along with negotiated rates," he said. "We're flexible." And in any case, "the exchange probably would have done it anyhow." When reminded of his earlier statement, Levy smiled. "That's all passé now."

Levy was an urbane individual, not given to public outbursts or talking off the cuff. In 1969, when speaking for the N.Y.S.E., he favored fixed commissions. Without them, he said, many firms—perhaps his own—would leave the Exchange, and this would damage liquidity at the central market, cripple the specialist system, and hinder the processes of self-regulation. As head of Goldman, Sachs he took a different point of view. Like Regan, he would trade at those markets where he could obtain the best deal.

The firms that specialized in dealing in large blocks—by 1971 known as "block positioners," and including Salomon Brothers, Shields & Co., Oppenheimer, and Bear Sterns, as well as Goldman, Sachs—tended to view the N.Y.S.E. as a convenience. They would be contacted by a client who wished to buy or sell a large block of stock. Then the brokerage would attempt to "position" it, contacting other institutions that might be interested. When the block or a large part of

* Donald Regan, *A View from the Street* (New York, 1971), pp. 170, 176–77.

it was accounted for, the positioner would bring the trade to the N.Y.S.E. floor and cross the transaction there. In such a case, the N.Y.S.E. provided little more than a place to do business, a location for a deal that could just as well have been executed elsewhere. These firms, along with the diversified giants like Merrill Lynch, would have preferred to see the death of all varieties of Rule 394 and conduct business in the best location for each trade, with no thought to liquidity or the N.Y.S.E.'s insistence on a goldfish bowl atmosphere. They sympathized with Weeden, though of course they could not indicate as much openly, for to do so would be to endanger good relations at the Big Board unnecessarily. In any event, the Third Market's leaders were doing well without their support. Still, the message was clear. When a former chairman of the Big Board could take such a casual attitude toward fixed commissions, it was a sign of drastic change on the Street.

Some N.Y.S.E. spokesmen knew that firms like Merrill Lynch and Goldman, Sachs were capable of charting their own courses and acting with few allies. Too, the Big Board needed the large commission houses more than they required the services of the trading floor. Fixed commissions, set high enough to assure good profits, would help the smaller firms which had minor large block business and did little or no underwriting. Such firms serviced the small investor more than they did the large institutional ones. These were the firms closely allied to the N.Y.S.E., to whom commissions were of vital importance, and the board worked for their interests. Ironically, the N.Y.S.E.—still the symbol for huge enterprise in the minds of most Americans—was acting for the concerns of relatively middle-sized and even small units, while the Third Market and firms of the magnitude of Merrill Lynch and Goldman, Sachs spoke of the virtues of competition in accents not unlike those of Donald Weeden.

In a marketplace where the big were increasingly shoving aside the small, it would appear that the N.Y.S.E. was on the losing side—that the men who had helped the Exchange survive in the 1930s through the introduction of a new kind of market had failed to adapt themselves to the dispensation of the 1960s and early 1970s. Of course, the N.Y.S.E. would continue, but in what form, to what degree? How far did the Third Market's reach extend? It was known that NASDAQ already had the capacity to execute orders as well as provide information to market makers. In periods of stress, such as that of 1969–1970, that market might outperform the specialist system, drawing trades in large numbers from a superheated Big Board. In time, large corporations might not seek N.Y.S.E. listing, considering it unnecessary to assure the marketability of their shares. One N.A.S.D. official, speaking to a *Wall Street Journal* reporter in late 1971 remarked, "Where do the exchanges get their listings? Suppose the over-the-counter market gets so perfected in its handling of transactions that it is just as good as that of the exchanges. Corporations, in thinking about getting listed on exchanges, wouldn't be trading a primitive market [O-T-C] for an automated market [N.Y.S.E.] as they do now, but would have to ask themselves whether it's worthwhile to trade one automated market for another automated market." * The implication was that by then NASDAQ methods would be superior to anything the N.Y.S.E. could develop, especially if they contained, in one form or another, the specialist system.

The initial implications of NASDAQ were comprehended in 1970, and the following year some Wall Streeters, guilty perhaps of overly active imaginations, wondered whether it was an opening wedge for an even more ambitious undertaking, the creation of a nexus between the first and third markets. Already several major Third Market firms were deeply involved in investment banking. First Boston, one of the oldest and most prominent underwriters, was then a Third Market firm. So was Blyth, an old-line house that had to sell its N.Y.S.E. seats when it was taken over by another corporation. Weeden was in the field, and additional ones were entering in force. The underwriting of new issues was more profitable than trading in old, and the entries were deemed natural.

The Third Market houses competed with N.Y.S.E. members for business, and also with one another. This was to be expected and was an aspect of the industry. At the same time, they were part of a powerful community, one which did not include the Big Board's specialists. If the second market—the exchanges—existed primarily to provide liquidity for the first, and Third Market firms were becoming more influential in that market, where did it leave the N.Y.S.E.? Might not a Third Market firm become the leading investment banker for an N.Y.S.E.–listed company at some time in the future and convince it to relinquish its listing? If this happened, what would follow? The implication was that eventually the Third Market could replace the N.Y.S.E. as the focus of the industry.

Such an idea was not taken seriously in 1971. But a decade earlier, few believed that NASDAQ would ever become operational. And there was another disquieting development. Late in the year, several Third Market–related brokerages appeared, offering to buy and sell listed securities for small investors at commissions lower than those charged by N.Y.S.E. houses.

Meanwhile, the S.E.C. pressed ahead with plans for negotiated commissions. Casey had proved far more vigorous than he had

* *Wall Street Journal*, October 12, 1971.

originally appeared and also less sympathetic to Big Board desires than anticipated. Having lost allies at the major commission firms, being weakened down the line in Washington and New York, and threatened with antitrust suits unless large institutions were admitted to membership, the N.Y.S.E. made a tactical retreat. It would accede to negotiated rates on a trial basis, with the understanding they would be phased in over a period of years with constant reviews by all concerned. Also, the Big Board wanted to link this agreement with the admission of institutions to membership. Then the large investment houses would patronize the BAS rather than NASDAQ. If the major commission firms would not stand with the specialists, the latter would seek new allies—and profits—among the institutions. In the end, however, this plan was dropped.

The S.E.C. decided that negotiated commissions on trades of over $500,000 would begin on April 1, 1971, and that the figure would be lowered in stages, with fully negotiated rates in effect by the spring of 1975. Thus, the N.Y.S.E. would have four years during which to fight the system, to defeat the Third Market in one way or another. At the time it was believed that unless this was done, fully negotiated commissions would mark the beginning of the end for N.Y.S.E. dominance in the nation's market structure. As it was, some firms were fearful of negotiations, even at high-level trades.

When the day arrived, quite a few members appeared confused. Jay Perry, in charge of Salomon's block-trading department, said, "I've just never seen such chaos down here." Loeb, Rhoades & Co. refused to negotiate rates for a while and lost orders as a result. Then that firm, like the rest, came around. The first shot in the revolution had been fired and there were no real casualties yet.

The commission-rate hearings had opened in 1968. For three years the N.Y.S.E. and the Third Market had struggled over the issue. By 1971, the contest had ended. Given Casey's earlier record, the Big Board hoped for his friendship in the future. A new battleground had to be found, however, and Capitol Hill appeared the likely location. Having fought the Third Market for support of the large brokerages and in the technological area, and having failed in both, the N.Y.S.E. would seek legislation either to destroy its rival or at least limit its growth. The Subcommittee on Securities of the Committee on Banking, Housing and Urban Affairs of the Senate would be the main arena, but its actions and decisions would be molded elsewhere.

The Lasker-Nixon connection was still strong; the Administration was deemed sympathetic to the N.Y.S.E. and, in any case, would want Lasker's help in raising funds for the 1972 election. If the President won a strong victory and in the process helped elect a Republican House and returned a strong G.O.P. contingent to the Senate, the Big

Board would benefit. Otherwise, so the reasoning went, antibusiness Democrats would be encouraged to mount an offensive against Wall Street, and given the symbolism of the times, the Big Board would be one of their prime targets. In part, at least, the fate of the district could be found in that of the Nixon Presidency.

The groundwork for this phase of the struggle was laid in 1970, when the Exchange asked outgoing Federal Reserve Chairman William McChesney Martin to prepare a study of the nation's markets and make recommendations for their futures. By that time Martin was a man widely respected for his integrity and knowledge of finance; the once boy-wonder president of the N.Y.S.E. had emerged as a giant figure whose judgments were taken seriously even by those who opposed his increasingly conservative views on a wide variety of subjects. Martin accepted the assignment, and began work in early 1971. The *Martin Report*, as it was called, was released on August 6 and immediately became a key document in the N.Y.S.E.–Third Market debate.

Most of the recommendations dealt with technical matters. Martin believed the N.Y.S.E. should broaden representation on the board, for example, and that brokers should not be permitted to manage mutual and closed-end investment trusts. He also opposed institutional membership on stock exchanges and would specifically exclude banks and insurance companies. On three key issues, however, he came down squarely on the side of the N.Y.S.E. Martin was strongly opposed to negotiated, variable commission rates, which he believed would lead to the destruction of many small firms. "An abrupt change to fully negotiated rates would be imprudent at a time when the industry needs continued earnings to accumulate and attract capital," he said. "The experiment now under way with negotiated commissions on transactions above $500,000 requires experience and analysis before the Securities and Exchange Commission and the exchanges proceed further." He also favored the specialist system over the procedures employed at the Third Market. "There has been a great deal of criticism of the role and function of specialists. However, no better system of maintaining a continuous and responsible market has been suggested. The capital resources of specialists, however, should be increased to meet the requirements of today's trading, and methods should be developed to encourage and enable specialists to improve performance of their functions in instances where securities are offered in unusually large volume."

Finally, Martin wrote of the need for a centralized stock exchange system. This did not mean the unification of all exchanges but rather cooperation between them. For example, "consolidation of certain computer facilities of the New York Stock Exchange and the

American Stock Exchange will provide maximum economy in their use." There would even be a "consolidated tape," by which was meant that the Big Board ticker would report all transactions on all exchanges—even those at rival markets.

This was the crux of the issue. Martin hoped for a strong O-T-C but favored the elimination of the Third Market. As he saw it, the over-the-counter traders would continue to deal in unlisted securities, but once they were accepted for listing on an exchange, all trading elsewhere would cease.

No one familiar with Martin's career as president of the N.Y.S.E. more than three decades before should have been surprised by the report. He had said it all then and apparently hadn't changed his mind. Critics charged him with possessing an ossified brain; defenders noted that consistency is a key element in integrity, a quality with which Martin had always been associated. In any case, the time bomb triggered in 1940 went off in 1971.

The regional exchanges and the Third Market were deeply critical of many aspects of the *Martin Report*, as were the large institutions that traded there. If all three of the Martin proposals were adopted, the Big Board would emerge with a clear-cut victory. Donald Weeden recognized this. "We're naturally disturbed by any report that calls for our elimination." Actually, Weeden & Co. and other Third Market firms would not be destroyed but instead be obliged to purchase Big Board seats and transact business in listed securities at Wall and Broad. Kenneth Foster, president of Prudential Insurance Co., noted that "The regional exchange is our one little out. We don't want to lose it."

Five months before the release of the *Martin Report*, on March 10, 1971, the S.E.C. published its *Institutional Investor Study Report*, which had come to a different set of conclusions. In the first place, the S.E.C. study favored variable rates. Next, the S.E.C., in principle, believed that the more market makers that existed for any stock, the better the public interest would be served.

> The participation of competing dealers in the central market will . . . reduce the element of monopoly power which has accompanied past efforts to establish a central market and will make it possible for potential abuses of such monopoly power to be controlled not only by regulation but to an increasing degree by competition. An essential characteristic of such a system would be the prompt reporting of all securities trades to the public on a comparable basis.*

* United States, Securities and Exchange Commission, *Institutional Investor Study Report*, House Doc. No. 92-64 (Washington, 1971), Vol. 1, pp. ix–xii.

Finally, the S.E.C. advocated the creation of "a strong central market system . . . to which all investors have access, in which all qualified broker-dealers and existing market institutions may participate in accordance with their respective capabilities, and which is controlled not only by appropriate regulation but also by the forces of competition. . . ."

The S.E.C.'s stress on competition was quite different from the *Martin Report*'s advocacy of the elimination of competition. Donald E. Farrar, who had directed the preparation of the *Institutional Investor Study Report*, noted that Martin had always said as much and favored the N.Y.S.E. becoming the sole major market in America. In 1941, for example, he had spoken out against the trading of N.Y.S.E.–listed stocks on the regionals, an effort that was defeated in the Multiple Trading Case. Thirty years later, he was attempting to do the same to the Third Market.*

Several S.E.C. staffers were highly critical of Martin, whose dislike of the O-T-C markets had been well known. Not only should he have refused to accept the assignment because of his biases, they thought, but having agreed to study the issues, Martin had come up with an implausible document—one the S.E.C. members considered far inferior to their own. "The initial reaction around here is a bit of disappointment that it is such a poorly prepared study from a man of such stature as Martin," said one official, while another thought the quality of the document was unimportant since it would soon be forgotten. "The immediate reaction of the powers—that they are going to study the study—is completely in keeping with past patterns. We're all a bit skeptical." Policy was made by the chairman, however, and not the staff. Casey appeared pleased with the *Martin Report*, even though he still favored negotiated rates.

It was a difficult period for the Commission. Under the New Deal, the S.E.C. had been a mover and shaker in the district, sometimes forcing it to accept reforms. Then, for more than twenty years, the Commission played the role of policeman, and a rather ineffectual one at that. With the coming of Cary and Cohen, the reform sentiment was stirred. Budge and Casey were not activists, but the staff had become zealous and was hard to control. Until the S.E.C. had a different chairman, however, it would tread water.

The N.Y.S.E. was delighted with the report. Such a document, from so eminent a man, would certainly be studied in Congress. If the *Martin Report* was adopted *in toto,* the Third Market would be eliminated and the Big Board would emerge more powerful than ever before—the culmination of Martin's 1940 ambitions and 1971 study.

* Donald E. Farrar, "Implications of the Martin Report," *Financial Analysts Journal* (Vol. 27, No. 5, September/October 1971), pp. 14–15.

As though to indicate cooperation, the board set about reordering the Exchange's government, combining the offices of president and chairman; no longer would there be any question as to who had power or spoke for the N.Y.S.E. The board's membership would be reduced from thirty-three to twenty, with ten "inside" directors and ten from outside the industry. Steps were initiated to implement Martin's recommendations regarding the strength of specialist units. After a decade of searching for a means to combat the Third Market, the N.Y.S.E. affixed itself to the *Martin Report*, which would become its agenda for reform and its program for action.

At the Amex, President Paul Kolton watched developments warily. A former N.Y.S.E. executive himself and a veteran of the Street, Kolton understood the terms of the conflict and the stakes. Historically, the Amex had allied itself with the Big Board in all matters involving a common front against outsiders. Yet in recent years, the A.S.E. had become more independent, often prodding the N.Y.S.E. into action and leading it into change. On this occasion, however, Kolton joined with the Big Board. Noting that under the provisions of the report the Amex would remain separate, though closely allied with the N.Y.S.E., he hoped to maintain his exchange's individuality while at the same time obtaining the best deal possible in any new system that might evolve.

Former Amex President Ralph Saul, then a vice-president at First Boston, thought that "Martin's recommendations on the composition of the governing board would go a long way to making the exchange the quasi-public institution it should be." Clearly an ambitious man, Saul was believed interested in becoming the first chairman of the N.Y.S.E. under the new dispensation. For that matter, Kolton, who had already won the respect of the district for his abilities at the Amex, was also being discussed as a possible "czar."

There was some support for Martin, too. But the former N.Y.S.E. and F.R.B. head was never interested in the position, and any chance he might be drafted for it died when his report became an object of criticism by S.E.C. and Third Market personnel and spokesmen.

Meanwhile, Robert Haack, the forgotten leader, served out the rest of his term in relative silence. On taking office in 1968, he had said, "My job is to move these people into the twenty-first century." The Exchange was finally moving, but not in the direction he thought it would. The N.Y.S.E. had problems and no policy in 1968. The problems were not as serious in 1971, due in part to Haack's work, and a policy and strategy had been evolved, not of his making.

In late October, to no one's surprise, Haack announced he would step down as president when his term expired in 1972.

CHAPTER 18

Into the Chrysalis

In 1971, as the debris of the brokerage house collapses was being cleared, Wall Street leaders discussed several plans regarding the future of the district. There were those who thought the Big Board, once reformed and automated, would continue to dominate the market structure. On the opposite side was a handful of Third Market enthusiasts who were equally convinced that given the proper breaks and a fair contest their method of trading would, in some ways, supplant the specialist system. The regionals walked a tightrope. They had done well by providing a location where the Third Market firms could cross trades with institutions and even N.Y.S.E. members, and they didn't want to lose that business. At the same time, their leaders saw no gain to be had in angering the N.Y.S.E.'s top firms. Some optimists believed a merger of kinds could be worked out, and there were a few who wanted a knock-down-drag-out contest between the competing systems, with the victor taking the spoils. At that time, however, most conclusions were based more upon emotion and old loyalties than careful analysis and a long-range concept of self-interest.

Conditions changed rapidly during the next two years, and ideas evolved at a surprising pace. Such documents as the *Institutional Investor Study Report* and the *Martin Report*, as well as heated debates and discussions throughout the district and in Washington, had resulted in agreements between rivals on the one hand and sharpened differences on the other.

The N.Y.S.E., with the *Martin Report* as both its holy writ and guide, favored a single, centralized marketplace from which competition would be excluded through a variety of devices. Under such a system, it would dominate the regionals, maintain its power over the Amex, and eliminate the Third Market.

Several Third Market leaders developed a rival approach, one based upon sections of the *Institutional Investor Study Report*, which they molded to their needs. They favored a variety of unified market, one which would provide economic benefits to those who utilized it and at the same time do away with some of the objections to the Third Market. Under their plan, both their market and the N.Y.S.E. would be permitted to trade in whatever securities they accepted and would compete with one another for business. All transactions would be reported on a unified tape, to be developed by a committee consisting of members of all markets. Thus, the Third Market would continue to compete with the Big Board, but the arena would be clearly defined—not quite the goldfish bowl atmosphere talked of at the N.Y.S.E., but close enough, with the S.E.C. at hand to make certain the laws were observed.

In these ways, both major systems accepted the idea of a unified marketplace, the difference between them being that the N.Y.S.E. wanted to eliminate competition and the Third Market to retain it.

Generally speaking, the S.E.C.'s professional staff was closer to the Third Market concept than it was to that put forth by the N.Y.S.E. Given two structures competing with one another in terms of efficiency, service, and liquidity, the public interest would be served. Such a compromise would combine the benefits of size with those of rivalry.

Not all S.E.C. members felt that way, however. One of the commissioners, James Needham, had a plan of his own, a variation of the N.Y.S.E. proposal which appealed to the Exchange's leaders. Under the direction of the Commission, he said, all exchanges would be united into a single structure, a new stock corporation. "The shares of the new corporation would be issued to all members of exchanges *pro rata* based on the reflective values of their seats. Simultaneously, the existing exchange organizations would transfer their net assets and operational and self-regulatory responsibilities to the new corporation and go out of existence." In this way, the N.Y.S.E. would lose its identity, join with the regionals and the Amex, and so become part of a larger structure, one that might be called "the United States Stock Exchange."

The N.A.S.D. would become the focal point for a second part of the system. It too would organize a market, which might well be based upon NASDAQ, as the exchanges would utilize the specialists. In the end, the nation would have two markets under a single rubric. Each would compete with the other for listings, with the S.E.C. making certain the rules were obeyed. Most importantly, under the Needham plan each market would have its own list of securities; there would be no competition between them.

> Each market will have the right to determine whether to trade a security. However, it will be up to the issuer of the security to

> determine in which market the security will be traded exclusively. This decision should be left to the issuer because it is an important property right. Further, this procedure will create much-needed competition in applying such shareholder services as transfer facilities, mailing of shareholder reports, and payment of dividends as well as in the market-making function. Both market systems will be fully automated.*

Behind the rhetoric of competition, Needham would give the N.Y.S.E. all it desired. If his plan were accepted, the N.Y.S.E. would retain its list and the Third Market traders would be banned from dealing in those issues. What Needham had done was to take the language of reform and competition and combine it skillfully with the essence of the N.Y.S.E.'s position. It was a masterful job, one that was noted with approval at the Big Board.

It was against this backdrop that the N.Y.S.E. sought its first leader under the new dispensation. Outgoing chairman Ralph DeNunzio, a force at the commission firms and a moderate, was considered a possibility, but immediately took himself out of the running. So did Saul and Kolton. All knew that the new chairman would have to be a person with important political connections and demonstrated abilities at swaying legislators. Given the anticipated Nixon victory in November, he should also be close to the President and able to influence him on the Exchange's behalf. S.E.C. Chairman Casey should recognize this and so should his successors. The new chairman's major task would be to make certain Congress passed a measure to create a centralized exchange system that excluded the Third Market and to work with the S.E.C. to assure the elimination of that rival. Men from the Street—like Saul, Kolton, and DeNunzio—were mentioned more out of courtesy than anything else; they understood this, and so did the press corps.

By late spring and early summer, the list was rumored to have narrowed to those members of the Nixon Cabinet who had indicated a desire to leave government after Election Day. Former Secretary of Commerce Maurice Stans, active at the Committee to Re-elect the President, was high on the list, as was Secretary of State William Rogers. In early July knowledgeable Wall Streeters were sure the chairmanship would go to Secretary of Defense Melvin Laird, and it appears Laird was sounded out and said he didn't want to go to Wall Street. Others may also have been contacted—the "rumor list" was long, as it always is under such circumstances. And almost all the names on it were prominent political figures. So it came as a surprise

* "The Mood of Reform at the New Big Board," *Business Week* (No. 2196, April 3, 1971), p. 59.

when, in mid-July, the Exchange announced that James Needham had been offered the post and had accepted.

Although hardly considered a top candidate for the position, Needham was a known quality and quantity, a man with whom the Exchange's leaders could feel comfortable, and who knew his way around Washington. Those close to him at the S.E.C. considered him intelligent, quick, and with a keen sense of what constituted good public relations. He was also flamboyant and aggressive, but lacked the kind of subtlety and diplomatic skills it had been felt the next chairman should possess. Needham had a facile mind and was being placed in a newly created position in order to deal with unprecedented problems and choices. When his predecessors—Martin, Schram, Funston, and even Haack—had taken office, the Wall Street news corps had a good idea of why and how they had been selected, could even predict their behavior in office, and knew the problems they had to face and their approaches to them. The situation was not as clear with Needham, and so the prognostications were more guarded than might have been expected.

This was not to say that Needham was devious, for he met often with the press and testified candidly before congressional committees. Those who opposed him conceded that he was an honest and open man, one with a high degree of integrity. His major faults, they said, were an overly developed sense of ambition and an undeveloped ability to differentiate between pragmatism and expediency. Needham would do all within his power to assure the ultimate victory of the N.Y.S.E., and he had the abilities to develop a strategy, mobilize his forces, conduct tactical advances and retreats, and deal intelligently with both allies and opponents. This was what the N.Y.S.E. wanted, and what it got.

A medium-sized, somewhat stocky, handsome man, Needham had played football at Cornell while majoring in accounting. His early career was not particularly distinguished, although Needham did well financially and had a minor reputation in the profession. In 1969, at the age of forty-two, he was the partner in charge of the New York office of A. M. Pullen & Co., a North Carolina accounting firm, and a member of the governing council of the American Institute of Certified Public Accountants. Considered an expert in the area of auditing, and having written and spoken of problems of standards, he was believed interested in rising at the AICPA and eventually heading the organization. That seemed to be the limit of his ambition at the time.

President Nixon had inherited a reformist, activist S.E.C., and had pledged during the campaign to take government "off the back" of Wall Street. Seeking a conservative-to-moderate appointee to the

Commission, and wanting an accountant to balance the preponderant number of lawyers, Nixon asked Secretary of Commerce Stans, himself an accountant, for suggestions, and Stans took the problem to Len Savoie, the AICPA's executive director. It was Savoie who recommended Needham for the position, one which he accepted.

Needham did not get along well with the S.E.C. staff; the conservative accountant might have expected to be out of place among so many liberal lawyers. He tended to distrust "lawyers and their legalistic solutions to business problems," while many on the staff viewed Needham as shallow and opportunistic. "Needham has an absolute blind spot when it comes to comprehending the legal obligations of people who manage other people's money," said one. "And this blind spot is colored by antipathy to the entire notion of regulation." Needham's defenders replied that he antagonized the staff because he held different views on certain parts of the *Institutional Investor Study Report* and believed both in self-regulation and the virtues of a central market for listed securities.

To be sure, Needham's unpopularity at the S.E.C. served him well at the N.Y.S.E., as did his proposals regarding the future of the industry. When he was named to the chairmanship, some of his former colleagues charged him with selling out in order to obtain the job. An S.E.C. commissioner received a salary of $38,000; the N.Y.S.E. chairmanship paid $200,000 per year with an additional $100,000 for expenses, and Needham had a five-year contract. This was not so; nor, for that matter, was the accusation that he had actively campaigned for the position. Rather, Needham's views throughout his career had been of the type preferred by the N.Y.S.E.'s leadership. They picked the man; he didn't select the job.

The choice was well received in the district. DeNunzio told reporters, "We've crossed the bridge from the old Exchange to the new. Jim's knowledge and the Exchange's new public thrust will give the Exchange the momentum to become the hub of the central market system of the 1970s and 1980s." "Needham knows the capital and operational problems of the industry," said Robert Gardner, president of Reynolds Securities, and William Martin made one of his rare passes at humor, remarking, "Goodness knows that industry needs accounting." A. Jones Yorke, one of the new chairman's few close supporters at the S.E.C., believed the selection was excellent. "It's important that a man like Needham can bring pure business management expertise to the vast reorganization going on now."

Needham realized he had not been the first choice for the position but was certain that he was at least as qualified as any other person considered. During his first months in office he publicized the Exchange in a fashion not unlike that of Funston, holding meetings in various cities and making an overseas trip, as though negotiating for the financial community with foreign powers. He conducted regular press conferences, and although Needham did not win fast friends from among the Wall Street news corps, he was respected and his word believed. At the same time, he led an effective lobbying campaign in Washington for the Big Board. As far as the N.Y.S.E. was concerned, he combined the ideology of a Keith Funston with the knowledge of a William Martin. By the end of the year, the Exchange—Needham insisted it be referred to by that name, as though there were no other—congratulated itself on having selected the right man, even though he had come to the position somewhat by happenstance. Needham, for his part, clearly was enjoying himself and was confident of success. When, during a Chicago address, a bell sounded by mistake, he joked that "this isn't the Major Bowes Amateur Hour. I've got some time left. I'll be here another ten years." Thus, he assumed, and with good reason, that his contract would be renewed in 1977—and by then there would be some form of U.S.S.E. for him to direct.*

During the late 1960s and into the 1970s, the N.Y.S.E. had appeared confused and indecisive. It had misunderstood the technological issues involved in its contest with the Third Market, miscalculated the impact of institutions upon trading and markets, and waited too long to initiate reforms—and when the Exchange did change, it often did so in the wrong ways. When Haack tried to sway the Establishment in the direction of change, it balked; he wanted to go too far, thought the floor leadership and a majority on the Board. Haack appeared to threaten their basic beliefs, and he even utilized the rhetoric of the S.E.C. in his criticisms. But his analyses of the problems were sound, though his proposed responses were unacceptable at the time they were presented and even after he left the Street.

Conditions were different by 1973. The *Martin Report* had provided the Big Board with a program and approach with which to attack the Third Market, one that could be legislated into existence and enforced by government agencies. In Needham the Exchange had found the right man to lead it in New York and Washington. At Haack's farewell dinner, the incoming chairman said—in a paraphrase of Winston Churchill— "I do not intend to preside over the dissolution of the New York Stock Exchange." In fact, Needham's earlier suggestion had been that the Exchange indeed be dissolved and become part of the new central system, but those present understood what he meant, and they appreciated the thought. During the Haack period, the powers on the floor had tried to defend the structure that had been perfected in the 1940s with the ideology of the 1950s—they utilized the words of

* For a perceptive view of Needham, see Richard E. Rustin, "Four Months Later—Big Board's Chairman," *Wall Street Journal*, December 18, 1972.

Funston to preserve the market in which Coleman and Stott had reigned. It would be different in the mid-1970s. Adopting some of the techniques of its rivals, determining its own strong points and then stressing them, and exerting political pressures to the fullest, the Big Board would reformulate the issues in the contest and then engage in combat on a more realistic basis.

Needham's main task was to reassert the Big Board's domination of the nation's securities markets. When he accepted the post in mid-1972, it appeared that this could be accomplished if and when Congress passed and the President signed a new securities act based upon the recommendations of the *Martin Report.* Within a few months, however, the picture became far more convoluted, with additional issues appearing, old problems becoming aggravated, and new complications muddying the waters. By then it was said that Needham knew how to grasp a nettle, but he had only two hands, and there were too many bushes.

The chairman had hoped to unify the exchange community against the Third Market. While it was true that the Big Board had interests which conflicted with those of the regionals, especially in the area of institutional memberships, a unified central market might benefit all, at the expense of the Third Market.

The leading regional exchanges had a different view of the matter. They considered their trading methods and technologies more advanced than those of the N.Y.S.E., and likely to remain so. Third Market firms and institutional investors utilized the regionals for trades in N.Y.S.E.–listed stocks, and this helped boost volume and profits. As recently as 1965, the regional exchanges accounted for little more than 10 percent of the trading volume in listed shares and 13 percent of their dollar value. By 1972, the portion was more than 15 percent and the dollar value over 18 percent. As some at the regionals saw it, the N.Y.S.E. needed them more than they needed the N.Y.S.E. They were also convinced they could compete effectively against the Big Board in block trades, the result of a more enlightened view and more efficient methods. Finally, there was the ancient dislike of New York, a sentiment particularly strong at the Pacific Coast and Midwest exchanges. Neither had much interest in a N.Y.S.E. crusade against the Third Market. Indeed, if Needham won his battle, the regionals would become part of the still nebulous U.S.S.E., one that was certain to be led by New York. A Third Market victory, on the other hand, would mean a continuation of their independence and, presumably, their prosperity. The specialists at the regionals competed against their New York counterparts for business, while large brokerage houses functioned at all the leading exchanges and were increasingly independent of the N.Y.S.E. The regional brokerages saw little to be gained under

Big Board domination and they tended to oppose the merger plans. There appeared no way by which Needham could change this situation.

Even the Amex, which so often in the past had functioned as a silent ally, questioned Needham's leadership. While it was true that the Amex did not compete with the N.Y.S.E. in the trading of listed securities, like the regionals it could in time lose its identity and come under the direct control of N.Y.S.E. people in the proposed unified market. Already there was talk of a merger of the N.Y.S.E. and the Amex as a preliminary step, phrased in such a way as to indicate a N.Y.S.E. takeover of the smaller market. All of this disturbed Kolton, who spoke out on the matter in early 1973. Noting that the *Martin Report* called for a consolidated tape, but that this did not mean a single trading floor for all stocks, he recommended the creation of a "national board of exchanges," to which each market would send representatives and which would determine policy for the emerging central system. Needham opposed the establishment of such a body, which he believed would add an unnecessary layer to an already overly complicated structure. "My position is very simple," he said, "To me, it's an exercise in futility." To Kolton and the regionals, however, it appeared a further sign of Needham's desire to centralize power at the N.Y.S.E.—at their expense, not that of the Third Market. When it served their interests, the Amex and the regionals would fight the O-T-C traders, but they would not bow to the wishes of the N.Y.S.E. and work against its enemies in order to remain in the good graces of any Wall Street Establishment. For it was clear by then that if ever there had been an Establishment of that kind, it had become fractionalized in the 1960s and certainly was no longer symbolized by the N.Y.S.E.

Stock prices were high in the late summer of 1972, as Needham familiarized himself with the Exchange's personnel and problems. The Dow Industrials, which had slipped to 889.15 on January 26, rose to close at 973.51 on August 14, before pausing for the pre–Election Day period of uncertainty. There was little of that in 1972, however. Democrat George McGovern, generally viewed as an antibusiness candidate whose demonstrated knowledge of finance was limited, was a decided underdog. If McGovern were to be elected, so it was believed, stocks would fall sharply. There was no chance of this, and when Nixon won in a landslide prices rose, going past the 1,000 mark, and reaching 1,036.27 on December 11, before settling down toward the end of the month. Then, with the conclusion of the Vietnam War, they rose again, peaking at 1051.70 on January 11, 1973.

It was the last gasp of bullish exuberance, the celebration of the end of the most divisive period in the nation's history in a century. But there was no delight in the nation, nor on Wall Street—nor, for that matter, was there a belief that the overwhelming Nixon victory would somehow help unite the country. Inflation was still a major threat, and although the Administration had pledged to keep it under control, the cost of living was rising rapidly, at a rate close to that of the postwar era. Interest rates were escalating too, and yet they appeared to have no effect on prices.

Then it became evident that the break-in at Democratic headquarters during the campaign, an episode the White House had dismissed as being of minor importance, had been carefully planned. The network of wrongdoing that came under the umbrella term of "Watergate" began to dominate news stories, and confidence in the President declined rapidly. In fact, all of government was distrusted by the public, if the polls were to believed, and even the press, which helped break the stories, was disliked for having done so.

To the "three I's"—Inflation, Interest Rates, and Impeachment—were added meat shortages in the summer and a fuel crisis in the fall, and still more inflation. By the end of 1973, serious and sober people were wondering whether the world was not on the edge of a major crash, one to which the 1929–1933 collapse would appear almost secondary.

Corporate profits were excellent in 1972 and 1973, but several speculative bubbles burst, resulting in a general apprehension about the state of the economy. The illegal involvement of some businesses and businessmen in the Nixon campaign, combined with the windfall profits of major petroleum companies after the Arab oil boycott, added to the general woes caused by inflation and high interest rates. The economic and political agonies the nation underwent in 1973 and early 1974 were scarcely less traumatic than those suffered through during the Vietnam War. Then came the impeachment debates, followed by the Nixon resignation and the uncertain early days of President Ford. As one commentator put it, the nation appeared to have a compound fracture of the spirit. Nor was this the full extent of the problem, for the economy began to decline in the second half of 1974, as anti-inflationary programs had their impact. By early 1975, it was evident that the nation had entered its worst recession since the 1930s, and the future appeared bleak.

As always, such forces and sentiments were reflected in the prices of common stocks. The Dow Industrials fell in 1973, and then prices collapsed in 1974. It was not a sudden 1929-like crash, however. Rather, prices dropped in a series of sharp declines, each of which was followed by a slight recovery, and then a further loss of public confidence. Investors were whipsawed by an erratic market, one which many specialists appeared to have abandoned, in which the price of a stock could and often did fall by between 30 and 50 percent in a single session. The Dow was at 851.90 on August 22, 1973. It rose to 987.06 by October 26, only to drop to 788.31 on December 12.

Amazed at such behavior, small investors deserted the market in droves. Some speculated in gold, others purchased commercial paper, and quite a large number needed the money to compensate for rising prices caused by inflation. By late 1974 the Dow was below 600, where it had been sixteen years before. Much of the great bull market of the postwar era had been wiped out, and the national mood was far closer to what it had been in the early 1930s than the late 1950s. By then, it was apparent that an entire generation of investors had lost faith in the market. Once more, it seemed that Wall Street was on its way to becoming irrelevant, and in early 1975, there was talk of the need for another Reconstruction Finance Corporation. As had been the case in the mid-1930s, there were hundreds of vacant suites in the district, low volume, and lower spirits. For all his good qualities, Gerald Ford appeared more like Herbert Hoover than Dwight Eisenhower, while the nation awaited the coming of a forceful leader, perhaps another F.D.R.

Throughout the postwar bull market, reformers had warned that a day of judgment was coming, that a replay of the 1930s would soon begin. But stocks had rebounded after each correction in the 1940s, 1950s, and 1960s; there was no crash, no panic, and certainly no great depression. This had been so even in 1969–1970, the most serious of the crisis periods. But the weaknesses exposed in that time of troubles were different from the others in that they were chronic, while the bull market was aged, prices already high on a historical basis, and the forces of inflation at work eroding values. At first this was not recognized, or if it was, tended to be ignored or considered unimportant. Stock prices rebounded and went on to record highs. Then, of course, came the long-term collapse.

There was no dramatic moment of truth in 1973–1974, such as Black Tuesday had been in 1929. Nor was there a symbolic Wall Street villain like Whitney to castigate. Those seeking misdeeds and criminals found them in Washington, not New York, and their activities had been far more destructive than manipulations or the theft of securities, and had more serious consequences for the nation's morale. Those who had lost their money in 1929–1930 left the Street in shock and anger; their 1973–1974 counterparts were dismayed and bewildered and, if anything, were confused rather than embittered.

For there was no major depression; instead inflation raged on, apparently unable to be halted. And not all stocks fell equally. Indeed, a large group of seasoned growth issues not only refused to fall but actually rose to new highs, as though in defiance of all the old laws of investing and markets.

The reason was no mystery. The large funds, deeply committed to certain common stocks, were unable to sell them. A major trust might own huge blocks—Morgan Guaranty controlled over $2 billion of I.B.M. alone. Such a holding could not be marketed. Indeed, the bank would have been unable to sell the shares over a period of months, if it came to that, without causing I.B.M.'s price to fall drastically. The large trusts and funds owned many such blocks of stock in firms like Xerox, Polaroid, American Telephone & Telegraph, Pfizer, Kresge—about fifty or so major growth companies. Unable to dispose of them, and in most cases still believing the issues to be sound investments, the trusts were obliged to support their prices by interceding on the buy side when they began to decline. If I.B.M. collapsed, for example, the net asset value of hundreds of large trusts and funds would likewise shrink. The well-being of millions of Americans who knew little of the stock market was bound up in the fortunes of I.B.M.'s stock, for their pensions and savings were based on its ups and downs.

This phenomenon, given the name "Two-Tier Market" in early 1973, confounded and confused the district's analysts. A perfectly sound and growing firm, not a member of the "favorite fifty," might sell for six times earnings and pay a dividend to return 8 percent. A new enterprise of great promise might not be able to float stock, and so either would go under or accept a merger offer from some other company. Meanwhile, Polaroid, with no appreciable earnings growth for a period of five years, sold for over one hundred times earnings and paid a dividend of below 1 percent. Polaroid, of course, was in the first tier; the other two firms were consigned to the second.

How long could this continue? What would happen when and if the roof caved in? The Two-Tier Market had few defenders, but the critics didn't know what to do about it, or, for that matter, whether any action should be taken.

The collapse came in late 1973 and continued into 1974. Almost all of the top-tier favorites fell—I.B.M., Avon, Disney, Tampax, McDonald's, Motorola, and Polaroid among them. And when they sank, they did so spectacularly, often losing more than 10 to 20 percent of their values in a single session. The mutual funds, which owned large amounts of these issues, declined sharply. According to a major rating service, 543 regularly monitored mutuals had fallen by over 15 percent in the June 1969 to June 1974 period, while an investor who placed equal amounts of money in a savings account and the average fund in 1964 would have done better at the bank.

Those who owned funds in this period knew this. Many sold their shares, accepting losses and vowing never again to become involved in the stock market. Their sales obliged the mutuals to dispose of stock to provide cash for the transactions. In 1972, for the first time since the end of World War II, net redemptions exceeded net sales, and the margin widened in 1973 and 1974. Fearing both a continued decline in stock prices and a massive redemption wave, many of the mutuals withdrew from stocks in these years, putting most of their liquid assets in commercial paper and Treasury notes. This, too, served to depress prices. Wall Street observers noted that if and when the mutuals decided to purchase securities once more, their combined power could spark a major bull rally. There was no sign of this happening, however. Instead, prices drifted lower, rallied, declined sharply, rebounded, and then repeated the process.

These problems, along with inflation, high interest rates, and political uncertainties, affected the N.Y.S.E. adversely, and provided Needham with more problems than he had anticipated on taking office in 1972. Even the two major issues of that year—negotiated commissions and the central market—were complicated by events of 1973–1974.

The commission houses and investment banks, which had appeared so powerful in 1968, were battered in 1969–1970, recovered somewhat in 1971–1972, and then, before they could consolidate their gains, were dealt a series of blows in 1973–1974. Costs were up, as the result of automation, reforms, insurance, modernization, the addition of new facilities and inflation. Business was poor, as volume stagnated and then declined, prices fell, and the market for new issues shriveled. In 1972, some $808 million a month in new flotations came out of Wall Street; in 1973, the monthly average was $649 million, and during the first half of 1974, $260 million.

Not only were the nation's businesses unable or unwilling to come to Wall Street to float new stock and bond issues but more than a few were buying back their already issued stock, which in 1974 was selling at bargain prices. The 1960s had been noted for mergermania and "going public." During the early 1970s, several large conglomerates attempted to divest themselves of their holdings, while a handful of consultant firms, led by Randall Fields, advised public companies as to the best methods of "going private"—they would purchase virtually all of their stock and, in some cases, withdraw from the N.Y.S.E. to await a better day for public ownership.

According to the S.E.C. timetable, the N.Y.S.E. established the principle of negotiated rates on orders above $300,000 in value on April 24, 1973, and many large commission firms began experimenting with negotiated commissions in 1974. Merrill Lynch had its "Sharebuilder" program and Paine, Webber its "Econo-Trade," and the latter firm considered a flat annual rate to cover all trading within certain limits. These new plans and others like them differed from ordinary brokerage, however. Under the Merrill Lynch program, for example, the client would submit his order, which would be filled the day following the arrival of the cash with which to pay for it, and the certificates were held by the firm, not the individual. Still, the discounts were sizable. Under the "regular way," the commission on a $500 sale was $15.84, while Sharebuilder cost $12.25 and Econo-Trade, $14.36. The large brokerages considered these plans temporary, experiments preparing the way for fully negotiated commissions in 1975, at which time many of them planned to institute "unbundling" programs. The client would then pay extra fees for all services above and beyond bare brokerages—research, investment of dividends, bookkeeping, etc. In mid-1974, it appeared unbundling and negotiated commissions might actually help the large houses. The smaller ones, on the other hand, might be forced to close down.

If the medium-sized and small firms were being crushed by the larger N.Y.S.E. brokerages, all of them faced major threats from O-T-C houses and the banks. By 1974, there were some twenty trading firms—among them Marquette de Bary, Odd Lot Securities, Source Securities, and Rose & Co.—which belonged to the N.A.S.D., bought and sold listed issues over NASDAQ, and offered brokerage services to clients at sharply reduced rates, in most cases even lower than those for Sharebuilder and Econo-Trade. Since these O-T-C houses did not provide research papers or other services, their overhead was low, and while N.Y.S.E. firms lost money when volume declined, they were able to show consistent profits—from brokerage as well as trading. In 1974, Third Market leader Donald Weeden noted, perhaps in a joking fashion, that there was no reason why stock transactions could not be executed at rates similar to those at Off Track Betting parlors. No one suggested commissions would fall to that level, but the thought was chilling to N.Y.S.E. member firms.

The banks posed a more serious threat, since they were larger and better equipped to operate in this kind of market than most commission firms. Not only did they sponsor closed-end trusts, real estate investment trusts, small business investment corporations, and old-line trusts of various kinds, but they also underwrote revenue bonds and, in 1974, initiated investment plans under which clients could establish funds in one or several of a specified group of securities. The bank would execute orders for its depositors, usually collecting a 5 percent service charge on each transaction (maximum, two dollars), plus a small brokerage fee. One firm, Investment Data Corporation, set up "Franchises" in several large banks, among them Chase Manhattan and Security Pacific. Needham accused the banks of unfair competition and violations of federal law, and the S.E.C. investigated. But Senator William Proxmire, known as a critic both of banks and exchanges, drew up a bill which, if passed, would enable banks an even larger role in the market.

If this were not enough, most large banks competed with the market for funds in a more direct fashion, by offering investors what appeared to be a safe and profitable alternative to stocks. In 1961, First National City Bank introduced the first certificates of deposit, large-denomination notes which matured in thirty to one hundred and twenty days, were negotiable, and carried high rates of interest. As inflation intensified and the demand for money grew, the interest rates shot up, while both stocks and bonds fell. In mid-1974, a large investor could purchase a certificate of deposit from a major bank that matured in a few months and paid over 12 percent interest. Or he could invest in securities, some of which returned 8 percent, but whose prices were declining. Given the alternative, such people went to certificates of deposit. By then, too, several "money-market mutuals" had made their appearance—led by Reserve Fund and Dreyfus Liquid Assets—which invested in certificates of deposit and federal bills, were offered and bought without commissions, and charged a fee of around one-half of one percent. In mid-1974, these funds paid between 9 and 10 percent, compounded daily. Certificates of deposit and money-market mutuals were criticized for having drawn money from the home mortgage market, and this certainly was the case, but they also provided one-time stockholders and speculators with a safe haven for their funds—and one from which they would not emerge until inflation subsided and stocks began to rise.

Given this increased use of certificates of deposit—which went to stoke the market for short-term funds—and the inability of investment banks to sell large new issues of stocks and bonds, several medium-sized corporations withdrew from the capital markets and turned to short-term financing instead, while others sought government help. By late 1974 it appeared that together the major banks and the government might be capable of fueling American industry, with the capital markets performing a decidedly secondary role. To some economists, this seemed a significant structural change in American capitalism, one which, if it continued for long, could turn Wall Street into the kind of desert it had been in the late 1930s.

Banks, trust companies, the Third Market and the regionals challenged the N.Y.S.E. for the patronage of large and small investors. Similarly, a new market appeared to offer an arena for the Exchange's more speculative element, as well as a vehicle for those wanting to enter into hedging operations.

For a century, speculators had purchased options on securities—the right to buy or sell a stated number of shares of a specific stock at an agreed upon fixed price until a stated expiration date. Once acquired, the option was held for the term of the contract. On April 26, 1973, after several years of planning, the Chicago Board of Trade opened the Chicago Board Options Exchange, which initially dealt in buy options for a list of twenty-seven N.Y.S.E. securities. This provided the options market with liquidity, and the publicity given the new "Chicago Board Options" and the opportunity it gave to small speculators to "bet" on the fortunes of relatively high-priced issues combined to make the C.B.O.E. an instant success. In September, after only five months of operation, the Board reported that it had traded 15 million option shares—approximately 60 percent of the N.Y.S.E. volume in the twenty-seven stocks—and had a volume that was 4 percent of the Big Board's for all securities. Not only was the C.B.O.E. drawing business from New York but the selling of options into the market, to provide the dealers with "merchandise," proved profitable in the down market. Many investors concentrated on this aspect of investment and speculation rather than buying and selling at the N.Y.S.E. Some students of the subject claimed the C.B.O.E., not the over-the-counter market in listed securities, deserved the title of Third Market, since it was truly one step removed from the secondary market.

All of these factors placed the brokerages under pressure, more than most could easily bear. At a time when it was thought that the "break-even" point for the community was 16 million shares a day, many were not only losing money but, given the state of the market, were without hope of survival. In 1973–1974 over 250 brokerages, most of them small and not members of the exchanges, went out of business. In 1973 and the first half of 1974, fifty Big Board member firms either were liquidated or merged. Wall Streeters who had been dismissed in 1971 and rehired in 1972, were let go again in 1973 and 1974.

At one time it had appeared that an enervated specialist community would be obliged to bow before the onslaughts of powerful brokerages and a vigorous Third Market. By the mid-1970s, the commission houses were in serious difficulties, while several of the most prominent Third Market operations were showing deficits—Weeden & Co., for example, lost $3 million in 1973. If investors and speculators were sullen and disheartened in 1974, the district's personnel feared for their positions.*

It was against this backdrop of gloom that Needham attempted to win favorable legislation for the Exchange. Even here the timing was

* As well they might. In the period from January 1969 to April 1974, employment in the securities industry in New York declined from 105,200 to 75,000—a 28 percent drop.

wrong. The clash between Needham and Weeden took place at the Senate's Subcommittee on Securities of the Committee on Banking, Housing and Urban Affairs, when the Watergate hearings and impeachment talk dominated the interest of Washingtonians. Needham had expected the S.E.C. to play a significant role in the debates and, given direction from the White House, come out in favor of a measure from which the Exchange would benefit. But the Executive branch was in no position to exert that kind of pressure in 1973–1974, while the leadership at the S.E.C. was shaky. Casey had left office in 1973, to be succeeded by G. Bradford Cook who, before he could do very much, was shown to have been implicated in one of the many scandals of the period. After ten weeks in office, Cook resigned, to be replaced by Ray Garrett, a conservative Chicago securities lawyer, who took over in August 1973. Shortly thereafter Garrett came out in favor of negotiated rates and other reforms supported by the Third Market. "Those who cannot adjust to the future, for whatever reason, will have to drop out," he told a group of industry leaders. "Those are harsh words, but then, these are harsh times."

Not only had Needham lost whatever support he had had at the S.E.C. but he was deserted by the commission firms. Ever since coming to office he had insisted that the large brokerages would leave the Big Board when and if fully negotiated rates were put into effect. This would destroy the Exchange as a central market, he claimed, and with the diminution of liquidity, the investment function of Wall Street would be seriously damaged. This had been more of a problem in 1972 than it was in 1974, of course, since at the latter time business was so bad. In any case, many of the men Needham had claimed would lead their organizations out of the N.Y.S.E. denied they would do so. Andrew Sage of Lehman Brothers said his firm "would not quit the N.Y.S.E. due to the phasing out of fixed minimum commission rates; nor would it decrease the quality or quantity of its research and advisory services." James Davant of Paine, Webber, Jackson & Curtis indicated the same; "I do not foresee that Paine, Webber would either dispose of its N.Y.S.E. memberships or decrease its research services under a system of competitive rates," while William Salomon, whose firm by that time had emerged as the largest block house, said Salomon Brothers has "no plans to resign our Exchange membership after the advent of fully negotiated rates" and expressed "disbelief that there would be a mass exodus of other Exchange members." Even Gustave Levy seemed to have changed his mind. Conceding that at one time he had strongly opposed negotiated rates, Levy remarked, "Upon further reflection since that time, and as a result of our experience with negotiated commissions on large trades, I have changed my views regarding the wisdom and desirability of moving to negotiated commission rates. I came to the view that it would not necessarily follow that the competitive determination of commission rates on transactions of all sizes would have the adverse effects I had alluded to in my 1968 testimony. I have rejected the view, and do not now believe, that the advent of fully negotiated commission rates would be likely to cause my firm to leave the N.Y.S.E. . . ." *

Third Market and N.Y.S.E. advocates argued their cases before the subcommittee, and attracted little attention. Even the senators often failed to show up for the sessions, being involved in Watergate and related affairs. Chairman Harrison Williams could rarely get more than three of the seven members of his subcommittee to be there at the same time. Senators Lowell Weicker, Edward Brooke, and William Proxmire were either absent or flitting in and out of the room. Only Senator Joseph Biden attended regularly, often enlivening the sessions with a grim humor born of boredom. In the end, the subcommittee would report a measure to the full committee, which then would make recommendations to the Senate. The final bill would either create a unified structure containing the Third Market or establish a central system without the Third Market. It was the culmination of a generation of conflict and contention, but in 1974 the issue somehow did not appear as significant as it had a decade earlier. The combination of Watergate, runaway inflation, astronomical interest rates and a moribund condition at all markets placed the matter in an entirely different perspective.

This new situation had damaged the Third Market, but it had done more harm to the N.Y.S.E. For in 1974, Needham and others still spoke of the necessity to protect the small investor, who they anticipated would shortly return to the market, eager to invest and speculate. That this would happen again—at least in the next few years—was not at all certain. Despite his problems, the middle-class American had more disposable and discretionary income in the mid-1970s than ever before in history. But he had lost his taste for stocks. The institutions were in command, not only at the Third Market and the regionals but at the N.Y.S.E. itself.

Some observers noted that the dichotomy constructed between small investors and institutions was false and deceiving. The large institutions, after all, usually consisted of many small investors—and big ones too—in the aggregate. It made little sense to view the investor who purchased 100 shares of General Motors as a "little guy," and a $2 billion mutual fund, which owned 100,000 shares of General Motors and dealt in large blocks, as an institution, when that same person often owned shares in the mutual. Small investors would continue to

* United States Congress, Senate, *Hearings before the Subcommittee on Securities of the Committee on Banking, Housing and Urban Affairs*, 93rd Cong., 2nd Session (Washington, 1974), pp. 7–11.

dominate the market, but they would do so through institutions, and not necessarily on their own. A large number of middle-class Americans would hold shares in mutual funds, participate in pension plans, belong to union welfare programs, and own insurance policies. The trustees for this community—the institutional managers—would buy and sell large blocks on the N.Y.S.E. and elsewhere. This seemed the direction of the securities markets in America in the mid-1970s. One columnist likened it to a person crossing New York Harbor in a rowboat and being swamped by the liners and freighters. For that kind of trip, you would want to be carried on a large ship, perhaps along with other former owners of rowboats. The same reasoning was applied to the markets of the 1970s. It was not that People's Capitalism was dead, but rather that it was taking on a corporate guise. The world had changed considerably since the early days of Keith Funston. The N.Y.S.E. would have to take cognizance of this alteration.

In testimony before the Subcommittee on Securities in 1974, Harry Keefe, president and founder of Bruyette & Woods, an O-T-C house, said as much. He noted that during the past year, some 800,000 stockholders had left Wall Street. N.Y.S.E. and Third Market people had been saying that this was due to poor market structure, each blaming the other. Keefe disagreed.

> I don't think this has a damn bit to do with the auction system and the stock exchange market. I think it has to do with the basic economic structure of our country. I don't need to save for my retirement, I don't—unlike my father.
>
> I don't need to save for sickness and I don't need to save for education. We have developed a social philosophy that does this.
>
> So much of the incentive for the individual to participate in the stock market has been removed, which is why I started a firm to deal exclusively with institutions because I felt that is where the action was going to be.
>
> I submit that the individual investor no longer has incentives he had twenty years ago to participate in the market. He no longer has the incentive to save for retirement. His company is doing that for him.
>
> Institutions, if they dominate the market, and they certainly do in the major stocks, cause supply-and-demand imbalances that necessitate a dealer function. That has been overlooked in these discussions. That is what my firm does; we operate as a principal to offset the imbalance of large supply-and-demand situations. To be a dealer takes capital, and in any institutionally dominated market, lots of it.
>
> If this committee has not already done so, I think you would

> find it very interesting to get the financial statements of some specialist firms. As I stated my firm has $8 million in capital, I believe Don Weeden's has $37 million. Some of the specialists against whom I compete have capital significantly less than $1 million.

In Keefe's view—to use the metaphor of the situation of the harbor—the O-T-C houses were oceanliners, while the specialists, like the small investors, were too much akin to rowboats. Given their small capital and the buffeting they took in a market dominated by block traders, it was little wonder that they often seemed to have abandoned their stocks in periods of distress. Grow or die, Keefe seemed to be saying, and the situation was not of his making, nor, for that matter, controllable by Needham, Weeden or even Congress itself.

> I submit that unless the gentlemen of the Congress and the Senate change our basic tax laws and unless this nation undergoes a basic change in social philosophy and does away with social security, pensions, medicare, Blue Cross, and state universities, we will have collectivized savings with huge pools of money moving around in large dollar amounts.
>
> I do not deny that we must protect the small investor, but I also submit that we have an obligation to the schoolteacher whose sole savings are in a retirement fund. That fund, too, should have an efficient market in which to operate, and if the auction market were efficient the Third Market would never have arisen.*

The demise of Wall Street had been predicted and feared, on many occasions, by a host of critics and supporters, since the New York financial district rose to prominence in the 1830s. Throughout the nineteenth century, the N.Y.S.E. had competed against rivals, both within the city and elsewhere, and on occasion it appeared weak and indecisive, on the point of fading if not vanishing entirely. Yet both the district and the Exchange survived and prospered and, in the aftermath of World War I, became the focus not only of American finance but of the money markets of the world, a situation that continued even after the Great Crash of 1929.

Throughout this period the N.Y.S.E. evolved, slowly changing its institutions, at times because of internal pressures but more often as a result of demands from the outside, from Washington and its rivals. Such a change and accommodation was made in the 1930s, during the New Deal. On that occasion the alterations came as a response to the

* *Ibid.*, pp. 145–46.

reform impulse and also as an adjustment to the different variety of investor and speculator interested in securities in that period. To some, the accommodations appeared unwise, a sign of weakness. But the N.Y.S.E. survived, to flourish again in the 1950s and 1960s.

A similar situation presented itself in the mid-1960s. It was not as obvious as the problems of the Great Depression and so went unrecognized at the time—a period when Wall Street was more concerned with another crash than with any new threat. Then, when the difficulties were comprehended, it took the Exchange several years to formulate a response and find a leader to put it into operation. And all the while the problems changed, became convoluted, were displaced by new issues, and complicated by extraneous matters. That the financial district would survive was never in doubt, and serious people did not believe the district could function well without a major exchange structure of one kind or another.

But what would it be? In the early 1970s, as it had in the mid-1930s, the N.Y.S.E. entered a chrysalis from which would emerge some new or hybrid form. As with so many other institutions in America at mid-decade, its final shape remains a mystery.

An Essay on Sources and Methodology

The body of published material on the history of the nation's securities exchanges is not very large. There are, of course, many books and articles on the stock market crash of 1929, almost all by people who have little understanding of the functioning of the markets in that period, or by apologists for one persuasion or another, trying to draw moral or political lessons from the event. Before the turn of the century, and for a while afterward, Wall Streeters would compose their memoirs, and a few even contributed histories of the N.Y.S.E. In the last two generations, however, the field has attracted few scholars. Vincent Carosso, an exception, has written *Investment Banking in America, A History* (Cambridge, 1970), and is currently at work on a history of Morgan & Co. John Brooks, whose perceptive essays on the Street appear regularly in the *New Yorker*, has contributed several studies which, however, tell us more about individuals and the ways they operate than about the development of institutions. Dana Thomas's *The Plungers and the Peacocks* (New York, 1967) is in the same vein. John Kouwenhoven has published *Partners in Banking, An Historical Portrait of a Great Private Bank, Brown Brothers Harriman* (Garden City, 1968), and, of course, there are a large number of articles on special topics in the journals, the *Business History Review* in particular.

Yet we lack a major biography of William McChesney Martin, surely one of the most important Americans of the past half century. Nor is there an adequate work on Charles Merrill, a key figure in the national experience from several points of view. There are two books on the early history of the S.E.C., but no full-scale treatment of the Commission. Were it not for the fact that William O. Douglas left the S.E.C. for the Supreme Court, and had a distinguished career on the bench, this most important of the agency's leaders would doubtless have been ignored. We have no histories of Lehman Brothers, Kuhn, Loeb, or Merrill Lynch. There is next to nothing on the history of the over-the-counter market; nothing at all has been written about the history of the National Association of Securities Dealers. There are literally hundreds of doctoral dissertation topics to be had in the field of securities markets history, but few conduct research in the area.

This requires mention, for it means that scholars lack a firm monographic foundation upon which to build. Nor is there a fellowship of scholars with whom to consult. Most academicians interested in the securities markets are conducting research on the subject of price behavior. Others are concerned with the efficiency of the markets. Both have only a peripheral interest in learning how the markets became the way they are, the origins and developments of institutions, the roles of individuals, and related matters that interest historians.

What all of this means is that the scholar seeking to write a history of the N.Y.S.E. must plunge directly into the documents, not quite certain what he will uncover, perhaps even without knowing what questions to ask of them. When he does find books and articles of interest, they often will turn out to have been written by scholars in disciplines other than his, and will not speak directly to the issues he is addressing. Furthermore, he knows that few will be able to challenge his interpretations in an informed manner. For example, the writer of an assessment of the Presidency of Theodore Roosevelt will find that there are dozens of capable historians prepared to review his work critically and intelligently. Those who do know of the presidency of William McChesney Martin—at the N.Y.S.E.—are not scholars, tend to rely upon memory rather than research, and often are not certain how to respond to requests for criticism.

Having said all this, and thus warning the reader, I should indicate that the best single source for a study of the Exchange's history is at the N.Y.S.E.itself—or, more properly, its warehouse on 55 Hudson Street. There, on the tenth floor, are several thousand large cardboard containers—"Bekins boxes." When filled with documents, one weighs around fifty pounds. Each is packed with documents, needless to say.

The boxes are numbered, their contents noted on a master list. The would-be researcher must first obtain permission from the Exchange to conduct his work in the files. Having done this, he will have to go through the list and select those boxes he believes contain the information he wants. Then he will retrieve the boxes from the tenth floor (more often than not the ones desired are below others and covered with dust), and go through the contents, which are uncatalogued.

There are three varieties of material of interest to historians in the boxes. First, the Exchange maintains a series of clippings scrapbooks. For the most part, these are drawn from newspapers throughout the nation, and in the past were used for public relations purposes. The books are fairly complete and so should save the time involved in going through the microfilms of newspapers. In addition, since the books contain out-of-town as well as New York clippings, they have material not easily found elsewhere.

Some of the minutes of Exchange committees have been stored in the boxes. Most, however, are at the Exchange's main library at 25 Broad Street. These are of little value, since the secretaries usually took note only of decisions, rarely of debates.

Finally, several boxes contain documents prepared for internal use at the Exchange. These include position papers, memos, reaction papers and committee correspondence. Much of this material is quite valuable, not to be found elsewhere. Included are transcripts of hearings as well as decisions. Without such documents, the first two sections of this book could not have been written.

Other material may be found at the main library. In the files there are copies of every major address delivered by N.Y.S.E. presidents since 1928, as well as other speeches and articles by key Exchange leaders. The library has a file of Exchange constitutions, indices, manuals, fact books, and the like. Most important, it is run by an excellent staff, people who are quite helpful.

Shortly after its formation in 1934, the S.E.C. began publishing important information regarding the securities industry. The quality of research and publications was high in the 1930s, and then declined. The same could be said of the nature and content of congressional committee hearings on Wall Street–related topics.

The situation changed in the 1960s, both at the S.E.C. and in Congress. Several key studies made during this decade are listed in the bibliography at the end of this essay. Special mention should be made of the various reports of the Senate Subcommittee on Securities of the Committee on Banking, Housing, and Urban Affairs, especially in the 1971–1974 period. Chaired by Harrison Williams, the subcommittee was charged with writing a new securities law. In the process of its hearings, the subcommittee amassed a great volume of data and testimony on the nature of the securities markets, especially in the post-1963 period. Its four-part *Securities Industry Study* is basic reading for anyone involved in the development of the market structure and the origins of present problems. Indeed, the high quality and volume of government scholarship and the lack of interest on the part of private scholars is enough to challenge the prejudices of an ardent philosophical anarchist, and the intelligence of the questioning—especially by Senators Brooke, Williams, Proxmire, and Biden—is a rebuke to those who believe government is run by second-rate hacks. One need only turn from a reading of the Watergate transcripts to a dialogue between Senator Biden and a Wall Streeter to experience the low and high of Washington life in our time.

The Leslie Gould Collection at Hofstra University was consulted on several occasions. One of the most noted business journalists of his day, Gould conducted extensive correspondence with many political and financial leaders—some of whom appear in the present work. Although there are no startling revelations to be found in the papers, they do help flesh out certain sections.

Mr. Richard Callanan of the N.Y.S.E. staff has maintained a "chronology of the N.Y.S.E." for more than forty years. It is a month-by-month—at times even day-by-day—record of events important in Exchange history. Locating both Mr. Callanan and his chronology was most fortunate for me. The collection helped provide a backbone for this book, while Mr. Callanan graciously read the entire manuscript, offering helpful suggestions, making corrections and, when necessary, arranging for meetings with others at the Exchange.

In the process of my research, I had the opportunity to interview several N.Y.S.E. members and others in the financial community. On occasion I have asked some to read chapters and offer comments. These were of only limited value for a variety of reasons, a disappointment since discussions with old Curb Exchange personnel were so helpful in another of my works on the district. Most N.Y.S.E. members appear wary of interviewers, especially those from academia. They have short memories, active imaginations, and tend to exaggerate. Generally speaking the very important people either are reluctant to talk frankly and say little, or tend to parrot a line. The unimportant are often fearful of endangering their positions, and say what is expected of them. The middle echelon will talk, again on occasion, but insist on total anonymity when they do so. These interviews provided "color" material but little else. Similarly, those who read chapters had little to offer, one way or another.

There were, of course, exceptions. Mr. Callanan has already been mentioned. Mr. Fred Seisel of Weeden & Co., who read the last section with care, shared with me his knowledge of the Third Market, of political cross-currents within the district, and his insights on legislation.

After having completed the manuscript I gave copies to several of my students at Hofstra who had volunteered to read the chapters and offer frank comments on it. Throughout the period of research and writing, I have become immersed in the jargon and politics of the district. I was concerned that the end product of my efforts might be intelligible to a relative few in the Wall Street community and Washington but confusing and boring to all others. The book was written with the lay reader in mind, and so my students' reactions were extremely important to me.

They reported little difficulty with the first two sections but lost their ways in the third, especially those chapters dealing with current crises and conflicts. Of course, this was a yeasty and complicated period, more than any previous one in the N.Y.S.E.'s history, and merits a book of its own. In the end, I attempted to stress the major issues at the expense of the minor, and tried to write the book in standard American English rather than utilize the colorful, handy, and sometimes impressive jargon of the district. If the work has still confused, the fault is mine. And should some readers find it too simple, I plan to write a study on the post-1963 period and hope to rectify whatever failings are found here.

The following is a selected bibliography of works consulted in the course of conducting research into the history of the N.Y.S.E. since 1935. As indicated above, the bulk of my material derives from the Exchange's files, at its warehouse and the library.

BOOKS

Abbott, Charles C. *Financing Business During the Transition.* New York, 1946.

Armour, Lawrence A., and the staff of *Barron's*, eds. *How to Survive a Bear Market.* Princeton, 1970.

Baruch, Hurd. *Wall Street: Security Risk.* Washington, 1971.

Baum, Daniel Jay, and Ned B. Stiles. *The Silent Partners.* Syracuse, 1965.

Black, Hillel. *The Watchdogs of Wall Street.* New York, 1962.

Brooks, John. *The Go-Go Years.* New York, 1973.

———. *Once in Golconda: A True Drama of Wall Street, 1920–1938.* New York, 1969.

———. *The Seven Fat Years.* New York, 1958.

Bullock, Hugh. *The Story of Investment Companies.* New York, 1959.

Carosso, Vincent. *Investment Banking in America.* Cambridge, 1970.

Cox, Edwin B. *Trends in the Distribution of Stock Ownership.* Philadelphia, 1963.

Crane, Burton. *The Sophisticated Investor.* New York, 1959.

DeBedts, Ralph. *The New Deal's SEC: The Formative Years.* New York, 1964.

Doughen, Joseph, and Peter Binzen. *The Wreck of the Penn Central.* Boston, 1971.

Douglas, William O. *Go East, Young Man.* New York, 1974.

Elias, Christopher. *Fleecing the Lambs.* Chicago, 1971.

Ellis, Charles D. *Institutional Investing.* Homewood, Ill., 1971.

———. *The Second Crash.* New York, 1973.

Friend, Irving, *et al. Investment Banking and the New Issues Market.* Philadelphia, 1965.

Fuller, John G. *The Money Changers.* New York, 1962.

Funston, G. Keith. *Wanted: More Owners of American Business.* Boston, 1954.

Goldsmith, Raymond W., ed. *Institutional Investors and Corporate Stock—A Background Study.* New York, 1973.

Graham, Benjamin. *The Intelligent Investor.* New York, 1973.

Hazard, John W., and Milton Christie. *The Investment Business: A Condensation of the S.E.C. Report.* New York, 1964.

Hughes, John Emmet. *Ordeal of Power: A Political Memoir of the Eisenhower Years.* New York, 1963.

Jones, Jesse with Edward Angly. *Fifty Billion Dollars: My Thirteen Years with the RFC (1932–1945).* New York, 1951.

Kaplan, Gilbert Edmund, and Chris Welles. *The Money Managers.* New York, 1969.

Krefetz, Gerald, and Ruth Marossi. *Money Makes Money, and the Money Money Makes Makes More Money: The Men Who Are Wall Street.* New York, 1970.

Krooss, Herman, and Martin R. Blyn. *A History of Financial Intermediaries.* New York, 1971.

Loeser, John C. *The Over-the-Counter Market.* New York, 1940.

Loll, Leo M., and Julian G. Buckley. *The Over-the-Counter Securities Markets.* 3rd ed. Englewood Cliffs, 1973.

Mayer, Martin. *The New Breed on Wall Street.* New York, 1969.

———. *Wall Street: Men and Money.* Rev. ed. New York, 1959.

Miller, Norman C. *The Great Salad Oil Swindle.* New York, 1965.

Nadler, Marcus, Sipa Heller and Samuel S. Shipman. *The Money Market and Its Institutions.* New York, 1955.

Ney, Richard. *The Wall Street Gang.* New York, 1974.

———. *The Wall Street Jungle.* New York, 1970.

Parrish, Michael E. *Securities Regulation and the New Deal.* New Haven, 1970.

Paul, Randolph E. *Taxation in the United States.* Boston, 1954.

Raw, Charles, Bruce Page and Godfrey Hodgson. *"Do You Sincerely Want to be Rich?": The Full Story of Bernard Cornfeld and IOS.* New York, 1971.

Regan, Donald T. *A View from the Street.* New York, 1972.

Robbins, Sidney M., and Nestor Terleckyj. *Money Metropolis: A Locational Study of Financial Activities in the New York Region.* Cambridge, 1960.

Robbins, Sidney M. *The Securities Markets: Operations and Issues.* New York, 1966.

Robinson, Roland I., and Dwayne Wrightsman. *Financial Markets: The Accumulation and Allocation of Wealth.* New York, 1974.

Sederberg, Arelo. *The Stock Market Investment Club Handbook.* Los Angeles, 1971.

Smigel, Erwin O. *The Wall Street Lawyer: Professional Organization Man?* Bloomington, 1964.

"Smith, Adam." *The Money Game.* New York, 1967.

Smith, Gene. *The Life and Death of Serge Rubinstein.* New York, 1962.

Smith, Ralph Lee. *The Grim Truth About Mutual Funds.* New York, 1963.

Sobel, Robert. *Amex: A History of the American Stock Exchange.* New York, 1973.

Timmons, Bascom N. *Jesse Jones: The Man and the Statesman.* New York, 1956.

Tyler, Poyntz, ed. *Securities, Exchanges and the SEC.* New York, 1965.

Vatter, Harold. *The U.S. Economy in the 1950's.* New York, 1963.

Wendt, Paul F. *The Classification and Financial Experience of the Customers of a Typical New York Stock Exchange Firm from 1933 to 1938.* Maryville, Tennessee, 1941.

West, Richard R., and Seha M. Tinic. *The Economics of the Stock Market.* New York, 1971.

Weston, J. Fred, ed. *Financial Management in the 1960s.* New York, 1966.

Wise, T. A., and the editors of *Fortune. The Insiders.* New York, 1962.

Zahorchak, Michael. *Favorable Executions: The Wall Street Specialist and the Auction Market.* New York, 1974.

GOVERNMENT PUBLICATIONS AND DOCUMENTS

United States. 84th Cong. 1st Sess. Senate. Committee on Banking and Currency. *Factors Affecting the Stock Market.* Washington, 1955.

———. 84th Cong. 1st Sess. Senate. Committee on Banking and Currency. *Staff Report.* Washington, 1955.

———. 84th Cong. 2nd Sess. Joint Economic Committee. *Institutional Investors and the Stock Market.* Washington, 1956.

———. 87th Cong. 1st Sess. Joint Economic Committee. *Variability of Private Investment in Plant and Equipment.* Washington, 1962.

———. 87th Cong. 2nd Sess. Joint Economic Committee. *1962 Supplement to Economic Indicators.* Washington, 1962.

———. 87th Cong. 2nd Sess. House of Reps. Committee on Interstate and Foreign Commerce. *A Study of Mutual Funds.* Washington, 1962.

———. 88th Cong. 1st Sess. House of Reps. *Report of the Special Study of the Securities Markets of the Securities and Exchange Commission.* Washington, 1965.

———. 92nd Cong. 1st Sess.–93rd Cong. 2nd Sess. Senate. Committee on Banking, Housing and Urban Affairs. Subcommittee on Securities. *Hearings.* Washington, 1971–1974.

———. 93rd Cong. 2nd Sess. Senate. Committee on Banking, Housing and Urban Affairs. Subcommittee on Securities. *Securities Industry Study*. 4 vols. Washington, 1972.

———. Securities and Exchange Commission. *Institutional Investor Study Report* (H.R. Doc. 92-64) 3 vols. Washington, 1971.

PERIODICALS

Barron's
Business Week
Dun's
The Exchange
Financial Analyst's Journal
Forbes

Fortune
Harvard Business Review
Institutional Investor
Newsweek
Time

NEWSPAPERS

New York Herald-Tribune
New York Herald
New York Sun

New York Times
New York Tribune
Wall Street Journal

Index

Index